GREAT LAKES SHIPPING LOG
1980-1989

A Chronicle of Shipping on the Great Lakes and St. Lawrence Seaway During the 1980s.

By Raymond A. Bawal, Jr.

INLAND
EXPRESSIONS

Clinton Township, Michigan

Published by Inland Expressions

Inland Expressions
42211 Garfield Rd. #297
Clinton Township, MI. 48038

www.inlandexpressions.com

First Edition 2019

Copyright © 2019 by Inland Expressions

All rights reserved. Except for use in a review, no part of this book may be reproduced in any manner. No photographs, scans, or any other form of reprint in any publications, PDF files, web sites, or any other electronic or written form without expressed permission from the publisher. Please do not encourage or participate in the piracy of copyrighted material only purchase authorized copies of this publication.

ISBN-13 978-1-939150-21-9

Design by Inland Expressions

TABLE OF CONTENTS

Preface i
Introduction iii
Chapter One
    The 1980 Shipping Season... 1
Chapter Two
    The 1981 Shipping Season... 23
Chapter Three
    The 1982 Shipping Season... 44
Chapter Four
    The 1983 Shipping Season... 64
Chapter Five
    The 1984 Shipping Season... 83
Chapter Six
    The 1985 Shipping Season... 105
Chapter Seven
    The 1986 Shipping Season... 130
Chapter Eight
    The 1987 Shipping Season... 158
Chapter Nine
    The 1988 Shipping Season... 187
Chapter Ten
    The 1989 Shipping Season... 214
Chapter Eleven
    Conclusion 242
Appendices 245
Index 253

Author's Preface

The primary purpose of this book is to offer the reader a single source that provides an historical account of Great Lakes and St. Lawrence Seaway shipping activity spanning an entire decade. To gather this information without such a reference, it would be necessary to comb through several different journals published by various maritime historical societies. Such a line of research would also require an examination of several different books, newspaper archives, and various online databases to produce an accurate result. As one of the most dynamic periods in modern Great Lakes shipping history, it was felt that the 1980s represented an appropriate subject for this work.

To prevent the finished product from becoming little more than a chronological listing of events required the subject matter be presented in a method that provides sufficient detail while also maintaining a high level of readability. One of the key decisions made during the early stage of this project was to include historical synopses for many of the vessels removed from the lake fleet during this period.

A common problem encountered during the research phase of this work was determining precise dates for particular events. In some cases, this proved somewhat confusing as journals and published references often give contradictory or incomplete details, sometimes within the same volume. Therefore, achieving the highest level of accuracy required a determined effort to locate the primary source material used by these publications when such inconsistencies occurred. After reviewing a large amount of this information, often in the form of newspaper reports, it became apparent that many of these minor discrepancies stem from simple typographical errors or the use of publication dates rather than the actual date of the event.

Another difficulty in this endeavor was that certain occurrences appearing in some marine journals go unreported in others. Crosschecking these events was further complicated by a growing scarcity in the reporting of marine matters by many of the region's newspapers during the latter part of the twentieth century. This was particularly true while attempting to verify minor incidents that resulted in no significant damage or financial loss.

The following explanation is provided to assist those readers who may be somewhat unfamiliar with Great Lakes shipping operations in making the distinction between a calendar year and a navigation season. Although tanker traffic continued throughout the winter months on a routine basis during the 1980s, annual shipping seasons are defined in this book as beginning with the spring fitout and ending with the closing of the locks and subsequent laying up of the last active dry bulk carriers. Consequently, most shipping seasons actually stretch into the next calendar year while still being referred to in terms of the year in which they began. For example, the 1989 navigation season did not end until late January of 1990.

It should be noted that most of the dates appearing in this book are expressed with only a month and day to minimize the redundant use of the year covered by each individual chapter. However, dates that fall outside of the period that is the topic of any particular chapter always contain the year. As such, events occurring during 1980 in Chapter One will be expressed with only the month and day while those that took place prior to or subsequent to that year, but appearing in that chapter, will be in the month/day/year format.

For purposes of brevity, the use of state and province names in relation to particular communities located in the Great Lakes and St. Lawrence Seaway region only appear in the first instance of each chapter with the exception of places that share common names such as Sault Ste. Marie, Michigan, and Sault Ste. Marie, Ontario. Furthermore, exceptions are also made when there is the possibility that some confusion may arise. For example, the cities of Erie, Pennsylvania, and Superior, Wisconsin, both of which share their names with bodies of water. Similarly, locations beyond the normal scope of lake vessel operation are provided with full geographical descriptions regardless of how many times each may appear in each chapter.

In an effort to attain an adequate measure of conciseness within the text, some fleet names such as Algoma Central Railway Marine Division and the Columbia Transportation Division of the Oglebay Norton Company, are typically shortened to Algoma Central Marine and Columbia Transportation respectively.

To simplify comparisons and maintain consistency, seasonal cargo movements are expressed in the terms of net tons. However, the unit of gross tons is often used when referring to cargo records, particularly those in the movement of iron ore, and the carrying capacity of individual ships.

All of the images used in this book come from my personal collection. Whenever possible, an acknowledgement crediting the photographer noted on the print or slide is included at the end of the image caption.

With the beginning of the 1980s now forty years in the past, it is likely that many readers will have no recollection of this period. As such, it is hoped that this book provides an insightful portrayal of that turbulent decade.

Raymond A. Bawal, Jr.
October 2019

Introduction

The 1980s were a difficult time for the Great Lakes shipping industry. The economic recession during the early years of that decade resulted in the idling of a significant portion of the lake fleet as cargo tonnages spiraled downward. Especially hard hit by the economic downturn was the domestic steel industry, which not only faced reduced demand in the construction and manufacturing sectors but also increased foreign competition. As steel production plummeted, so too did the movement of iron ore on the Great Lakes. This decline was as dramatic as it was sudden. Within just a few years of reaching its third highest level since the end of the Second World War with shipments during the 1979 season totaling 103 million net tons, this all-important commodity fell to its lowest point since the Great Depression. Although improving market conditions generated a recovery, the iron ore trade never again breached prerecession levels throughout the balance of the decade.

Losing half of its annual volume over the course of the decade, shifting trade patterns in the movement of grain also figured prominently in reduced commercial activity on the Great Lakes. This was especially detrimental to Canadian shipping companies due to their reliance upon grain shipments routed from Lake Superior to ports on the St. Lawrence River.

Regardless of economic factors, the seeds of change had been sown in the decades leading up to the 1980s, among which included major investments by the American and Canadian governments to improve the canal infrastructure that supports shipping on the Great Lakes.

Whereas the completion of the St. Lawrence Seaway in 1959 ushered in a new era of shipbuilding in the Canadian fleet so too did the 1969 opening of the Poe Lock at Sault St. Marie, Michigan, in the U.S. fleet. Replacing an older lock of the same name, the dimensions of this lock permitted the passage of thousand-foot ships with carrying capacities more than twice that of the then largest vessels plying the waters of the Great Lakes. In addition, it also made possible the lengthening of a dozen existing U.S. flagged steamers thereby providing ship owners a method of increasing capacity with a minimal investment.

The harsh economic realities of the early eighties, however, brought shipbuilding on the lakes to an abrupt halt. Reaching its conclusion in 1981, a flurry of new construction had added 27 dry bulk freighters to the U.S. fleet since 1972 of which 13 were in the thousand-foot class. On the opposite side of the border, Canadian shipyards continued turning out lake freighters until 1985.

The introduction of more efficient carriers with higher carrying capacities and faster turnaround times represents a significant factor in the downsizing of the Great Lakes shipping industry during the 1980s. Simply put, a smaller number of ships could now

Introduction

carry the same amount of cargo over a given period of time. Coupled with drastically reduced cargo demands, this only accelerated the obsolescence of older vessels.

Every decade in the twentieth century brought about change to shipping operations on the Great Lakes. What makes the 1980s especially unique is that the sale of surplus tonnage included ships that were in excellent condition with many years of service life remaining. In fact, some were able to depart for the scrap yard under their own power despite having been idle for extended periods. The scrapping of vessels of only 20 to 30 years in age stood in stark contrast to the historical precedent of those built strictly for Great Lakes service having a normal lifespan of around 60 to 70 years. Even with the accelerated wear and tear associated with additional canal transits and exposure to saltwater, ships trading regularly through the St. Lawrence Seaway usually have operational careers of about 40 years.

Apart from struggling to keep their carriers active, several Great Lakes vessel operators demonstrated a commitment to the future of the shipping industry by making significant capital investments to modernize their fleets. This included the conversion of many U.S. flagged ships to self-unloaders during the trying times of the early 1980s.

Given the remarkable transformation of the Great Lakes shipping industry, there can be little doubt that the 1980s was a defining point in the history of commerce on the Inland Seas.

Chapter One
The 1980 Shipping Season

During the final days of 1979, two veteran carriers suffered what could have easily been career-ending accidents. The first took place on December 25 of that year when the 81-year old cement carrier *E. M. Ford* sank at Milwaukee, Wisconsin, after a winter storm of unexpected ferocity tore the steamer from its moorings the previous afternoon. Repeatedly slammed into a dock for several hours by high winds, the vessel finally settled to the bottom in approximately 30 feet of water after suffering severe hull damage. Just four days later, a fire sparked by a welder's torch ravaged the forward section of the 74-year old self-unloader *Nicolet* at its winter layup berth in Toledo, Ohio. Despite being among the oldest vessels on the lakes at the time, both ships, in a remarkable turn of events, received extensive repairs and went on to see several years of further service.

It was also during the latter part of the 1979 shipping season that the Erie Sand Steamship Company sold the 221-foot cement carrier *Loc Bay* to the Cement Transit Company (Medusa Cement). Shortly following this transaction, in early 1980, Medusa renamed this vessel *Badger State* (3). Although acquired specifically for the movement of cement between the company's facility at Charlevoix, Michigan, and its terminal at Manitowoc, Wisconsin, this vessel never entered operation for its new owner and instead spent the rest of its career as a cement storage vessel.

In January of 1980, Upper Lakes Shipping announced the awarding of a $4 million contract to its Port Weller Dry Docks division at St. Catharines, Ontario, to convert the 28-year old bulk carrier *James Norris* to a self-unloader. Entering the shipyard on September 2 of that year, the primary purpose of this major reconstruction was to permit the steamer to deliver limestone loaded at Colborne, Ontario, to the St. Lawrence Cement plant at Clarkson, Ontario.

As is the normal practice within the industry, several Great Lakes based shipping companies took advantage of the 1979-80 winter layup to perform repairs and upgrades to their vessels. Significant among these was the installation of sewage treatment plants aboard many ships belonging to the large United States Steel (USS) fleet. This program involved the steamers *B. F. Affleck*, *Arthur M. Anderson*, *Sewell Avery*, *Cason J. Callaway*, *Philip R. Clarke*, *John Hulst*, *William A. Irvin*, *Horace Johnson*, *Rogers City*, *George A. Sloan*, *Robert C. Stanley*, *Ralph H. Watson*, and *Homer D. Williams* along with the diesel powered *Calcite II*, *Thomas W. Lamont*, *Eugene W. Pargny*, *Myron C. Taylor*, and *Eugene P. Thomas*. Interestingly, several of these vessels were near the end of their useful lives. In fact, the *Affleck* and *Hulst* had just entered what was to be their final layups while the *Irvin* had been idle since the end of the 1978 season.

Over a six-day period beginning on March 10, three separate fires damaged two retired vessels and another still under construction. The first took place during the dismantling of the *James A. Farrell* at the Hyman-Michaels yard in Duluth, Minnesota, when a cutting torch ignited a wooden bulkhead in the bow section of the former USS steamer. Four days later, cutting operations also proved to be the culprit of a fire that broke out aboard the *Clarence B. Randall* (2) while a crew worked on converting the 552-foot vessel to a floating dock at Milwaukee. Confined to the after quarters, the blaze damaged three staterooms and the galley. Lastly, on March 16, a small rubbish fire singed a five-foot section of conveyor belt on the *Burns Harbor* as that vessel neared completion at the Bay Shipbuilding yard in Sturgeon Bay, Wisconsin.

Early in the year, the Soo River Company renamed its recently purchased steamer *George D. Goble* to *Robert S. Pierson*. Launched at Toledo in 1924 as the *William K. Field* for the Minnesota Transit Company, a subsidiary of the Reiss Steamship Company, this vessel later sailed as the *Reiss Brothers* before its acquisition by the American Steamship Company in 1969 and subsequent renaming to *George D. Goble* the following year. Sold to the Kinsman Marine Transit Company in 1972, this ship engaged in that fleet's pattern of ore, stone, and grain movements until the end of the 1979 season when it passed into Canadian registry as a result of the aforementioned transaction.

During this same timeframe, the Soo River Company also sold the *Pierson Independent* for scrapping following that vessel's short career with the fleet that ended with a serious grounding accident the previous October. Towed out of Hamilton, Ontario, on May 2 and given the uninspired name *Company*, the veteran steamer arrived at Santander, Spain, for dismantling on June 11.

With the pending conclusion of the Republic Steel iron ore contract looming large on the horizon, the late 1970s and the early 1980s was a difficult period for the Cleveland-Cliffs Steamship fleet. In 1980,

The Carryore Ltd. steamer *Menihek Lake* was involved in testing the use of shunters in the Welland Canal during the early part of the 1980 shipping season. (Author's Collection)

however, Cliffs managed to secure a floating contract with the Wisconsin Steel Corporation to transport iron ore into that firm's steel mill at South Chicago, Illinois. Concurrent with this agreement, the company finalized a bare-boat charter agreement involving the steel company's 600-foot steamer *Maxine*, which, in the end, it never operated.

Another preseason transition involved the Erie Sand Steamship Company, which entered into a charter agreement with the American Steamship Company to operate the self-unloader *Consumers Power* (3). This arrangement allowed the former fleet to replace the carrying capacity lost with the retirement of the *J. F. Schoellkopf, Jr.* at the end of the 1979 shipping season.

In March, Davie Shipbuilding Limited announced it would construct a new tanker for its Branch Lines division at a cost of $21 million. Built with an ice strengthened hull and a 96,000-barrel carrying capacity, this vessel was launched on November 29, 1981 and entered service in August of the following year as the *L'Erable No. 1* (2) for Societe Sofati-Soconav which by that time had completed its purchase of the Branch Lines fleet.

Continuing a robust period of U.S. flagged construction, the Bay Shipbuilding Corporation laid the keel for Hull No. 726 at Sturgeon Bay on March 3. Contracted to the Oglebay Norton Company's Columbia Transportation Division, this vessel became that fleet's first 1,000-foot vessel, *Columbia Star*. That same day, the shipyard also prepared for the arrival of the heavily damaged *E. M. Ford* in tow of the tugs *John M. Selvick* and *Lauren Castle* following a salvage operation that successfully raised the venerable cement carrier off the bottom of Milwaukee Harbor on January 20. Even as these shipyard activities took place in Wisconsin, Ford Motor Company's *Henry Ford II* departed its winter quarters at Dearborn, Michigan, to begin the early season coal shuttle between Toledo and the auto company's steel making complex on the Rouge River.

Three weeks later, on March 24, the crane vessel *Yankcanuck* (2) became the first ship to pass through Soo Locks at Sault Ste. Marie, Michigan, for the 1980 shipping season. On the same date, the Welland Canal connecting Lake Erie and Lake Ontario opened to commercial traffic with Canada Steamship Lines' *H. M. Griffith* and *Tadoussac* (2) making the first upbound and downbound passages through the canal respectively.

On March 25, tugs moved the *Menihek Lake* out of the dry dock at Port Weller Dry Docks in preparation to beginning a series of trials connected to its charter to the St. Lawrence Seaway Authority as part of that agency's shunter program in the Welland Canal. This followed some testing conducted the previous year with the retired steamer *Marinsal* (ex-*Peter Robertson* (2)) on a temporary charter from Marine Salvage Ltd. in which two propulsive units (one at the bow and another at the stern) maneuvered the ship through the canal. The goal of this project was to validate a method of relieving congestion in the Welland Canal by expediting lock passages through the system. Loaded with a cargo of ballast sand, the *Menihek Lake* operated in this arrangement until the completion of the project on May 9 with the removal of the shunters and the steamer's subsequent return to duty with the Carryore Limited fleet.

While fitting out at Toronto, Ontario, during late March, the discovery of cracks in the starboard boiler of Quebec & Ontario Transportation's *Marlhill* signaled the end of

Boiler problems led to the retirement of the steamer *Marlhill*. (Photo by Tom Salvner)

the 72-year old steamer's operational career. Subsequently sold for use as a grain storage barge in Mexico and with its cabins removed over the following winter, the retired vessel remained at Toronto until departing the lakes along with its former fleet mate *Lac Des Iles* in May of 1981.

A pair of early season incidents took place on April 8 when the *Canadian Prospector* went aground on Crossover Shoal in the St. Lawrence Seaway about nine miles west of Brockville, Ontario, while to the north, the *Fort York* received some bow damage when high winds forced it against a dock at Thunder Bay, Ontario. Freed from the bottom the following day, the *Canadian Prospector* went to Port Weller Dry Docks the following week for bottom repairs before reentering service on April 30.

On April 12, Interlake Steamship's *Mesabi Miner* established a Lake Erie cargo record by loading 46,915 net tons of coal at Conneaut, Ohio, for delivery to Port Washington, Wisconsin. With heavy ice continuing to complicate shipping operations in western Lake Superior well into the spring, the *Seaway Queen* rubbed the bottom while in the harbor entrance channel at Thunder Bay on April 16.

Christened at Bay Shipbuilding on April 16, the maiden voyage of American Steamship's *American Mariner* began ten days later when the 730-foot motor vessel sailed from Sturgeon Bay bound for Escanaba, Michigan, to load taconite pellets for Ashtabula, Ohio. The *American Mariner* was the first of three new U.S. flagged vessels to enter service that season, the others being the thousand-footers *Burns Harbor* and *Edgar B. Speer*.

Following an extensive reconstruction that included a new bow and cargo section, Upper Lakes Shipping christened the *Canadian Navigator* during a ceremony at Port Weller Dry Docks on April 19. Originally built in 1967 for saltwater trading as the *Demeterton* and given the name *St. Lawrence Navigator* upon entering the fleet in 1975, the refurbished vessel began sea trials on April 21.

Another early season mishap occurred on April 22 when Canada Steamship's *Hochelaga* suffered a boom collapse while unloading at Windsor, Ontario. Following the removal of its remaining cargo and the damaged remnants of the unloading boom, the steamer departed three days later to operate in the grain trade. After serving in this role for nearly six months, the *Hochelaga* finally entered the Port Arthur Shipbuilding yard at Thunder Bay on October 14 of that year for the installation of a new unloading boom.

While attempting to enter Taconite Harbor, Minnesota, to load ore on April 23, Bethlehem Steel's *Arthur B. Homer* went aground following a bow thruster failure. Freed from the bottom a short time later, the 826-foot steamer went to the Fraser Shipyards at Superior, Wisconsin, for drydocking and repairs before resuming what was to become its final operational season. Just two days after its fleet mate grounded at Taconite Harbor, the *Sparrows Point* took on its first cargo as a self-unloader when it departed Fraser Shipyards to load taconite at the nearby Burlington Northern Dock. The reconstruction of the *Sparrows Point* from its original gearless configuration proved to be the only one of its type undertaken by Bethlehem Steel during a decade-long fleet modernization program that also included the lengthening of one steamer and the construction of three thousand-foot vessels.

During the waning days of the first full month of 1980 shipping season, the Cleveland-Cliffs steamer *Tom M. Girdler* went aground near Light No. 2 in Lake St. Clair north of Detroit, Michigan, on April 27. Freed later that afternoon, the vessel continued its voyage with no reported damage. On the same day the *Girdler* suffered its minor mishap, the *Goderich* (2) entered service for the Soo River Company when it departed Toronto. Acquired after becoming surplus tonnage in the Upper Lakes Shipping fleet, the 550-foot vessel made one round trip voyage before being renamed *Soo River Trader* at Toronto on May 9.

Loaded with 55,502 gross tons of taconite, the *James R. Barker* opened a new chapter in Great Lakes shipping history when it arrived at Lorain, Ohio, on May 2 with the initial shipment for Republic Steel's new pellet transshipment complex. With Republic's steel mills located up the winding Cuyahoga River in nearby Cleveland, Ohio, the construction of this facility permitted the transfer of iron ore carried down the lakes by 1,000-foot ships into smaller vessels capable of navigating the constricted channels leading to its unloading docks. Taking full advantage of the economic benefits provided by larger vessels that first entered service during this period, this process eliminated the costly practice of transporting the iron ore from the upper lakes aboard lower capacity ships capable of transiting the Cuyahoga River. In the coming months, this new trading pattern was to have an adverse impact upon the company's three converted C4 bulk carriers, *Tom M. Girdler*, *Thomas F. Patton*, and *Charles M. White*, which it had on charter to the Cleveland-Cliffs Steamship Company.

Sold to Marine Salvage Ltd. for dismantling, two McKeil Work Boats Ltd. tugs towed the *J. F. Schoellkopf, Jr.* out of Erie,

Pennsylvania, on May 2 en route to Ramey's Bend on the Welland Canal, where the trio arrived the following day. Subsequently resold for scrapping overseas, the tugs *Cathy McAllister* and *Helen M. McAllister* towed the former Erie Sand self-unloader down the canal on June 17 for Quebec City, Quebec. Departing from that port ten days later, the *J. F. Schoellkopf, Jr.* began a month-long journey across the Atlantic and the Mediterranean before arriving at La Spezia, Italy, for scrapping on July 29.

On May 5, the steamer *Sharon* went hard aground in the Trenton Channel of the Detroit River. Despite the efforts of the tugs *Kinsale*, *Maine*, *Maryland*, *Shannon*, *Tug Malcolm*, and *William A. Whitney*, the American Steamship self-unloader refused to budge until finally coming free from the bottom on May 7 after lightering a portion of its cargo. Its operational career at an end, the *Sharon* went into permanent layup the next day at nearby Monroe, Michigan.

While undergoing repairs from damage sustained in a devastating fire on Lake Superior in June of 1979 that cost seven lives, an explosion of a carbon dioxide cylinder aboard the *Cartiercliffe Hall* at Collingwood, Ontario, on May 7 left one person dead and another injured. Valued at $6 million, the shipyard completed the extensive reconstruction of the vessel's superstructure just six days later.

Its construction delayed by a labor dispute, the American Ship Building Company launched United States Steel's second thousand-footer, *Edgar B. Speer*, at Lorain on May 8. Christened on June 4, the *Speer*

A grounding accident in the Detroit River put an abrupt end to the operational career of the steamer *Sharon*.
(Author's Collection)

underwent sea trials in late August but did not embark on its maiden voyage to load taconite at Two Harbors, Minnesota, until September 19 of that year due to a weakened demand for ore.

On May 9, Columbia Transportation's self-unloader *Robert C. Norton* (2) laid up for the final time when it tied up at the Hans Hansen Dock in Toledo. The following day, its fleet mate *Sylvania* also arrived at that port to close out its long career. While the *Sylvania* went to the scrap yard three years later, the *Norton* languished at Toledo for nearly a decade and a half before being sold for dismantling in 1994.

While loading grain at the Globe Elevator in Superior, Wisconsin, on May 13, a loading spout fell into the cargo hold of S & E Shipping's *Alastair Guthrie*. Occurring late in the evening, the minor incident inflicted no injuries among the vessel's crew or those working at the elevator.

Possessing a fleet committed to supplying its raw material transportation needs, the decline in domestic steel production prompted the United States Steel Corporation to layup several ships during the middle of May. This included the *Eugene W. Pargny*, *Eugene P. Thomas*, *Ralph H. Watson*, and *Homer D. Williams*. With economic conditions continuing to deteriorate, the fleet's list of idled units had grown by the end of the month to include the *Sewell Avery*, *Thomas W. Lamont*, and *Robert C. Stanley*. Of these vessels, the *Eugene W. Pargny* and *Ralph H. Watson* never operated again.

Bound for Toronto with sugar on May 17, the Cuban freighter *Carlos Manuel De Cespedes* struck the canal-sized motor vessel *Roland Desgagnes* in the St. Lawrence River just above the Eisenhower Lock. This accident took place when the saltwater vessel suffered a steering failure and swung into the port bow of the *Desgagnes*, which was carrying a payload of grinding balls from Sault Ste. Marie, Ontario, for Sept-Iles, Quebec. Following the collision, both vessels continued their respective voyages with the *Roland Desgagnes* receiving repairs at Sorel, Quebec, at the end of the month.

During mid-May, two classic lakers began their final voyages to the scrap yard. On May 18, the tug *Salvage Monarch* towed the retired Misener Transportation steamer *Royalton* out of Hamilton for Quebec City. Six days later, the same tug pulled the *Marinsal* out of Hamilton to join the *Royalton* in preparation for a tandem overseas scrap tow. Retired from active service in 1975, the former carrier, which last sailed as the Kinsman fleet's *Peter Robertson* (2), had thus far avoided an appointment with the cutting torch thanks to its previously mentioned charter to the St. Lawrence Seaway Authority for shunter testing in the Welland Canal. Towed out of Quebec City on May 31 by the West German ocean tug *Hanseat*, both vessels arrived at La Spezia, Italy, for scrapping on June 25.

On May 19, tugs towed the forward cargo section of American Ship Building's Hull No. 909, out of that firm's Toledo yard for its primary facility at Lorain, a transit repeated the following day by the hull's bow section. As the Interlake Steamship Company's third and final thousand-foot vessel, the *William J. De Lancey* became not only the longest ship ever built for service on the Great Lakes but also the last ship ever constructed by this prolific shipbuilder over its long history.

Following a tow up the lakes from South Chicago, the tug *Wilfred M. Cohen* pulled the steamer *C. H. McCullough, Jr.* into Thunder Bay on May 20 for scrapping at the Western Metals yard. Built in 1907, this ship had enjoyed a long career with the Interlake Steamship Company prior to its sale to the Cement Transit Company (Medusa Cement) in 1970. Intended for conversion to a cement carrier, the *C. H. McCullough, Jr.* operated in the bulk trades through the 1975 shipping season before a subsequent survey in 1978 found the steamer unfit for its planned reconstruction.

Suffering steering difficulties during its departure through the Duluth Ship Canal on May 24, the 730-foot *Lake Winnipeg* rubbed the north pier with sufficient force to break loose a section of concrete and topple a lamppost. Loaded with a cargo of wheat for Baie-Comeau, Quebec, this vessel's misfortunes continued two days later when it went aground near Espanore Island in northern Lake Huron. Freed on May 27, tugs towed the *Lake Winnipeg* into the St. Marys River for a structural inspection before the steamer made a subsequent visit to Port Arthur Shipbuilding at Thunder Bay for hull repairs from both the grounding and the earlier incident at Duluth. Later caught up by a labor dispute, this vessel spent much of the remaining shipping season in the shipyard.

Christened at Sturgeon Bay on May 24, the *Burns Harbor* became the third thousand-foot vessel commissioned by the Bethlehem Steel Corporation. Although beginning sea trials on July 7, the soft demand for iron ore delayed the maiden voyage of this vessel until September 28 of that year when it sailed from Sturgeon Bay to Superior, Wisconsin, to load taconite pellets for Burns Harbor, Indiana.

On May 27, Canada Steamship Lines commissioned the 730-foot *Nanticoke* at Collingwood. The only Canadian flagged vessel of new construction to enter Great Lakes service during the 1980 season, the

The *Joseph H. Thompson* required a tow into Two Harbors, Minnesota, after losing power on Lake Superior.
(Author's Collection)

Nanticoke began its maiden voyage on June 12 when it departed the shipyard bound for Marquette, Michigan, to load a cargo of iron ore pellets for delivery to Hamilton.

In late May, the American Steamship Company awarded the American Ship Building Company a contract to repair the extensive fire damage suffered by the self-unloader *Nicolet* at Toledo in December 1979. Operated by American Steamship's Gartland Steamship Company subsidiary, this reconstruction culminated with the 1905-built motor vessel to reentering service at the beginning of the 1981 shipping season.

During the month of May, Group Desgagnes Inc. acquired the package freighter *Eskimo* from the Canada Steamship Lines following that ship having spent the previous season idle at Collingwood. Following a refit at Lauzon, Quebec, the 21-year old vessel entered service for its new owners as the *Mathilda Desgagnes*.

While en route to Cleveland with iron ore on June 1, the *Joseph H. Thompson* lost electrical power in western Lake Superior. Towed into Two Harbors by the tug *Edna G.* the crew of the 714-foot bulker managed to restore power around 8:30 that evening. Following an inspection by the U.S. Coast Guard, the steamer resumed its downbound trip.

The string of steering failures that had already caused a number of accidents on the Great Lakes/St. Lawrence Seaway system thus far in the season claimed another victim on June 2 when the *Seaway Queen* grounded in the St. Clair Cutoff Channel near the mouth of the St. Clair River. Proving minor in nature, the steamer suffered no serious damage in the stranding.

Following an extensive refit, the recently renamed tanker *Congar* (3) began running sea trials in Toronto Harbor during early June prior to reentering service later that month. Acquired by Johnstone Shipping Limited in 1979 as the *Tegucigalpa* after its sale to a Honduran buyer fell through, the steamer had originally entered service for the Imperial Oil fleet in 1948 as the *Imperial London*.

At the beginning of summer, the continued softening of raw material transportation demands for the steel and construction industries led to another massive round of layups within the U.S. fleet. The lack of available cargoes that had already sidelined a large percentage of the United States Steel fleet also prompted Columbia Transportation to send its self-unloaders *Crispin Oglebay* (2) and *J. R. Sensibar* to the wall at Toledo. With its damaged steamer *Sharon* removed from service earlier in the season, the American Steamship Company also laid up the *John J. Boland* (3) and *Richard J. Reiss* (2). Other vessels entering layup during this period included Interlake Steamship's *Samuel Mather* (6), Kinsman's *Merle M. McCurdy*, and the *Tom M. Girdler* of the Cleveland-Cliffs fleet. In addition to these vessels, Huron Cement had already placed the *Lewis G. Harriman* into an indefinite layup at Alpena, Michigan, after the 57-year old cement carrier suffered boiler problems while entering that port near the beginning of the season.

In spite of the worsening economic conditions, several U.S. flagged shipping companies were in the process of upgrading their fleets at the beginning of the 1980s. This included the conversion of many existing straight deck bulk carriers built during the 1950s and early 1960s into self-unloaders. Due in large part to its signing of a long-term contract to transport iron ore for Republic Steel, the Interlake Steamship Company had good reason to be especially

Sold to Group Desgagnes during the spring of 1980, the former Canada Steamship Lines package freighter *Eskimo* was renamed *Mathilda Desgagnes*. (Author's Collection)

optimistic about the upcoming decade. As such, the company continued the process of modernizing its fleet with the construction of a third thousand-foot vessel and the self-unloading conversions of the *Elton Hoyt 2nd* (2) and *Charles M. Beeghly*, the latter of which arrived at Fraser Shipyards at Superior, Wisconsin, for its reconstruction in late June.

Following a relatively quiet month, a string of accidents befell a number of vessels in the Canadian fleet during the last ten days of June. The first took place on June 20, when the steamer *Brookdale* (2) went aground in the Detroit River just below the Canadian Salt Company Dock at Windsor. Refloated two hours later, the elderly Westdale Shipping self-unloader was soon back to work. Four days later, the *Cartiercliffe Hall* lost steering and ran aground in the St. Lawrence Seaway near Cornwall, Ontario, while upbound with a load of iron ore. Assisted by three tugs, the 730-foot vessel floated off the bottom the following day and sailed to Prescott, Ontario, for a survey before continuing on to Conneaut.

Near five o'clock in the morning of June 25, the most significant accident to occur on the St. Clair River in several years transpired when the steamer *Montrealais* and the motor vessel *Algobay* came together in a spectacular head-on collision abreast St. Clair, Michigan, which surprisingly caused no injuries to the crews of either vessel. Taking place in dense fog, the collision heavily damaged the bow of the *Montrealais*, which was downbound with taconite for Hamilton. Upbound in ballast to load salt at Goderich, Ontario, the *Algobay* required temporary patching at nearby Sarnia.

Proceeding about six miles downstream from the collision site later that day, the *Montrealais* anchored just below Recors Point before being cleared to continue downbound the following morning. Lightering at Port Colborne, Ontario, to reduce its draft in order to transit the Welland Canal, the 730-foot steamer discharged its remaining cargo at Hamilton before tying up at Port Weller Dry Docks on July 1 for repairs reaching $1.2 million. Meanwhile, fleet mate *Gordon C. Leitch* took aboard the ore unloaded at Port Colborne and delivered it to Hamilton.

Bearing the scars of its unfortunate meeting with the Upper Lakes Shipping bulk carrier, the *Algobay* received permanent repairs at Port Colborne by Herb Fraser & Associates before it resumed trading during mid-August. Its extensive bow reconstruction completed, the *Montrealais* reentered service in late September.

While downbound in the St. Clair Cutoff Channel on June 27, Algoma Steel's *Yankcanuck* (2) went aground following a steering gear failure. Freed the following day, the 324-foot crane vessel was able to continue its trip to Windsor. Towed out of Port Dover, Ontario, during the latter part of June, the *Inland Transport* went to Port Maitland, Ontario, for scrapping. Retired following a grounding accident in 1972, the former Hall Corporation tanker had languished at Sarnia until its purchase by Harry Gamble Shipyards and subsequent tow to Port Dover four years later.

During the summer, United States Steel drastically reduced the size of its fleet through the sale of seven steamers for scrapping. The vessels involved were the *Eugene J. Buffington*, *D. M. Clemson* (2), *Thomas F. Cole*, *Alva C. Dinkey*, *D. G. Kerr* (2), *Governor Miller*, and *J. P. Morgan, Jr.*, all of which spent their entire careers in the steelmaker's fleet and had been idle at the Twin Ports for several years. Within the same timeframe, USS also sold the *Peter A. B. Widener* for duties described separately in this chapter.

Towed out of Duluth on July 13, the *Eugene J. Buffington* and *J. P. Morgan, Jr.* were the first of these ships to depart on their scrap tows. Departing Quebec City in a tandem tow on October 4 of that year, both vessels arrived at Bilbao, Spain, eighteen days later following a safe crossing of the Atlantic. Scrapping of both veteran carriers began one month later.

Following a short tow up Lake Superior from Duluth by the tugs *Daryl C. Hannah* and *Tug Malcolm*, the *Thomas F. Cole* arrived at Thunder Bay on July 31 for scrapping by the Western Metals Corporation. Sold to the same company for dismantling, the *D. M. Clemson* (2) was towed out of Superior, Wisconsin, by the *Tug Malcolm* four days later to join its former fleet mate at Thunder Bay.

Having loaded cargoes of scrap metal at Milwaukee during their voyage off the lakes, the *Alva C. Dinkey* and *Governor Miller* departed Quebec City in tow of the ocean tug *Cathy B.* on October 18. Arriving off El Ferrol del Caudillo, Spain, on November 12, scrapping of the *Dinkey* began the following month. After splitting the tow, the *Cathy B.* delivered the *Governor Miller* to Vigo, Spain, on November 28 where the youngest USS steamer sold that season was to meet an identical fate.

While being towed out of the Duluth by the tug *Tusker* on September 22, the *D. G. Kerr* (2) struck the north pier of the Duluth Ship Canal near the same spot hit by the *Lake Winnipeg* earlier in the season. Although the retired steamer suffered little harm, this incident, along with that involving the Canadian vessel, inflicted some $200,000 worth of damage to the pier. Later, while at Sydney, Nova Scotia, awaiting a tow across the Atlantic to Spain, the *D. G. Kerr* (2) broke free

The Ford Motor Company's *Benson Ford* was one of several veteran carriers laid up during summer due to depressed demand. (Photo by James Hoffman)

of its moorings during an autumn storm on November 19. Loaded with approximately 5,000 tons of scrap iron prior to its departure from Duluth, the *Kerr* went adrift until grounding in a shallow section of the harbor. Released from its stranding with no apparent damage, the old steamer subsequently sank approximately eight miles east of Santa Maria Island in the Azores on December 16 while in tow of the supply ship *Federal 6*.

On July 1, the steamer *Frank R. Denton* departed Superior, Wisconsin, with a record 540,000 bushels of malting barley destined for Oswego, New York. Three days later, and just weeks after leaving Port Weller Dry Docks following an extensive refit, the *Cape Breton Miner* went aground in the St. Lawrence River near Prescott while loaded with a cargo of salt from Windsor for Montreal, Quebec. Released the following day, the 680-foot self-unloader returned to Port Weller Dry Docks later that month for bottom repairs.

Angered by plans to reduce personnel, a strike by lock operators closed the five Canadian Seaway locks between Montreal and Lake Ontario to commercial traffic on July 7. During the work stoppage, however, the striking workers permitted the passage of recreational vessels through the locks. By the time the Canadian Labor Relations Board ordered the employees back to work two days later, the labor dispute had delayed the transits of 45 vessels through the Seaway.

Launched by the Bay Shipbuilding Corporation at Sturgeon Bay on July 14, the *American Republic* became the last vessel built for the American Steamship Company during a fleet modernization program that began during the early 1970s that resulted in the construction of ten vessels. Built primarily to satisfy a contract signed with Republic Steel to move taconite from the steelmaker's pellet terminal at Lorain to its mills at

Cleveland, this ship featured several unique design features to facilitate its operation in the twisting confines of the Cuyahoga River. With final work on the vessel completed over the winter, the *American Republic* entered service in May 1981.

On the morning of July 16, a strong windstorm caused widespread damage throughout the Detroit area. Knocking two bridge cranes out of service at Ford Motor Company's River Rouge Complex in Dearborn, the high winds also toppled an unloading rig at Great Lakes Steel on nearby Zug Island. Continuing its path of destruction, the storm knocked out power to the Dix and Jefferson Avenue bridges spanning the Rouge River, thereby closing the busy waterway to navigation. With their path to the Rouge Plant blocked, the Ford Motor Company's *Henry Ford II* and *William Clay Ford* were forced to anchor in the Detroit River. When power to the bridges was finally restored on July 21, the number of vessels in the Detroit River awaiting passage had grown to include the *Benson Ford* and *Richard J. Reiss* (2).

Across the river loading salt at Windsor, the *Brookdale* (2) lost its unloading boom during the same storm. Interestingly, this incident took place just one month after the steamer had grounded in the same general vicinity. The damaged vessel proceeded to Buffalo, New York, where it unloaded before entering a permanent layup at Toronto on July 20. Its advanced age and condition prohibiting the cost of repairs, Westdale Shipping sold the *Brookdale* (2) for scrapping later that fall. Towed out of Toronto on October 10, the retired self-unloader went first to Port Colborne and finally to the scrap yard at Port Maitland, where dismantling began a short time later. Over the following winter, Herb Fraser & Associates installed the boilers removed from the scrapped vessel into the Quebec & Ontario Transportation steamer *Lac Ste. Anne* at Port Colborne.

The threat of the same labor strike that was to delay the repair of the *Lake Winnipeg* at the Port Arthur Shipbuilding also prompted the early sailing of Halco's *Frankcliffe Hall* (2), which was undergoing a conversion to a self-unloader at the yard. Its reconstruction incomplete, the steamer loaded a cargo of potash on July 17 before departing Thunder Bay for further work at Hamilton.

While upbound in the St. Lawrence Seaway with a cargo of iron ore, Halco's *Lawrencecliffe Hall* (2) struck the south tower of the St. Louis de Gonzague Bridge near Valleyfield, Quebec, at around 9:30 in the evening of July 21. Immediately shutting down all traffic in the area, the accident inflicted heavy damage to both the bridge and the bulk carrier, the latter of which sustained a large hole in its port bow that extended far below the waterline. With 35 ships awaiting passage, temporary repairs to the bridge allowed navigation through this section of the Seaway to resume two days later. Suffering a considerable amount of flooding through its punctured hull, the *Lawrencecliffe Hall* (2) settled to a draft of 31 feet. After lightering, the vessel went to Valleyfield to unload its remaining cargo before departing on July 29 for Montreal. Entering the dry dock at the Vickers Canada Ltd. yard on August 11, the 15-year old motor vessel returned to service on September 25. All told, the accident resulted in approximately $2 million worth of damage to the bridge and a similar amount to the *Lawrencecliffe Hall* (2).

On July 22, the Upper Peninsula Shipbuilding Company (UPSCO) at Ontonagon, Michigan, laid the keel for a 120-foot tugboat under contract to the State of

Michigan. Intended for the establishment of a cross-lake railcar service between Michigan and Wisconsin ports using the integrated tug/barge (ITB) concept, this project also included the planned construction of four 437-foot barges by the same yard. Mired by scandal involving officials at UPSCO, the shipyard ceased work in 1982 with the tugboat and one barge still under construction. Having lost millions in the affair, the State of Michigan would eventually abandon the project.

The depressed demand for the movement of raw materials sent further vessels to the wall during July. This included the laying up of Inland Steel's *E. J. Block*, *L. E. Block*, and *Philip D. Block* at Indiana Harbor, Indiana, and Ford Motor Company's *Benson Ford* at Dearborn. Other vessels entering periods of inactivity during this same period included American Steamship's *St. Clair* and Pringle Transit's *Paul Thayer*.

Rededication ceremonies took place for the newly refurbished *E. M. Ford* at Sturgeon Bay on July 31. Having survived what could have been a career ending sinking at Milwaukee seven months earlier, the veteran cement carrier went back to work in the cement trade one week later. Although relegated to cement storage and transfer duties at Carrollton, Michigan, after the 1996 season, the 428-foot vessel lasted until being sold for scrapping in 2008.

August of 1980 witnessed the demise of the three C4 conversion steamers owned by the Republic Steel Corporation. Brought to the lakes following their reconstruction from saltwater transports built during World War II, these vessels became redundant with the opening of the steel company's pellet

Shown downbound on the St. Marys River, the *Tom M. Girdler* was one of three C4 conversion lake freighters sold for scrap during the 1980 season. (Author's Collection)

transshipment facility at Lorain and the end of its iron ore hauling contract with Cleveland-Cliffs. As previously stated, this ore movement pattern from loading facilities on the upper lakes to Republic Steel's docks at Cleveland relied entirely upon self-unloading vessels. With a limited carrying capacity of only 15,000 gross tons, or only about 1/4 that of a thousand-foot laker, these steamers were among the fastest on the lakes, the latter achieved, however, at the cost of high fuel consumption of their steam turbines.(See Appendix A for further information)

The *Tom M. Girdler* and *Charles M. White* operated briefly during the early part of the season before laying up at Lorain on June 4 and June 17 respectively. Although the *Thomas F. Patton* fitted out at Toledo that year, a subsequent change in orders resulted in this ship not entering service. Declared surplus, Republic Steel wasted little time disposing the three sister ships for scrapping overseas. Retaining their black hulls and olive drab cabins, but devoid of any Cleveland-Cliffs markings, these distinctive ships departed the lakes following careers that spanned only three decades.

Pulled out of Toledo on August 13 by tugs *Helen M. McAllister* and *Salvage Monarch*, the *Thomas F. Patton* became the first of the trio to begin its final voyage. After passing through the Welland Canal, the scrap tow continued across Lake Ontario before transiting the St. Lawrence Seaway to reach Quebec City. Returning to Lake Erie, the same tugs towed the *Charles M. White* from its layup berth at Lorain on August 24 to begin a repeat voyage to Quebec City. Embarking upon their third scrap tow in as many weeks, the *Helen M. McAllister* and *Salvage Monarch* maneuvered the *Tom M. Girdler* past the breakwaters at Lorain on September 4.

On September 8, the German tug *Fairplay IX* towed the *Thomas F. Patton* and *Charles M. White* out of Quebec City bound for the Atlantic Ocean. After rounding Cape of Good Hope, the tow arrived at Karachi, Pakistan, on December 23, from which the two retired steamers went to India for scrapping a short time later. Clearing Quebec City on September 15 in tow of the German tug *Hanseat*, the *Tom M. Girdler* became the first of these three ships to reach the scrap yard when it arrived at Bombay, India, on December 13.

Having signed a long-term contract with the Canadian Wheat Board to move grain on the Great Lakes and St. Lawrence Seaway, Algoma Central Marine announced its ordering of a 730-foot gearless bulk carrier from Collingwood Shipyards during the summer of 1980. The first ship built for this fleet without a self-unloading capability since the commissioning of the *Algocen* (2) in 1968, the *Algowest* was to enter service two years later.

On August 4, engine problems forced the *Gordon C. Leitch* to drop anchor in lower Lake Huron. Towed to Point Edward, Ontario, the following day by the tug *Glenada*, the Upper Lakes Shipping steamer resumed its upbound voyage to Thunder Bay three days later. During this same timeframe, two separate accidents took place on the Welland Canal. The first occurred on August 4 when Bridge 19 lowered early and struck the *Scan Crusader*, thereby resulting in significant damage to the bridge. The next day, a crewman attempting the board the 730-foot self-unloader *Jean Parisien* of the Canada Steamship Lines fell to his death at Lock 7 in the canal.

Even while struggling to survive the loss of its ore hauling agreement with Republic Steel, Cleveland-Cliffs explored the possibility of building a thousand-footer after winning an initial bid to secure a major

The *Edward B. Greene* following its conversion to a self-unloader. (Photo by Tom Salvner)

floating contract to haul coal for the Detroit Edison Company during the late 1970s. In contrast to the prevailing preference of utilizing diesel engines for new construction, the Cliffs project incorporated steam propulsion. When falling demand during the early 1980s delayed the implementation of this arrangement, however, Cleveland-Cliffs quietly dropped any further work toward building a new lake freighter. In the end, the coal contract eventually went to the Interlake Steamship Company in 1984. Despite these challenges, the fleet did invest in converting the *Edward B. Greene* to a self-unloader when that steamer arrived at the American Ship Building Company yard at Toledo on August 7 for its reconstruction.

Although quickly extinguished, a small fire that broke out on the *Cape Breton Miner* at Port Weller Dry Docks on August 11 left one firefighter injured. The following day, a more serious accident took place aboard another Canadian flagged vessel when the *Ralph Misener* suffered a crankcase explosion and engine room fire while sailing on the Saguenay River approximately six miles from Port Alfred, Quebec. Taking place while the 730-foot vessel was carrying a cargo of petroleum coke loaded at Chicago, Illinois, the explosion and subsequent fire left five of its crew injured, two of which later died. The dead included the ship's chief engineer who passed away the following day at a hospital in Quebec City. Towed first into Port Alfred to unload its cargo on August 13, the *Ralph Misener* later went to the Vickers Canada Ltd. shipyard at Montreal for repairs before returning to service in October.

Idled by a broken crankshaft since the 1973 season, the Ann Arbor Railroad car ferry *Arthur K. Atkinson* reentered service on Lake Michigan with a recommissioning ceremony taking place at Manitowoc on August 16 and a similar celebration at Frankfort, Michigan, the following day. This voyage had come a week later than planned due to problems with the vessel's electrical system. Its $500,000 repair project subsidized through a combination of federal and state funds from Michigan and Wisconsin to improve cross-lake rail ferry service, the *Arthur K. Atkinson* operated until April of 1982 when car ferry service from Frankfort was suspended.

The recent string of misfortune in the Canadian fleet continued on August 20 when the package freighter *Fort Chambly* went aground near Six Mile Point in the St. Marys River. After offloading some fuel, the 463-foot vessel came off the bottom with the assistance of four tugs and USCGC *Katmai Bay* on August 21. That same day, a fleet mate of the *Fort Chambly*, the *Sir James Dunn*, grounded near Champlain, Quebec. Refloated with tug assistance on August 22, the bulk carrier proceeded to Montreal for a survey before continuing to unload at Hamilton. Although requiring a shipyard visit for repairs, the *Sir James Dunn* returned to duty late in the season before laying up for the winter at Midland, Ontario.

Sent to the shipyard early due to depressed demand, Columbia Transportation's *Courtney Burton* arrived at Sturgeon Bay on August 25 for conversion to a self-unloader over the coming winter. This reconstruction was to be one of four such conversions performed by Bay Shipbuilding for this fleet during the early 1980s, the others involving the *Armco*, *Middletown*, and *Reserve*.

On August 30, the tug *Daniel McAllister* towed the retired Quebec & Ontario Transportation steamer *Helen Evans* out of Hamilton. With the assistance of the *Cathy McAllister*, the scrap tow proceeded through the St. Lawrence Seaway to Quebec City. A few weeks later, on September 17, the *Helen Evans* departed in tow of the seagoing tug *Captain Ioannis S.* in tandem with Upper Lakes Shipping's former steamer *Thornhill*. Retired in 1976, the latter vessel saw subsequent use as a storage barge prior to its scrap sale. Following a stop at Halifax, Nova Scotia, after the *Captain Ioannis S.* encountered mechanical problems, the two lake vessels arrived at Mamonal, Columbia, for dismantling on October 30.

Having been laid up at Calcite, Michigan, since 1973, the tugs *Ohio* and *Sainte Marie II* towed the *Irvin L. Clymer* upbound through the Soo Locks on September 24 en route for a refit at Fraser Shipyards. Towed across Lake Superior by the *Ohio*, the 63-year old self-unloader safely reached Superior, Wisconsin, despite the tow seeking shelter on September 25 after encountering heavy weather east of the Keweenaw Peninsula. Spending the winter at the shipyard, the *Irvin L. Clymer* reentered service the following spring.

Following a relatively quiet period devoid of any serious accidents but one during which several retired carriers made their final voyages to the scrap yard, one minor mishap occurred on September 25 when American Steamship's *Saginaw Bay* hit the Sixth Street Bridge at Marinette, Wisconsin. Operating in its 63rd year, this self-unloading steamer entered its final layup after delivering a cargo of iron ore to Cleveland on December 16 of that same year.

On October 4, Bethlehem Steel laid up the *Arthur B. Homer* at Erie, Pennsylvania, due to a combination of reduced demand and the entry into service of the steelmaker's third thousand-footer, *Burns Harbor*, in late

September. Its future sealed by a new breed of larger carriers equipped with self-unloading equipment and a general downsizing of the domestic steel manufacturing base, this steamer remained idle at Erie until its sale for scrapping in 1986. The poor economic conditions in early fall also prompted United States Steel to send three of its "Super" class steamers to the wall when it laid up the *Benjamin F. Fairless*, *Irving S. Olds*, and *Enders M. Voorhees* at Duluth with storage cargoes of grain.

In tow of the tug *Ohio*, the Seaway Towing Company's *Peter A. B. Widener* passed downbound through the Soo Locks on October 5 bound to load grain at Zilwaukee, Michigan. Acquired from the United States Steel Corporation earlier that year, this 601-foot vessel had been idle since the 1974 shipping season. Prior to entering service for the Duluth based company, the *Widener* went to Fraser Shipyards in September for conversion to a barge. The loading operation at Zilwaukee having proved a prolonged affair, the *Ohio* towed the former steamer downbound past Detroit on October 28 en route to Sorel. Assisted by the tugs *South Carolina* and *Ste. Marie II*, the *Ohio* and *Widener* passed through Welland Canal on October 30 before high winds delayed the voyage across Lake Ontario for several days. Later, the barge sustained some damage in a collision with the Swiss tanker *Rhone* after becoming uncontrollable in strong currents at Montreal on November 7. This incident, along with the onset of unfavorable weather conditions, prompted Seaway Towing to cancel plans for the *Widener* to move another grain cargo before the close of the 1980 shipping season.

While transiting the Detroit River on October 6, the *Lac Des Iles* suffered a steering failure and went aground near Grassy Island. Freeing itself without major difficulty, the 75-year old steamer operated for a few more weeks before going to Port Weller Dry Docks, where it entered the dry dock on November 17. Found to be beyond economical repair, the *Lac Des Iles* sailed to Toronto under its own power the next day. Acquired by Marine Salvage Ltd. shortly afterwards, this vessel remained at that port until its subsequent resale for off-lakes use the following spring.

Continuing its long association with the Algoma Central Railway's Marine Division, Collingwood Shipyards launched the *Algowood* at its Collingwood yard on October 7. Destined to make its maiden voyage in April of the following year, this 730-foot motor vessel was the eighth self-unloader built by that shipyard for Algoma since the construction of the *Roy A. Jodrey* in 1965.

On October 11, the *Quedoc* (2) was damaged in a collision with the Greek saltwater freighter *George L.* on Lake St. Louis in the St. Lawrence River. With damage to its starboard bow extending up to the pilothouse, the 605-foot steamer went to Port Weller Dry Docks for repairs over the following winter. Just four days after the *Quedoc* (2) suffered its mishap, the *Nipigon Bay* suffered an equally serious accident when it grounded near Brockville in the St. Lawrence River. Opening a 100-foot gash in its hull, the steamer went into Port Arthur Shipbuilding at Thunder Bay on October 24 for repairs estimated to be in the range of $500,000. Returning to that yard over the upcoming winter, the *Nipigon Bay* received a 5-foot high trunk deck to increase its cubic capacity for carrying grain.

The *Gulf Canada* suffered minor damage in a collision with the Greek flagged freighter *Megalohari II* at Montreal on October 17. Subsequent repairs to the tanker stemming from this accident took place at

Charlottetown, Prince Edward Island.

Arriving at Taconite Harbor on October 21, the *Elton Hoyt 2nd* (2) loaded its first cargo following the completion of its self-unloader conversion by the American Ship Building Company at Toledo. This reconstruction was the second such project undertaken by Interlake Steamship since the mid-1970s, the first being the conversion of the *Herbert C. Jackson* in 1975.

On the first day of November, high winds and heavy seas in the Straits of Mackinac pushed the *Chief Wawatam* into its dock at St. Ignace, Michigan. Causing some $87,000 in damage, the incident took the venerable car ferry out of service until mid-December.

A pair of incidents involving Great Lakes tankers occurred over a two-day period in early November. Occurring on November 3, the first involved the *Lakeshell* (3) when that vessel grounded at Marathon, Ontario, on the north shore of Lake Superior. Stranding on the harbor's bottom after striking a dock, the tanker managed to free itself without any significant damage. The next day, the steamer *Amoco Wisconsin* blew a cylinder head and went adrift off the Leelanau Peninsula in northern Lake Michigan while carrying 48,000 gallons of gasoline. Towed into Grand Traverse Bay by the U.S. Coast Guard, two Selvick Marine tugs, one of which was the 98-foot *Lauren Castle*, arrived later in the day to take the disabled tanker to Traverse City, Michigan. Colliding with the *Amoco Wisconsin* in the darkness near 1:30 in the morning of November 5, however, the *Lauren Castle* sank in approximately 300 feet of water with the loss of one life. Its hull punctured in the collision, the tanker began losing about 12 gallons of gasoline per hour until its crew brought the leak under control a short time later. Operating in the twilight of its career, the *Amoco Wisconsin* received repairs and went on to operate for two more seasons.

The awarding of its construction contract announced jointly by Bay Shipbuilding and Columbia Transportation the previous September, the launch of the *Columbia Star* took place at Sturgeon Bay on November 8. Coming near the end of a robust period of vessel construction on the American side of the lakes, the *Columbia Star* not only represented the sixth, and thus far last, thousand-footer built at Sturgeon Bay but also the final ship ever constructed for Oglebay Norton's Columbia Transportation Division.

Suffering mechanical problems in Lake Erie on November 11, Erie Sand's *Lakewood* (2) required a tow by the tug *Ohio* first into Fairport, Ohio, and later to Cleveland, where the sand sucker went to the G. & W. Industries Dock for repairs. Requiring a further tow to Port Weller Dry Docks following the discovery of a misaligned shaft, the *Lakewood* (2) entered the dry dock on November 21 before clearing the shipyard two days later under its own power.

While upbound in the Detroit River on November 12, the *J. L. Mauthe* suffered a 4-foot gash in its port bow after losing steerage near Zug Island. Anchoring temporarily off the Delray Power Plant, the 647-foot laker went to Nicholson Terminals for repairs before resuming its voyage.

The notorious heavy weather common across the Great Lakes region during late autumn made its presence known when Quebec & Ontario Transportation's *Meldrum Bay* found itself at the mercy of heavy seas in Lake Superior just after passing upbound at Whitefish Point on November 29. Although the encounter ravaged the navigational equipment in the vessel's pilothouse and left one crewmember injured, the 31-year old steamer managed to reach port safely.

As the shipping season entered its final weeks, three separate groundings took place on December 1. Two of these incidents occurred on the St. Marys River when the *Wolverine* (2) stranded near Nine Mile Point and the *Frank A. Sherman* ran onto the bottom just above Pt. Louise. In both instances, the vessels managed to free themselves without any reports of significant damage. Meanwhile, to the south, the *Buffalo* (3) suffered a power failure and went aground near Peche Island in the upper Detroit River. Freeing itself from the bottom a short time later, the motor vessel briefly anchored outside the shipping channel below Belle Isle for repairs before continuing to Cleveland.

On December 4, Halco's *Hallfax* nearly sank during a storm in the Gulf of St. Lawrence. Battling for survival in 50-knot winds near Miscou Island, the 445-foot self-unloader began rolling in excess of 35 degrees after a steering cable parted. Responding to calls of distress, a Canadian Armed Forces helicopter managed to remove seven of the vessel's crew before the deteriorating weather conditions curtailed any further airlifts. Surviving its brush with disaster, the *Hallfax* arrived at Sept-Iles in tow of the tug *Irving Beach* two days later. Having sustained further damage when its port propeller and shaft snagged a towline, the battered vessel went into an indefinite layup at Sorel, where it remained until being sold for off-lakes use the following year.

In early December, Johnstone Shipping purchased the *D. C. Everest* from American Can of Canada Limited. Sailing from Thunder Bay later that month with a Johnstone crew and a storage cargo of wheat, the canal-sized motor vessel arrived at Toronto on December 23, where it was renamed *Condarrell* in early 1981.

Carrying a cargo of scrap metal loaded at Holland, Michigan, the barge *Maitland No. 1* departed the Great Lakes during December in tow of the tug *John Roen V* after Bultema Marine Transportation sold the former car ferry for off-lakes use. Purchased to move scrap between Port Everglades, Florida, and Progreso, Mexico, the Trio Shipping Group placed the pair into Honduran registry following their arrival at Quebec City. As such, the company renamed the barge *Trio Trado* and the tug *Trio Bravo*. The *Trio Trado* never made it Florida, however, as it capsized and sank in the Atlantic Ocean on January 10, 1981 while in tow of an ocean tug that had taken over that role after the *Trio Bravo* proved inadequate for the task. Successfully completing its voyage to Florida, the *Trio Bravo* subsequently sank at Port Everglades on January 21, 1981. Refloated, but with its cabins destroyed, the tug sat derelict until its intentional scuttling off Fort Lauderdale, Florida, in 1982.

On December 8, the motor vessel *Kingdoc* (2) grounded while departing Pugwash, Nova Scotia, with a load of salt. With the tug *Point Valiant* assisting, the freighter came free from the bottom the next day with no reported damage.

While transiting the St. Marys River on December 12, the *Imperial St. Clair* hit the ice boom at Mission Point, approximately 2½ miles below the Soo Locks. That same day, a crane at the McLouth Steel Plant at Trenton, Michigan, struck the after mast of the *Rogers M. Kyes*. Disabling all of the vessel's radar and radio equipment, this mishap required a trip to Nicholson Terminals at nearby Ecorse, Michigan, for repairs.

Having filled the gap left in the Westdale Shipping fleet during the latter months of the shipping season by the sudden retirement of the *Brookdale* (2), the *John A. Kling* of

The *Detroit Edison* (2) suffered a serious grounding at the end of the 1980 season. (Author's Collection)

American Steamship's Reiss Steamship Company subsidiary laid up at Toronto on December 15 following its sale to the Canadian shipping company. Over the upcoming winter layup, Westdale renamed the 561-foot self-unloader *Leadale* (2).

A little more than a month and a half after grounding at Marathon, the *Lakeshell* (3) stranded on Telegraph Rock in the Parry Sound Channel of Georgian Bay on December 19. With the incident occurring in near gale force conditions, the tanker spilled about 100 gallons of gasoline and remained firmly stuck until floating free two days later after discharging a portion of its cargo of diesel fuel into the *Imperial Sarnia*.

As winter tightened its hold upon the Great Lakes region, a pair of incidents on December 22 left two lake freighters damaged. The most serious of these involved American Steamship's *Detroit Edison* (2), which went aground on Grays Reef in northern Lake Michigan. Freed from the stranding with 350 feet worth of bottom damage, the tugs *Adrienne B.* and *Lenny B.* towed the stricken steamer to Charlevoix for a preliminary inspection before continuing across the lake to Sturgeon Bay for repairs at Bay Shipbuilding. A second, but far less serious, accident that day left the *H. M. Griffith* with a one-foot gash on the forward port side when it hit the stern anchor of its docked fleet mate *T. R. McLagan* while maneuvering at Quebec City.

Departing Cleveland for the final time on December 22, the retired Cleveland-Cliffs motor vessel *Raymond H. Reiss* sailed to Ramey's Bend in the Welland Canal following its sale to Marine Salvage Ltd. for scrapping. Arriving at its destination later that same day, the *Reiss* was the only diesel-powered vessel ever operated by that fleet throughout its nearly 120-year involvement in shipping on the Great Lakes.

Commercial shipping operations at the Soo Locks concluded on December 30 with the downbound passage of United States Steel's *Cason J. Callaway* with a cargo of taconite for Gary, Indiana. The following day, Algoma Central Marine's *Algoway* (2) became the last ship to transit the Welland Canal for the 1980 season when it cleared Lock 8 upbound for Cleveland with a cargo of stone. Demonstrating the capabilities of vessels belonging to the thousand-foot class, the *Edwin H. Gott* established a new benchmark at Sault Ste. Marie, Michigan, that year by carrying 2.6 million net tons of iron ore through the Soo Locks during a single season.

During the season, the giant grain firm James Richardson & Sons Ltd. transferred the two ships in the Mohawk Navigation Company to a marine subsidiary of its Pioneer Grain division named Pioneer Shipping Ltd. Involving the bulkers *Senneville* and *Silver Isle*, this transaction did not alter the management arrangement for these vessels that had been in place with Misener Transportation since the 1970 season. Although the *Senneville* received Pioneer Shipping's distinctive orange and yellow paint scheme in 1980, the *Silver Isle* retained its blue and green Mohawk fleet colors for another two years.

Among the ships sailing their last during the 1980 shipping season were the steamers *Sharon* and *Arthur B. Homer*, which first entered service in 1957 and 1960 respectively. Reflecting the dire economic conditions facing the inland shipping industry during the early 1980s, these ships had sailed on the lakes for only two decades before becoming obsolete. Although a grounding accident in May of that year played a role in the premature retirement of the *Sharon*, itself a conversion of a saltwater tanker built in 1945, it is likely the steamer would have been repaired had the poor business climate not intervened. In the case of the *Arthur B. Homer*, Bethlehem Steel had gone to the expense just five years earlier to lengthen the vessel from 730' to 826' thereby making it one of the longest ships on the lakes. Surpassed in length only by the *Roger Blough* and the growing list of thousand-footers then entering service, the lack of a self-unloading capability and the decline of the steel industry soon condemned this vessel to an early date with the scrap yard. These two vessels joined others that remained idle during the season, notable among which included Columbia Transportation's "Maritime" class steamers *Ashland* and *Thomas Wilson* (2) and the package freighter *Fort Henry* of Canada Steamship Lines.

Chapter Two
The 1981 Shipping Season

Following a period of heavy scrap sales, the 1981 shipping season was to witness a significant decline in the pace of fleet reductions with the only U.S. flagged vessel sold for dismantling that year escaping the cutter's torch through the misfortune of an even more elderly Canadian steamer. Although iron ore shipments grew slightly in comparison to the previous season from 81.7 to 83.8 million net tons, losses in the coal, grain, and stone trades resulted in overall dry bulk commerce on the lakes declining by three percent to 181.1 million net tons.

A pair of accidents in the St. Lawrence River on February 2 left three Canadian flagged tankers damaged. The first of these involved the *Edouard Simard* and *James Transport*, which both suffered bow damage in a collision near Portneuf, Quebec. Belonging to the Branch Lines fleet, the *Edouard Simard* went to Montreal, Quebec, for repairs, where Halco's *James Transport* also had its injuries mended later in the season. Another Branch Lines tanker ran into trouble that same day when the *Arthur Simard* rubbed the bottom just downstream of Trois-Rivieres, Quebec, while on a voyage from Montreal to Sept-Iles, Quebec. Holed in three tanks, the tanker went to Trois-Rivieres, where it unloaded part of its cargo ashore and the remainder into Halco's *Chemical Transport* before sailing to Montreal for repairs. Spending the next three months in the shipyard, the *Arthur Simard* returned to service on May 14.

On February 26, sparks from a welder's torch started a serious fire aboard Halco's *Montcliffe Hall* at Point Edward, Ontario. Despite spreading to engulf the pilothouse and two decks of the superstructure, the blaze spared the bulk carrier's engineering spaces. As such, the reconstruction process, although costing in excess of $1 million, proceeded rapidly at Point Edward with the vessel reentering service just three months later on May 26.

Barely a month following its collision with the *Edouard Simard*, trouble once again struck the *James Transport* when the tanker suffered an engine room fire on March 5 while in the Gulf of St. Lawrence. Extinguished by carbon dioxide, the fire left the vessel without power for about an hour as the crew waited for temperatures in the engine room to drop. With power restored, the unlucky Halco tanker sailed the following day to Gaspe, Quebec.

During the early part of the year, United States Steel entered into an agreement with Fraser Shipyards to convert the steamers *Arthur M. Anderson*, *Cason J. Callaway*, and *Philip R. Clarke* to self-unloaders at its Superior, Wisconsin, shipyard over the 1981-82 winter layup. This significant project followed the lengthening of these three vessels, along with the *John G. Munson* (2), at the same yard between 1974 and 1976.

Preseason activity in the Canadian fleet included the *Frankcliffe Hall* (2) having its funnel heightened to address draft issues

The *James Norris* at Port Weller Dry Docks for conversion to a self-unloader. (Photo by Tom Salvner)

associated with the large self-unloading structure installed in front of its stern cabins the previous year and the *Cape Breton Miner* receiving an extensive refit at Port Weller Dry Docks. Meanwhile, the conversion of the *James Norris* to a self-unloader at that yard continued throughout the early winter layup period following the steamer's removal from the dry dock the previous November. This work was completed in mid-March with the *Norris* returning to service on April 2 when it sailed to Colborne, Ontario, to load stone for Clarkson, Ontario.

Other Canadian shipyard projects during the early months of the year included improvement work to the *Northern Shell* at the Versatile Vickers Inc. yard in Montreal to prepare that vessel for an 87-foot lengthening slated for later that spring at a cost of $4.6 million. Built at Helsingor, Denmark, in 1970 as the *Olau Syd* and later operating under the name *Axel Heiberg*, Hall Corporation Shipping Ltd. assumed the management of this tanker after it came into Canadian registry in 1974 and placed it into service as the *Frobisher Transport*. Identifying a capacity gap within its fleet, Shell Canadian Tankers Ltd. purchased this vessel in 1977 after it had proven somewhat unsuited for Hall's trade routes. Returning to Versatile Vickers on May 22, the *Northern Shell* emerged from the shipyard in October with a new length of 550 feet. This reconstruction made it one of the largest tankers on the Great Lakes, its size only marginally exceeded by the *Gulf Canada*.

Prior to the spring fit out, Bethlehem Steel sold its surplus "Maritime" class steamer *Lehigh* (3) to the Soo River Company.

Renamed *Joseph X. Robert* while still at its layup berth at Erie, Pennsylvania, during late March this vessel entered service under its new ownership early the following month. During this same timeframe, Canada Steamship Lines sold the package freighter *French River* to Mount Royal Marine Repairs Ltd. of Montreal after having operated that vessel on a sporadic basis since 1973. Placed into a newly formed subsidiary, Societe Jensen Marine Ltee. and renamed *Jensen Star*, the 404-foot vessel began its first trip following the sale on April 8 when it departed Kingston, Ontario, bound for a refit at Montreal.

In another transaction involving the Canadian fleet, Halco sold its two oceangoing chemical tankers *Canso Transport* and *Coastal Transport* to Chemical Sol Shipping Ltd. and Chemical Mar Shipping Ltd. respectively. Employed in saltwater operations following their acquisition just one year earlier, neither vessel is known to have visited the Great Lakes while members of the Halco fleet.

On the morning of March 25, the *Richelieu* (3) made the first upbound passage through the St. Lawrence Seaway while later that afternoon the *Ralph Misener* became the first downbound ship through the waterway. Even as the Seaway opened, the *Agawa Canyon* made the season's maiden upbound transit of the Welland Canal. Locking downbound through the Soo Locks during the early morning hours of March 26, Halco's *Cartiercliffe Hall* heralded the beginning of the shipping season on the upper lakes. Throughout the remainder of the month and well into April, however, heavy ice conditions hampered shipping operations on eastern Lake Erie especially among low powered vessels. Consequently, an extensive ice field off the southern entrance to the Welland Canal at Port Colborne, Ontario, proved a difficult obstacle to many older vessels. Arriving off the piers on April 9 after sailing across the lake from Erie, Pennsylvania, the *Joseph X. Robert* struggled for a full day to reach Wharf 10 on the canal to complete fitting out for the season.

A weather system that brought high winds to southeastern Michigan over a three-day period at the beginning of April created problems for a pair of ships tied up at the Nicholson Terminal & Dock Company on the Detroit River. The first incident took place when the thousand-footer *George A. Stinson* snapped its lines on April 1 followed by a similar mishap three days later in which the *Adam E. Cornelius* (3) also broke free of its berth in strong winds. Apparently minor in nature, neither episode resulted in any reports of damage.

The discovery of a crack in a boiler during the fitting out of the *Soo River Trader* at Toronto, Ontario, in early April put the future of the 75-year old steamer into extreme jeopardy. Having sailed to Hamilton, Ontario, on just one boiler, three McKeil Work Boats Ltd. tugs later towed it to Port Colborne on April 28. Despite the advanced age of the vessel, the Soo River Company contracted Herb Fraser & Associates to perform the necessary boiler repairs to allow the *Soo River Trader* to resume operation in the grain trade at the beginning of June.

A little more than fifteen months after suffering extensive damage in a December 1979 fire at Toledo, Ohio, the motor vessel *Nicolet* departed that port on April 4 following the completion of repairs. As stated in the previous chapter, this accident had caused considerable damage to the vessel's forward section. Carried out by the American Ship Building Company, the reconstruction of the burned-out forward cabins included the installation of a square pilothouse.

On April 5, the *Leadale* (2) sailed on its first voyage as a member of the Westdale Shipping fleet. That same day, one of this vessel's fleet mates, *Nordale*, grounded above Lock 3 in the Welland Canal. Apparently undamaged in the incident, the 596-foot self-unloader broke free from the bottom about 30 minutes later. Just three days later, another incident on the canal led to some brief localized power disruptions at Port Colborne when the *Chicago Tribune* (2) snapped some electrical lines near the Robin Hood Mill.

While downbound with a load of wheat from Thunder Bay, Ontario, for Trois-Rivieres on April 10, the *Sir James Dunn* went aground just above Mission Point in the St. Marys River. The following day, a fleet of tugs consisting of the *Barbara Ann*, *Miseford*, *Olive L. Moore*, *Ste. Marie I*, *Ste. Marie II*, and *W. J. Ivan Purvis* managed to refloat the gearless bulk carrier, which then resumed its voyage. Having suffered side tank damage, the *Dunn* paid a subsequent visit to Thunder Bay for repairs.

Algoma Central Marine's *Algowood* began its maiden voyage on April 16 when it sailed from Owen Sound, Ontario, bound to load stone at Stoneport, Michigan, for delivery to Sarnia, Ontario. That day, however, proved far less fortunate for the *Canadian Prospector* when that vessel went aground near Varennes, Quebec, the result of which was a trip to Port Weller Dry Docks at St. Catharines, Ontario, on April 28 for two weeks worth of repairs.

A labor strike by the Marine Engineers Beneficial Association (MEBA) representing ship officers, engineers, and stewards beginning on April 16 affected the operation of nearly 90 percent of the U.S. flagged fleet. This included ships in the Bethlehem Steel, Columbia Transportation, Inland Steel, Interlake Steamship, and United States Steel fleets. The work stoppage continued until both sides reached an agreement eleven days later.

While working at the mouth of the Saginaw River on the morning of April 20, a fire broke out aboard the U.S. Army Corps of Engineers dredge *Hains* when one of its engines overheated and ignited some lubrication oil. Although quickly extinguished, the blaze injured five crewmembers and took the dredge out of service for four weeks.

Launched by Collingwood Shipyards at Collingwood, Ontario, on April 28, the *Lake Wabush* became the first straight deck bulk carrier built from the keel up for Great Lakes service since the construction of Hall Corporation's *Ottercliffe Hall* in 1969. Built for Nipigon Transport Ltd., this 730-foot vessel took on its first cargo on July 27 when it loaded a record 1,024,383 bushels of wheat at Thunder Bay for delivery to Baie-Comeau, Quebec.

Throughout the month of April, work continued on two retired Quebec & Ontario Transportation steamers, the *Lac Des Iles* and *Marlhill*, for voyages off the lakes following their sale for use as grain storage barges at Tampico, Mexico. In preparation for this new duty, both ships had their engines and cabins removed at Toronto. On April 29, the tug *Daniel McAllister* towed the *Marlhill* out of that port bound for Quebec City, Quebec, before making a repeat voyage five days later with the *Lac Des Iles*. Departing Quebec City in a tandem tow behind the tug *Irving Birch* on May 16, neither ship made it to Mexico with the *Marlhill* sinking in heavy seas 150 miles east of Norfolk, Virginia, on May 30 and the *Lac Des Iles* foundering two days later at a position 62 miles southeast of

Virginia Beach, Virginia.

In early May, the Duluth, Missabe & Iron Range Railway retired the steam-powered tugboat *Edna G.* following a long career of assisting ore carriers at Two Harbors, Minnesota. The 95-foot vessel languished at that port until its sale to the city of Two Harbors in June 1984 for use as a floating museum, a role in which it continues to serve today.

A minor grounding on May 3 in the Amherstburg Channel of the Detroit River resulted in no damage to the tug *Olive L. Moore* or the barge *Buckeye* (2). Barely a month following a similar incident involving the *Chicago Tribune* another power disruption occurred along the Welland Canal when, on May 7, the *Ontario Power* snapped an electrical cable that shut down the east side of the waterway's Flight Locks for a brief period.

On May 7, the Malcolm Marine tug *Barbara Ann* towed the *Peter A. B. Widener* upbound through the Welland Canal bound for Buffalo, New York, following the barge's eventful Seaway trip the previous autumn. Remaining at that port during the first half of the upcoming summer, a subsequent tow near the end of July took the former USS steamer to Chicago, Illinois.

While preparing to dock at Detroit, Michigan, with 12,000 tons of gravel on May 8, a power failure caused Columbia Transportation's *J. Burton Ayers* to go aground in the Detroit River. Remaining stuck off the city's downtown district for about six hours, three Gaelic Tugboat Company tugs managed to free the 620-foot self-unloader from the river's muddy bottom without any reported damage.

The next day, the recent spate of trouble on the Welland Canal continued when a towing cable between the tug *John Purves* and barge *Mel William Selvick* snapped while the pair was upbound below Port Robinson, Ontario. Taking the barge back in tow, the two vessels continued their transit of the canal only to have the line snap once again as they were passing the downbound *J. N. McWatters* (2). Shearing to port, the *Mel William Selvick* struck the side of the Misener Transportation steamer before going sideways in the canal. Although causing minimal damage, the incident halted all traffic through the area until the *Purves* managed to secure another line aboard the cement barge.

On May 10, the longest ship ever built for Great Lakes service began its maiden voyage when the Interlake Steamship Company's 1013-foot *William J. De Lancey* departed Lorain, Ohio, bound for Lake Superior. Reflecting the primary purpose that led to its construction, the motor vessel sailed to Silver Bay, Minnesota, where it loaded 55,944 gross tons of taconite pellets for delivery to Republic Steel's pellet terminal back at Lorain.

Outbound from Duluth, Minnesota, with a load of ore on May 13, the *Cliffs Victory* went aground just inside of Minnesota Point. Luckily, two tugs managed to pull the unique steamer free a short time later without any damage. Three days later, another incident at the Twin Ports left the *Leon Falk, Jr.* with light damage when the 730-foot vessel ran into an ore dock while maneuvering in Superior Harbor during high winds.

Elsewhere at the Twin Ports, the *Irvin L. Clymer* reentered service following an extensive refit at Fraser Shipyards, a process that included the installation of a bow thruster unit salvaged from the wrecked Cleveland-Cliffs steamer *Frontenac* (2). Several hours after departing Duluth with a load of iron on May 16, however, the self-unloader began taking on water in a ballast tank while

During the spring of 1981, the *Irvin L. Clymer* returned to service following a lengthy layup.
(Photo by Tom Salvner)

encountering 35 mph winds and 10-foot waves. Limping back to port, an inspection identified a loose rivet as the cause of the flooding. Quickly repaired, the *Clymer* soon departed to resume its voyage down the lakes.

Early season trouble continued to plague Duluth-Superior Harbor on May 19, when U.S. Steel's *Robert C. Stanley* lost its propeller while attempting to tie up at the Duluth, Missabe & Iron Range Railway ore loading dock. With the steamer towed to the nearby Fraser Shipyards for repairs, the recovery of the propeller and its hub took place a short time later. Entering layup at Superior, Wisconsin, on November 25 of that year, this was to be the last active season for the "Maritime" class steamer.

During mid-May, the combination of a U.S. coal strike and diminished grain exports prompted Upper Lakes Shipping to begin sending several of its vessels to the wall. Continuing through the summer months, these layups grew to include the *Canadian Olympic, Gordon C. Leitch, James Norris, Frank A. Sherman, Red Wing,* and *Wheat King* at Toronto and the *Hilda Marjanne* at Hamilton. All of these ships returned to service later that season, however, following the onset of the annual fall grain rush.

One of the most maneuverable vessels ever constructed for service on the Great Lakes, the *American Republic* sailed on its maiden voyage when it cleared Sturgeon Bay, Wisconsin, on May 21 bound for Escanaba, Michigan, to load taconite. Built specifically to navigate the narrow confines of the Cuyahoga River leading to the unloading docks of the Republic Steel Corporation at Cleveland, Ohio, this unique ship has several design features to assist its operation in constricted waterways. Despite the dedicated nature of its construction, the carrying capacity of 634-foot vessel allowed it to serve effectively in other trading patterns as needed. Two days following the departure of the *American Republic*, Columbia Transportation's *Courtney Burton* sailed from Bay Shipbuilding following the completion of its conversion to a self-unloader.

On May 27, Upper Lakes Shipping's newest vessel, *Canadian Pioneer*, was float launched at Port Weller Dry Docks. That same day, a work crew removed the forward cabins from the grain storage barge *D. B. Weldon* (2) at Goderich, Ontario, for use as a maritime museum, the opening of which took place in July of the following year. Dating back to 1907, the 552-foot vessel had last sailed as the *Shelter Bay* for Trico Enterprises Ltd. (managed by Quebec & Ontario Transportation) prior to its sale to Goderich Elevators Ltd. for non-transportation use in 1978.

The final unit of the thirteen member class of 1,000-foot ships commissioned by various operators between 1972 and 1981, Columbia Transportation's aptly named *Columbia Star* entered service when it left Sturgeon Bay on May 30 to load taconite pellets at Silver Bay for delivery to Lorain. As of 2019, this vessel, now sailing as the *American Century*, remains the last powered U.S. flagged freighter built thus far for Great Lakes service.

A slight improvement in business conditions toward the beginning of summer allowed some U.S. fleets to place vessels into service that had thus far remained idle that season. This included the fitting out of Interlake Steamship's *Samuel Mather* (6) and Columbia Transportation's *Crispin Oglebay* (2) and *William A. Reiss* (2).

While approaching its dock in Toronto Harbor at 9:30 in the evening of June 2, the ferry *Trillium* suffered a mechanical breakdown and rammed the floating restaurant ship *Normac*. Pushed into its dock, the stricken vessel began taking on water through a series of small punctures on its starboard side as the nearly 300 diners aboard at the time scrambled to safety. Following a successful evacuation, the Toronto Fire Department kept the *Normac* afloat with pumps until the installation of a temporary patch. Two weeks later, however, the former passenger and freight ferry sank to the harbor bottom when the makeshift repair gave way. With its superstructure removed early the following year, the hull of the *Normac* remained on the bottom until its raising at the insistence of the Toronto Harbor Commission in June of 1986.

The fleet of ships operated by the United States Steel Corporation entered a significant new chapter in its history when, on June 5, the steel maker announced the reformation of its Great Lakes marine operations into a wholly owned subsidiary named USS Great Lakes Fleet. In addition to supplying the raw material transportation needs for U.S. Steel, the fleet would also actively pursue outside contracts to haul cargoes in competition with other shipping companies. In conjunction with this reorganization came the creation of a second subsidiary, USS Great Lakes Fleet Services, to provide management services for other vessel owners.

After spending some time anchored in the St. Marys River due to heavy fog on June 14, the *A. H. Ferbert* (2) struck bottom while attempting to turn around near Sault Ste. Marie, Michigan. Freeing itself a short time later, the 639-foot steamer continued its downbound journey to Lorain after divers placed a temporary patch over a 10-foot tear in its bow. That same day, the onset of high water levels that limited bridge clearances over the Maumee River began complicating shipping operations at Toledo. The swollen river delayed several Canadian grain carriers over the next four days, including the *Canadian Hunter*, *A. S. Glossbrenner*, *T. R. McLagan*, and *Soo River Trader*.

Near 10:30 in the evening of June 15, Inland Steel's *Joseph L. Block* came across the fish tug *Ramona*, which had broken down in Lake Michigan south of Kenosha, Wisconsin, at a location about 14 miles northeast of Grosse Point Light. The 728-foot self-unloader remained with the powerless vessel until the arrival of the U.S. Coast Guard four hours later. Interestingly, just two months later, on August 13, the *Joseph L. Block* came to the aid of another powerless vessel on Lake Michigan when it discovered a 24-foot yacht about five miles off Chicago that had been drifting since the previous night. Following the arrival of a police boat about 40 minutes later, the self-unloader continued its voyage to Indiana Harbor, Indiana.

Over a four-day period during mid-June, three Canadian vessels experienced mishaps in the upper lakes region. The first of these claimed the bulk carrier *Nipigon Bay*, which punctured some shell plating in a minor grounding while shifting along a dock at Thunder Bay on June 15. Only three days later, the *Algoway* (2) was somewhat more fortunate in managing to free itself without damage after running aground off Drummond Island in the St. Marys River. Lastly, the *Senneville* sustained hull damage at Thunder Bay on June 19 when it touched bottom while departing Saskatchewan Pool No. 4.

On June 18, just three days after passing upbound through the Soo Locks on its first trip of the season, the *Samuel Mather* (6) suffered an engine failure in Lake Superior just a few hours after departing Superior, Wisconsin, with a cargo of iron ore. Towed into Fraser Shipyards, the completion of repairs allowed the steamer to resume what was to be its final operational season.

The steamer *A. H. Ferbert* (2) required hull repairs after hitting the bottom of the St. Marys River. (Photo by Tom Salvner)

During the spring of 1981, Columbia Transportation sold the *J. R. Sensibar* to Johnstone Shipping Ltd. of Toronto. Following the sale, it was dry-docked at the American Ship Building Company yard in Toledo. Renamed *Conallison*, the tugs *Barbara Ann* and *Daryl C. Hanna* towed the 75-year old self-unloader to Windsor, Ontario, on June 19 for further work. First entering service for Johnstone on July 26 when it departed for Drummond Island to load stone for Sarnia, this vessel was to have a brief, but eventful, career in Canadian registry.

As their usual trade routes involved the transportation of raw materials from loading ports on the upper lakes to their owner's steel making facility at the southern end of Lake Michigan, visits by Inland Steel vessels to Lake Erie ports were uncommon. One such occurrence took place on June 24, however, when the steamer *L. E. Block* paid a visit to Conneaut, Ohio, with a load of iron ore.

On June 28, the Greek flagged freighter *Interspirit* encountered some trouble while downbound in the Seaway from Chicago with a cargo of petroleum coke for a port in the United Kingdom when it ran into an approach wall at the Iroquois Lock. Although escaping any serious damage, the vessel did require temporary patching at Montreal prior to beginning its transatlantic voyage.

While conducting one of its regular trips out of Tobermory, Ontario, on June 29, the ferry *Chi-Cheemaun* went aground at South Baymouth, Ontario, in heavy fog. Found to have sustained considerable bottom and propeller damage, it was immediately withdrawn from service. With the busy summer tourist season at its height and with the dry docks at Collingwood and Thunder Bay unavailable, the ferry required an unusual tow to the Bay Shipbuilding yard at Sturgeon Bay for repairs. These were completed quickly, however, with the *Chi-Cheemaun* resuming its normal sailing schedule on July 10.

As it sailed upbound in the Welland Canal on July 7, the *Condarrell* lost power and slammed into the wall at Lock 2. Receiving the necessary repairs at Toronto, the canal-sized vessel returned to service on July 12.

Mechanical trouble once again struck a classic carrier on Lake Superior when at eight o'clock in the morning of July 23 the motor vessel *Eugene P. Thomas* suffered a major engine failure west of the Apostle Islands. Coming just five weeks after the *Samuel Mather* (6) experienced similar difficulties in the same general section of the lake, this incident left the 603-foot bulk carrier powerless approximately nine miles north of Bark Point, Wisconsin. Having loaded a cargo of iron ore earlier that morning at Two Harbors, the *Cason J. Callaway* arrived during the early afternoon hours to tow the *Eugene P. Thomas* to Duluth. Arriving off the Twin Ports at seven o'clock that evening, the pair was met by the Great Lakes Towing tugs *North Dakota* and *Vermont*, which towed the disabled vessel into the harbor. In need of major repairs, the *Eugene P. Thomas* went into an indefinite layup at Duluth the following day.

During the summer, Misener Holdings awarded Govan Shipyards Ltd. of Govan, Scotland, a contract for three 730-foot gearless bulk carriers. Capable of operating in both the Great Lakes and saltwater trades, these vessels arrived on the lakes during the 1983 season with two, *Canada Marquis* and *Selkirk Settler*, entering service in the Misener Transportation fleet and a third, *Saskatchewan Pioneer*, with Pioneer Shipping. The ordering of this trio of ships reflected a growing trend among the major Canadian fleets during this period of building ships capable of operating on the lakes during the regular navigation season and on ocean routes during the winter months.

Barely four months after first entering service in Westdale Shipping colors, the *Leadale* (2) went aground at the west end of the South Shore Canal of Lake St. Louis in the St. Lawrence River on August 1. Remaining stuck for the next three days, a fleet of five tugs managed to pull the vessel free after it had lightered 2,400 tons of its salt cargo. A subsequent survey at Montreal immediately following the accident revealed damage to the ship's bottom plates along with its bow thruster and propeller.

The string of mechanical breakdowns among older vessels on the upper lakes continued on August 3 when a blown piston forced the *Soo River Trader* to anchor in the upper St. Marys River. Having already experienced boiler problems at the beginning of the season, the steamer managed to continue its upbound voyage to Thunder Bay following temporary repairs. Nine days later, another Soo River Company ship ran into trouble when the *E. J. Newberry* required tug assistance after grounding in Lake St. Francis near Valleyfield, Quebec.

During its departure from Port Cartier, Quebec, on August 21, the Philippine flagged bulker *Asean Knowledge* struck the *Canadian Navigator*. While the ocean vessel suffered no harm, the incident inflicted minor bow damage to the Upper Lakes self-unloader, which required repairs before sailing for Ashtabula, Ohio.

The recipient of some engine work during the previous winter layup, Misener Transportation's 58-year old steamer *George M. Carl* (2) found itself involved in a minor grounding just above the Iroquois Lock in the St. Lawrence Seaway on August 25. That same day, Lakespan Shipping Ltd. inaugurated a new RO/RO (Roll-On/Roll-Off) ferry service across Lake Ontario between Oshawa, Ontario, and Oswego, New York, using a former saltwater ferry named *Lakespan Ontario*. Intended to provide commercial trucking firms with an alternative to the lengthy highway route around the lake, this service never managed to gain wide acceptance. As such, it is unsurprising that the *Lakespan Ontario* only carried four trailers on its maiden voyage in this role. The insufficient demand convinced company officials to reduce the initial twice a day crossing schedule to only three times per week a short time later.

During late summer, a slackening demand for iron ore led to a number of lake vessels being idled. Faced with weak market conditions, USS Great Lakes Fleet took the opportunity to send the *Cason J. Callaway* and *Philip R. Clarke* into early layups at Fraser Shipyards to begin their conversions to self-unloaders. Making their last voyages as straight deck bulk carriers, both steamers passed upbound through the Soo Locks on August 26. In early November, the third unit of this class slated for conversion over the coming winter, *Arthur M. Anderson*, joined its sister ships at Fraser when poor economic conditions also cut short that steamer's season.

Carrying a load of wheat for delivery to Halifax, Nova Scotia, Trico Enterprise's *Thorold* (4) went aground south of Clark Island in the St. Lawrence River on August 31. Responding to scene, an initial effort to release the 410-foot vessel by the tug *Robinson Bay* proved fruitless. Following a lightering operation, four McAllister tugs managed to free the *Thorold* (4), which, once reloaded, resumed its voyage a few days later.

On the first day of September, grain

handlers went on strike at the Cargill Limited Elevator in Thunder Bay. Coming after more than six months of fruitless negotiations between the Canadian Lakehead Grain Elevator Workers union and the Lakehead Terminal Elevators Association, the labor dispute quickly expanded to include all 13 grain terminals at the port and their 1,600 workers by the following day. With shipping operations at Canada's single most important grain loading port on the lakes seriously disrupted, the grain handlers ratified a tentative agreement to end the two-week strike on September 16.

A pair of incidents on September 2 left one saltwater visitor unharmed and a classic laker disabled. At seven o'clock that morning, the British flagged cargo vessel *Sandgate* went aground near the mouth of the Detroit River. Freed 12 hours later with the assistance of two Gaelic Tugboat Company tugs, the 5-year old vessel sailed to Port Colborne, where a survey revealed no damage. Meanwhile, the *Irvin L. Clymer* suffered rudder damage during one its calls to the International Salt Company Dock at Cleveland. Arriving later in the day, the *Enders M. Voorhees* towed the 64-year old self-unloader to the American Ship Building Company's Toledo yard for repairs.

Returning from an uncommon run up the St. Lawrence Seaway, the Ford Motor Company's *John Dykstra* docked at Dearborn, Michigan, on September 5 with a load of iron ore from Sept-Iles. On its downbound voyage, the steamer had taken on a cargo of export coal at Conneaut for Quebec City. During mid-October, the *Dykstra* made a repeat trip through the Seaway when it, along with fleet mate *Ernest R. Breech*, loaded grain at Toledo for delivery to Baie-Comeau. After discharging their cargoes, both ships went to Port Cartier for iron ore before

The Ford Motor Company's *John Dykstra* made at least two appearances in the St. Lawrence Seaway during the second half of the 1981 shipping season. (Photo by James Hoffman)

returning to Dearborn. Taking advantage of the fall grain rush, USS Great Lakes Fleet also sent some of its "Super" class steamers down the Seaway during this same timeframe.

On September 10, the Gaelic Tugboat Company tugs *Donegal* and *Kinsale* moved the long retired tanker *Panoil* (2) from Nicholson Terminal's main slip at Ecorse, Michigan, to that firm's south slip for scrapping. Having served as a bunker barge at the terminal since 1952, dismantling proceeded quickly with only the lower section of its hull remaining two months later.

The worsening state of the steel industry sent several U.S. flagged vessels to the wall during late August and early September. Over a 15-day period no less than five ships entered layup due to the lack of demand, four of which never sailed again. On August 28, Columbia Transportation's *William A. Reiss* (2) ended its 56-year operational career when it tied up at Toledo. Less than one week later, on September 3, USS Great Lakes Fleet's *Thomas W. Lamont* and *Sewell Avery* went into layup for the final time at Duluth and Superior respectively. Having a difficult time finding cargoes for its handful of active ships, Cleveland-Cliffs laid up the *Cadillac* (4) at Toledo on September 7, its days of service on the lakes having ended. Entering an early layup at Sturgeon Bay on September 12, the *Roger Blough* joined the growing list of USS Great Lakes Fleet vessels taken out of service when it began a period of idleness that was to last for the next six years.

Shortly after clearing the MacArthur Lock at Sault Ste. Marie, Michigan, while upbound at two o'clock in the afternoon of September 15, Algoma Central's *E. B. Barber* collided head-on with Bethlehem Steel's *Lewis Wilson Foy*, which was downbound on the approach to the Poe Lock. Although the 574-foot self-unloader suffered little more than a scuffed hull that was repaired over the following winter at Collingwood, the much larger thousand-footer came away from the incident with three holes in its starboard bow, including one measuring 3' x 4' located approximately 12 feet above the waterline. Released by the U.S. Coast Guard a short time later, both vessels resumed their respective voyages with the *E. B. Barber* sailing to Thunder Bay with its load of limestone and the *Lewis Wilson Foy* proceeding to Burns Harbor, Indiana, to deliver a cargo of taconite pellets.

Over the course of seven days during mid to late September, three separate incidents took place involving saltwater vessels. While making a 180-degree turn in the St. Clair River after departing Sarnia on September 18, the Japanese flagged *Silver Magpie* went aground off Marysville, Michigan. Remaining stranded overnight, four tugs pulled the chemical tanker free the following day with no reported damage. While attempting to moor at Quebec City in 20-knot winds on September 23, the Greek flagged freighter *Armonia* came away from an altercation with a dock at Section 51 with an oil leak and a punctured hull. Another Greek vessel ran into trouble two days later when the *Rea* suffered a creased hull after striking the approach wall to the Poe Lock at Sault Ste. Marie, Michigan.

A short time after arriving at Port Colborne from Thunder Bay with the barge *D. D. S. Salvager* in late September, the tug *Tusker* was struck by the *Algocen* (2) (incorrectly quoted in some early accounts as the *A. S. Glossbrenner*). Although initial reports cited the failure of the Clarence Street Bridge (Bridge 21) to open in time for the downbound *Algocen* (2) as a factor in this incident, a subsequent investigation proved this not to be the case. The impact of the 730-foot

The self-unloader *Conallison* during its short time in the Johnstone Shipping fleet. (Photo by Tom Salvner)

bulker left the *Tusker* with a damaged Kort nozzle, thus requiring a tow across Lake Ontario by the tug *Bagotville* to Kingston, where it arrived on September 26 to be repaired by the Canadian Dredge & Dock Company. On September 29, another minor casualty occurred on the Welland Canal when the prop wash of a passing vessel pushed the cement carrier *Robert Koch* into a concrete abutment at the Glendale Avenue Bridge (Bridge 5) just below the Flight Locks.

The month of October started out with a pair of groundings on the St. Lawrence River, the first of which involved the *Algobay* near St. Nicolas, Quebec, on October 2 and a similar mishap the following day when the Greek freighter *Saronis* stranded at the west end of Lake St. Pierre. Refloated with the assistance of three tugs on October 4, the *Saronis* went to Sorel, Quebec, for a survey before resuming its voyage to Cuba.

While downbound in the Welland Canal with a cargo of corn for Cardinal, Ontario, on October 6, Westdale Shipping's *Erindale* hit the east abutment of the Allanburg Bridge (Bridge 11) after suffering an steering failure. With the *Erindale* entering an early layup at Toronto on October 12, this accident led to the reactivation of Johnstone Shipping's *Conallison*, which departed that city on October 17 after being out of service for nearly two months. Around this same time, Westdale also renewed its charter agreement with the Canada Steamship Lines for the self-unloader *Hochelaga* that had been sitting idle at Thunder Bay.

Loaded with coal for Quebec City, the 730-foot *Jean Parisien* ran aground in the American Narrows section of the St. Lawrence River about a mile west of Alexandria Bay, New York, shortly after six o'clock in the morning of October 10. Sustaining a significant amount of bottom damage and flooding, the self-unloader took on a heavy list to port. The precarious condition of the Canada Steamship Lines vessel prompted the evacuation of all those aboard with the exception of the captain and four other men. Refloated two days later with the assistance of the tugs *Christine E.*, *Daniel McAllister*, and *Robinson Bay*, the *Jean Parisien* paid a subsequent visit to the Versatile Vickers yard at Montreal for repairs. Taking place in the same general area as where Algoma Central's *Roy A. Jodrey* sank following a similar grounding in 1974, this accident delayed the transit of about 25 ships through the area.

Three days after the *Jean Parisien* suffered its misadventure, a far less serious episode on the St. Lawrence River left the *Ungava Transport* aground near St. Zotique, Quebec. Loaded with gasoline from Clarkson for St. Romuald, Quebec, and subsequently freed with the assistance of three tugs, the Halco tanker suffered no damage in the stranding.

A third incident in four days on the St. Lawrence River, and another involving a 730-foot motor vessel belonging to the Canada Steamship Lines, took place on October 14 when the *Louis R. Desmarais* rubbed bottom near Brockville, Ontario. Although reporting a holed starboard ballast tank, the 4-year old self-unloader continued its trip to Hamilton about five hours later at a reduced speed to allow pumps to control the flooding. That same day, the recent parade of U.S. flagged straight deckers into shipyards for self-unloading conversions continued with Columbia Transportation's *Armco* arriving at Sturgeon Bay for its conversion over the upcoming winter. On October 16, the *Middletown* joined its fleet mate when it also entered Bay Shipbuilding for reconstruction to a self-unloader.

Passing Port Huron, Michigan, as it sailed up the St. Clair River at 12:45 in the morning of October 15, the tug *John Purves* lost control of the cement barge *Mel William Selvick*. Forced toward the Michigan shore by strong river currents, the barge crashed into the former Peerless Cement Dock just downstream of the Blue Water Bridge before swinging around and striking the dock with its stern. With holes punched in its bow and stern, the *Selvick* began taking on water. Secured to the dock, the quick action of the U.S. Coast Guard and Port Huron Fire Department in bringing additional pumps to the scene prevented the cement barge from sinking. Towed to Detroit with temporary patching, the *Mel William Selvick* unloaded its cement cargo before receiving permanent repairs at Toledo.

With the fall grain rush in full swing, an altercation between the *Meldrum Bay* and the McCabe Elevator at Thunder Bay on October 16 left the Quebec & Ontario Transportation steamer with some hull damage. A third incident involving a Canada Steamship Lines vessel in just eight days occurred on October 18 when the *Frontenac* (5) sustained some bottom plate damage after running across a shoal near Point Iroquois in the upper St. Marys River.

The Upper Peninsula Shipbuilding Company float launched the unnamed tug under construction for the State of Michigan at its yard in Ontonagon, Michigan, on October 21. As related in the previous chapter, this vessel was intended for use in an ill-fated plan to develop a barge based railcar service on Lake Michigan to replace the existing car ferry system. Consequently, it never entered service on the waters of the Great Lakes.

On October 24, the saltwater tug *Gulf Commander* and the 550-foot barge *Oceanport* ran aground in the St. Lawrence River following the latter vessel's construction at the Bay Shipbuilding Corporation for the Ocean Barge Corporation, an off-lakes operator.

Having sailed from Sturgeon Bay eight days earlier, the pair had stopped at Conneaut to load an outbound cargo of coal. Apparently representing little more than a minor setback on their trip out of the lakes, the tug and barge freed themselves a short time later with no reports of damage.

While transiting Lock 4 in the Welland Canal on October 26, the Branch Lines tanker *Leon Simard* ran into the yacht *Medicine Man*. Although the yacht took on some water, it nonetheless remained afloat with no injuries resulting from the incident.

Removed from service after making a couple of trips earlier in the season, Paterson's canal-sized motor vessel *Troisdoc* (3) left Cardinal in tow of the tug *Daniel McAllister* on October 28. Arriving at Kingston the following day, the *McAllister* moored the idle vessel next to the barge *Wittransport II* alongside the La Salle Causeway. Built for the Hall Corporation of Canada in 1947 as the *Northcliffe Hall* and later sailing as the *Cape Transport*, the latter vessel had provoked the ire of local residents as it sat derelict at the port. Just two days after its arrival, this animosity may have sparked an incident in which a group of vandals cut the *Troisdoc* (3) free on Halloween night. Quickly retrieved, the 259-foot vessel remained tied up along the La Salle Causeway until November 5 when the *Daniel McAllister* moved it to a different layup berth.

Departing Port Weller Dry Docks on October 28, the *Canadian Pioneer* first entered service when it sailed for Conneaut to load coal for delivery to Nanticoke, Ontario. Three months earlier, a small fire had broke out on this vessel when, on July 16, sparks from a welder's torch ignited a section of conveyor belt. Encountering serious vibration issues while conducting sea trials in mid-October, this vessel required some adjustments at the shipyard before resuming trials later that month. The *Canadian Pioneer* was the first of two self-unloading vessels built for Upper Lakes Shipping during the early 1980s designed for both ocean and Great Lakes operations, the other being the *Canadian Ambassador*.

While unloading grain at Owen Sound on October 29, the discovery of a cracked boiler aboard the Soo River Company's *H. C. Heimbecker* resulted in the 76-year old steamer's retirement. Sold to Triad Salvage of Ashtabula for dismantling, the 569-foot vessel departed on its final voyage the following day. Sailing downbound on Lake Huron, the *Heimbecker* made an unscheduled stop at Goderich on October 31 following the death of a crewmember. Proceeding at reduced speed due to its boiler problems, the classic bulk carrier arrived at Ashtabula on November 2, where dismantling began almost immediately.

Ironically, the unexpected retirement of the *H. C. Heimbecker* provided the steamer *Maxine* a second lease on life. Triad Salvage had acquired the *Maxine* on August 14 of that year during an auction of assets in connection with the Wisconsin Steel (Envirodyne Inc.) bankruptcy. With the trade in value of the *Heimbecker* taken into consideration, the Soo River Company acquired this ship from the scrap firm for a purchase price of $240,000. At the time of this transaction, the *Maxine* was sitting at South Chicago, Illinois. Renamed *J. F. Vaughn* and towed out of that port on November 15 by the *Tug Malcolm*, it loaded a storage cargo of soybeans at Toledo before being delivered to Hamilton in preparation of entering service the following spring.

Late in the evening of November 1, the *Roland Desgagnes* ran aground near Harsens Island at the southern end of the St. Clair

One of the most recognizable ships to ever sail the Inland Seas, the *Cliffs Victory* laid up for the last time in 1981. (Author's Collection)

River. The prevailing heavy fog conditions in that area not only delayed the refloating of the canal-sized motor vessel but also closed the river to all traffic. Freed the following afternoon with the assistance of the tugs *Kinsale*, *Shannon*, and *William A. Whitney*, the *Desgagnes* suffered no lasting effects from the incident and continued its upbound voyage a short time later.

Following a long history of shipbuilding and repair activity stretching back to its founding in 1890 as the Chicago Shipbuilding Company, the American Ship Building Company closed its South Chicago yard on November 2. Located on the Calumet River and becoming part of the American Ship Building Company with the merger of several shipyards in 1899, the last ship serviced by the facility was the *Cliffs Victory* of the Cleveland-Cliffs Steamship Company. The 5-year survey conducted on that steamer during its autumn visit reflected an optimistic appraisal for its future operation despite the strengthening recession in the steel industry. Laid up for the last time at the end of the season, the *Cliffs Victory* sat at South Chicago until its sale for scrapping four years later.

Backing into a coal loading dock at Conneaut, the *Nordale* suffered propeller and rudder damage on November 3. Towed across Lake Erie to Port Colborne for repairs, the self-unloader paid a return visit to the northern Ohio port six days later to load coal.

While on a voyage from Duluth to Spain with barley, the Spanish flagged bulker *Monte Zalama* made an unscheduled stop at Cleveland on November 3 to address a leak in the vessel's No. 2 cargo hold. This required a trip to Detroit to offload a portion of its cargo to permit the repairs necessary for the vessel to resume its trip off the lakes on November 11.

Another saltwater visitor ran into trouble on November 5, when the Indian freighter *Ramdas* was found to have suffered hull damage after striking both walls in Lock 3 of the Welland Canal. Built at Gdansk, Poland, the previous year, it was inbound with a load of containers bound for Chicago at the time of the incident.

Pushed back three days due to high winds, the launch of Hull #222 took place at Collingwood on November 9. Built for the Canada Steamship Lines as the *Atlantic Superior*, the construction of this ship took the unusual approach of having the work split between Collingwood Shipyards and Port Arthur Shipbuilding at Thunder Bay, both of which were divisions of Canadian Shipbuilding & Engineering Ltd. but separated by a distance of 530 miles. After spending the upcoming winter at Collingwood, tugs towed the 600-foot stern section to Thunder Bay the following spring for joining to a 130-foot forward section.

Laid up at Toledo since the end of the 1979 season, Medusa Cement's "Maritime" class steamer *Pioneer* (3) arrived at Sturgeon Bay on November 12 in tow of the *Tug Malcolm*. Throughout the following winter, the Bay Shipbuilding Corporation converted the former Bethlehem Steel bulk carrier to a cement transfer vessel for use at South Chicago.

Its charter to Westdale Shipping cancelled after only three trips, the *Conallison* closed out its operational career when it tied up at Toronto on November 13. During its short time in Johnstone Shipping ownership, this self-unloader encountered a seemingly endless string of difficulties. This included one episode in which the problem plagued vessel reportedly took more than eight days to discharge a cargo of coal due to problems with its unloading equipment. Just six days before its retirement, the *Conallison* suffered one final misadventure when it fouled a buoy in the Detroit River on November 7 while departing the Canadian Salt Company Dock at Windsor.

Carrying a load of potash, American Steamship's *Sam Laud* ran aground in the West Neebish Channel of the St. Marys River on November 15. Offloading some of its cargo into fleet mate *Adam E. Cornelius* (3), the 634-foot self-unloader came free the following day with tug assistance. Both vessels proceeded downbound to De Tour, Michigan, where the *Cornelius* (3) reloaded the lightered cargo back into the *Laud*, which continued its voyage to Zilwaukee, Michigan, following an inspection on November 17.

Encountering heavy seas in Lake Erie on November 18 while loaded with 1,634 tons of pig iron, the barge *G.L.M. 507* sank approximately 12 miles south of Long Point. Owned by Great Lakes Marine Contracting Ltd. of Port Dover, Ontario, the barge was on a voyage from Port Colborne to Cleveland when it began breaking up. The loss of the barge triggered an aerial search for debris until poor weather forced its suspension several days later.

During the waning days of November, three separate incidents involving saltwater vessels took place on the Great Lakes-St. Lawrence Seaway system, the first being the stranding of the *Walka Mlodych* near Buoy 46Q in the St. Lawrence River on November 20 following an engine failure. With power restored, the Polish freighter managed to free itself a short time later. Following a damage survey at Quebec City, the vessel departed two days later for Poland.

Downbound from Thunder Bay on November 25, the Liberian flagged *Gemini Pioneer* sustained propeller damage when it touched bottom in the Welland Canal. Following a stop at Montreal, the ocean carrier resumed its voyage to a port in the United Kingdom on November 28. That same day, the *London Earl* grounded off Pointe-aux-Trembles, Quebec, in the St. Lawrence River. Refloated on November 30 by five tugs, the British freighter went to nearby Montreal for a survey before sailing for Hamburg, West Germany, on December 2.

Poor economic conditions during the month of November forced the Interlake Steamship Company to idle two of its steamers when it laid up the *John Sherwin* (2) at Superior, Wisconsin, on November 16 and the *Samuel Mather* (6) at De Tour, Michigan, just seven days later. Although Interlake sold the latter vessel for scrap in 1987, the *John Sherwin* (2) has remained idle to this day.

On November 29, Davie Shipbuilding Ltd. launched a 444-foot ice-strengthened tanker at Lauzon, Quebec, it had originally laid down for its Branch Lines Division. As Dome Petroleum had purchased Davie Shipbuilding the previous June with no intention of operating its own fleet of tankers, ownership of this vessel passed to Societe Sofati-Soconav prior to it entering service the following August as the *L'Erable No. 1* (2).

During the latter part of the season, Halifax Industries Ltd. lengthened Halco's *James Transport* at its yard in Halifax, Nova Scotia. Originally built by Davie Shipbuilding Ltd. in 1967, the insertion of a new 40-foot midsection increased the tanker's overall length to 411'5" and boosted its carrying capacity from 66,000 tom 73,500 barrels.

Two minor incidents during the first three days of December involved a pair of Greek registered vessels, the first of which took

The steamer *John Sherwin* (2) entered a long-term layup at Superior, Wisconsin, during the autumn of 1981.
(Photo by James Hoffman)

place on December 1 when the *Hellas in Eternity* grounded in the St. Lawrence River. Able to free itself a few hours later, the 11-year old vessel made a brief stop at Quebec City before sailing for Bordeaux, France. Two days later, the *Irene Diamond* encountered some difficulty when it struck a railroad bridge at the Upper Beauharnois Lock. This mishap happened when the captain of the vessel tried to move astern in the lock only to have the engine not respond to his command to stop. The quick action of the lock operator prevented the backing vessel from damaging the lock gates. Coming to rest against the railroad bridge crossing the canal, the *Irene Diamond* remained in that position until being released the next day with tug assistance, after which it sailed to Contrecoeur, Quebec, for an inspection.

Making a rare trip east of Lake Erie, Columbia Transportation's *J. Burton Ayers* passed through the Welland Canal on December 4 with coal for Hamilton. The following day, another unusual caller on the canal presented itself in the form of the Gartland Steamship Company's *Nicolet* with coal for Oshawa.

Arriving at Toledo following a tow from Ashtabula on December 15, the *William P. Snyder, Jr.* joined the long list of idle Cleveland-Cliffs vessels at that port. This vessel was later included in a proposal to utilize some that fleet's idle carriers to carry coal and containers through the St. Lawrence Seaway. Other vessels considered for use in such a role were the *Willis B. Boyer*, *Cadillac* (4), and *Champlain* (3). Although Cleveland-Cliffs reportedly approached a number of shipyards to perform these conversions, the project never proceeded past the preliminary stage.

While being maneuvered by the tug *Manco* on December 16, the barge *Huron* lost a dozen railcars into the Detroit River in a partial sinking at Windsor. Although the cargo of the railcars consisted primarily of raw beans, a number of 55-gallon drums containing the toxic compound ethyl oxazoline created some local environmental concerns until their recovery. Responding to the scene, a crew from the U.S. Coast Guard icebreaking tug *Bristol Bay* used pumps to stop water from flooding into further compartments as divers descended below the surface to secure the open deck hatches. Prevented from sinking completely, a salvage operation to recover the 106-year old barge began the next day. Repaired despite its advanced age, the *Huron* resumed its duties on the Detroit River two months later.

The most serious accident of the 1981 season occurred during the early hours of Christmas Day when a fire broke out aboard Halco's 355-foot tanker *Hudson Transport* in the St. Lawrence River during a voyage from Montreal to the Magdalen Islands. Loaded with 40,000 barrels of bunker C oil, the crew first discovered the blaze at 2:55 in the morning while the vessel was about five miles off Metis-sur-Mer, Quebec, in the lower section of the river some 200 miles below Quebec City. Although the crew managed to anchor the burning vessel, it could do little to prevent the flames from spreading throughout the ship's cabins. Of the 21 crewmembers aboard the *Hudson Transport* at the time of the accident, six lost their lives when a life raft lost its buoyancy while another died after falling into the cold water when he attempted to leap aboard a life raft.

Despite burning for nearly two days, the fire spared the ship's engine room and cargo holds. Taken in tow, the heavily damaged tanker arrived at Baie-Comeau on December 27, where it transferred a portion of its

The *Cadillac* (4) was one of several idle Cleveland-Cliffs bulk carriers considered for use in the coal and container trades through the St. Lawrence Seaway. (Photo by James Hoffman)

undamaged cargo to fleet mate *Gaspe Transport*. Towed into Montreal by the tug *Captain Ioannis S.* on January 3, 1982, a survey placed the value of damages to the 19-year old vessel at between one and two million dollars. Deciding against repairs, Halco abandoned the *Hudson Transport* to the underwriters a short time later. As will be related in subsequent chapters, however, this vessel survived a scrap sale to begin a new career in the form of a tank barge.

A far less serious accident on the afternoon of December 25 left the *Canadian Mariner* with minor bottom damage when it hit bottom in the lower St. Marys River. Temporarily patched after taking on some water, the steamer continued its downbound voyage to become the last vessel through the Welland Canal for the 1981 season two days later. On December 30, the *John A. France* (2) closed the Soo Locks when it passed downbound with a load of grain from Thunder Bay for Tiffin, Ontario. Earlier that month, on December 4, Algoma Steel's *Yankcanuck* (2) made that year's final passage through the Canadian Lock on the opposite side of the St. Marys River at Sault Ste. Marie, Ontario.

Near the end of the season, Canada Steamship Lines, now part of the CSL Group following its sale by the Power Corporation in August of that year, announced the cessation of its long established package freight service. This resulted in the fleet immediately putting the *Fort Chambly*, *Fort Henry*, *Fort St. Louis*, *Fort William*, and *Fort York* up for sale. Of these, the *Fort St. Louis* had just returned to the lakes that spring following a long-term charter on the East Coast.

As the year ended, the poor economic conditions that forced ship owners on both sides of the border to remove several of their units from service during the season showed no signs of improvement. Reflecting the severity of the recession, no less than 30 lake carriers entered what was to become their final layups as they joined a growing ghost fleet of idled vessels languishing in various ports around the lakes. Although some of these carriers had reached the end of their productive lives, several of those destined for an early retirement had seen less than 30 years of service. With the average Great Lakes vessel commonly enjoying an operational career in excess of 50-60 years in length, such ships were comparatively young.

The 1981 season also marked the end of the massive wave of new vessel construction in the U.S. flagged dry cargo fleet stretching back to early 1970s among which included thirteen vessels of the thousand-foot class. Combined with a large number of lengthening and self-unloading reconstructions carried out over the same period, the introduction of these new vessels during a time of diminishing demand was to delegate several American ships to the scrap yard that may have otherwise survived the economic downturn.

Regardless of the challenges faced thus far in the decade, the consequences of the economic recession of the early 1980s upon the steel industry was to make its full fury known in 1982 when shipping companies on both sides of the border faced the worst season for iron ore shipments on the lakes since the Great Depression.

Chapter Three
The 1982 Shipping Season

The Great Lakes shipping industry has faced few challenges as great as those symbolized by the global economic recession of the early 1980s. By 1982, poor economic conditions had severely crippled the industrialized might of North America with a large number of manufacturing facilities idled or operating on vastly reduced schedules. Particularly hard hit during this period, the automotive industry not only faced a weakened demand but also stiff foreign competition in its home market. As one if its largest customers, falling car production dealt a heavy blow to both U.S. and Canadian steel manufacturers, which not only faced deep cuts associated with a depressed construction sector but also a battle to retain market share in the face of imported steel. Leading to a massive downturn in the movement of raw materials, this combination of economic factors produced one of the darkest years in the modern history of commerce on the inland seas.

While grain movements in 1982 remained virtually unchanged from the previous season at 28.2 million net tons, shipments of iron ore plummeted by nearly 49 percent to 43.1 million net tons compared to 83.8 million net tons just one year earlier. Likewise, coal loadings fell from just over 39 million net tons in 1981 to 36.7 million net tons in 1982 while the stone trade suffered even higher losses with shipments of that commodity declining from 24.5 million net tons to only 15 million net tons over the same period. Overall, bulk commerce on the lakes for the season fell by 27 percent from the previous year to 142 million net tons.

At the beginning of 1982, a restructuring move by the Ford Motor Company resulted in the creation of a wholly owned subsidiary named the Rouge Steel Company, which included not only the corporation's steel making operation at Dearborn, Michigan, but also its marine division of four straight deck bulk carriers and one self-unloader.

Even as rumors of its potential sale circulated throughout marine circles, the Branch Lines Division of Davie Shipbuilding Ltd. initiated a fleet wide renaming program at the beginning of 1982. As such, its tankers received the following name changes: *Arthur Simard* to *Le Cedre No. 1*, *Edouard Simard* to *Le Chene No. 1*, *Jos. Simard* to *Le Frene No. 1*, *Leon Simard* to *L'Orme No. 1*, *Ludger Simard* to *Le Saule No. 1*, and *Maplebranch* (2) to *L'Erable No. 1*. Of these vessels, the *L'Erable No. 1* passed out Canadian registry early in the season with its sale to a Panamanian buyer that placed it into ocean service as the *Tlatoani*.

On January 8, the gradual drawdown of Lake Michigan car ferry operations continued with Chessie System's *Badger* (2) beginning the final run on the railroad's Ludington, Michigan, to Manitowoc, Wisconsin, route. This closure left Kewaunee, Wisconsin, as the last destination served by Chessie from Ludington, which at one time also featured a route to Milwaukee, Wisconsin. A further reduction in cross-lake ferry traffic took place just four months later, when, on April 26, the Michigan Interstate Railway Company halted all service with the Ann Arbor Railroad ferries from Frankfort, Michigan, thereby ending that community's long association with railcar ferry operations.

Sustaining ice damage at Chatham, New Brunswick, on January 16, the *Mathilda Desgagnes* sailed to Quebec City, Quebec, before paying a subsequent visit to Halifax, Nova Scotia, for dry-docking in early February. Following the completion of rudder stock repairs, the 360-foot freighter cleared that port to begin a transatlantic voyage to Algeria.

Over the 1981-82 winter layup, several Canadian ship owners carried out work to repair or upgrade their existing vessels. One of the most significant projects undertaken during this period took place at St. John, New Brunswick, when Algoma Central's *Algosea* received a major refit and repowering at Saint John Shipbuilding and Dry Dock Ltd. Completed in May, this work took place just prior to that vessel entering service in a 15-year charter to Soquem Incorporated to carry salt from the Magdalen Islands in the Gulf of St. Lawrence to ports in Quebec and on the Great Lakes.

A second repowering in the Canadian fleet that year involved the tanker *Seaway Trader*, which had its original 1,200 ihp Skinner Unaflow steam engine replaced by a 2,100 bhp diesel engine. Owned by Shediac Bulk Shipping Ltd., this vessel dated back to its original 1948 construction at Collingwood, Ontario, as the *Imperial Collingwood*. Although serving primarily on the St. Lawrence River and in the Maritime Provinces of eastern Canada, the *Seaway Trader* made several trips into the Great Lakes following the completion of its repowering.

Other winter layup activity included Misener Transportation's 678-foot bulker *John O. McKellar* (2) receiving boiler repairs to rectify damage caused by the use of contaminated feed water in the St. Lawrence River the previous April and the fitting of a bow thruster into Carryore Limited's *Menihek Lake*. At Toronto, Ontario, the Soo River Company steamer *Joseph X. Robert* received a condenser salvaged during the scrapping of the *Brookdale* (2). This installation proved less than ideal, however, with the "Maritime" class vessel experiencing some problems with the unit, which in combination with other mechanical difficulties left it sidelined for much of the early season.

Having completed its first season as a self-unloader, the *James Norris* received some engine work while in its winter quarters at Hamilton, Ontario. Meanwhile, poor economic conditions curtailed Upper Lakes Shipping's plan to have its Port Weller Dry Docks division convert the *Gordon C. Leitch* to a self-unloader at St. Catharines, Ontario, over the winter. Instead, fleet managers sent that steamer, a sister ship to the *James Norris*, into layup at Toronto with a storage cargo of grain at the end of the 1981 season. Benefiting from its conversion, the *Norris* plied the waters of the Great Lakes for another 30 years while the *Leitch* never sailed again.

The unfavorable economic outlook reportedly prompted Westdale Shipping to back out of negotiations to purchase the *Saginaw Bay* from the American Steamship Company along with similar talks with Canada Steamship Lines (CSL) concerning the possible acquisition of the *Hochelaga*.

While transiting the St. Lawrence River on February 5, Halco's recently lengthened tanker *James Transport* went aground near Batiscan, Quebec. Refloated about 10 hours

The tanker *Seaway Trader* downbound at Port Huron, Michigan. (Photo by Tom Salvner)

later with the assistance of the tug *Captain Ioannis S.* from Quebec City, the 15-year old tanker was dry-docked at Sorel, Quebec, on February 15 for repairs. Just five days after the *James Transport* suffered its mishap, another Canadian flagged tanker found itself in trouble when ice and strong currents pushed the *Texaco Brave* (2) into the Quebec Bridge spanning the lower St. Lawrence River. Sustaining radar and communication equipment damage when its aft mast struck the bridge, the tanker continued downstream a short distance to Quebec City for a survey.

Having sat idle at Cleveland, Ohio, for several years, the retired excursion steamer *Canadiana* broke free of its moorings and sank at Collision Bend in the Cuyahoga River on February 17. Coming to rest with its pilothouse and upper deck above the surface of the water, the sunken vessel developed a persistent fuel oil leak in late July that required the mobilization of a specialized U.S. Coast Guard team to prevent a major discharge from its fuel tanks. The 72-year old *Canadiana* remained in its sunken condition until finally raised from the bottom in May of the following year.

On February 20, Port Weller Dry Docks launched the Canadian Coast Guard medium icebreaker *Des Groseilliers*. Christened on August 7, the $64 million vessel began sea trials one month later before entering service in late October when it sailed first to Toronto and then Cornwall, Ontario, before proceeding to Quebec City, its assigned homeport. Capable of Arctic operations, the *Des Groseilliers* continues to serve primarily in the St. Lawrence during the winter months although it also performs occasional ice-breaking duties on the Great Lakes.

Awarded a construction contract the previous November, the Bay Shipbuilding Corporation laid the keel for a 414-foot tank barge at Sturgeon Bay, Wisconsin, on March 15. Named *Amoco Great Lakes*, this vessel was the barge component of an articulated tug-barge (ATB) unit ordered by the Amoco Oil Company to modernize its Great Lakes operations. With construction of a 115-foot tug, *Amoco Michigan*, beginning on May 17, the christening of the ATB *Amoco Great Lakes/Amoco Michigan* took place on August 5.

Delivered to Amoco Oil on September 1, the combined unit with the tug in its notch has an overall length of 454' and a 75,000-barrel carrying capacity.

While on a voyage from Montreal, Quebec, to Sept-Iles, Quebec, with a cargo of Bunker C fuel oil on March 17, the *Lakeshell* (3) had its hull ripped open by an ice floe in the St. Lawrence River. The incident occurred near Trois-Rivieres, Quebec, with the tanker leaking a reported 21,000 gallons of Bunker C fuel oil into the river. Discharging its remaining cargo at Sept-Iles, the *Lakeshell* (3) returned to Montreal for repairs.

During the final days of March, N. M. Paterson & Sons Ltd. sold its 315-foot bulk freighter *Prindoc* (3) to the Southern Steamship Company for off-lakes use. Based in the Cayman Islands, the new owners renamed the 16-year old motor vessel *Hankey* prior to its departure from Montreal on April 10 to load bagged cement at Hamilton. Clearing the latter port on April 14, it then proceeded to Valleyfield, Quebec, to load fertilizer and finally to Cacouna, Quebec, for wood pulp before sailing for Guatemala.

Addressing CSL's decision to abandon its package freight operations at the end of the previous season, the Ontario government put forth a proposal calling for the use of one of the company's package freighters to serve three of the province's ports, these being Sault Ste. Marie, Thunder Bay, and Windsor. The plan also included service to two Ohio ports, namely Ashtabula and Toledo. When the government refused to subsidize the vessel's operation as a safeguard against any potential operating losses, however, the company quickly abandoned any further consideration toward reestablishing a limited package freight service.

The opening of the Soo Locks at Sault Ste. Marie, Michigan, on April 1 reflected the dire state of the Great Lakes shipping industry that season as no commercial vessel transited the locks until the *Benjamin F. Fairless* passed upbound under the escort of the U.S. Coast Guard icebreaker *Mackinaw* on April 9. This stood in stark contrast to the usual lineup of anxious lake ships awaiting the opening of locks to begin the annual movement of raw materials to the lower lakes. Its first trip of the season having begun at Milwaukee, the *Fairless* struggled with ice in Whitefish Bay for two days before opening the season at Duluth, Minnesota, when it arrived to load grain on April 12.

Likewise, a combination of heavy ice and poor economic conditions delayed the first commercial passages through the Welland Canal from March 29 to April 5. On that date, Algoma Central's *Algobay* made the first upbound transit of the canal en route to load salt at Windsor, Ontario, while its fleet mate *Algosoo* (2) made the first downbound passage of the season.

The *Richard J. Reiss* (2) became an early season casualty on April 8 when ice tore open a 28-inch hole in its bow plating in the Straits of Mackinac. Loaded with coal from Toledo, Ohio, for delivery to Charlevoix, Michigan, and under the escort of the USCG *Mackinaw* at the time of the incident, the "Maritime" class self-unloader went to anchor off Bois Blanc Island. Ballasted down at the stern to raise the affected area out of the water, the *Reiss* (2) made a brief stop at Calcite, Michigan, before sailing to Ecorse, Michigan, where it offloaded its cargo into the *Detroit Edison* (2) on April 12. With the latter vessel rerouted to deliver the cargo of coal to Charlevoix, the *Richard J. Reiss* (2) headed to the American Ship Building Company yard at Lorain, Ohio, for repairs.

Touching bottom in the St. Lawrence River on April 9, Halco's *Steelcliffe Hall* suffered some bottom damage while downbound from Prescott, Ontario, to Port Cartier, Quebec. Arriving at its destination on April 13, the 730-foot bulk carrier received a damage survey before departing two days later.

On April 12, another Halco 730-footer, *Frankcliffe Hall* (2), became the largest ship to unload at the Victory Soya Mills grain elevator at Toronto. During this process, the crew used the self-unloading boom to shift its soybean payload to cargo holds that the elevator's unloading leg could reach.

A second mishap in the Straits of Mackinac in less than a week took place on April 14 when the 469-foot Yugoslav freighter *Alka* went aground while on a voyage in ballast from Detroit, Michigan, to Chicago, Illinois. Freeing itself the next day without any damage, the frequent saltwater visitor was soon on its way. This incident was not to be the only misfortune to befall the *Alka* during its freshwater travels that season, however, as on July 5 of that same year it sustained minor damage when struck by the Panamanian bulker *Gerdt Oldendorff* at Chicago.

Having just entered service the previous October, Upper Lakes Shipping's *Canadian Pioneer* lost power and went aground while upbound in the Amherstburg Channel of the Detroit River on the morning of April 14. Carrying a partial load of grain and sailing to Windsor to finish loading at the time of the incident, the self-unloader suffered some flooding in its bow thruster compartment. Remaining hard aground after an initial attempt by four tugs failed to dislodge the year old vessel, the *Canadian Pioneer* was refloated with tug assistance on April 16 after lightering into the Soo River Company steamer *E. J. Newberry*. Proceeding to Windsor for an inspection, permanent repairs took place during a subsequent visit to Port Weller Dry Docks.

A separate mid-April casualty claimed CSL's *Tadoussac* (2), which opened up an 18-foot tear during a run in with ice while downbound on Lake Superior from Superior, Wisconsin. The damage apparently went unnoticed until the motor vessel was sailing back across the lake on April 16 after unloading at the Algoma Steel mill in Sault Ste. Marie, Ontario. The necessary repairs were completed at Thunder Bay, Ontario.

The recent chain of incidents involving Canadian flagged vessels thus far in the month continued on April 17 when the *Chemical Transport* grounded near Dark Island in the upper St. Lawrence River. Reportedly caused by a channel marker pushed out of position through a combination of wind and ice, the stranding caused some damage to the tanker's forward pump room and one of its twelve cargo tanks, the latter of which leaked a small amount of its cargo, a gasoline additive, into the river. Once refloated, the *Chemical Transport* sailed to Prescott, where it transferred its cargo to the *James Transport* before proceeding to Montreal for tank cleaning and finally Sorel for repairs.

Never achieving the traffic levels necessary to sustain a profitable operation, Lakespan Shipping Ltd. laid up the *Lakespan Ontario* at Oshawa, Ontario, on April 23 following its decision to abandon truck ferry service across Lake Ontario between that city and Oswego, New York. With the ferry making its first trip on that route the previous August, this short-lived service had lasted only eight months. Clearing Oshawa on July 27 following its sale to a saltwater operator, the *Lakespan Ontario* remained idle at Montreal until departing for the British Isles on November 21.

Two days after clearing Ashtabula, Ohio, the Greek flagged freighter *Salamis* went aground in Lake Michigan about one mile offshore of Muskegon, Michigan, on April 28. Freed with tug assistance, the ocean vessel docked at Muskegon later that same day for a damage survey.

Its conversion to a cement storage and transfer vessel complete, Cement Transit Company's (Medusa Cement) *C.T.C. No. 1* left Sturgeon Bay on April 27 in tow of the tugs *Minnie Selvick* and *John M. Selvick*. Arriving at South Chicago, Illinois, this vessel began fulfilling its new duties in the cement trade that were to last until its sale in 2010 to the Grand River Navigation Company. As of 2019, it remains inactive on the Calumet River at South Chicago.

One final grounding accident before the end of the month left Nipigon Transport's *Lake Manitoba* with $155,000 worth of damage when the 730-foot gearless bulker hit bottom at Thunder Bay on April 29.

In late April, Moore-McCormack's *Mormaclynx* arrived at American Ship Building Company's Lorain yard for a lengthening reconstruction that included the insertion of a 115-foot midsection. This was to give the saltwater vessel an overall length of 665'9" and the capacity to carry 628 containers. Spending the next six months in the shipyard, the 18-year old ship conducted sea trials in its newly lengthened configuration during late October before sailing to Cleveland to load containers for South America. While coming to anchor to await passage through the Welland Canal, however, the *Mormaclynx* suffered a propeller shaft bearing failure that necessitated a trip back to Cleveland on November 10 to unload before paying a return visit to the shipyard. With repairs completed, a second attempt at transiting the Welland Canal revealed further shaft bearing problems. Although managing to clear the lakes before the onset of winter, the *Mormaclynx* ran into further trouble on December 9 when it experienced an overheated shaft bearing while sailing in the Atlantic bound for Norfolk, Virginia. This round of difficulties resulted in a stop at Baltimore, Maryland, for additional repairs.

On May 1, the *Soo River Trader* delivered the first cargo of powdered cement to the St. Lawrence Cement Company's new terminal at Duluth. Two days later, a fire damaged the unused officer quarters aboard the railcar barge *Scotia II* at Sarnia, Ontario.

Towed by the tugs *Wilfred M. Cohen* and *Miseford*, the stern section of the *Atlantic Superior* departed Collingwood Shipyards on May 5. After crossing Georgian Bay, the trio proceeded up Lake Huron and through the Soo Locks before transiting the length of Lake Superior to Thunder Bay. Joined to a 130-foot bow section at Port Arthur Shipbuilding, the completed 730-foot *Atlantic Superior* entered service on June 25 with its departure from Thunder Bay to load taconite at Superior, Wisconsin, for delivery to the Algoma Steel mill at Sault Ste. Marie, Ontario.

Fresh off the dry dock at Port Weller Dry Docks, the *J. F. Vaughn* entered service for the Soo River Company when it passed upbound through the Welland Canal on May 7. Acquired the previous autumn from Triad Salvage of Ashtabula following the retirement of the *H. C. Heimbecker*, this steamer went to Chicago to load corn for a St. Lawrence River port. Later encountering boiler problems on its inaugural downbound trip for Soo River, however, the *Vaughn* stopped at Sarnia on May 15 for repairs.

A fire that struck the Cargill Limited Elevator at Baie-Comeau, Quebec, on May 14 not only inflicted approximately $1 million in damage but also forced a three-month closure of the facility. This resulted in the

Canadian Wheat Board rerouting several Canadian vessels to Port Cartier and Quebec City.

Poor economic conditions led to USS Great Lakes Fleet idling one-quarter of its active carriers during mid-May when it sent the *Cason J. Callaway*, *Benjamin F. Fairless*, and the *T. W. Robinson* into early layups. Arriving at Calcite on May 23, the 57-year old self-unloader *T. W. Robinson* never sailed again.

Even as lake commerce struggled with depressed markets during the middle of May, the Pittsburgh & Conneaut Dock Company Dock at Conneaut, Ohio, loaded 150,000 tons of metallurgical coal destined for Japan into a quick succession of six CSL self-unloaders. These loadings involved the *Louis R. Desmarais*, *Manitoulin* (5), *Nanticoke*, *Jean Parisien*, *Tadoussac* (2), and *Tarantau*, which transported the coal down the Seaway for a mid-stream transfer into the large (89,000-grt) seagoing combination carrier *Sir Alexander Glen* at Sept-Iles. Developed in large part to bypass lengthy delays at U.S. East Coast ports, this transshipment mirrored a similar operation conducted the previous August in which six CSL vessels loaded 160,000 net tons of coal into the saltwater vessel *Yemanja* at that same port.

After delivering coal to Detroit Edison's Conners Creek Power Plant in Detroit during the late afternoon hours of May 17, the *Wolverine* (2) grounded near the entrance to the channel leading to the plant from the Detroit River. Arriving a few hours later, two Gaelic Tugboat Company tugs managed to free the 630-foot self-unloader the following day after which it departed for Toledo.

Sailing into the unfamiliar waters of Lake Ontario, American Steamship's *Adam E.*

The *Adam E. Cornelius* (3) made an unusual visit to Toronto, Ontario, during the spring of 1982.
(Photo by James Hoffman)

Cornelius (3) paid a rare visit to Toronto on May 20 with a load of salt. The next day, the *Canadian Prospector* ripped open some hull plating when it touched bottom while departing Saskatchewan Pool No. 15 at Thunder Bay.

Loaded with grain from Duluth, the Spanish flagged bulker *Lekeitio* went to anchor near De Tour, Michigan, after losing a thrust bearing on May 24. Towed to Sturgeon Bay five days later, the draft of the saltwater vessel required Bay Shipbuilding to conduct repairs as it sat anchored in the bay. Following six weeks of work, the *Lekeitio* departed Sturgeon Bay on July 10.

Upbound with salt from Pugwash, Nova Scotia, for Montreal on the evening of May 26, the *Roland Desgagnes* ran aground in the St. Lawrence River about 75 miles northeast of Quebec City near the village of Pointe-au-Pic, Quebec. Floating free with the onset of high tide a few hours later, the severity of the damage inflicted by the rocky bottom quickly became apparent as water flooded into the canal sized motor vessel. Called to the scene, the Canadian Coast Guard survey vessel *Ville-Marie* rescued all fifteen crewmembers from the foundering ship before it sank in 300 feet of water at four o'clock in the morning of May 27.

During the last week in May, two vessels went aground in the St. Clair River. The first mishap took place on May 26 when Rouge Steel's *Ernest R. Breech* stranded near Marine City, Michigan, in dense fog. Freed the following day by the tugs *Barbara Ann*, *James A. Hannah*, *Shannon*, *Tipperary*, and *Tug Malcolm*, the steamer departed for its owner's steel making complex on the Rouge River. A second such episode occurred at the south end of the river on May 28 when the downbound Portuguese freighter *Nacional Aveiro* ran aground in the St. Clair Cutoff Channel after suffering a power failure. With power restored a short time later, the vessel managed to free itself from the muddy river bottom without any reported damage.

An electrical fault sparked a fire aboard the Seaway Towing tug *Comanche* at De Tour on May 28. Racing through the vessel's superstructure and destroying its pilothouse, the blaze left the tug a smoldering wreck. Stationed at Sault Ste. Marie, Michigan, for several years, the 82-year old tug was bound for new duties at Kenosha, Wisconsin, at the time of the accident. Towed back to Sault Ste. Marie, the burned-out tug was abandoned to the underwriters on June 14. Later ending up at Muskegon, the *Comanche* lasted another three and a half years in idleness until sinking in Lake Michigan on December 12, 1985 after encountering heavy weather while in tow off Ludington.

As the month of May drew to a close, work neared completion at Bay Shipbuilding on a pair of self-unloader conversions under contract to Oglebay Norton's Columbia Transportation Division. First out was the *Armco*, which left Sturgeon Bay on May 29 followed four weeks later by the *Middletown* on June 25. Due to a lack of demand, Columbia originally intended to operate both steamers for only a few voyages before placing them into layup. These plans changed, however, when the *Armco* had to return to Bay Shipbuilding following the discovery of a crack in its unloading gear during early July, thereby allowing fleet managers to keep the *Middletown* in service.

With its new tug-barge combo nearing completion at Sturgeon Bay, the Amoco Oil Company sent the steamer *Amoco Wisconsin* into layup alongside fleet mate *Amoco Illinois* at Essexville, Michigan, on June 3. Their lengthy operational careers over, both vessels remained tied up at that location until being

Bethlehem Steel's *Lewis Wilson Foy* sustained significant damage in an accident at Taconite Harbor, Minnesota. (Photo by Tom Salvner)

sold for dismantling three years later.

Shortly following the completion of its repowering at Saint John Shipbuilding, the *Algosea* sailed into the lakes to load grain at Thunder Bay. While attempting to enter the Welland Canal at 9:30 in the morning of June 6, the self-unloader sustained heavy bow damage when it rammed the east pier of the canal entrance at St. Catharines. Given permission to proceed to Thunder Bay with its badly mangled bow, the *Algosea* went to Port Arthur Shipbuilding for repairs before reentering service in late July when it cleared that port with potash for Baltimore, Maryland. Shortly after delivering that cargo, the 12-year old vessel entered service on its long-term charter to carry salt from the Magdalen Islands. Reflecting its new duties, the ship was renamed *Sauniere* and given new stack colors.

Straying into shallow water after losing power, the *Edward B. Greene*, one of only two vessels operated by the Cleveland-Cliffs fleet that season, went aground while upbound in the St. Clair Cutoff channel on June 8. With power restored and with no damage suffered in the stranding, the 767-foot self-unloader freed itself about four hours later. One day later, the Greek freighter *Captain Panapagos D. P.* managed to avoid serious damage at Thunder Bay when it came away from an encounter with a dock at Saskatchewan Pool No. 15 with little more than some creased hull plating.

After serving as a floating warehouse for Peterson Builders Inc. at Sturgeon Bay for nearly three decades, the *G. A. Boeckling* departed that city on June 9 in tow of the tug *William A. Whitney*. Greeted by a large crowd, the retired passenger steamer arrived at Sandusky two days later, where a volunteer group had spearheaded a restoration effort to save the vessel. While work toward this goal began swiftly, including the installation of two new pilothouses in late August to replace the original structures removed during its time as a storage vessel, a subsequent fire in 1989 put an unfortunate end to the project.

On June 14, the tugs *Barbara Ann* and *John M. Selvick* towed the Columbia Transportation steamer *Reserve* upbound past Detroit en route to Sturgeon Bay. Idle at Toledo since the beginning of the season due to economic circumstances, the 767-foot carrier arrived at Bay Shipbuilding four days later to begin its conversion to a self-unloader, the last such reconstruction ever carried out by that fleet.

Entering the Chenal Ecarte from the St. Clair River near Port Lambton, Ontario, on June 15, the Quebec & Ontario Transportation Company motor vessel *Franquelin* (2) made its way to the narrow Sydenham River to reach Wallaceburg, Ontario. There it loaded the initial shipment at a newly opened grain facility operated by the Hazzard Grain Company. Assisted by the tug *Glenada*, the 349-foot vessel departed for Cardinal, Ontario, the following day with a load of corn.

The tanker *Imperial Acadia* went aground off Port au Basques, Newfoundland, on June 25 while loaded with one million gallons of diesel oil. Ripping a hole in its No. 3 tank, the ship spilled approximately 84,000 gallons of diesel oil into the river, with about half that amount being recovered. Freed from the bottom the following day, the 16-year old tanker offloaded its remaining cargo before sailing under its own power to Halifax, Nova Scotia, for repairs.

On July 2, the ongoing saga connected with the construction of an Integrated Barge Rail Ferry System for the Michigan Department of Transportation entered a new phase with the closure of the Upper Peninsula Shipbuilding Company (UPSCO) at Ontonagon, Michigan. Citing the state's failure to make timely payments, the move by shipyard officials led to the immediate layoff of more than 350 workers and was just the latest development in an ongoing dispute over the escalating costs associated with the construction of a single tug and four barges. During late November, with talks now concentrating on the completion of the tug and the first barge, both sides continued blaming one another for the impasse with state officials accusing UPSCO of not allowing an audit of company records and neglecting to provide a month-by-month schedule with costs for the two vessels.

A serious accident involving one of the thirteen thousand-foot ships in service on the lakes took place on July 6 when Bethlehem Steel's *Lewis Wilson Foy* suffered considerable flooding when it backed hard into a breakwall at Taconite Harbor, Minnesota. Towed to Duluth, an underwater survey revealed extensive hull plating, rudder, propeller, and shaft damage. Sailing across Lake Superior under its own power, the *Foy* passed down the St. Marys River on July 9 with the assistance of the tugs *Chippewa* and *Seneca* while making its way to Sturgeon Bay. With repairs estimated at $2.5 million, the self-unloader arrived at Bay Shipbuilding three days later. Faced with the loss of the *Lewis Wilson Foy* for the balance of the season, Bethlehem Steel kept the *Stewart J. Cort* in service rather than laying it up later that summer as originally planned.

On July 7, the *Amoco Indiana* punctured its hull in an altercation with a lock wall while transiting the Canadian Lock at Sault Ste.

Marie, Ontario. By the time of this accident, the 465-foot vessel had become the last steam-powered tanker operated by the Amoco Oil Company on the Great Lakes following the retirement of the *Amoco Wisconsin* the previous month. After leaking several hundred gallons of gasoline into the canal, the 45-year old vessel sailed across the St. Marys River to Sault Ste. Marie, Michigan, to discharge half of its cargo. Proceeding to Mackinaw City, Michigan, with temporary patching, the *Amoco Indiana* finished offloading before continuing to Bay Shipbuilding for permanent repairs. Returning to service a few weeks later, the steamer made a few uncommon voyages down the St. Lawrence Seaway to Montreal in November of that year as it neared the end of what was to be its last operational season as a tanker.

While locking upbound at Sault Ste. Marie, Michigan, on July 18, the 620-foot straight deck bulk carrier *Golden Hind* accidentally discharged some of its bunker fuel into the MacArthur Lock. With the spill contained within the confines of the lock, the cleanup operation proceeded quickly with officials granting the vessel permission to resume its trip to Lake Superior a short time later.

Surrendered by Halco to the underwriters earlier that year, Marine Salvage Ltd. of Port Colborne, Ontario, purchased the heavily damaged *Hudson Transport* on July 23. Towed out of Montreal five days later, the burned-out tanker went to Sorel before the scrap company placed it up for sale in December of that year.

Nearly three months following its launching on April 28, Algoma Central's *Algowest* entered service when it sailed light from Collingwood on July 21 bound for Owen Sound, Ontario, to disembark some shipyard personnel before continuing up the lakes. Loading its initial payload at Thunder Bay, the gearless bulker left that port on July 26 with a cargo of barley for delivery to Quebec City.

Having abandoned a proposal to employ shunters to improve traffic flow in the Welland Canal, the St. Lawrence Seaway Authority placed both of its testing units up for sale during the summer of 1982. Sold to a marine contracting company based in British Columbia, the two shunters made their way to Toronto in tow of the tug *Glenside* for shipment aboard the Malaysian saltwater vessel *Rimba Balau* early that autumn. While arriving at the Polson Quay Slip to load these craft on October 1, however, high winds pushed the *Rimba Balau* into the Danish heavy-lift ship *Kathrine Sif* with sufficient force to mangle its port bow and inflict significant damage to the folding hatches of the latter vessel, which were in their open position at the time of incident.

On July 30, the *William J. De Lancey* established a cargo record at Escanaba, Michigan, when it loaded 62,701 gross tons of iron ore for delivery to Indiana Harbor, Indiana. Just eight days later, the Interlake Steamship thousand-footer surpassed its own benchmark by carrying 63,007 gross tons of ore pellets over the same route.

A slowdown in export shipments of grain from St. Lawrence River ports during July resulted in several Canadian flagged vessels entering layup at various ports around the lakes as they joined other units that had remained idle since the beginning of the season.

As shipping managers coped with depressed markets, the summer months also witnessed a substantial decline in the already small number of active U.S. flagged lakers. The austere economic conditions proved so difficult that one point in mid-July the USS Great Lakes Fleet could only find enough work to keep six of its 31 vessels in operation. This included the *Philip R. Clarke* and *Edwin H. Gott* in the ore trade and the fleet's stone carriers *Calcite II*, *Irvin L. Clymer*, *John G. Munson* (2), and *Myron C. Taylor*. One example of the fleet's significantly reduced trading patterns during this timeframe was a dramatic 35-day absence of its ore carriers on the Detroit River extending between the upbound passage of the *Philip R. Clarke* on July 21 and the downbound transit of that same vessel on August 25.

Extremely hard hit by the recession, the Cleveland-Cliffs Steamship fleet went through most of the summer with only the *Edward B. Greene* in service until the reactivation of the *Walter A. Sterling* during mid-August. With the balance of its fleet composed of older and less efficient gearless bulk carriers, these two steamers were to remain the only active vessels operated by Cleveland-Cliffs until the cessation of its marine operations at the end of the 1984 shipping season.

Even as it endured some of its darkest days, the Great Lakes shipping industry continued its longstanding practice of embracing the latest technological advancements. During the summer, the American Steamship Company had a satellite navigation system installed aboard its thousand-footer *Indiana Harbor*. From outward appearances, the most noticeable feature of this system was a large white dome antenna housing installed atop the starboard side of vessel's pilothouse that made it easily distinguishable from its similarly designed fleet mate *Belle River*.

On the first day of August, the tanker *L'Erable No. 1* (2) embarked upon its maiden voyage when it departed Quebec City to load a cargo of fuel oil at Sarnia for delivery to Montreal. Launched the previous November, ownership of this vessel was transferred to Societe Sofati-Soconav following that firm's acquisition of the Branch Lines tanker fleet from Davie Shipbuilding Ltd. in a $43 million transaction announced on August 3.

Possessing a fleet built entirely upon the acquisition of surplus bulk carriers, the Soo River Company experienced an increasing state of financial instability as the season progressed. The poor state of the company's accounts reached its climax in mid-summer when its largest creditor, the Canadian Imperial Bank of Commerce, initiated foreclosure proceedings due to a lack of payments. This resulted in the filing an assignment in bankruptcy on August 6 and the appointment of the Toronto based firm Peat Marwick Limited as receiver. With the *Joseph X. Robert* having been idle at Toronto with mechanical problems since July, the receiver attempted to keep the remaining members of the fleet operating even as various creditors moved to seize the vessels at Canadian ports. Although initially producing only mixed results with the prompt release of the *J. F. Vaughn* and *Robert S. Pierson*, this effort eventually managed to get the *Howard F. Andrews*, *Pierson Daughters*, *Joan M. McCullough*, and *E. J. Newberry* back into service before the end of the month. Following its inception in 1975, the Soo River Company had purchased eleven secondhand vessels, two of which it subsequently sold for scrap.

Within days of the bankruptcy filing, the Canadian grain company Parrish & Heimbecker Limited offered to purchase the fleet for $2.5 million in a deal that took effect on September 16. This transaction resulted in the creation of that firm's P. & H. Shipping Division and the wholesale renaming of the former Soo River Company steamers in the following manner: *Howard F. Andrews* to

The *Howard F. Andrews* was one of nine vessels involved in the bankruptcy of the Soo River Company. (Photo by Al Sweigert)

Elmglen, Joan M. McCullough to *Birchglen, E. J. Newberry* to *Cedarglen, Judith M. Pierson* to *Fernglen, Robert S. Pierson* to *Spruceglen, Pierson Daughters* to *Beechglen, Joseph X. Robert* to *Willowglen, Soo River Trader* to *Pineglen,* and *J. F. Vaughn* to *Oakglen.* Although returning to service at some point during the balance of the season, the *Elmglen, Fernglen, Pineglen,* and *Spruceglen* all made their final operational voyages before the end of the year. Sending the *Spruceglen* into layup at Goderich, Ontario, on December 13, P. & H. Shipping sold the 58-year old steamer to the Goderich Elevator & Transit Company over the upcoming winter layup for use as a storage barge.

Three weeks following its accidental fuel discharge in the MacArthur Lock, the *Golden Hind* encountered trouble again on the St. Marys River when it lost power while approaching the turn into the Little Rapids Cut above Mission Point on August 10. Downbound with barley for Owen Sound, the steamer ran over both of its forward anchors dropped in an attempt to bring the powerless vessel to a halt and a navigational buoy before grounding on the Canadian side of the river. After lightering some of its cargo, the tugs *Chippewa, Wilfred M. Cohen, John McLean,* and *Rod McLean* managed to refloat the *Golden Hind* the following day.

Grounding just after midnight on August

11, the motor vessel *New York News* (3) spent a few hours on a sandbar at Ogdensburg, New York, until freed later that day by the Simjac Marine tugs *Constructor* and *Newfie Queen*.

Launched by Bay Shipbuilding on April 22, the 610-foot self-unloading barge *Erol Beker* departed Sturgeon Bay on August 14 in company with the tug *April T. Beker* that had arrived at the shipyard following its construction by the Marinette Marine Corporation at Marinette, Wisconsin. Built for the Beker Shipping Company of Greenwich, Connecticut, to transport wet phosphate rock from Tampa, Florida, to ports on the Mississippi River, the pair made an uneventful delivery trip off the lakes. A subsequent name change five years later resulted in the tug and barge being renamed *Beverly Anderson* and *Mary Turner* respectively. Nearly thirty years following their original construction, in December 2011, Rand Logistics Inc. purchased the two vessels for operation in its U.S. flagged subsidiary, the Grand River Navigation Company. This transaction resulted in another name change during the summer of the following year with the *Beverly Anderson* being renamed *Defiance* and the *Mary Turner* becoming *Ashtabula*. Following an extensive refit at Bay Shipbuilding, the duo entered service in the bulk commodity trades in October of 2012.

In mid-August, USS Great Lakes Fleet's *Benjamin F. Fairless* returned to duty in the ore and grain trades following a three-month layup. Remaining active until tying up alongside its fleet mate and sister ship *Enders M. Voorhees* at Duluth on October 4 of that year, the idling of the 639-foot steamer later that season closed out that fleet's long association with operating gearless bulk carriers stretching back over eight decades.

Over a span of five days in late August, two Canadian flagged vessels were involved in separate accidents, one of which took place far north of the Great Lakes region. While on a voyage from Montreal to Little Cornwallis Island in the Canadian Arctic on August 21, Paterson's *Soodoc* (2) sustained some ice damage that prompted a subsequent visit to Halifax, Nova Scotia, in mid-September for rudder repairs. In a second incident just five days later, a combination of high winds and a strong current forced the 730-foot steamer *Quebecois* aground in the Mission River at Thunder Bay.

With the low demand for raw material movements extending to effect the operation of even the newest and largest vessels on the lakes, Interlake Steamship sent the *James R. Barker* into layup at De Tour during late August. There it joined its much smaller fleet mate, *Samuel Mather* (6), which had not fitted out for the season. With the downturn in the ore trade continuing into the following month, the American Steamship Company also withdrew one of its thousand-footers from service when the *Indiana Harbor* entered a temporary layup at Ashland, Wisconsin, near the end of September.

After spending more than 20 years delivering sand pumped from the bottom of Saginaw Bay to Chevrolet's Saginaw Grey Iron Foundry at Saginaw, Michigan, for that facility's mold-making operations, Erie Sand Steamship's *Niagara* (2) made its final trip on the Saginaw River on August 31. Retired from further service, the 85-year old self-unloading sand sucker headed downbound to enter its final layup at Erie, Pennsylvania, the following day.

An accident on September 6 left one person missing when the tug *Daryl C. Hannah* and its barge collided with a 22-foot fishing boat near Harsens Island in the lower part of the

St. Clair River. A nearby boat managed to rescue two other persons thrown into the water from the stricken craft.

After sitting idle at Toronto since December 12, 1980, Upper Lakes Shipping sold the *Pointe Noire* to Newman Steel of St. Catharines on September 16. Due to the depressed state of the scrap market at the time, the steamer sold for only $56,000. Four days after the sale, the tugs *R. & L. No. 1* and *Glenevis* towed the 600-foot bulk carrier upbound through the Welland Canal bound for dismantling at Port Maitland, Ontario.

Bound for a Spanish port, toxic fumes from an oil-soaked cargo of steel shavings loaded aboard the Greek freighter *Pola Dyo* at Detroit left two sailors dead as the saltwater vessel was sailing in eastern Lake Erie on the morning of September 24. In addition to the fatalities, six other crewmen along with ten Port Colborne firefighters required medical treatment at an area hospital.

During the early morning hours of December 6, 1977, a fire broke out aboard the cruise ship *Royal Clipper* as that vessel sat moored at Montreal. Capsizing at its berth during firefighting operations, the ship rested on the harbor bottom in a partially sunken condition for nearly five years until refloated by McAllister Towing & Salvage Ltd. on September 26, 1982. Towed out of that port by the tugs *Salvage Monarch* and *Helen M. McAllister* on November 20, the burned-out vessel transited the Welland Canal three days later bound for scrapping at Port Maitland.

In late September, the Michigan Legislature approved an appropriation to operate the railcar ferry *Chief Wawatam* across the Straits of Mackinac that included a maximum monthly subsidy of $45,000. At the time, the 71-year old vessel had been laid up at Sault Ste. Marie, Michigan, since April 26 for roof repairs and a 5-year inspection. In a deal that took effect on December 1, a newly formed subsidiary of the Michigan Northern Railway, appropriately named The Boat Company, assumed responsibility for operating the ferry. Departing from the Carbide Dock on October 21, the *Chief Wawatam* sailed to St. Ignace, Michigan, before making its first trip under this arrangement between that city and Mackinaw City on December 22.

Downbound in the Thousand Islands section of upper St. Lawrence River with a load of wheat for Quebec City on September 29, the recently commissioned *Atlantic Superior* ran aground about one mile west of Wellesley Island. After lightering approximately 2,000 metric tons of its cargo into the barge *Mapleheath*, the self-unloader came off the bottom two days later with the assistance of the tugs *Christine E.*, *Daniel McAllister*, and *Robinson Bay*. Proceeding to Quebec City, the *Atlantic Superior* unloaded the remainder of its cargo before sailing for Thunder Bay. Arriving at that port, the 730-foot vessel entered the dry dock at Port Arthur Shipbuilding on October 9 for two weeks' worth of repairs.

At 4:15 in the afternoon of September 30, another Canadian vessel, this one in the twilight of its career, ran into trouble when P. & H. Shipping's *Cedarglen* went aground in the St. Clair River just downstream of the Blue Water Bridge. Upbound with a cargo of iron ore at the time of the incident, the 57-year old steamer came to rest on the Canadian side of the river abreast Point Edward, Ontario. Assisted by the locally based Sandrin Brothers tug *Glenada*, the *Cedarglen* broke free of the bottom two hours later with no lasting effects.

With the onset of the fall grain rush, S. & E. Shipping (Kinsman Lines) placed five of its six steamers into service during early October after operating for most of the season with only one-half of its vessels active. These reactivations left only the *C. L. Austin* sidelined at Duluth with a storage cargo of grain.

During early October, the barge *Buckeye* (2) damaged one of its deck-mounted cranes while loading iron ore at Marquette, Michigan. Pushed by the tug *Olive L. Moore*, the barge stopped at Sault Ste. Marie, Michigan, on its downbound voyage to have the boom removed for transport to Escanaba. With the completion of the necessary repairs, the pair sailed to the latter port for the reinstallation of the crane boom later that autumn.

On October 14, the Indian flagged bulker *Jalagodavari* suffered some unspecified damages at Montreal. After receiving temporary repairs, the 3-year old ship continued upbound for the lakes one week later.

In a manner similar to that employed during the construction of the *Atlantic Superior*, Collingwood Shipyards launched the 610-foot stern section of the *John B. Aird* on October 21. Built for Algoma Central Marine, the partially completed vessel was to remain at Collingwood over the winter while awaiting a tow to Thunder Bay the following spring for joining to a 120-foot bow section built by Port Arthur Shipbuilding.

Elsewhere along the shores of Georgian Bay as the aforementioned launching festivities took place at Collingwood on October 21, the P. & H. Shipping steamer *Fernglen* took on a load of barley some 35 miles west of that city at Owen Sound. In an unusual twist, this cargo consisted of the same payload delivered to the elevator earlier that season by this vessel while sailing as the *Judith M. Pierson* for the Soo River Company.

Far away from its usual trade route on Lake Erie, American Steamship's highly maneuverable self-unloader *American Republic* paid a rare visit to Sault Ste. Marie, Ontario, on October 23 when it delivered coal to the Algoma Steel Mill. Eight days later, a barge towed by the Pitts Engineering Construction Ltd. tug *Kay Cole* lost some rocks in the upper St. Marys River. This incident led to the U.S. Coast Guard imposing a temporary one-way traffic restriction through the affected area while a cleanup operation cleared the shipping channel of any obstructions.

With rumors of its impending demise having circulated since the beginning of the season, reports of Johnstone Shipping Ltd. entering into receivership during late October came as little surprise to marine observers. Founded in 1962, this shipping company had operated primarily in the tanker trades throughout its 20-year history. At the time of its bankruptcy, the Johnstone Shipping fleet consisted of the self-unloader *Conallison*, the tanker *Congar* (3), and the canal-sized crane vessel *Condarrell*, all of which had been idle at Toronto during the 1982 shipping season.

Encountering high winds while on a voyage to Port Cartier with a load of grain on November 12, the *Quebecois* went aground in the St. Lawrence River. Refloated the following day, the bulk carrier came away from the stranding with no reported damage. On November 18, another Upper Lakes Shipping steamer, the 730-foot *Canadian Leader*, established a cargo record when it loaded one million bushels of grain at Huron, Ohio.

During its downbound transit of the Welland Canal on the morning of November 21, the saltwater vessel *Grigorousa* struck Bridge 3A (Carlton Street) just upstream of Lock 2 at St. Catharines. While the impact mangled the sidewalk section of the bridge, which was in its closed position at the time of the incident, the structure was otherwise unharmed. Likewise, the *Grigorousa* came away from the bridge allision with only slight damage.

Towed out of its layup berth at Hamilton on November 28 by the tugs *Helen M. McAllister* and *Salvage Monarch*, the CSL package freighter *Fort William* began its voyage to Collingwood Shipyards for conversion to a self-unloading cement carrier. Following a weather delay at Port Colborne, the tow proceeded to Windsor. Departing from that port behind the McLean tug *Wilfred M. Cohen*, the 17-year old ship arrived at Collingwood on December 4. Spending the next seven months at the shipyard, this vessel entered service for Lake Ontario Cement in June of the following year as the *Stephen B. Roman*.

During late autumn, the Rouge Steel Company swapped the names of two of its vessels when it renamed the *Benson Ford* to *John Dykstra* (2) and the *John Dykstra* to *Benson Ford* (2). With the former lake freighter having been retired at the end of the 1981 season and retained for use as a source of spare parts for its sister ship *Henry Ford II*, this transition allowed the name Benson Ford to be carried on by an active member of the fleet.

On December 1, the tugs *Barbara Ann* and *Tug Malcolm* towed the *C. L. Austin* out of Duluth bound for Buffalo, New York. Idle throughout the season, the 604-foot vessel had taken aboard 400,000 bushels of surplus government grain that summer as a storage cargo subsequently determined to be of poor quality. With no offloading facilities available at the Twin Ports and with its survey expired, the *Austin* required a tow to Buffalo to remove the unwanted grain. Towed

The package freighter *Fort William* was towed to Collingwood, Ontario, during the autumn of 1982 for conversion into a cement carrier. (Authors Collection)

A late season accident on the Welland Canal ended the career of the self-unloader *Leadale* (2).
(Photo by Wendell Wilke)

downbound through the Soo Locks on December 3, the 71-year old steamer arrived at its destination four days later, where it was to remain until sold for dismantling in early 1984.

Operating in foggy conditions on December 2, the tanker *L'Erable No. 1* (2) ran aground in the St. Lawrence River above Beauharnois, Quebec. Refloated the following day, the stranding delayed the transit of at least a dozen vessels through the area. Having just entered service in August, Sofati-Soconav renamed this tanker *Hubert Gaucher* before the end of the year.

The second of a pair of vessels capable of Great Lakes and unrestricted ocean service built by Port Weller Dry Docks for Upper Lakes Shipping during the early 1980s was float launched at St. Catharines on December 3. Named *Canadian Ambassador* and to enter service the following summer, the design of this vessel closely followed that of the *Canadian Pioneer*.

An overheated diesel pump sparked a small fire aboard the tanker *Seaway Trader* at Massena, New York, on December 4. Although a call went out to the local fire department for assistance, the vessel's crew managed to extinguish the blaze without outside help.

Two U.S. flagged straight deck bulk carriers made rare visits to Thunder Bay during early December to load grain. On December 5, the *William A. McGonagle* became the first Kinsman steamer into that port in several years, while the arrival of the *J. L. Mauthe* around the same time reportedly signified the first visit by an Interlake Steamship Company vessel in nearly two decades. Both ships took aboard cargoes for delivery to Buffalo.

At 7:30 in the evening of December 7, the Westdale shipping fleet suffered a major casualty when the *Leadale* (2) struck a cement dolphin while backing away from the Moore-McLearly Dock #6 at Thorold, Ontario, after delivering a cargo of road salt from Cleveland. Opening up a large hole in its stern plating, water quickly flooded into the 60-year old ship through its still open tunnel access hatches. Although all 30 crewmembers aboard the *Leadale* (2) at the time of the accident managed to reach safety, the vessel settled on the bottom in 27 feet of water about 20 minutes later. With its hull temporarily patched, Ship Repairs and Supplies Ltd. managed to raise the self-unloader on December 19. Towed to Port Colborne three days later by the tugs *Glenevis* and *Stormont*, a subsequent damage survey persuaded Westdale Shipping to sell the *Leadale* (2) to Marine Salvage Ltd. for demolition the following spring.

During its voyage across Lake Superior on December 10, Rouge Steel's *Ernest R. Breech* touched bottom while attempting to enter the Keweenaw Waterway. In another minor mishap on the largest of the five Great Lakes just two days later, a battle with heavy ice at Thunder Bay left Upper Lakes Shipping's *Canadian Navigator* with some damaged bow plating.

Barely more than two weeks after moving the *Fort William*, the tug *Wilfred M. Cohen* towed another CSL vessel from Windsor to Collingwood when it departed the former port on December 21 with the steamer *Quetico*, which had remained idle that season. Assisted by the tug *John McLean*, the purpose of this tow was to deliver the 730-foot self-unloader to Collingwood Shipyards for conversion back to its original straight deck bulk carrier configuration.

After more than a quarter century of inactivity at various Lake Michigan ports since making its final voyage in 1956, scrapping of the self-unloading suction sand dredge *American* began in Lake Calumet during the autumn of 1982. This work came to an abrupt halt in December, however, when the vessel took on water and sank. With refloating efforts beginning in November of the following year, final dismantling of the 255-foot steamer took place in 1984.

With the 1982 shipping season entering its final days, the Welland Canal closed on December 23 with the upbound passage of CSL's *Rimouski* for Port Colborne and the downbound voyage of its fleet mate *Baie St. Paul* for Hamilton. On December 25, the *Indiana Harbor* and *Algorail* (2) made the final downbound and upbound transits through the Soo Locks respectively despite the official closing of the canal not taking place until two days later.

During 1982, the U.S. Army Corps of Engineers (USACE) had withdrawn two of its four self-propelled hopper dredges from service on the Great Lakes with the decommissioning of the *Lyman* that summer followed by the *Hoffman* in September. While the *Lyman* joined the James River Reserve Fleet near Norfolk, Virginia, the *Hoffman* remained in layup at Cleveland until towed off the lakes in 1986 for use as a naval gunnery target. Reflecting the USACE's newly established policy of shifting dredging duties to private contractors, these retirements left only the hopper dredges *Hains* and *Markham* in service on the lakes.

On December 31, 1982, the Cleveland-Cliffs Steamship Company transferred the steamers *Willis B. Boyer*, *Champlain* (3), and *William P. Snyder, Jr.* to American Bulk Shipping and the *Cadillac* (4) to Craig Maritime Inc., both of which were firms operating out of Los Angeles, California. The primary purpose of this transaction was to operate these ships in the bulk and container trades between points on the Great Lakes and the St. Lawrence

The *William A. McGonagle* paid a rare visit to Thunder Bay, Ontario, near the end of the 1982 season.
(Photo by Tom Salvner)

River under a charter agreement with Seaway Lines Inc. of Cleveland. Although this resulted in the removal of all Cleveland-Cliffs markings from the four vessels a short time later, none ever operated in such a manner.

Reflecting upon a dismal season, Great Lakes shipping operators could do little more than hope for better times ahead. Although the iron ore trade would improve significantly in 1983, it was to still fall far short of the 83.8 million net ton benchmark for the decade established during the 1981 season. With the volume of ore movement never fully recovering to the latter level throughout the balance of the decade, further challenges lay just a few years in the future when a dramatic decline in the grain trade beginning in 1985 resulted in shipments of that commodity being cut nearly in half over the next four years. This drop in tonnages played a significant role in the rapid downsizing of the Great Lakes fleet that was to take place over the upcoming seasons.

With many of their contemporaries remaining idle at various ports around the lakes or operating on greatly reduced schedules, several lake vessels made their last operational voyages during the 1982 shipping season. This included the *Amoco Wisconsin, Frank R. Denton, Detroit Edison* (2), *Benjamin F. Fairless,* and *T. W. Robinson* in the U.S. fleet and the Canadian flagged steamers *Sir James Dunn, Elmglen, Fernglen, Georgian Bay, John E. F. Misener, Nipigon Bay, Paterson, Pineglen,* and *Spruceglen*. Largely reflecting a depressed scrap market, only one vessel, the steamer *Pointe Noire,* was sold for dismantling during the 1982 shipping season.

Chapter Four
The 1983 Shipping Season

During the early months of 1983, iron mine operators in the Lake Superior region reported their intention of running these facilities at approximately 40 percent capacity at the beginning of the upcoming shipping season. Although a meager figure in comparison to the production capabilities of the mines, this low level of activity nonetheless represented an improvement over the previous year. In addition, the Great Lakes shipping industry also faced a reduction in U.S. grain export shipments brought about by a combination of governmental policies to restrict the size of the crop that year and competition from shippers operating on the Mississippi River.

On January 26, Upper Lakes Shipping (ULS) purchased the package freighters *Cabot* and *Chimo* from Clarke Transport Canada Inc., both of which had become redundant after container traffic had taken over the normal trading routes of these vessels between Montreal, Quebec, and ports in Newfoundland. With no intention of operating the two ships in their current configuration, ULS made this acquisition as part of a major reconstruction project involving its gearless bulkers *Hilda Marjanne* and *Northern Venture*. Rebuilt into bulk carriers in 1961 from saltwater tankers dating back to the later part of World War II, both steamers had relatively new cargo sections but aged, and troublesome, power plants. Meanwhile, the *Cabot* and *Chimo*, built in 1965 and 1967 respectively, had more modern and reliable 6,100 bhp Sulzer diesel engines. Therefore, the reconstruction of the package freighters incorporating the cargo sections of the *Hilda Marjanne* and *Northern Venture* would provide ULS with two refurbished motor vessels at a minimal expenditure.

In simple terms, these reconstructions, performed by Port Weller Dry Docks at St. Catharines, Ontario, involved the removal of the forward cargo sections from the package freighters and the sterns of the two bulk freighters. Once the unwanted sections were removed, the shipyard then brought the two remaining halves together in the dry dock to form a newly rebuilt vessel. One of the more interesting aspects of this joining was the 19-foot difference between the 56-foot beam of the package freighters and the 75-foot beam of the bulkers. To avoid an extensive reworking of the stern section, the difference in width required the insertion of a 25-foot hull section to blend both halves into a single hull form. With the project retaining the machinery, wheelhouse, and accommodations of the package freighters, the reconstruction process included the removal of the forward cabins from the *Hilda Marjanne* and *Northern Venture*. As rebuilt, both vessels had identical mid-summer carrying capacities of 26,000 gross tons.

At the time ULS purchased the two coastal package freighters, the *Hilda Marjanne* and *Northern Venture* were in winter layup at Hamilton, Ontario, the former of which had a storage cargo of grain. While work began on removing the cabins from the *Northern Venture* early that spring, the *Hilda Marjanne* went into operation near the beginning of season before going back into layup at Hamilton on June 13. Accounts of these reconstructions will appear later in this chapter.

In another move by ULS early that year, the shipping company sold the self-unloader *Cape Breton Miner* to a Mexican firm named Naviera Mazahua S. A. de C. V. This steamer had operated in the movement of grain from Houston, Texas, and New Orleans, Louisiana, to Tampico, Mexico, for ULS's saltwater subsidiary, Mar-Bulk Shipping Ltd., since 1981. Reregistered in the Republic of Vanuatu and renamed *Mazahua*, it remained in operation for Mar-Bulk following the change of ownership. A near sister ship, *Ontario Power*, also working in the movement of grain in the Gulf of Mexico, was subsequently transferred to Mar-Bulk Shipping later that same year and renamed *Thornhill* (2).

With U.S. flagged construction having come to an abrupt halt, the American Ship Building Company announced a further reduction in its operations on February 3 with the closing of its yard at Toledo, Ohio. This news came just sixteen months after the company had shuttered its shipyard at South Chicago, Illinois. Although it had produced ships in the past, the use of the Toledo yard in the years leading up to its closure involved primarily maintenance and repair work. In addition to such projects, however, the facility had also performed the self-unloading conversions of the *Elton Hoyt 2nd* (2) and *Edward B. Greene* along with the construction of several hull sections for the thousand-footers built by the company at Lorain, Ohio, during the same timeframe.

During the early months of the year, three separate incidents took place aboard laid up vessels as work continued to prepare them for the upcoming shipping season. While in its winter quarters at Milwaukee, Wisconsin, on February 2, the *John G. Munson* (2) suffered a minor fire in its machine shop that resulted in three men requiring treatment at a local hospital.

An accident of a far greater magnitude occurred at Thunder Bay, Ontario, on February 18 when an explosion and subsequent fire killed three workers engaged in welding operations in the forward section of the bulker *Richelieu* (3) at Port Arthur Shipbuilding. In another fatal mishap just two weeks later, on March 5, a shipkeeper assigned to Algoma Central Marine's self-unloader *Algobay* fell to his death at Point Edward, Ontario.

As one of the earliest ships to enter service each season throughout the 1980s, Rouge Steel's *Henry Ford II* opened Toledo on March 7 when it arrived to load coal for Dearborn, Michigan. Departing its winter layup berth at Toronto, Ontario, on March 18, the Canada Steamship Lines (CSL) cement carrier *Metis* opened that port for the 1983 season when it returned with a load of cement from Picton, Ontario. Converted to carry cement in 1966, this was to be the 27-year old ship's final season as a powered vessel.

Serving exclusively on a route between Thunder Bay and Superior, Wisconsin, the railroad ferry *Incan Superior* opened the Twin Ports on March 24 when it arrived on its first crossing of the season. Having operated for nine seasons in the movement of wood products from Canada to the United States across western Lake Superior, the 382-foot motor vessel reached a significant milestone in mid-April of that year when it completed its 1,000th voyage between those two ports.

Originally planned for March 28, a

malfunctioning hydraulic valve in the Poe Lock at Sault Ste. Marie, Michigan, forced officials to delay the scheduled opening of the Soo Locks until the following day when the CSL self-unloader *Tarantau* passed upbound for Sault Ste. Marie, Ontario. On March 31, the same fleet's *Nanticoke* opened the St. Lawrence Seaway when it passed downbound with a load of grain.

Early season activity included work on a project to prepare Shell Canadian Tankers Limited's *Arctic Trader* for use in the bunkering role following that firm's decision in late 1982 to replace the considerably smaller *Bayshell* (2) in that service at Montreal. Outfitted with new blending, heating, and fuel metering systems along with the necessary handling equipment to refuel vessels, the 25-year old tanker assumed its new duties on June 4 as the *Rivershell* (3). Meanwhile, Shell reassigned the *Bayshell* (2) to perform bunkering tasks at Hamilton.

The opening of the shipping season led to a number of incidents during the month of April. The first such event took place on April 5 when CSL's *Frontenac* (5) struck an underwater object at Toledo. This mishap resulted in the self-unloader requiring a subsequent tow to Thunder Bay by the tugs *Barbara Ann* and *Tug Malcolm* for bottom repairs.

While downbound in the St. Marys River on the morning April 6, an encounter with an submerged obstruction in the West Neebish Channel opened a 250-foot gash in the hull of the Cleveland-Cliffs steamer *Walter A. Sterling*. Faced with a considerable amount of flooding, the crew intentionally beached the 826-foot self-unloader to prevent its sinking in the river. Unloading 11,000 tons of its taconite payload into the *Henry Ford II* the following day, the salvage effort succeeded in refloating the stricken vessel at 12:58 in the morning of April 8. Escorted by the tug *Chippewa*, the *Sterling* proceeded to Huron, Ohio, to discharge its remaining cargo before entering the American Ship Building Company yard at Lorain for repairs.

With the *Walter A. Sterling* out of service, fleet managers sent its crew to fit out the *Edward B. Greene* at Toledo. That vessel, however, also experienced trouble when a week and a half later, on April 17, it suffered reduction gear problems off Crisp Point in eastern Lake Superior while downbound with taconite from Marquette, Michigan. Limping across Whitefish Bay, the *Edward B. Greene* anchored for the night near Waiska Bay to await a tow to Sault Ste. Marie, Michigan, the following day by the tugs *Chippewa* and *W. J. Ivan Purvis*. The cost of rectifying the extensive machinery damage reportedly approached $250,000.

Over a period of nine days during early to mid-April, four separate incidents took place within the Canadian fleet. On April 7, the Paterson fleet's *Soodoc* (2) was involved in a minor mishap when it snagged a submarine cable at Levis, Quebec. Five days later, CSL's *Jean Parisien* touched bottom in the St. Lawrence Seaway near Montreal while on a voyage to Port Cartier, Quebec. Although experiencing a small amount of flooding, the 730-foot self-unloader continued to its destination, where it arrived on April 15 before proceeding back up the lakes for repairs at Thunder Bay. The latter port had itself been the scene of another incident on April 13, when the *Algowood* went aground in the Mission River after being forced out of the navigation channel by ice. Rounding out these occurrences, the *Canadian Leader* had a run-in with the pilings of a railroad bridge at Toledo on April 16 that inflicted slight damage to the steamer and the bridge.

On April 15, N. M. Paterson & Sons Ltd.

The *Whitefish Bay* following its conversion back into a gearless bulk carrier. (Photo by Marc Dease)

sold the *Troisdoc* (3) to Transportacion Maritima Peninsular S. A. for off-lakes use under the Mexican flag as the *Koba*. Idle since early in the 1981 shipping season, the canal-sized motor vessel departed Kingston, Ontario, on May 8 before clearing the Seaway the following day bound for its new saltwater duties.

Following the completion of its unusual conversion from a self-unloader back to a straight deck bulk carrier at Collingwood Shipyards, the steamer *Whitefish Bay* departed Collingwood, Ontario, on April 15 to load grain at Thunder Bay. With its hull repainted to match the red and white color scheme common to CSL gearless bulk carriers at the time, this vessel retained the raised forward hatches and pilothouse bridge wings installed at the time of its conversion into a self-unloader in 1969. Later that season, on June 1, the *Whitefish Bay* carried the one billionth metric ton of cargo to pass through the Eisenhower Lock since the opening of the St. Lawrence Seaway in 1959.

One day following the departure of the *Whitefish Bay*, the stern section of the *John B. Aird* left Collingwood Shipyards for Port Arthur Shipbuilding in tow of the tug *Wilfred M. Cohen*. Joined by the tug *John McLean* while passing through the Soo Locks on April 17, the tow proceeded across Lake Superior to arrive at Thunder Bay two days later. There, the shipyard joined the 610-foot aft section containing all of the vessel's accommodations and power plant to a 120-foot forward section built by that yard.

Departing Port Weller Dry Docks on April 16 following bow repairs stemming from its encounter with the east abutment of the Allanburg Bridge in the Welland Canal during the autumn of 1981, the tug *Glenevis* towed the Westdale Shipping steamer *Erindale* to Hamilton for additional boiler and engine work prior to reentering service a few weeks later. Previously towed to the shipyard from its layup berth at Toronto on March 30, the reactivation of this ship resulted directly from the company's decision to scrap the *Leadale* (2) following that vessel's sinking at Thorold, Ontario, the previous December.

Pushed by strong winds, the *Agawa Canyon* slammed hard into the Lake Superior & Ishpeming Railroad Dock at Marquette on April 18. This episode left the self-unloader with significant damage to its forward cabins while also wrecking nine loading chutes on the ore dock. That same day, the Greek bulker *Atlantic Hawk* struck a bridge on the Calumet River in an incident that left both the ocean visitor and the span with minor damage.

On April 19, a strange incident occurred on the St. Clair River when a 16-year old stowaway jumped from the Panamanian freighter *Yerel* just as that vessel was passing beneath the Blue Water Bridge. Plucked from the 40-degree water by the locally based pilot boat *Huron Belle*, the authorities returned the youth to the ship at Green Bay, Wisconsin. Remarking upon the frequent problem of stowaways sneaking aboard at African ports, the captain reported his company would arrange to send the young man back to Conakry, Guinea, once the *Yerel* docked at Chicago, Illinois.

During one of its usual visits to the Great Lakes Steel Dock at Zug Island in River Rouge, Michigan, on the night of April 19, the *George A. Stinson* suffered a self-unloading boom collapse when the kingpin holding the system's hydraulic cylinder atop the belt casing at the front of the superstructure suffered a catastrophic failure. Breaking free of its mount, the large cylinder punched a hole through the ship's spar deck as the now unsupported 260-foot long boom crashed down across the port side of the thousand-footer and onto the adjacent dock. Despite the seriousness of the accident, there were no injuries among the vessel's crew. With the mangled wreckage removed, the *Stinson* resumed operation in early May using a makeshift chute to discharge its cargoes while awaiting the installation of a new unloading boom, which took place at Bay Shipbuilding on September 20.

While downbound with grain for Halifax, Nova Scotia, on April 22, the motor vessel *Thorold* (4) grounded south of Crysler Shoal in the upper St. Lawrence River. Remaining stuck for three days, the 410-foot bulk carrier finally came free on April 25 with the assistance of the tugs *Daniel McAllister*, *Robinson Bay*, and *Salvage Monarch* after lightering 1,050 tons of its cargo into the barge *Mapleheath*.

Having served in a storage capacity at Goderich, Ontario, since its retirement as a powered vessel in late 1962, the tug *W. J. Ivan Purves* towed the barge *R. G. Sanderson* through the Soo Locks on April 24 bound for scrapping by Western Metals Ltd. at Thunder Bay. The acquisition of the *Spruceglen* by Goderich Elevators Ltd. (formerly the Goderich Elevator & Transit Company Ltd.) at the end of the previous season had made the former lake freighter, along with the *Lionel Parsons* and *D. B. Weldon* (2) serving in the same capacity at that port, redundant. With all three sold to Western Metals for dismantling, the *Lionel Parsons* and *D. B. Weldon* (2) arrived at Thunder Bay in tow of the *W. J. Ivan Purvis*

Entering service for Misener Transportation during May of 1983, the *Selkirk Settler* was designed for both Great Lakes and ocean service. (Photo by Tom Salvner)

on June 3 and June 11 respectively.

As it transited the Welland Canal on April 27, the steamer *Willowglen* ran into the embankment after suffering a steering failure. Though minor in nature, the mishap caused a temporary blockage to traffic through the waterway.

During the month of April, Peterson Builders Inc. of Sturgeon Bay, Wisconsin, purchased the idle Ann Arbor Railroad ferry *Viking* (2) for use as a floating warehouse. Towed across Lake Michigan from Frankfort, Michigan, by the tug *American Viking*, the 58-year old vessel arrived at the Wisconsin port on May 11.

A brief encounter with the bottom of the St. Lawrence River near Port Cartier on May 4 left the coastal freighter *Jacques Desgagnes* with no lasting damage. That same day, the sand sucker *Lakewood* (2) required a tow into Erie, Pennsylvania, by the tugs *Montana* and *Pennsylvania* after encountering mechanical trouble off Conneaut, Ohio. Initially moored at the Erie Marine yard, the 80-year old vessel required a subsequent tow to Lorain on May 24 by the tug *Ohio* for permanent repairs by the American Ship Building Company.

After resting on the bottom of the Cuyahoga River at Cleveland, Ohio, for nearly fifteen months and following a partial refloating on February 25, a salvage crew finally raised the sunken excursion steamer *Canadiana* from the muddy river bottom on May 5. Secured to a dock at Collision Bend, it remained at Cleveland until clearing for Ashtabula, Ohio, on June 21 in tow of the tug *Jiggs*. The 216-foot vessel managed to elude the scrapper's torch, however, when a group operating under the name Friends of the

Canadiana arranged for its tow to Buffalo, New York, the following year as the first step of a challenging restoration project.

Previously christened on April 15 along with a sister ship, *Canada Marquis*, at Glasgow, Scotland, Misener Transportation's new bulk carrier *Selkirk Settler* arrived at St. Catharines on May 5 following an 11-day transatlantic voyage. The first of three vessels contracted to Govan Shipyards designed for operation on both the Great Lakes and saltwater, a formal commissioning ceremony for this 730-foot ship took place the following day. Encountering some difficulties on its maiden voyage up the lakes, however, the *Selkirk Settler* later anchored in Detroit River on May 8 for unspecified repairs lasting two days.

Winds reaching as high as 60 mph caused the U.S. flagged ocean freighter *Marjorie Lykes* to go out of control as it attempted to dock at Milwaukee on May 7. Pushed sideways into a breakwater, the wayward freighter prompted officials to close the nearby Hoan Bridge to all traffic at 6:59 that evening. Struggling in the blustery conditions, it took a fleet of six tugs nearly 11 hours to secure the *Marjorie Lykes* to its dock.

A rather infrequent caller to the Detroit River, Bethlehem Steel's *Burns Harbor* made what was likely its first visit to Zug Island on May 10 when the thousand-footer delivered a cargo of iron ore to Great Lakes Steel. On the opposite side of the river, USS Great Lakes Fleet's *John G. Munson* (2) paid an equally uncommon call to the Canadian Salt Company Dock at Windsor, Ontario, that same day.

Falling victim to high winds and a strong current at Thunder Bay on May 13, the *Algocen* (2) came away from a scrape with the wall at Manitoba Pool No. 3 without any apparent damage. Just four days later, the tanker *Hubert Gaucher* slammed into the Polish bulk carrier *Ziemia Bialostocka* while attempting to dock at Sorel, Quebec. With both vessels damaged in the incident, the *Gaucher* had its injuries mended at Montreal while the owners of the *Bialostocka* deferred repairs to a later date.

Running aground after experiencing a power failure near the Lake Erie entrance to the Welland Canal at Port Colborne, Ontario, on May 24, the Nipigon Transport bulker *Lake Nipigon* blocked traffic through the canal until pulled free by tugs the following day. Suffering bow and bottom damage in the stranding, the converted saltwater vessel cleared the Welland Canal on May 27 bound for Quebec City, Quebec, to unload its grain cargo before receiving repairs at Montreal.

Arriving at Cardinal, Ontario, with a load of corn on May 30, the Quebec & Ontario Transportation steamer *Outarde* (3) suffered propeller damage when it grounded on a mud bank about 1,000 feet from the Canada Starch Elevator. The 56-year old vessel remained stuck until released the next day by the tugs *Daniel McAllister* and *Salvage Monarch*.

Towed from Sorel by the *James E. McGrath* and *R. & L. No. 1* the *Cabot* arrived at Hamilton on April 27 before a subsequent tow by the same tugs delivered the package freighter to Port Weller Dry Docks on May 17 to begin its conversion to a bulk carrier for ULS. Put into the dry dock two weeks later, shipyard workers soon began cutting the hull apart just in front of the superstructure to separate the vessel's forward and stern sections, the latter of which was moved to the adjacent building berth on June 14.

Its forward cabins and stern removed at Hamilton, the forward section of the *Northern Venture* reached Port Weller Dry Docks on June 25 prior to entering the dry

The *Northern Venture* prior to its reconstruction. (Author's Collection)

dock the following day for joining to the *Cabot*'s severed stern section. On July 1, the tug *R. & L. No. 1* towed the unneeded forward hull section of the package freighter to Port Maitland, Ontario, for scrapping, where dismantling of the *Northern Venture*'s power plant section, which dated back to 1944, also took place.

Performed in the manner described near the beginning of this chapter, the conversion process also included the heightening of the wheelhouse to improve visibility over the significantly longer cargo section of the bulk carrier's new configuration. Christened as the *Canadian Explorer* on October 29 and conducting sea trials on Lake Erie two days later, the newly converted motor vessel entered service on November 2 when it cleared Port Weller Dry Docks to load corn at Duluth, Minnesota.

In an incident reminiscent of that involving the *Troisdoc* (3) a year and a half earlier, vandals damaged the laid up barge *Wittransport II* at Kingston in early June. As related in Chapter 2, the presence of the former Hall Corporation canal-sized tanker along that city's La Salle Causeway had proven very unpopular with local residents with many demanding its immediate removal. While the previous episode had left the *Troisdoc* (3) unharmed, this instance resulted in the stern of the *Wittransport II* settling to the bottom. In the end, the barge remained at Kingston until departing during May of the following year.

As the *John B. Aird* neared completion at Port Arthur Shipbuilding, a June 1 accident caused the death of two men electrocuted while working inside of a ballast tank. Christened just two days later, the 730-foot self-unloader departed Thunder Bay on June 13 with a load of coal for delivery to Nanticoke, Ontario.

Carrying a cargo of wheat, the *Willowglen* went hard aground while backing away from Saskatchewan Pool No. 6 at Thunder Bay on June 2. Departing from Saskatchewan Pool No. 7A to aid its stranded fleet mate, the

Birchglen spent a short time aground after also finding the bottom. Meanwhile, the *Willowglen* remained stuck fast until pulled free by six tugs on June 3 with minor damage. This was, however, not the only difficulty encountered by the "Maritime" class steamer that month as just two weeks later, on June 16, mechanical problems resulted in it requiring a tow through the upper reaches of the St. Clair River and into Lake Huron by the locally based *Tug Malcolm*. Spending much of that summer tied up at Port Colborne for repairs, the *Willowglen* returned to service during early August.

Laid up since the end of the 1981 shipping season, the tugs *James E. McGrath* and *R. & L. No. 1* towed the 54-year old self-unloader *Nordale* out of Toronto on June 4 bound for scrapping at Port Colborne. Built at Midland, Ontario, in 1929 for the Canada Steamship Lines and converted to a self-unloader in 1958, this steamer had carried only two names during its career, the other being *Stadacona* (2).

Christened at Port Weller Dry Docks on June 11, the *Canadian Ambassador* completed sea trials later that month before entering service when it sailed from the shipyard on July 6 for Conneaut to load coal destined for Nanticoke. This vessel was the second of two self-unloading ships built for Upper Lakes Shipping during the early 1980s capable of both freshwater and ocean operations. Sharing nearly all of the same design characteristics of its sister ship, *Canadian Pioneer*, including identical overall dimensions and number of cargo hold compartments, this ship had a slightly larger cubic capacity and a 8,796 bhp Sulzer diesel engine rather than a 9,000 bhp Doxford diesel engine like that used to power its predecessor.

Sold to Sullivan Marine of Cleveland, the former Ford Motor Company motor vessel *John Dykstra* (2) left its layup berth on the Rouge River on June 23 in tow for a dock on the Detroit River previously owned by the Semet-Solvay Company. There, workers removed the bulk carrier's diesel engine in preparation for its planned conversion to a self-unloading barge. Launched in 1924 as the *Benson Ford* and retired at end of the 1981 season following a long and productive career, this reconstruction was never completed.

On June 23, Gulf Canada Limited's *Gulf Gatineau* became disabled approximately 65 miles northeast of Halifax, Nova Scotia. Taken in tow by the tug *Point Carroll*, the 7-year old tanker arrived at that port for repairs the following day.

Carrying imported steel for delivery to Detroit, Michigan, and Chicago, the saltwater bulker *Nosira Madeleine* ran aground in the Detroit River near Amherstburg, Ontario, on June 26. Refloated a short time later, the saltwater vessel continued to Detroit before clearing that port on June 29 to discharge its remaining cargo at Chicago.

An altercation with a dock wall during a visit to Saskatchewan Pool No. 4 at Thunder Bay on June 28 left the 730-foot self-unloader *Algobay* with some ruffled hull plating. Two days later, the *Canadian Transport* tied up at Sarnia, Ontario, with significant engine damage after a contaminant worked its way into the power plant's fuel and lubrication systems. The cost of rectifying this damage apparently approached $1 million.

The looming threat of a strike at Collingwood Shipyards prompted the early departure of the *Stephen B. Roman* on June 30 when that vessel sailed for Toronto, where it was to receive final work on its conversion to a cement carrier. Operating for Lake Ontario Cement Limited, the former package freighter entered service on Lake Ontario a short time later hauling cement from Picton to Toronto and Rochester, New York. Having become redundant with the arrival of the *Stephen B. Roman* on these routes, the canal-sized motor vessel *Metis* entered an indefinite layup at Kingston on August 1.

Taking place even as it celebrated its 100th anniversary of operation, a labor strike that began at the Collingwood Shipyards on the first day of July came during a difficult time for the Great Lakes shipbuilding industry. With opportunities of contracting new vessels becoming increasingly scarce, the work stoppage, which lasted until early September, delayed the launching of CSL's *Prairie Harvest* from July 14 to mid-October.

The tally of summer incidents continued to grow on July 1 when Halco's *Frankcliffe Hall* (2) brushed the wall while passing through the MacArthur Lock at Sault Ste. Marie, Michigan. Coming away from the encounter with some hull damage, the steamer made a stop at Port Weller Dry Docks two days later for minor dockside repairs.

With the Chessie System continuing the process of winding down its ferry routes across Lake Michigan originating at Ludington, Michigan, a pair of businessmen from that city formed the Michigan-Wisconsin Transportation Company to acquire the railroad's three remaining car ferries. This transaction included the *Badger* (2), *City of Midland 41*, and *Spartan* (2), the latter of which last operated in 1979. On July 1, the newly formed company put the oldest of these steamers, *City of Midland 41*, into service between Ludington and Kewaunee, Wisconsin. One week later, the *Badger* (2) returned to operation after passing a U.S. Coast Guard inspection when it began carrying automobiles and passengers on the summertime Ludington-Milwaukee route.

Registered at St. Catharines on June 22, the *Canada Marquis* departed Glasgow, Scotland, on July 11 to begin its transatlantic delivery voyage to the Great Lakes. The second of two such vessels built for Misener Transportation, this vessel is noted as having passed upbound past Detroit for the first time on July 25, the same day that a third ship of this class, which was consigned to the Misener managed Pioneer Shipping Ltd. fleet, was first registered at Thunder Bay. That vessel, *Saskatchewan Pioneer*, arrived on the lakes later that autumn.

In a second mishap to take place that month at the Soo Locks involving a Canadian vessel, the *Chicago Tribune* (2) rammed a pier while passing through the canal on July 20. Left with a rumpled bow, the 319-foot motor vessel docked at Sault Ste. Marie, Michigan, for repairs before resuming its voyage. Three days later, the tanker *Seaway Trader* suffered a minor grounding in the St. Lawrence River from which it managed to free itself with no reported damage.

During the early morning hours of July 24, an unusual event took place at Detroit when the aft mast of American Steamship's *Roger M. Kyes* rubbed against the bottom of the I-75 Rouge River Bridge as that vessel attempted to reach the Detroit Lime Company Dock. During its departure that evening with the assistance of the tugs *Shannon* and *Wicklow*, the crew of 680-foot self-unloader discovered that the severely bent mast would not clear the support beams of the bridge. Returning to the Detroit Lime Dock, the *Kyes* remained trapped in the Rouge River overnight until a crew from the Nicholson Terminal & Dock Company removed the damaged mast the following day.

On July 25, a minor incident occurred on the Welland Canal when the saltwater freighter *Ruder Boskovic* struck the wall at

Lock 4. Although the vessel received no damage, the mishap brought upbound traffic in the canal to a standstill for one hour.

Having sat at Sault Ste. Marie, Michigan, in a slowly deteriorating condition since August of 1972, the retired salvage tug *Favorite* departed that city on the morning of July 29 in tow of the tug *Chippewa* for scrapping at De Tour, Michigan. Built in 1919 and already in a state of disrepair when first donated by the Great Lakes Towing Company to expand the *Valley Camp* museum, Le Sault de Sainte Marie Historic Sites Inc. found itself unable to justify the considerable expense necessary to restore the historic tugboat. Towed down the St. Marys River, the *Favorite* arrived safely at De Tour, where dismantling began almost immediately.

With trading patterns normally focused on the lower lakes, the Westdale Shipping steamer *Erindale* made an uncommon passage through the Soo Locks on August 2 while en route to Thunder Bay. Just three days later, the only other vessel operated by Westdale, the 596-foot self-unloader *Silverdale*, cleared Toronto on its first trip of the season.

While on a voyage to Port Cartier with a load of grain for the Canadian Wheat Board, the *Senneville* ran aground near Cornwall Island in the St. Lawrence River on August 3. Taking place at a difficult bend in the channel, the swift river current complicated efforts to refloat the 730-foot vessel. With the tugs *Leonard W.*, *Cathy McAllister*, *Helen M. McAllister*, and *Robinson Bay* assisting, the *Senneville* remained hard aground until finally pulled free on August 5 after lightering a small portion of its cargo into the barge *Mapleheath*. Departing the following day, the bulk carrier sailed to Montreal to unload before proceeding to Port Weller Dry Docks for bottom repairs.

On August 4, the tug *Ohio* towed American Steamship's *John T. Hutchinson* from Cleveland to Toledo where it joined a large number of laid up vessels at that port. Idle since December 18, 1981, the 620-foot self-unloader remained inactive until its sale for scrapping in 1988. Reflecting the soft demand for raw material movements in the U.S. fleet that month, Rouge Steel laid up the *Benson Ford* (2) and *William Clay Ford* at its Dearborn facility near Detroit even as its *Ernest R. Breech* was in the dry dock at Sturgeon Bay for a 5-year inspection.

Two months following the *Willowglen* grounding, another P. & H. Shipping steamer ran into difficulty at Thunder Bay when the *Beechglen* struck the ore dock at the port on August 8. Presumably minor in nature, the incident resulted in no reported damage to either the dock or the 680-foot bulk carrier.

While being towed up the Maumee River at Toledo on August 14, the Liberian flagged bulk carrier *Grand Faith* snapped an electrical line with its mast while passing through the Conrail railroad bridge. Although coming through this episode without any lasting effects, the saltwater vessel required a subsequent survey at Tenerife in the Canary Islands during early September to assess damage sustained when it hit a jetty in the St. Lawrence Seaway.

The steamer *Montrealais* presented an unusual appearance on August 16 when it passed through the Welland Canal with a deck load of 360 TEU (20-foot equivalent unit) intermodal containers taken aboard at Detroit for Montreal. Although lake ships had carried a small number of containers on rare occasions, this was by far a much large consignment than had ever been attempted before. On this unorthodox voyage, the 730-foot bulker also carried a cargo of grain

The bulk carrier *Royalton* (2) while operating under charter to Misener Transportation. (Author's Collection)

destined for delivery to Trois-Rivieres, Quebec.

In mid-August, Misener Transportation entered into a charter agreement with the Royal Bank of Canada, which was managing the Halco fleet, to operate the bulk carrier *Ottercliffe Hall* for the remainder of the year and through the 1984 shipping season. This arrangement resulted in the renaming of this ship to *Royalton* (2) at Thunder Bay in early October. Despite receiving Misener stack markings, the vessel retained its black hull with the Halco billboard lettering painted over to reflect the charter.

Bound for Oshawa, Ontario, with salt, USS Great Lakes Fleet's *Calcite II* made a rare passage through the Welland Canal on August 24 while making the first of several trips to Lake Ontario that autumn with deliveries to both Oshawa and Toronto. Near the end of the season, the company's *Myron C. Taylor* also made an uncommon transit of the canal on December 1 with a cargo of silica sand for Hamilton.

A strange episode played out at Duluth on August 29, when the *Philip R. Clarke* snagged an automobile on the harbor bottom after dropping anchor near the Duluth Port Terminal in high winds. Pulled from 30 feet of water, the vehicle contained the bodies of a man and woman reported missing five years earlier. Following the discovery, the *Clarke* went to the C. Reiss Coal Company Dock to have the badly crumpled wreck removed from its anchor.

Following an eventful voyage into the Great Lakes, in which it smacked the wall at Lock 8 in the Welland Canal on August 25 and rubbed up against one of the entrance piers while arriving at Duluth five days later, the Liberian flagged freighter *Xenia* underwent a survey at that port on September 7. In addition to these incidents, the inspection also evaluated the vessel for damage sustained in an August 11 grounding accident at Camden, New Jersey.

As the reconstruction of the *Cabot* into the *Canadian Explorer* neared its conclusion at Port Weller Dry Docks, the *Chimo* arrived at the shipyard on September 17 following its tow from Hamilton by the tugs *James E. McGrath* and *R. & L. No. 1*. Dry-docked on October 9, cutting of the package freighter's hull progressed along the same lines as that of its sister ship. On November 17, the tugs *Glenside* and *Stormont* towed the surplus forward section of the *Chimo* into Port Maitland for scrapping following a two-day delay due to poor weather.

Meanwhile, the tugs *Bagotville* and *G. W. Rogers* delivered the forward section of the *Hilda Marjanne* to Port Weller on November 7 following the removal of that vessel's forward cabins and stern section at Hamilton, that latter of which was taken to Port Maitland later that year for dismantling. Placed on the shipyard's building berth on December 16, work on joining the forward section of the former bulk carrier to the stern of the package freighter continued over the winter to culminate with the converted vessel entering service for ULS as the *Canadian Ranger* the following May.

A relatively quiet period in terms of accidents ended on September 22 when a fire aboard the *Alastair Guthrie* damaged 140,000 bushels of barley in the steamer's No. 4 cargo hold. Sailing eastbound on Lake Superior at the time, the blaze required a return to Duluth, where the steamer offloaded the affected cargo. This incident occurred as the *Guthrie* was one of the few U.S. flagged straight deckers operating in the grain trade even as it neared the end of its days as a powered vessel.

Sidelined due to poor economic conditions following its reconstruction at Bay Shipbuilding the previous year, Columbia Transportation began fitting out the *Reserve* during September. Departing Sturgeon Bay late that month, the 767-foot steamer passed upbound through the Soo Locks on September 30 while making its first voyage as a self-unloader.

While transiting the St. Lawrence River on October 4 with a load of marble chips, the *Sam Laud* went aground off Ogdensburg, New York. Managing to break free of the bottom without requiring assistance, the American Steamship self-unloader resumed its upbound voyage to Chicago a short time later.

The longstanding struggle to keep the *Chief Wawatam* operating across the Straits of Mackinac entered a new chapter when, on October 5, the tugs *John M. Selvick* and *Soo Chief* towed the classic car ferry out of Mackinaw City, Michigan, for Sturgeon Bay. There, the 72-year old vessel entered the dry dock at Bay Shipbuilding five days later for a survey and various minor repairs necessary for its continued operation in a project financed by a $300,000 grant approved by the Michigan Legislature that June. Recertified by the U.S. Coast Guard, The Boat Company placed the *Chief Wawatam* back into service on December 20.

Arriving on the lakes following a transatlantic voyage from Glasgow, Scotland, the *Saskatchewan Pioneer* passed up the Welland Canal for the first time on October 9 while bound for Thunder Bay. Built for Pioneer Shipping Ltd., this ship had that fleet's distinctive orange and yellow color scheme, thus making it easily distinguishable from its virtually identical sister ships *Canada Marquis* and *Selkirk Settler*. Departing Thunder Bay on October 13 with its maiden cargo, this ship demonstrated the inherent versatility of this class to perform ocean voyages the following month when it loaded grain at Duluth on November 16 for direct shipment to Le Havre, France. This capability allowed all three vessels to continue producing revenue by operating on saltwater during the winter months as the balance of their fleet mates sat idle.

Sold by the Quebec & Ontario Transportation Company to a Panamanian operator, Progress Overseas Co. S.A., in April of that year, the *Baie Comeau II* sailed from Sorel on October 11 for the Gulf of Mexico under the name *Agia Trias*. Acquired by its former owner in 1977 to operate primarily in the coastal and ocean trades, the 387-foot vessel had rarely ventured into the Great Lakes.

The *Algolake* experienced a short spell of misfortune during early autumn in a pair of mishaps, the first of which happened on October 12 when the 6-year old self-unloader ripped its hull open at Thunder Bay. Just six days later, it suffered propeller and Kort nozzle damage while downbound on Lake Superior. Assisted through the Soo Locks by three tugs on October 19, the *Algolake* went to Port Colborne for repairs after discharging its cargo of coal at Nanticoke.

During mid-October, two saltwater vessels sustained damage in separate incidents on the Welland Canal, the first of which took place on October 12 when the Indian bulker *Vishva Bhakti* punctured its hull during an encounter with the wall at Lock 6. Five days later, a similar misadventure at Lock 2 left the Yugoslav registered *Marko Marulic* with a crumpled bow. On October 18, another ocean freighter, the Liberian flagged *Pegasus*, had trouble while transiting the St. Lawrence Seaway when it slammed into the downbound approach wall to the Snell Lock in an incident requiring temporary repairs at Montreal.

Its launch postponed since summer due to a labor strike, CSL's *Prairie Harvest* finally slid into the water at Collingwood Shipyards on October 18. At 736'6" in length, this vessel was the largest ever constructed for Seaway operation up to that time. Although built as a straight deck bulk carrier due to a large obligation by its owner to move grain for the Canadian Wheat Board, the design of the *Prairie Harvest* included several features to simplify its conversion to a self-unloader at a future date, a provision acted upon by CSL in 1988. In addition, this ship evolved from technical discussions between the Canadian Coast Guard, Canadian Shipbuilding & Engineering Ltd., and Lloyds of London that resulted in its designation as a "Caribbean Class" vessel capable of voyages to the U.S. eastern seaboard and, as the term implies, the Caribbean. With final work continuing over the winter, this vessel entered service at the beginning of the 1984 shipping season.

Bethlehem Steel's only operational steamer, *Sparrows Point*, damaged a 100-foot section of its bottom plating and 32 internal frames when it grounded in the St. Marys River on October 18 while approaching the Drummond Dolomite Inc. stone dock on Drummond Island, Michigan. Following an inspection by the U.S. Coast Guard, the 698-foot self-unloader sailed to Bay Shipbuilding for repairs.

Having sat idle since late August of the previous year due to the general recession, Interlake Steamship's *James R. Barker* departed De Tour upbound for the Soo Locks on October 30. Crossing Lake Superior, the thousand-footer entered Fraser Shipyards at Superior, Wisconsin, two days later for rudder repairs.

On October 31, the tugs *Arkansas* and *Wyoming* towed Columbia Transportation's venerable self-unloader *Sylvania* from the Frog Pond at Toledo following that vessel's sale to Triad Salvage earlier that month. Arriving at Ashtabula in tow of the tug *Ohio* the next day, final dismantling of the 78-year old steamer took place during 1984.

Striking both the ship arrester and lock gates at the Lower Beauharnois Lock on November 1, the saltwater vessel *Paulina C.* caused a traffic disruption in the Seaway until the lock reopened the next day following repairs. Cleared to leave the scene of the mishap, the Greek bulker sailed to Montreal for repairs to its bulbous bow. Another incident in the same area took place a few days later when the British flagged *Martha Envoy* spent a few hours aground in the Beauharnois Canal on November 5.

The *Canadian Ambassador* took aboard an unusual cargo at Port Weller Dry Docks on November 10 when it loaded four large wooden fenders for delivery to the Lower Beauharnois Lock for use in repairing the damage caused by the *Paulina C.* in the accident described above.

Over the course of autumn, Marine Salvage Ltd. acquired the *Conallison* in an action resulting from court proceedings to dissolve the assets of the bankrupt Johnstone Shipping fleet. At 77 years old, this vessel had spent only a brief, but tumultuous, period of service under the Canadian flag. Within this same timeframe, the salvage company also came into possession of the defunct fleet's crane ship *Condarrell*.

Towed out of Toronto by the tugs *Glenevis* and *Stormont* on November 22, the *Conallison* arrived at the scrap firm's Port Colborne yard the next day, where it was to remain until resold for scrapping overseas the following summer. Meanwhile, having determined the possibility existed of selling the *Condarrell* to an operator for further use, Marine Salvage put the canal-sized freighter on the market. Receiving a reprieve from the scrap yard, this vessel remained tied up at

The *Horace Johnson* was scrapped at Thunder Bay, Ontario. (Author's Collection)

Toronto until its sale to McKeil Work Boats Ltd. of Hamilton in late 1987.

Further transactions involving obsolete carriers during the closing weeks of the shipping season included USS Great Lakes Fleet's sale of the steamers *John Hulst* and *Horace Johnson* to the Western Metals Corporation of Thunder Bay for dismantling. At the time both of these ships had been laid up at Duluth for several years. Towed up Lake Superior, the *John Hulst* arrived at Thunder Bay on November 23 with the *Horace Johnson* making the same trip exactly one week later. These two vessels made their final journeys to the scrap yard just a few weeks before Western Metals went into the receivership on December 13. With Shearmet Recycling Ltd. purchasing the bankrupt scrap firm a short time later, dismantling of the *Johnson* began in June of 1984 while the final demolition of the *Hulst*, which had some initial cutting done before Western Metals closed, proved to be a protracted affair not completed until September of 1986.

In an event similar to that involving the *Marjorie Lykes* earlier in the season, high winds once again played havoc with a saltwater vessel at Milwaukee when the Indian flagged bulker *Jalatapi* sustained damage when pushed hard against a dock while loading on November 27. Experiencing no significant delay in relation to the incident, the ocean freighter cleared a short time later for Montreal, where it arrived on December 6 to load additional cargo.

Glancing off a pier while entering the MacArthur Lock at Sault Ste. Marie, Michigan, at 8:45 in the evening of November 27, the downbound saltwater vessel *Anangel Spirit* collided with American Steamship's *Indiana Harbor*, which was in the process of exiting the adjacent Poe Lock while upbound in ballast for Two Harbors, Minnesota. The collision left an 8-foot tear measuring approximately four inches wide in the bow of the thousand-footer while the Greek owned freighter suffered a 8-foot dent in its bow plating. Loaded with barley and wheat, the *Anangel Spirit* cleared the Soo shortly afterwards for a St. Lawrence River port while the *Indiana Harbor* had to back into the Poe Lock to lock downbound before proceeding downstream to the Carbide Dock for an inspection and temporary repairs.

During the latter part of the season, Westdale Shipping committed its two elderly vessels to the movement of coal between points in southern Ontario as that firm neared the end of its final year of operation. This resulted in the *Erindale* transferring a considerable amount of coal from Toronto's Hearn Generating Station to the nearby Lakeview Generating Station at Mississauga, Ontario, after the former facility retired its last remaining coal-fired units. Meanwhile, the *Silverdale* made several trips carrying coal from Windsor to the Lambton Generating Station located on the St. Clair River at Courtright, Ontario.

An era of Great Lakes shipbuilding came to sudden close on December 1 when the American Ship Building Company shuttered the firm's last remaining facility on the lakes with the closure of its Lorain yard. This announcement came on the heels of the company abandoning its Toledo facility in February of that same year. During the final years of its Great Lakes operations, American Ship Building had encountered a string of labor issues and heavy financial losses even as U.S. flagged construction ground to a halt. In addition, the number of active vessels on the lakes that provided maintenance and repair revenue had undergone a significant decline during the same period.

A pair of mishaps at St. Lawrence River

ports during the first week of December left three Canadian lake vessels damaged. On December 1, the steamer *James Norris* sustained some bent plating in an altercation with a dock at Valleyfield, Quebec. Just five days later, the self-unloader *Jean Parisien* struck the bulk carrier *Montrealais* while attempting to dock at Quebec City in an incident in which both vessels reported light damage.

Sold for $1, the Michigan Department of Transportation transferred ownership of the car ferry *City of Milwaukee* to the City of Frankfort on December 6 for use in a preservation effort. This transaction came after a failed attempt to sell the retired vessel earlier that year in which all of the bids received fell far below its estimated $180,000 scrap value. The *City of Milwaukee* currently serves as a museum ship at Manistee, Michigan.

During mid-July, the Panamanian registered RO/RO (Roll-On/Roll-Off) vessel *Caribbean Trailer* had arrived on the lakes to inaugurate a service carrying truck trailer traffic between Windsor and Thunder Bay. Granted an exemption to operate on that route for the 1983 season from the Canadian government, the use of a foreign-flagged vessel between two domestic ports generated a considerable amount of opposition from both labor unions and some ship owners when this vessel entered service near the end July. Operated by Lakespan Shipping Inc., which was unrelated to a similarly named firm that previously offered a comparable service across Lake Ontario, the *Caribbean Trailer* ended what was termed a profitable season in late November. While making its way out of the lakes, however, the authorities detained the saltwater vessel at Port Colborne on December 12 due to an unpaid food bill until releasing it the next day. Service on this route resumed during the spring of 1984 with a Canadian flagged vessel.

Citing rising costs and lockage rates on the Welland Canal that favored large vessels, the Quebec & Ontario Transportation fleet issued a statement on December 16 announcing its intention to cease operations at the end of the season. Founded in 1914, the longstanding fleet consisted of eight bulk carriers at the time of its demise, these being the *Chicago Tribune* (2), *Franquelin* (2), *Golden Hind*, *Lac Ste. Anne*, *Meldrum Bay*, *New York News* (3), *Outarde* (3), and *Thorold* (4). As will be related in the next chapter, Group Desgagnes Inc. of Quebec City purchased the fleet in January of the following year.

As the shipping season entered its final days, traffic on the St. Lawrence Seaway drew to a close on December 18 when Algoma Central's *A. S. Glossbrenner* and Halco's *Steelcliffe Hall* made the respective final upbound and downbound transits of that waterway.

The *Philip R. Clarke* encountered a late season mishap while attempting to refuel on December 20 when it allided with the Shell Canada Ltd. fuel dock at Corunna, Ontario. Causing considerable damage to approximately 260 feet of the dock, the impact also opened a large gash in the starboard bow of the 767-foot self-unloader. Proceeding upriver following the accident, the *Clarke* went into the Sarnia Elevator Slip for temporary repairs. With a steel plate installed over a hole just below the anchor pocket, the steamer cleared Sarnia on December 23.

After completing a downbound transit of Lake Huron in heavy weather, the *Elton Hoyt 2nd* (2) anchored in the Detroit River on December 22 following the discovery of a crack in its deck plating. Departing the anchorage with tug escort after receiving minor repairs, the steamer was able to

The steamer *Golden Hind* was one of eight bulk carriers in the Quebec & Ontario Transportation fleet when that firm ceased operations. (Photo by Tom Salvner)

continue its voyage to Ashtabula.

As the lower lakes region began experiencing extremely cold temperatures in late December, increasingly tenacious ice conditions began impeding marine traffic in Lake Erie. The rapid onset of the wintry weather resulted in some vessels requiring tug assistance as thick ice began clogging the Welland Canal, through which CSL's *Black Bay* made the final complete transit of the 1983 season on December 25. The next day, Lock 2 sustained ice damage even as several vessels, their voyages suddenly curtailed by the adverse conditions on the canal, struggled to reach unplanned layup berths at Port Colborne.

On the morning of December 27, the *Edwin H. Gott* went aground in the Middle Neebish Channel of the St. Marys River while downbound with taconite for Gary, Indiana. A short time later, the tug *Chippewa* arrived to assist the grounded vessel while the U.S. Coast Guard also dispatched the *Mackinaw* and *Katmai Bay* to the scene. Refloated later that afternoon after lightering a portion of its cargo into American Steamship's *Roger M. Kyes*, the thousand-footer resumed its voyage. After unloading at Gary, the *Gott* sailed north to Sturgeon Bay, where it entered Bay Shipbuilding for repairs and a 5-year survey.

A broken valve allowed an estimated 13,000 gallons of water into the unfinished tug at the bankrupt Upper Peninsula Shipbuilding Company in Ontonagon, Michigan, on the evening of December 28. As mentioned previously, the tug was under contract to the Michigan Department of Transportation (MDOT) for the establishment of a tug/barge rail ferry service. With the vessel listing heavily, the Ontonagon Fire Department managed to bring the flooding under control the next morning with no serious damage reported. Following this incident, state officials agreed to perform periodic inspections of the partially built tug, which had sat largely untouched since the shipyard suspended operations in July 1982.

Near the end of the year, another transition within the Canadian fleet took place when, on December 28, the ships of the Upper Lakes Shipping fleet became part of ULS International Inc. in a move to recognize the company's continued growth into global markets. This corporate change had no significant impact upon the fleet's general operation.

Sizable gains in the iron ore trade during the autumn had led to the reactivation of three U.S. flagged vessels and the Lake Carriers' Association reaching an agreement with the U.S. Army Corps of Engineers to keep the Soo Locks open until January 8, 1984 with the stipulation of closing the canal plus or minus seven days from that date. The severity of the prevailing cold weather across the Great Lakes region at the end of the year, however, forced the closure of the locks on December 31 with the downbound passage of the *Algobay* for Burns Harbor, Indiana. The earlier than anticipated cessation of shipments from Lake Superior ports left an estimated 600,000 tons of iron ore undelivered.

The *Wilfred Sykes* closed out the season's list of casualties on January 6, 1984 when a furnace explosion inflicted substantial damage to its port boiler. Subsequent repairs over the winter layup had the 678-foot steamer back to work at the beginning of the 1984 season.

In comparison to the disappointing 1982 season, iron ore shipments for the year rebounded by 35 percent to reach 58.3 million net tons. Despite this remarkable turnaround, the amount carried nonetheless represented the third worst year for that commodity in the postwar era. While stone shipments grew by 3.3 million net tons, or 22 percent, from the previous year, the other primary bulk commodities, grain and coal, remained relatively unchanged over the same period. Taken as a whole, the partial recovery in ore shipments provided the primary impetus to push the season's total dry bulk commerce to just over 147 million net tons, an increase of nearly 15 percent compared to 1982 but still far below the ten-year average. During the 1983 season, Canadian tankers transported 29.1 million barrels of petroleum products while U.S. flagged vessels carried an additional 20.8 million barrels for a combined total of 50 million barrels.

Over the course of the 1983 shipping season, lake freighters established five new cargo records. Commerce on the Great Lakes attained a new benchmark that year with the *William J. De Lancey* carrying the largest single cargo ever moved on the lakes up to that time when it loaded 68,001 gross tons of taconite pellets at Escanaba, Michigan, for Indiana Harbor, Indiana. Other iron ore records established that season included the *Columbia Star* carrying the largest shipment of that steelmaking commodity through the Soo Locks with a payload of 62,968 gross tons and the *Lake Wabush* doing the same for the St. Lawrence Seaway with a 27,902 gross ton cargo. In addition, the *Belle River* pushed the coal record to new heights by transporting a 69,054 net ton cargo while the *Algowest* established a new record in the grain trade by loading 1,047,758 bushels of wheat at Duluth for Baie Comeau, Quebec.

Chapter Five
The 1984 Shipping Season

The same harsh conditions that led to the earlier than expected closure of the Soo Locks at the end of the 1983 season also curtailed winter tanker traffic on the lakes while also resulting in some difficult tug-barge transits in the lower lakes region. In addition, the breakup of ice in Lake Huron during the upcoming spring thaw resulted in a nearly month long ice jam in the St. Clair River at the beginning of the shipping season unlike anything experienced in several years.

A number of transitions took place within the Canadian fleet during the early months of the year. This included the sale of the *Texaco Warrior* (2) to Waterose Marine Ltd. of Cyprus for off-lakes use. Launched at Wallsend-on-Tyne, England, in 1970, this 312-foot tanker had first entered the Canadian fleet following its purchase by Texaco Canada Limited in 1975. Placed into service on the company's trade routes, the *Texaco Warrior* (2) operated on the lakes until laying up at Montreal, Quebec, on December 16, 1982. Renamed *Trader*, this vessel departed that city on January 12 en route to its new saltwater duties. This voyage proved anything but uneventful, however, as this vessel and the Sofati-Soconav tanker *Le Cedre No. 1* came together in a minor collision in the St. Lawrence River the next day. Following the accident, the *Le Cedre No. 1* sailed for Chatham, New Brunswick, while the *Trader* resumed its voyage to Nigeria.

Just months after chartering Halco's *Ottercliffe Hall*, Misener Transportation entered into a similar agreement with Nipigon Transport Limited to operate the 729-foot gearless bulker *Lake Nipigon* during the 1984 and 1985 navigation seasons. Originally slated for dry-docking at Thunder Bay, Ontario, over the winter layup, the onset of heavy ice conditions in the Welland Canal near the end of the previous season forced the *Lake Nipigon* into winter quarters at Hamilton, Ontario. Renamed *Laketon* (2) for the duration of this charter, this ship began its first voyage for Misener on April 6 when it departed Port Weller Dry Docks at St. Catharines, Ontario, following a brief survey.

In mid-January, Misener Transportation disposed of the oldest member in its fleet when it sold the *George M. Carl* (2) to Marine Salvage Ltd. for dismantling. Having been idle at Toronto, Ontario, since December 17, 1982, this steamer's lengthy career stretched back to 1923 when it first entered service as the *Fred G. Hartwell*. Renamed *Matthew Andrews* (2) in 1951, this 617-foot bulker came into the ownership of Scott Misener Steamships Ltd. in November 1962 after becoming excess tonnage in the Hanna Mining Company fleet. Given its last name the following year, the final disposition of this vessel will be related later in this chapter.

On January 20, Quebec & Ontario Transportation Company Ltd. announced it had sold the eight vessels in its defunct fleet to Group Desgagnes Inc. of Quebec City,

Quebec. With a long history of operating small bulk carriers, the *Chicago Tribune* (2), *Franquelin* (2), *New York News* (3), and *Thorold* (4) fit nicely into the company's established business practices and entered service early that spring. With no experience in operating large lake vessels, however, Desgagnes was unable to find work for the *Golden Hind*, *Lac Ste. Anne*, *Meldrum Bay*, and *Outarde* (3). Of these ships, only the *Golden Hind* saw any further service when it operated very briefly in late 1985.

Concentrating in the operation of elderly self-unloading vessels with high maintenance costs since 1977, the poor financial condition of Westdale Shipping Limited became untenable in February when creditors seized the *Silverdale* at Windsor, Ontario, and the *Erindale* at Port Colborne, Ontario. With the poor economic outlook offering little hope for a reversal of fortunes, the company had little choice but to declare bankruptcy a short time later.

Early in the year, Ontario-Lake Erie Sand Ltd. sold the sand sucker *W. M. Edington* to McKeil Work Boats Ltd., which renamed the 54-year old vessel *Niagara II*. Placed into service working the Niagara River and the western waters of Lake Ontario, the 182-foot diesel-powered ship operated a full season for its new owner before laying up for the winter at Hamilton on January 15, 1985.

Having snuck aboard the *William G. Mather* (2) at Toledo, Ohio, a vagrant from Salt Lake City, Utah perished in a fire he started in the steamer's aft cabins on February 8.

The bulk carrier *Lake Nipigon* operating under the name *Laketon* (2) during its charter to Misener Transportation.
(Photo by Tom Salvner)

Extinguished by a local fire crew, the blaze inflicted significant damage to the vessel's galley and dining areas. At the time of this incident, the Cleveland-Cliffs vessel had been idle for just over three years after laying up for the last time on December 21, 1980.

With the Soo Locks not scheduled to open for another six weeks and ore stockpiles beginning to run low, early season activity within the U.S. flagged fleet included Columbia Transportation's *Wolverine* (2) entering service on the ore shuttle up the Cuyahoga River at Cleveland, Ohio, in mid-February. A few weeks later, on March 7, the motor vessel *Richard J. Reiss* (2) docked at Toledo to load the first cargo of the season for the coal run between that port and the Detroit area upon which it was soon joined by the *Henry Ford II*.

The same day the *Richard J. Reiss* (2) sailed into Toledo, the USS Great Lakes Fleet began its season with the departure of the *Philip R. Clarke* from Milwaukee, Wisconsin, to begin carrying iron ore between Escanaba, Michigan, and Gary, Indiana. Joining its fleet mate in the Lake Michigan ore trade when it cleared Milwaukee on March 8, the *Cason J. Callaway* suffered minor rudder and steering gear damage when it encountered heavy ice in the Rock Island Passage and near Minneapolis Shoal. Arriving at Escanaba on March 10, temporary repairs kept the 767-foot self-unloader in service.

Operating without its barge, *Amoco Great Lakes*, the tug *Amoco Michigan* went aground near Whaleback Shoal in Green Bay on March 17. Experiencing its own trouble in the prevailing ice conditions, the tug *John M. Selvick* made a futile attempt to release the 2-year old vessel. Finally freed following the arrival of the U.S. Coast Guard icebreaking tug *Mobile Bay*, the *Amoco Michigan* made a subsequent visit to Bay Shipbuilding at Sturgeon Bay, Wisconsin, for repairs.

The series of early season mishaps continued on March 21, when the *John G. Munson* (2) suffered the loss of its port anchor and other bow damage when it ran into the outer breakwater at Lorain, Ohio. Having just opened the season at Conneaut, Ohio, two days earlier, the large self-unloader was engaged in the movement of ore pellets from that port to Lorain at the time of the accident. Successfully recovered from the lake bottom, the anchor lost in this incident was reinstalled later in the season.

The earlier misadventure with ice on its first voyage notwithstanding, the *Cason J. Callaway* arrived at Sault Ste. Marie, Michigan, late in the afternoon of March 25 in anticipation of being the season's first commercial vessel through the Soo Locks. With the U.S. Coast Guard icebreaker *Mackinaw* having locked through earlier to work the upper St. Marys River and Whitefish Bay, the *Callaway* transited the Poe Lock at 12:14 the next morning bound for Two Harbors, Minnesota.

Shipping operations on the Welland Canal began with the arrival of the upbound *Jean Parisien* from Hamilton on March 27 and the downbound passage of the *Ralph Misener* the following day. To commemorate the 25th anniversary of the opening of the St. Lawrence Seaway, an official ceremony took place aboard the latter vessel at Lock 3 before it continued eastbound to participate in a similar event held at the Eisenhower Lock on April 2.

Its fate foretelling what was to come with the significant downsizing of the Great Lakes fleet over the next several years, the Interlake Steamship Company sold the *E. G. Grace* to Marine Salvage Ltd. on April 4 for scrapping at Port Colborne. This vessel was one of sixteen bulk freighters built by the U.S.

Shown here laid up at Ashtabula, Ohio, the *E. G. Grace* was the first "Maritime" class steamer to be sold for scrap. (Photo by Tom Salvner)

Maritime Commission during World War II to meet the tonnage demands of that conflict and assist in modernizing the domestic lake fleet, which had saw little new construction since the onset of the Great Depression. As such, the *Grace* was the first member of this class sold for dismantling. On May 17, the tugs *Glenevis* and *Glenside* delivered the 41-year old steamer to Ramey's Bend on the Welland Canal, where dismantling took place over the next year and a half. Built by the American Ship Company at Lorain in 1943, the *E. G. Grace* spent its entire career in the Interlake Steamship fleet until engine problems, an affliction common among the six "Maritime" class vessels built with Lentz-Poppet power plants, sent it into a permanent layup at Ashtabula, Ohio, on December 25, 1976.

Clearing Collingwood, Ontario, on April 6, the newest addition to the Canada Steamship Lines (CSL) fleet, *Prairie Harvest*, began its maiden voyage when it sailed for Thunder Bay, where the gearless bulker loaded a cargo of wheat for delivery to Port Cartier, Quebec. While downbound in the Welland Canal with its initial payload on April 13, however, this vessel rubbed the west wall after losing power near Lock 7. Although delayed for about five hours, the gearless bulker came away from the incident with nothing more than some dented hull plates and a few patches of scuffed paint.

As mentioned at the beginning of this chapter, the spring thaw produced a prolonged ice jam in the St. Clair River just after the start of the shipping season. The winter that year was characterized by an extremely frigid January followed by a warm February and a cold March. By March 31, this cycle of freezing, thawing, and refreezing had created an area of ice cover on southern Lake Huron extending eastward along a roughly diagonal line from Port Hope, Michigan, to Bayfield, Ontario, which began the normal process of breaking up with the arrival of warmer spring temperatures. By April 4, strong northeast winds had pushed a large amount of this brash ice toward the Michigan shore as it followed the lake's natural flow into the St. Clair River. Moved along by a combination of river currents and northerly winds, the broken ice began to accumulate in the St. Clair Flats, an area consisting of numerous islands and narrow channels near the mouth of the river where it meets Lake St. Clair.

The buildup of ice brought about an abrupt halt to auto ferry traffic across the river between the United States and Canada along with service to Harsens Island from Algonac, Michigan. Operating exclusively between Marine City, Michigan, and Sombra, Ontario, the auto ferry *Daldean* had a close brush with disaster on April 7 when a sudden rise and fall in the river's water level left the 33-year old vessel in an awkward position atop a spile. Carefully extricated from its delicate predicament without further incident, the ferry was soon back to work.

As conditions worsened, a fleet of icebreakers consisting of units from both sides of the border deployed to the region to assist commercial vessels and minimize flooding in the communities bordering the lower reaches of the river. Over a three week period, the roster of government vessels involved in this operation grew to include the U.S. Coast Guard's *Biscayne Bay, Bramble, Bristol Bay, Katmai Bay, Neah Bay,* and *Mackinaw* which were joined by the Canadian Coast Guard's *Griffon,* and *Des Groseilliers.* Assisting in this effort were several privately owned tugs that not only included those of local operators but those as far away as the Escanaba based *Olive L. Moore.*

With 18 vessels reported trapped on April 13, the U.S. and Canadian Coast Guards closed the river to traffic two days later due to the heavy ice jam, which in some areas had built up to 10 feet in thickness. Reopened on April 16, all commercial vessel traffic on the St. Clair River was restricted to the convoy system. One of the vessels involved in these transits was Bethlehem Steel's *Stewart J. Cort*, which had just reentered service after being laid up at Erie, Pennsylvania, since the end of the 1982 season. During its upbound voyage, the *Cort* came to the assistance of the low powered (2,200 ihp) *Kinsman Independent* (2) near Algonac when the 600-foot steamer was unable to make headway in the ice-choked river. Falling in close astern of the thousand-footer, the Kinsman bulk carrier proceeded upriver in the path made through the ice by its escort's much wider 105-foot beam.

Although the majority of ships that transited the St. Clair River over the duration of the ice jam encountered little more than the usual complications associated with lost time, a handful went aground when forced out of the navigation channel. An early casualty involved the *Canadian Progress*, when high winds pushed the icebound 730-foot self-unloader into shallow water near Algonac on April 9. Just eight days later, the *Murray Bay* (3) spent a short time aground in the same general area while struggling to make its way down the river.

A more serious incident occurred on April 20 when the *George A. Stinson* grounded just north of Marine City. Downbound with taconite pellets, the best efforts of the tugs *Bantry Bay, Barbara Ann, Olive L. Moore,* and *Tug Malcolm* failed the budge the thousand-foot vessel. Sailing from Detroit, Michigan, the following day, the steamer *Paul H. Carnahan* worked its way upbound to tie up alongside its much larger fleet mate. After lightering into the *Carnahan*, the *George A. Stinson* finally floated free on April 24 without any reported damage. Interestingly, this unfortunate episode was the second stranding suffered by the large lake freighter on this particular voyage as it had previously grounded at Superior, Wisconsin, on April 12. In that particular mishap, the *Stinson* remained aground until being refloated three days later after offloading some of its cargo into the *Herbert C. Jackson*.

The prolonged nature of the ice jam created significant backlogs at various loading ports located in the upper lakes region. With few vessels arriving to load grain, a serious bottleneck developed at Thunder Bay when the elevators quickly ran out of space to accommodate further rail shipments from the Canadian prairie. The decreased ability to move cargo through the St. Clair River also resulted in the idling of some vessels, one such example being the decision by fleet managers at the American Steamship Company to send the motor vessel *St. Clair* (2) into a temporary layup at Ashland, Wisconsin, during late April.

As the ice jam entered its third week, the list of ships experiencing delays continued to grow in direct relation to the limited number daily transits taking place through the clogged St. Clair River. This resulted in a lengthy queue of vessels above and below the vital connecting channel that by April 20 included 18 ships in lower Lake Huron and another 64 awaiting passage in the Detroit River and western Lake Erie.

As the ice blockade entered its final days, the difficult navigation conditions claimed another victim when the *Tadoussac* (2) went aground on April 27 while sailing downbound as part of a six-ship convoy. Freed with tug assistance the following day, the Canadian flagged self-unloader was able to resume its voyage.

A combination of warmer temperatures and blustery weather with winds clocked as high as 47 mph over the weekend of April 28 finally provided the necessary conditions to begin breaking up the ice jam. Taking advantage of the shift in weather, the icebreaking fleet worked to keep ice moving into Lake St. Clair with the river reopening to unrestricted movements at three o'clock in the morning of April 30. With some ships having waited for more than a week to pass through the river, the traffic backlog cleared up over the next couple of days even as the icebreakers began returning to their home stations for a well-deserved rest. Near the end of this 24-day episode (April 5-29), the Lake Carriers' Association estimated the shipping industry was losing up to $1.7 million a day due to delays caused by the ice jam.

Returning to the chronological review of the 1984 season, the annual spring fit out continued during early April as crews in various ports across the Great Lakes region busily prepared their ships for another shipping season. As often occurs after a period of idleness, however, not all of these initial voyages proceeded without the occasional encounter with mechanical difficulty. For example, Bethlehem Steel's *Burns Harbor* experienced bow thruster problems shortly after departing its winter layup berth at Litton's Erie Marine Inc. yard at Erie, Pennsylvania, on April 7. Paying a return visit to the shipyard, the thousand-foot vessel finally cleared that port on April 13 following the completion of repairs.

The spring thaw also created some

headaches for shipmasters in the Welland Canal with the Liberian flagged bulker *La Liberte* sustaining minor hull damage on April 8 while passing through heavy ice at Lock 8. Continuing its voyage, which originated at Antwerp, Belgium, the ocean freighter tied up at Detroit the following day, thereby becoming the first saltwater ship into that port for the season.

The lower lakes region in no way held exclusive rights to early season difficulties as the winter months had also created a significant amount of ice cover in western Lake Superior. Extending some 15 miles into the lake and measuring up to 13 feet thick, this ice field caused significant problems for several ships arriving and departing the Twin Ports, among which included the steamer *Ernest R. Breech* and car ferry *Incan Superior* both which became stuck off Duluth, Minnesota, on April 11. Joined the following day by the *Benson Ford* (2), the U.S. Coast Guard imposed traffic restrictions through the area as the cutter *Mobile Bay* and local tugs worked to free the icebound vessels. By April 17, a shift in winds had sufficiently broken up the ice field to allow the resumption of normal navigation in that section of the lake.

While sailing upbound for Green Bay, Wisconsin, on April 13, the Panamanian flagged *Duteous* went aground off Light 2 in Lake St. Clair. With the tugs *Bantry Bay*, *Tipperary*, and *William A. Whitney* assisting, the bulk freighter finally floated off the bottom on April 17 after lightering 280 tons of its cargo into the motor vessel *New York News (3)*. Reversing course to reload its cargo at Windsor, the *Duteous* arrived at Green Bay on April 27 before receiving a subsequent damage survey at Burns Harbor, Indiana, early the next month.

Heavy ice was not the only hardship complicating marine traffic at the Twin Ports that spring as the *Benson Ford* (2) and *Federal Maas* both found a shoal in Duluth-Superior Harbor on April 15, the latter having just come up the lakes after being the first saltwater vessel into the port of Erie, Pennsylvania, six days earlier. Both ships came away from these encounters without suffering any serious damage.

Arriving at Grand Haven, Michigan, on April 24 a strong current forced the *Calcite II* into the harbor's breakwall. Although the impact ripped away a 6-foot section of the concrete structure, the 55-year old self-unloader came away from the mishap unscathed. That same day, the package freighter *Jensen Star* passed upbound through the Welland Canal bound for Windsor to begin carrying general cargo between that city and Thunder Bay over the same route as the foreign-flagged *Caribbean Trailer* had sailed the previous season. Returning to the lakes after spending a few years on saltwater, this vessel, the former *French River* of the Canada Steamship Lines fleet, commonly delivered newsprint and wood products to Toledo on its downbound voyages from Thunder Bay.

Purchased by Peterson Builders Inc. for non-transportation use, the retired car ferry *Arthur K. Atkinson* left Elberta, Michigan, on April 25 in tow for Kewaunee, Wisconsin, to await the availability of dock space at Sturgeon Bay. This same owner had acquired another former Ann Arbor Railroad car ferry, *Viking* (2), the previous year.

Shortly after departing Trois-Rivieres, Quebec, on April 26, the *Sauniere* went aground in the St. Lawrence River while carrying a load of phosphate consigned to Baltimore, Maryland. Refloated four hours later, the 14-year old self-unloader returned to port for an inspection. That same day, the

The motor vessel *Canadian Ranger* following its extensive reconstruction utilizing the stern of the package freighter *Chimo* and forward section of the steamer *Hilda Marjanne*. (Author's Collection)

Canadian Ranger emerged from Port Weller Dry Docks to begin sea trials on Lake Ontario following its extensive reconstruction involving the stern of the package freighter *Chimo* and forward section of the steamer *Hilda Marjanne*. Following some additional work at the shipyard, the 730-foot bulker began its maiden voyage in this configuration on May 6 when it sailed light to Toledo to load coal for delivery to Hamilton.

Improving market conditions at the beginning of the season allowed the Interlake Steamship Company to reactivate the *Charles M. Beeghly* after it had sat idle at Superior, Wisconsin, since 1982. Departing that port on April 27, this steamer suffered an unfortunate accident at the beginning of its first voyage after returning to service. This occurred just after eight o'clock that morning when a combination of ice, high winds, and strong currents forced the *Beeghly* off course and into shallow water while backing away from the Burlington Northern ore dock after loading 26,174 gross tons of taconite pellets. With its bow grounding in 20 feet of water, the stern of the 806-foot self-unloader swung around and struck the north pier of the Superior Entry. Inflicting damage to a 70-foot section of the pier, the impact opened an 8' x 5' gash in the vessel's hull about three feet above the waterline while also ripping away its stern anchor, which fell onto the breakwater.

Completely blocking the entry channel, the *Charles M. Beeghly* resisted the efforts of three tugs before finally breaking free some five hours later. Moved to the Duluth Port Terminal for an inspection, it went back across the harbor on May 1 to receive repairs at Fraser Shipyards. Estimated damage to the pier amounted to approximately $25,000 while that to the *Beeghly* approached $50,000, the latter of which cleared the shipyard on May 14. A subsequent investigation by the

U.S. Coast Guard absolved the vessel's master of any wrongdoing.

Converted into a barge at Hamilton by Port Weller Dry Docks with the addition of V-shaped frame installation at its stern, the cement carrier *Robert Koch* departed that port on April 28 in tow of the tug *R. & L. No. 1* to begin operating on a route between Clarkson, Ontario, and Oswego, New York. Previously serving primarily between Clarkson and Buffalo, New York, this vessel dated back to its construction as the coastal bulk carrier *Ethel Everard* by the Grangemouth Dockyard Company at Grangemouth, Scotland, in 1957. Rebuilt as a cement carrier and renamed *Guardian Carrier* in 1963, this 240-foot motor vessel saw subsequent service in the Pacific Ocean before coming to the Great Lakes following its sale to the St. Lawrence Cement Company of Mississauga, Ontario, in 1977. In lake service, the *Robert Koch* had a carrying capacity of 1,600 gross tons of cement, which remained unchanged after its conversion into a barge.

Laid up at Montreal since December 2, 1982, the *Nipigon Bay* arrived at Kingston, Ontario, on April 28 in tow of the tugs *Helen M. McAllister*, *Salvage Monarch*, and *Rival*. There it joined three other inactive fleet mates, the *Fort Henry*, *Fort York*, and *Hochelaga*.

The same weather system that helped break up the ice jam on the St. Clair River at the end of April with several days of sustained high winds also damaged a pair of Canadian flagged vessels as it swept across the Great Lakes region. Ripped from its

The laid up steamer *John E. F. Misener* broke free of its moorings during a windstorm at Port McNicoll, Ontario. (Author's Collection)

moorings at Port McNicoll, Ontario, on April 30, the gusty conditions blew the laid up steamer *John E. F. Misener* lengthwise across the small harbor basin. With its stern slamming into the adjacent grain elevator, this incident resulted in significant damage to that structure but left the Misener Transportation vessel with just a few dents as evidence of its misadventure. The next day, the bulker *Silver Isle* had some cracks develop in its spar deck while upbound in heavy seas on Lake Superior west of Caribou Island. Managing to reach the safety of Thunder Bay, the Pioneer Shipping motor vessel went into the dry dock at Port Arthur Shipbuilding for repairs before reentering service on May 16 when it loaded grain for a St. Lawrence River port.

Just weeks before the beginning of the season, P. & H. Shipping sold three of its steamers for dismantling. This transaction involved the *Elmglen*, *Fernglen*, and *Pineglen*, none of which had operated since the end of the 1982 shipping season. Towed out of Toronto by the tugs *Glenevis* and *Glenside*, the *Elmglen* became the first of this trio to make its final voyage to the scrapper's torch when it arrived at Port Maitland, Ontario, on May 3, where dismantling of the 75-year old steamer began on November 1. While the *Pineglen* joined its former fleet mate at the scrap yard later that autumn, the *Fernglen* was to remain at Toronto until April of the following year.

After sitting at Hamilton for nearly six years following its sale to United Metals for scrapping, dismantling of the *Pic R.* finally began during early spring. Originally built as the barge *James Nasmyth* by the F. W. Wheeler Company at West Bay City, Michigan, in 1896, this vessel had been in tow of the steamer *Mataafa* when that vessel stranded just off the Duluth Entry piers during a major storm on November 28, 1905. While the *Nasmyth* managed to ride out the fall gale without any damage or loss among its crew, nine of those aboard *Mataafa* lost their lives in the accident. Sold into the Canadian fleet in 1936 for use in the lumber trade, this ship became part of the Quebec & Ontario Transportation Company fleet in 1949. Renamed *Pic River*, the 382-foot barge underwent an unusual conversion to a powered freighter at Port Weller Dry Docks four years later. The motor vessel arrived at the scrap yard in Hamilton on October 25, 1978, where it was unofficially renamed *Pic R.* a short time later.

On May 9, the bunkering vessel *Rivershell* (3) was involved in a minor incident when it hit the anchored Philippine flagged *Saint Vincent* in the St. Lawrence River. The next morning, the tug *Daniel McAllister* towed the barge *Wittransport II* out of Kingston thus putting an end to that vessel's controversial presence along the La Salle Causeway. Taken to Deseronto, Ontario, the barge remained unused at the small port until sold to McKeil Work Boats Ltd. three years later.

Following several years of construction, the Detroit Edison Company prepared to place its Belle River Power Plant into operation during the summer of 1984. Built adjacent to the St. Clair Power Plant, which is located on the St. Clair River a few miles north of Marine City, this facility was designed to burn low-sulfur western coal brought down the lakes from Superior, Wisconsin. To supplement the tonnage already carried by the American Steamship Company fleet, the utility company awarded a long-term floating contract to the Interlake Steamship Company to meet the additional demand associated with the startup of the new power plant. This agreement called for the movement of approximately 1.5 million tons of coal in its first year followed by 3 million tons in subsequent years. Assigning its thousand-footers to this route, the first cargo carried by Interlake on this contract took place on May 9 when the *James R. Barker* arrived at the Superior Midwest Energy Terminal to load coal for St. Clair, Michigan, delivery.

Despite the austere economic climate facing the shipping industry during this period, N. M. Paterson & Sons Ltd. awarded Collingwood Shipyards a $30 million contract during mid-May to build a 736-foot gearless bulk carrier. With its keel laid on November 5, this vessel entered service in June of the following year as the *Paterson* (2). Earlier in the year, Paterson had sold the 291-foot coastal freighter *Lawrendoc* (2) to Transportacion Maritima Peninsular S. A. of Progreso, Mexico, for use in the Gulf of Mexico. Laid up at Collingwood at the time of its sale, the 22-year old motor vessel received a refit before departing on its trip off the lakes. Renamed *Contoy*, this ship cleared the Welland Canal on May 28 while downbound for its new saltwater duties.

Early in the season, the Cleveland-Cliffs steamers *Edward B. Greene* and *Walter A. Sterling* began making regular deliveries of iron ore from the Lake Superior region to the Rouge Steel Company Dock on the Rouge River at Dearborn, Michigan. With the *William Clay Ford* remaining committed to the movement of raw materials for its production requirements, this arrangement allowed the steelmaker to employ its two other straight deck bulk carriers, *Ernest R. Breech* and *Benson Ford* (2), more actively in outside trades. This resulted in the *Breech* spending much of the season carrying grain while the *Benson Ford* (2) made several trips to Hamilton with ore for the Steel Company of Canada (Stelco).

The Panamanian flagged bulker *Aegis Hispanic* ran into some minor trouble on May 20 when its engine quit near the Eisenhower Lock, thereby resulting in a three-hour traffic stoppage in the Seaway.

During late May, S. & E. Shipping (Kinsman Lines) bolstered its active fleet carrying capacity to meet the demands of the domestic grain market when it placed the bulk carrier *Alastair Guthrie* into service as a barge. Towed by the large Great Lakes Towing Company tug *Ohio*, the 62-year old vessel made several trips between Duluth and Buffalo in this configuration over the next four months before entering its final layup at the latter port on September 17 of that year.

Having returned to service earlier that spring after sitting idle at South Chicago, Illinois, since 1981, the steamer *John J. Boland* (3) made a rare trip down the Welland Canal on May 30 with a cargo of salt. That same day, the *Stephen B. Roman* suffered a minor grounding in Genesee River while outbound light from Rochester, New York. Stranding during the late afternoon hours, three tugs refloated the 19-year old cement carrier without any significant damage at four o'clock the following morning.

A minor mishap involving a saltwater vessel transiting the Seaway took place on May 31 when the Philippine flagged bulker *Valor* struck an approach wall at the Cote Ste. Catherine Lock. Following a damage inspection at Montreal, the ocean freighter was drydocked at Lauzon, Quebec, on June 11 for rudder repairs.

Taking steps to reduce its idle package freight fleet that spring after abandoning such operations at the end of the 1981 season, CSL sold the *Fort Henry* and *Fort York* to United Metals for scrapping at Hamilton. Laid up at Kingston since December 1980,

Sold for scrapping, the former Canada Steamship Lines package freighter *Fort Henry* was towed from Kingston, Ontario, to Hamilton, Ontario, during the summer of 1984. (Author's Collection)

the *Fort York* departed that port in tow of the tug *Glenevis* on May 31 bound for Hamilton, where the pair arrived the following day. Sailing back across Lake Ontario to Kingston, the same tug, along with its fleet mate *Glenside*, delivered the *Fort Henry* to the scrap yard on June 5. While the *Fort York* received a temporary reprieve from a date with the cutter's torch with its sale for use as a barge in the lumber trade the following year, dismantling of the *Fort Henry* did not begin until 1988.

Near the beginning of summer, Gulf Canada Limited sold the tanker *Gulf Canada* to Coastal Canada Marine Inc. Launched in 1952 by Collingwood Shipyards Ltd. as the *B. A. Peerless* for the British-American Transportation Company, this vessel was one of four 620-foot tankers built for the Canadian inland fleet during the early 1950s and the only one to remain a tanker throughout its entire career. The other members of this class were the *Imperial Leduc*, *Imperial Redwater*, and *Imperial Woodbend* that, within a few years of entering service, were converted into the bulk carriers *Nipigon Bay*, *R. Bruce Angus*, and *Golden Hind* respectively. Shortened by 72 feet at Port Arthur Shipbuilding in 1958 and renamed *Gulf Canada* in 1969, this vessel remained one of the largest tankers on the Great Lakes at the time of its sale. Renamed *Coastal Canada*, the 32-year old tanker operated primarily on the lower lakes although some voyages took it as far away as the East Coast and the Gulf of Mexico.

Sold to M&M Metals of Hamilton for scrapping following the bankruptcy of Westdale Shipping fleet, the tugs *Gotham*, *Manco*, and *Prescotont* pulled the self-unloader *Silverdale* away from the Consol Coal Dock at Windsor on June 2 and towed it a short distance upriver to the Sterling Fuels Slip. There, scrapping of the 59-year old steamer began a short time later.

A minor incident occurred in the Thousand Islands section of the St. Lawrence River on June 7 when Halco's 730-foot gearless bulker *Lawrencecliffe Hall* (2) went aground after losing engine power near Ironsides Island.

The summer of 1984 witnessed the return of passenger service on the Great Lakes, albeit on a small scale, with the arrival of the cruise ship *Caribbean Prince* of the American-Canada Line. Built by the Blount Marine Corporation at Warren, Rhode Island, the previous year, the 156-foot vessel passed upbound through the Welland Canal for the first time on June 10. Offering leisurely 12-day voyages between Wyandotte, Michigan, and Owen Sound, Ontario, with stops at several points between, the *Caribbean Prince* made four such trips before the unprofitability of the venture forced its reassignment to duties away from the lakes.

Following a few weeks devoid of accidents, CSL's Seaway-sized ocean self-unloader *Atlantic Superior* suffered a methane explosion in its forecastle on June 24 while anchored in Chedabucto Bay near Port Hawkesbury, Nova Scotia, with a load of coal. Although the blast and flash fire severely injured one member of its crew, the two-year old vessel suffered no significant damage in the incident.

Unable to stop while entering Lock 1 of the Welland Canal on June 26, the bulk carrier *Thorold* (4) ended up with a mangled bow when it severed an arrester cable designed to protect the lock gates. This incident, which could have had dire consequences for the shipping industry, came just two months after the 410-foot motor vessel first entered service for Group Desgagnes and closed the canal for 18 hours while the lock received minor gate repairs.

During the early hours of July 1, the *Nicolet* ran aground in Lake Michigan while attempting to reach the National Gypsum Company Dock at Waukegan, Illinois. Stranding around 4:30 that morning, the 79-year old self-unloader remained firmly stuck until refloated nineteen hours later with the assistance of tugs *G. W. Falcon*, *J. G. II*, *Bonnie G. Selvick*, and *William C. Selvick*.

The first day of July also witnessed USS Great Lakes Fleet Inc. reduce its large pool of laid up bulk carriers with the sale of the steamers *B. F. Affleck*, *Joshua A. Hatfield*, and *August Ziesing* to the Hyman-Michaels Company of Duluth for scrapping. Sharing similar carrying capacities in the 13,000 gross ton range common to 600-foot lake freighters with 60-foot beams built during the early part of the twentieth century, all three of these vessels had been laid up at that port since the 1970s. As will be related in subsequent chapters, however, the *Hatfield* was the only member of this trio broken up at Duluth with the other two vessels resold to Canadian scrap firms for dismantling.

On July 3, Misener Transportation Limited changed its corporate name to Misener Shipping Limited. At the time of this transition, the Misener fleet consisted of eight gearless bulk carriers. In addition, it also operated three vessels under a longstanding management agreement with Pioneer Shipping Ltd. and the chartered bulkers *Laketon* (2) and *Royalton* (2).

A minor casualty occurred at Superior, Wisconsin, on July 11 when the French flagged *Philippe L. D.* struck the Superior Midwest Energy Terminal Dock while being towed into the Great Northern "S" grain elevator. Coming away from the incident with a damaged stem and some bent hull frames, the ocean freighter made the short trip to Fraser Shipyards two days later for repairs. Around that same time, the *Philip R. Clarke* also entered that shipyard for the installation of two additional cargo hold bulkheads to permit the handling of a wider range of cargo types.

While sailing in southern Lake Michigan on July 24, Interlake Steamship's *Herbert C. Jackson* came to the aid of a cabin cruiser that had become disabled a day and a half earlier when it towed the small craft for 30 miles off Waukegan. Two days later, the *Chicago Tribune* (2) wandered out of the channel and went aground near the north end of Neebish Island while upbound in the St. Marys River. Managing to release itself shortly afterwards by pumping out ballast, the 319-foot vessel spent the night at Sault Ste. Marie, Ontario, for an inspection before continuing to Thunder Bay.

Just after departing the grain elevator at Sarnia, Ontario, on July 26 with the tug *Barbara Ann* assisting, the saltwater bulker *Timur Swallow* heavily damaged a seawall at Port Huron, Michigan, after going out of control in the strong current of the St. Clair River. Passing through the area at the time of the incident, the tanker *Jupiter* reportedly burned-out its clutch while taking evasive action to avoid a collision with the wayward freighter. Running into trouble the next day, the Greek flagged *Kasos* went onto to the Vidal Shoals in the upper St. Marys River but managed to free itself without any noted damage.

Sold to Triad Salvage for scrapping early that year, the steamer *C. L. Austin* departed Buffalo on July 30 in tow of the tug *Ohio* bound for Ashtabula, where it arrived the following day. Built by the Great Lakes Engineering Works at Ecorse, Michigan, in 1910 as the *Willis L. King*, this ship sailed for Jones & Laughlin Steel Corporation's wholly owned subsidiary Interstate Steamship Company and, after 1949, in the steelmaker's marine division until its sale to the Wilson Marine Transit Company near the end of the 1952 season. Acquired by the Kinsman Marine Transit Company in 1973, the 604-foot freighter closed out its operational career at Duluth in late 1981. It remained at that port until towed to Buffalo in December of the following year with a storage cargo of grain.

A member of the Canada Steamship Lines fleet experienced a minor mishap at 6:30 in the morning of August 5 when the *Baie St. Paul* ran aground above the Fighting Island South Light in the Detroit River. Arriving on the scene, the Gaelic Tugboat Company tugs *Bantry Bay* and *Wicklow* managed to free the 730-foot bulker, apparently without damage. The next day, the saltwater vessel *Federal Schelde* came down hard against the approach wall to the St. Lambert Lock in the St. Lawrence Seaway, thereby necessitating a damage survey at Montreal.

During the summer, Marine Salvage Ltd. sold the *Conallison* and *George M. Carl* (2) to the Spanish ship breaking firm Desguaces Vige for dismantling overseas. In preparation for the transatlantic tow, the tugs *Glenevis* and *Glenside* delivered these vessels to Quebec City with the pair towing the *Conallison* out of Ramey's Bend on August 9 before sailing back across Lake Ontario to pull the *George M. Carl* (2) out of Toronto nine days later. Departing Quebec City in tow of the Polish tug *Koral* on August 25, the two lake freighters survived their three-week voyage to arrive at Aviles, Spain, on September 17. Dismantling of both vessels at San Esteban de Pravia took place shortly afterwards with cutting beginning on the *George M. Carl* (2) on September 26 and that of the *Conallison* late the following month.

A crewman aboard the *Thorold* (4) was killed on August 12 when he fell between the ship and a wall near Lock 3 in the Welland Canal. This accident came just six weeks after this vessel suffered bow damage in the canal while transiting Lock 1.

On August 14, a federal judge in U.S. Bankruptcy Court approved the sale of the Upper Peninsula Shipbuilding Company (UPSCO) at Ontonagon, Michigan, to the Wedtech Corporation, a defense contractor based in New York. This ruling came after the Superior Shipbuilding Company, which was a competing bidder, and a vice president of UPSCO withdrew their objections to the $5.2 million deal, the closing of which took place at Grand Rapids, Michigan, on August 28.

During August, a pair of classic U.S. flagged carriers rejoined the active lake fleet. After being idle since the 1981 season, Huron Cement's *J. B. Ford* reentered service during the middle of the month with the 80-year old steamer delivering its first cargo to St. Joseph, Michigan, on August 19. The venerable 440-foot cement carrier was to operate for only one additional season before beginning a second career as a storage vessel. Despite a lull in the export market, the movement of domestic grain shipments from U.S. ports prompted the Kinsman Lines to reactivate the bulk carrier *Merle M. McCurdy* during this same timeframe when that steamer cleared Lorain on August 25 for Duluth.

Stranding in the St. Clair Cutoff Channel in upper Lake St. Clair at around six o'clock in the morning of August 21, the crane vessel *Yankcanuck* (2) spent about ten hours aground before managing to free itself from the muddy bottom at 4:15 that afternoon. Owned by the Algoma Steel Corporation, the 324-foot vessel suffered no damage in the incident.

A more significant grounding occurred on August 23 when American Steamship's *Roger M. Kyes* hit bottom in the Trenton Channel of the Detroit River while inbound for the McLouth Steel Dock at Trenton, Michigan. Ending up crosswise in the channel, the effort to release the 680-foot vessel quickly grew into a major salvage operation involving a fleet of ten tugs consisting of the Gaelic Tugboat Company's *Bantry Bay*, *Galway Bay*, *Newcastle*, *Shannon*, *Tipperary*, and *Wicklow* along with the *Barbara Ann*, *Olive L. Moore*, *Nebraska*, and *Wyoming*. The *Kyes* remained hard aground until finally refloated at 6:45 in the evening of August 25 after lightering some of its cargo into the *Richard J. Reiss* (2). Going to the Bay Shipbuilding yard at Sturgeon Bay for extensive bottom repairs, the 11-year old self-unloader returned to service on September 26.

A fire that broke out aboard the *Nanticoke* while discharging a cargo of grain at Quebec City on August 29 ravaged the self-unloader's conveyor and electrical systems. Taking an hour and half to extinguish, the blaze also inflicted considerable smoke damage to the vessel's accommodation spaces. Spending the next two weeks in port, the *Nanticoke* finally departed on September 13 bound for extensive repairs at Thunder Bay.

During the month of August, the *Chief Wawatam* made its final crossing of the Straits of Mackinac when it entered a permanent layup following the collapse of the Soo Line Dock at St. Ignace, Michigan. This came only eight months after the ferry had returned to service and less than year since it received a dry dock survey at Bay Shipbuilding the previous October. With the damaged loading apron considered beyond economical repair, the retired car ferry remained at Mackinaw City, Michigan, until its sale for conversion to a barge in late 1988.

The U.S. flagged saltwater cargo ship *Shirley Lykes* spent about an hour and a half aground in the St. Lawrence River near Iroquois, Ontario, on September 15 before freeing itself without any reported damage. Built by the Bethlehem Steel Corporation at Sparrows Point, Maryland, in 1962, this vessel operated in merchant duties until 1988 when it entered the U.S. Maritime Administration's National Defense Reserve Fleet. Sold for disposal in late 2004, Bay Bridge Enterprises dismantled the *Shirley Lykes* at Chesapeake, Virginia, the following year at a cost of $849,800.

On September 17, the Cleveland-Cliffs Steamship Company sold the steamer *Pontiac* (2) to Marine Salvage Ltd. for scrapping. Having spent several years of idleness at Toledo, the 67-year old vessel departed that port for Port Colborne on October 4 in tow of the Malcolm Marine tugs *Barbara Ann* and *Tug Malcolm*. Upon arriving at Ramey's Bend two days later, the bulk carrier was placed alongside the partially dismantled *E. G. Grace* where it was to remain until sold for scrapping overseas the following spring. Built by the Great Lakes Engineering Works at Ecorse, the 600-foot *Pontiac* (2) had first entered service on May 26, 1917 when it departed Toledo with a load of coal consigned to Sault Ste. Marie, Ontario.

The Liberian registered *Seatransport* hit the Eisenhower Lock on September 18 while downbound from Duluth in an incident that required a damage inspection at Montreal before continuing its voyage to Cartagena, Columbia.

After sitting unused at Kingston since the late 1960s, the Canadian Dredge & Dock Company Ltd. sold the *Dredge Primrose* to Acton Marine Salvage of Oshawa, Ontario. During its tow out of Kingston on September 19, however, the 69-year old dredge went aground and sank in the harbor leaving only its upper superstructure above the surface of the water. The sunken vessel created a significant oil slick when some of the Bunker C fuel in its storage tanks escaped. Resting on the bottom for the next six weeks, a subsequent salvage operation succeeded in raising the 136-foot *Dredge Primrose* on October 30. Returned to the yard of its former owner for repairs, the authorities subsequently seized the dredge as security against the recovery and environmental cleanup costs associated with the sinking. With Acton Marine Salvage going into receivership following the accident, the court ordered sale of the *Dredge Primrose* took place in September of 1985, but not before vandals had cast it adrift in July of that year. Purchased by Keen Kraft Marina Company Ltd. for conversion to a floating restaurant, the dredge arrived at Toronto in tow of the tug *Atomic* on October 3, 1985.

Continuing a busy season of scrap tows, the McKeil tugs *Glenevis* and *Glenside* pulled the steamer *Pineglen* out of Toronto on September 27 for dismantling at Port Maitland, where the trio arrived two days later. With its name shortened to *Neglen*, Port Maitland Shipbreaking Ltd. completed demolition of the 78-year old vessel over the upcoming winter.

On September 28, CSL sold the *St. Lawrence* (3) for scrapping in the Far East. Built by the Mitsubishi Zosen Shipyard at Nagasaki, Japan, in 1962, this gearless bulk freighter made its first trip through the St. Lawrence

Seaway in 1975 while sailing as the *Gaucho Taura* under the Liberian flag. Acquired by CSL and given its final name one year later, this 649-foot vessel operated primarily in the ore trade on the St. Lawrence River with an occasional foray into the Great Lakes until laying up for the last time at Thunder Bay in late 1981. Departing that port on October 22, the *St. Lawrence* (3) sailed first to Milwaukee and then Detroit to load scrap before continuing to Quebec City, where a Taiwanese crew replaced the Canadian crew that had brought it down the lakes. Clearing Quebec City under Cayman Islands registry on November 13, the motor vessel passed through the Panama Canal two weeks later before sailing across the Pacific to arrive at Dalian, China, on January 5, 1985 for dismantling.

Shortly after experiencing a loss of engine power while arriving at the Cargill B1 Elevator in Duluth on the evening of October 2, Halco's *Steelcliffe Hall* suffered a crankcase explosion that critically injured the vessel's chief engineer. After three other crewmembers moved the severely burned man to safety, the assistant engineer sealed and flooded the compartment with carbon dioxide to extinguish any remaining fire. While still in port, a second, but far less serious, accident took place aboard the 730-foot vessel just six days later when a crewman working in the engine room was injured when hit in the head by a falling 2' x 10' plank.

As it was refueling at Montreal on October 4, a faulty valve caused the Greek bulk carrier *Sifnos* to spill some 25 tons of Bunker C oil into the harbor. With approximately 20 percent of the fuel oil collecting in the

The bulk carrier *St. Lawrence* (3) sailed to Asia under its own power for scrapping. (Author's Collection)

immediate vicinity of the dock, the majority of the spill reached the nearby Boucherville Islands. The seriousness of the incident compelled the Canadian authorities to hold the ocean vessel in port for two days until its owner assumed responsibility for the environmental cleanup, the cost of which amounted to $350,000.

With a new bulk carrier on order from Collingwood Shipyards due for delivery the following year, N. M. Paterson & Sons Ltd. sold the steamer *Paterson* to Shearmet Recycling on October 9 for scrapping at Thunder Bay. Laid up at that port since the end of the 1982 shipping season, the career of this lake freighter had come full circle with its dismantling taking place not far from the site of its original construction by the Port Arthur Shipbuilding Company in 1953. Towed to Shearmet's yard on the Mission River, scrapping of the 574-foot vessel was completed on June 28, 1985.

Shortly before midnight on October 14, the Greek freighter *Amilla* went aground near Pointe aux Pins in the upper St. Marys River. After radioing word of this incident to the U.S. Coast Guard's Soo Control, the vessel's pilot suddenly collapsed and died. The *Amilla* later extricated itself from the bottom without damage by shifting ballast.

Ten months after selling the *George M. Carl* (2) for scrap, Misener Shipping Ltd. reduced its fleet further on October 15 with the sale of the *John O. McKellar* (2) to P. & H. Shipping. Fitting out at Owen Sound, where it had laid idle since the end of the previous season, the 678-foot steamer cleared that port on October 31 as the *Elmglen* (2).

Traversing Lake Erie in heavy fog on October 16, CSL's *Frontenac* (5) suffered minor damage when it came together with the tug *William A. Lydon* off Point Pelee. At the time of the collision, the *Lydon* was towing the scows *No. 73*, *No. 134*, and *No. 153*. Although the big self-unloader ripped a deep gash in the bow of *No. 73*, the scow remained afloat. Five days later, Algoma Central's *Algowood* spent a short time aground after losing power near Buoy 17 in Lake St. Clair before refloating itself.

At 10:30 in the evening of October 31, the railroad bridge that crosses the St. Marys Falls Canal at Sault Ste. Marie, Michigan, suffered a mechanical failure while being lowered for the passage of a train. Coming to a stop at an awkward angle that left one end of the 450-foot long lift span about 51 feet lower than the other, the tilted structure blocked all ship traffic through the MacArthur and Poe locks. As a temporary measure, the U.S. Army Corps of Engineers placed the Davis Lock into service to allow the transit of smaller vessels. After the bridge span was moved back to its raised position, traffic through the Soo Locks returned to normal on the afternoon of November 2 by which time the incident had delayed 19 vessels. A subsequent economic analysis prepared by the Corps of Engineers estimated the financial impact of the 2-day blockage to shippers at $1,115,000.

During October, the Cleveland-Cliffs Steamship Company took steps to exit the Great Lakes shipping business when it agreed to sell its last two active vessels, the *Edward B. Greene* and *Walter A. Sterling*, to the Rouge Steel Company. As stated earlier, both of these steamers had been actively engaged in the movement of raw materials into the steelmaker's complex at Dearborn since early in the season. This transaction resulted in the retirement of the *William Clay Ford* and *Benson Ford* (2), both of which passed downbound through the Soo Locks for the final time on December 13 before being laid up on the Rouge River. To free up

The *William Clay Ford* was retired at the end of the 1984 shipping season. (Photo by James Hoffman)

their names for the newly acquired Cliffs vessels, Rouge Steel renamed the *William Clay Ford* to *No. 266029* and *Benson Ford* (2) to *No. 265808* in early 1985 by simply utilizing each ship's Official Number assigned by the U.S. Government at the time of its construction. With the sale completed during November, the *Edward B. Greene* and *Walter A. Sterling* went to Fraser Shipyards at the end of the season for repainting and renaming to *Benson Ford* (3) and *William Clay Ford* (2) respectively over the 1984-85 winter layup.

While plans to utilize four Cleveland-Cliffs steamers in the container trade through the Seaway failed to materialize, Halco's *Maplecliffe Hall* made three such trips during the autumn months. Originating at Montreal, one of these voyages ended at Detroit the other two at Windsor. In order to carry shipping containers in both its cargo hold and topside, the vessel required the installation of specialized fastening devices along with additional tank top strengthening neither of which impaired its ability to carry grain.

Under the watchful gaze of an estimated 15,000 onlookers, Collingwood Shipyards launched the *Hon. Paul Martin* at Collingwood on November 1 thus signifying the last ship built by that yard for Canada Steamship Lines. Preceded by its fleet mate *Prairie Harvest*, the bow design of this vessel incorporated an underwater ram section that extended below the lowered booms at various locks on the St. Lawrence Seaway. This feature gave the pair overall lengths of 736'6" compared to the standard 730-foot carriers built for operation through that waterway system up to that time. Work on the ocean class self-unloader continued over the winter with the *Martin* entering service the following April.

On November 2, the tugs *Atomic* and

Elmore M. Misner towed the *Erindale* from its layup berth on the Welland Canal near Humberstone, Ontario, to the International Marine Salvage (IMS) yard at Port Colborne for scrapping. Wasting little time, work on breaking up the 69-year old self-unloader began later that month.

The *New York News* (3) sustained some hull damage on November 4 when it touched bottom while approaching the Eisenhower Lock. At the time of the mishap, the 349-foot motor vessel was on a voyage from Detroit to Baie Comeau, Quebec. Just three days later, another incident took place on the Seaway, this time involving a saltwater visitor, when the Greek flagged *Silver Leader* hit the Iroquois Lock. Downbound at the time, the bulk carrier sailed to Montreal for an inspection prior to resuming its voyage on November 8.

During mid-November, USS Great Lakes Fleet disposed of two more inactive bulk carriers when it sold the *Eugene P. Thomas* and *Homer D. Williams* to Shearmet Recycling for dismantling at Thunder Bay. Retaining their original names throughout their entire careers, both ships had not sailed since July of 1981. Operating far north of its homeport, the Port Huron based *Tug Malcolm* towed the *Williams* out of Duluth on November 12 bound for Thunder Bay before repeating this voyage with the *Thomas* five days later.

Towed across Lake Erie from Buffalo by the Great Lakes Towing Company tug *Ohio*, the Kinsman Lines steamer *Frank R. Denton* arrived at Ashtabula on November 14 following its sale to Triad Salvage for dismantling. With its scrapping slated to take place following that of its former fleet mate *C. L. Austin* acquired by Triad earlier that season, the 605-foot lake carrier sat untouched until finally moved to the scrapping berth on November 13, 1985. While being broken up, however, workers at the scrap yard removed the *Denton*'s pilothouse for display at the Ashtabula Maritime Museum.

On November 21, a mechanical failure that left the Larocque vertical lift bridge crossing the Beauharnois Canal at Valleyfield, Quebec, frozen in a partially raised position resulted in a significant bottleneck on the St. Lawrence Seaway. Illustrating the significance of this traffic blockage, the backlog quickly grew to include 98 ships just six days later. Battling frigid temperatures and high winds, workers successfully replaced a 2-foot long shaft in the bridge's pulley system that allowed the waterway to reopen to commercial traffic on the morning of December 10 by which time some 160 vessels were awaiting transit. In addition to idling grain elevators on Lake Superior and costing the shipping industry in excess of $1 million per day, the 18-day disruption also prompted officials to extend the closing dates of the St. Lawrence Seaway, Welland Canal, and Soo Locks.

Sold to Marine Salvage Ltd. the previous month, the motor vessel *Saginaw Bay* arrived at Ramey's Bend on November 22 following a tow from Cleveland by the tugs *Kansas* and *Ohio*. Joining the *E. G. Grace* and *Pontiac* (2), the former American Steamship Company self-unloader sat at the scrap yard until towed down the Seaway in July of the following year for scrapping overseas.

Slated for retirement, P. & H. Shipping's *Cedarglen* cleared Thunder Bay on December 10 with a load of grain for Goderich, Ontario. There, the 59-year old steamer became a grain storage barge following its acquisition by Goderich Elevators Limited. Serving in that role until replaced by the *Willowglen* nearly 10 years later, this vessel went to Port Maitland for dismantling in August of 1994.

Just one day after the St. Lawrence Seaway

reopened to traffic following the Larocque Bridge closure at Valleyfield, the saltwater vessels *Beograd* and *Federal Danube* collided in Lake St. Louis on December 11. Suffering only light damage, the *Federal Danube* continued its voyage to Toronto. Coming away from the unfortunate meeting with a holed hull, the *Beograd* was intentionally beached outside the navigation channel. Growing to include the offloading of cargo and the installation of pumps to control flooding, the effort to refloat the *Beograd* proved a lengthy endeavor not completed until December 22 when three tugs finally pulled the bulk carrier free. Arriving at Montreal on December 27, the Yugoslav vessel entered the Versatile Vickers dry dock four days later for repairs.

Another saltwater visitor ran into trouble on December 13 when the upbound Icelandic bulker *Akranes* tore open its hull on a shoal in the Thousand Islands section of the St. Lawrence River. Going to anchor near Clayton, New York, the ocean carrier received temporary patching before going to unload at Ogdensburg, New York.

During mid-December, the *Royalton* (2) was returned to the Halco fleet following the end of its 16-month charter to Misener Shipping. Reverting to its original name, *Ottercliffe Hall*, this 730-foot motor vessel rejoined the Misener fleet in 1988 as the *Peter Misener* following the demise of Halco.

Sold to the Upper Lakes Towing Company for conversion to a self-unloading barge after being idle since October of 1982, Hansand Steamship's *Joseph H. Thompson* departed Ecorse on December 15 in tow for Menominee, Michigan. This reconstruction progressed slowly over the balance of the decade with the *Thompson* reentering service as a barge during the latter half of 1990.

In the midst of a late season gale, the tug *Ohio* towed the *John Dykstra* (2) into Cleveland Harbor on December 21 following a voyage across Lake Erie that began at the former Semet-Solvay Dock on the Detroit River. Joined by the tugs *Iowa* and *Kentucky*, the tow continued into the Cuyahoga River with the former Ford Motor Company lake freighter being tied up at the Ontario Stone No. 4 Dock.

Near the end of the season, ULS International purchased the Halco tanker *Ungava Transport* and had its engine removed at Port Colborne over the upcoming winter. Around this same time, ULS and CSL entered into a joint venture named Provmar Fuels Inc., which purchased the hull to serve as a storage tanker in the bunkering trade at Hamilton. Moved to that port on April 6, 1985 by the tugs *James E. McGrath* and *R. & L. No. 1*, the former saltwater vessel received the name *Provmar Terminal* to reflect its new duties.

No less than 10 lake vessels went into their final layups during the 1984 shipping season. This included the U.S. flagged straight deck bulk carriers *E. J. Block*, *Benson Ford* (2), *William Clay Ford*, and *Alastair Guthrie*. With careers spanning several decades, the *E. J. Block* and *Alastair Guthrie* had reached the end of their useful lives, the former of which had been committed to serving an Inland Steel dock in a constricted location at Indiana Harbor, Indiana, for several years while the latter only operated as a barge in 1984. On the Canadian side, the *E. B. Barber*, *Cedarglen*, *Menihek Lake*, *Quedoc* (2), *Red Wing*, and *Senator of Canada* also made their last operational voyages. With the exception of the 1925 built *Cedarglen*, all of these ships had entered service on the Great Lakes between 1953 and 1960 although one, *Red Wing*, dated back to its original 1944 construction as a saltwater tanker.

Halco's *Ungava Transport* later became a storage barge in the bunkering trade. (Author's Collection)

Experiencing positive growth for the second straight season, the 64.1 million net tons of iron ore carried across the waters of the Great Lakes during the 1984 season not only exceeded that of the previous year by nearly 10 percent but also established a high point for that commodity not surpassed until the 1988 season. The coal and stone trades also recorded significant gains in comparison to the 1983 season with the former increasing by 18 percent to 43.1 million net tons and the latter achieving an even greater boost of almost 26 percent to 23.1 million net tons. Although remaining stable for the fourth year in a row within the 28 million net ton range, the grain trade was to encounter a dramatic reversal during the upcoming season when tonnages tumbled by nearly one-third. Combining these four major commodities along with shipments of cement and potash, overall dry bulk commerce on the lakes during 1984 reached 164 million net tons, a level not surpassed until 1988.

Chapter Six
The 1985 Shipping Season

Following two years of improving tonnages, shippers faced yet another season of decreased demand in 1985 when loadings of iron ore fell by nine percent to 58.4 million net tons while those of coal plummeted by nearly 16 percent to 36.3 million net tons. While the stone trade gained some traction with an eight percent improvement to 24.9 million net tons, the grain trade fell to a level not seen since the 1974 season. The lack of demand for this commodity proved so extreme that by late summer, port officials at Thunder Bay, Ontario, predicted a 30 to 40 percent decline in shipments that season. This forecast proved largely accurate with the combined grain loadings across the lakes for the season amounting to only 20 million net tons, a decline of nearly 29 percent in comparison to the previous year.

Regardless of sluggish market conditions, above average water levels allowed lake vessels to establish four new cargo records during the season, the largest being a 69,701 gross ton load of taconite carried by the *Lewis Wilson Foy* from Escanaba, Michigan, to Indiana Harbor, Indiana. Meanwhile, the *Columbia Star* reached a new milestone for that same commodity at the Soo Locks when it locked through with a 64,188 gross ton cargo taken aboard at Silver Bay, Minnesota, for delivery to Toledo, Ohio. Operating in the trade for which it was designed, the *Belle River* pushed the coal record to new heights with a 70,522 net ton payload. Entering service during late June, the Canadian bulker *Paterson* (2) wasted no time in proving itself a prodigious grain carrier when it loaded a record setting 1,058,867 bushels of wheat.

Reflecting the dramatic downsizing of the lake fleet that characterized the shipping industry during the decade, vessel owners sold 22 of their units for dismantling during the 1985 season. Remarkably, these sales included the first two ships in the 730-foot class sent to the cutting torch that until 1972 were among the largest ships operating on the Great Lakes and St. Lawrence Seaway.

The most significant modernization project undertaken within the U.S. fleet during the 1984-85 winter layup was the repowering of the *George A. Sloan* by Fraser Shipyards at Superior, Wisconsin. This conversion involved the replacement of the vessel's original 2,500 ihp triple-expansion steam engine with a 4,500 bhp Caterpillar 3612 diesel engine along with the installation of a tail shaft and controllable-pitch propeller salvaged during the dismantling of the *Raymond H. Reiss*. Other work at the shipyard that winter included the repainting of the *Benson Ford* (3) and *William Clay Ford* (2) into Rouge Steel colors.

Losing power during a voyage from Montreal, Quebec, to the Magdalen Islands, Desgagnes Transport's *Thorold* (4) caused a few anxious moments on the evening of January 5 when it nearly floated into the Quebec Bridge near Quebec City, Quebec. Encountering further trouble on the St. Lawrence River while returning to Montreal with a load of salt on January 14, the 410-foot bulk carrier sustained significant bow and bottom damage when it ran aground on Red Islet. Escorted by the tug *Captain Ioannis S.*, the damaged vessel limped to Quebec City before going to Davie Shipbuilding at Lauzon, Quebec, for repairs. Before reentering service that spring, Desgagnes renamed the former ocean freighter *Catherine Desgagnes*.

During this same timeframe, Desgagnes Transport Inc. acquired the crane equipped motor vessel *Federal Pioneer*. Renamed *Cecilia Desgagnes*, the 374-foot bulker entered service for this fleet on March 4 when it cleared Sorel, Quebec, for Baie Comeau, Quebec.

Operating in the movement of grain between Hamburg, West Germany, and Leningrad, Russia, during the winter months, Misener Shipping's *Selkirk Settler* suffered minor shell plating damage at the latter port in a collision with the Russian freighter *Komsomolets Latvii* on January 17. With permanent repairs from this episode deferred until a later date following a survey at Hamburg, the 730-foot vessel resumed working in the grain run along with its sister ship *Canada Marquis*.

The explosion of several propane gas cylinders in a storage shed at Montreal on the afternoon of January 31 singed the hull of the Canada Steamship Lines (CSL) gearless bulk carrier *Black Bay*. Heard up to three miles away, the blast killed one man and injured three others but inflicted only superficial damage to the 22-year old steamer.

During early March, the Toledo-Lucas County Port Authority purchased the former American Ship Building Company shipyard at Toledo for $500,000. In late July, the Authority's board of directors approved a 5-year lease agreement with Merce Industries

The *George A. Sloan* was repowered by Fraser Shipyards in Superior, Wisconsin, during the winter of 1984-1985.
(Photo by Tom Salvner)

Inc. to operate the facility, which was to be reopened as the Toledo Shipyard. Less than a month later, Merce signed a contract with St. Marys Holdings Inc. for the construction of a 360-foot self-unloading cement barge christened the following May as the *St. Marys Cement*.

Returning to service after wintering at Ecorse, Michigan, the cement carrier *S. T. Crapo* once again played the role as a harbinger of spring when it arrived to unload at Detroit, Michigan, on March 16. Just two days later, Rouge Steel's *Henry Ford II* opened the port of Toledo when it loaded coal for Dearborn, Michigan.

On March 17, Provmar Fuels Inc. purchased the 201-foot tanker *Metro Sun* from the Shediac Coastal Carrier Corporation of Shediac, New Brunswick, for use in the establishment of a bunkering service at Hamilton, Ontario. Built by the Grangemouth Dockyard Company at Grangemouth, Scotland, in 1965 as the *Partington*, this vessel later operated as the *Shell Scientist* and had been idle at Halifax, Nova Scotia, since the summer of 1984. Renamed *Hamilton Energy*, the small tanker made its way into the lakes after the opening of navigation and tied up below Lock 1 on the Welland Canal during mid-April to undergo a refit. Reconfigured to refuel ships in the western end of Lake Ontario, this vessel cleared the canal for Hamilton on June 11 prior to performing its first bunkering assignment six days later with the fueling of the CSL bulk carrier *Simcoe* (2).

An early season accident took place on March 23 when the tug *James A. Hannah* ran into its own barge while breaking ice in the Straits of Mackinac. Sustaining some damage in the collision, the 149-foot vessel went to Sault Ste. Marie, Michigan, for repairs. Later that same year, on December 17, the namesake of this tug and founder of the Hannah Inland Waterways Corporation passed away at the age of 92.

At the end of the previous season, the *Paul H. Carnahan* laid up at Duluth, Minnesota, with a storage cargo of cement loaded during a rare visit to Clarkson, Ontario, in late December of that year. With the steamer's impending return to service drawing near for what was to be its final operational season, the St. Lawrence Cement Company began offloading this unusual payload on March 25. Five days later, the *Jensen Star* departed Windsor, Ontario, for Thunder Bay to begin its second year of service between those two ports even as the U.S. Coast Guard's *Mackinaw* began icebreaking operations on Whitefish Bay in preparation for the new season.

Upbound after wintering at Hamilton, the *Algowest* opened the Welland Canal on April 1 with its transit commemorated by a ceremony held at Lock 3. The Soo Locks opened to commercial navigation that same day with the upbound passage of the *John B. Aird* through the Poe Lock bound for Thunder Bay. This voyage did not go without incident, however, as the Algoma Central vessel sustained forepeak damage while working through ice in Whitefish Bay just hours later.

While downbound from Thunder Bay on its first voyage following the completion of major repairs from an onboard fire at Quebec City the previous August, CSL's *Nanticoke* rubbed the bottom of the St. Marys River near Johnson Point on April 2. Proving much less serious than its earlier mishap, the 5-year old vessel sustained only light damage in this incident. The next day, another 730-foot Canadian self-unloader ran into trouble when the *Algolake* grounded in Lake St. Clair following an engine room fire.

Without any prospect for their future use,

Desgagnes Transport decided early in the year to sell three of the four lake steamers it acquired with the purchase of the Quebec & Ontario Transportation fleet in early 1984. This resulted in the sale of the *Lac Ste. Anne*, *Meldrum Bay*, and *Outarde* (3) to ULS International for dismantling, none of which ever operated for Desgagnes.

Laid up since December 1982, the *Lac Ste. Anne* departed Hamilton on April 1 in tow of the tugs *James E. McGrath* and *R. & L. No. 1*. Pulled up the Welland Canal to Port Colborne, Ontario, the tugs docked the 61-year old vessel in the old canal below Lock 8, where it remained until moved to the scrapping berth by the tugs *Atomic* and *Elmore M. Misner* on November 23. With work beginning quickly afterwards, a salvage crew finished breaking up the old bulk carrier early the following year.

Beginning its maiden voyage, CSL's *Hon. Paul Martin* cleared Collingwood, Ontario, on April 6 bound for Thunder Bay to load grain for Quebec City. Held up by a system of heavy weather that closed the navigation track broken through the ice on Whitefish Bay by the *Mackinaw*, the self-unloader anchored briefly at Sault Ste. Marie, Michigan, before continuing its upbound trip into Lake Superior on April 7. Five days later, the *Martin* encountered the type of minor mechanical difficulty commonly experienced by newly commissioned vessels when winch problems delayed its inaugural passage through the Welland Canal at Lock 7.

After spending an unusual winter layup at Thunder Bay, Interlake Steamship's *J. L. Mauthe* made an equally uncommon visit to Toronto, Ontario, on April 8 when it arrived with a split shipment of grain for delivery to the Canada Malting and Victory Soya

The former Cleveland-Cliffs steamer *Walter A. Sterling* sailing on the St. Marys River in Rouge Steel Company colors as the *William Clay Ford* (2). (Photo by Tom Salvner)

elevators. Carried between two Canadian ports, not only did this consignment require government approval but was also reportedly the first grain cargo brought into that port by a U.S. flagged lake freighter in more than two decades. On the same day the *J. L. Mauthe* reached Toronto, a minor incident took place at a nearby Lake Ontario port when the *Algowood* ran aground while entering Hamilton Harbor. A pair of tugs soon freed the 730-foot self-unloader from the bottom, which apparently escaped its predicament unscathed.

Departing Fraser Shipyards on April 9, the *Benson Ford* (3) entered service for the Rouge Steel Company when it moved the short distance across St. Louis Bay to the Duluth, Missabe & Iron Range Railway Dock in Duluth to load iron ore for Dearborn. Exactly one week later, the *William Clay Ford* (2) began an identical voyage when it also left the shipyard to load pellets at Duluth for its owner's steelmaking complex on the Rouge River.

A buildup of sediment just inside the Duluth Entry created some problems for marine traffic at the Twin Ports when it claimed four victims over a period of eight days during mid-April, none of which suffered any appreciable damage. Swinging slightly north of the channel while departing Duluth, American Steamship's *Indiana Harbor* became the first to find this area of shoaling when it spent about four hours aground on April 14. The same location collected the Panamanian bulker *Blue Pine* four days later and the *William J. De Lancey* on April 21. The U.S. Army Corps of Engineers began clearing operations on April 22 but not before a fourth, and final, occurrence took place when the *Belle River* ran onto the shoal that same day.

Entering the waters of Georgian Bay with the characteristic splash of a side launching on April 18, the motor vessel *Paterson* (2) became the last lake freighter launched by Collingwood Shipyards. The following day, work began on the only other new construction project in the shipyard's order book with the keel laying of a $50 million icebreaker for the Canadian Coast Guard.

Upbound in the St. Lawrence River with a load of iron ore on April 23, the *Canadian Progress* lost steering and went aground off Galop Island near Ogdensburg, New York. Pulled free the following day by the tugs *Daniel McAllister*, *Robinson Bay*, and *Salvage Monarch* after lightering into the *James Norris*, the self-unloader went to Prescott, Ontario, for a damage survey before resuming its voyage.

While unloading at Detroit on April 26, the Liberian freighter *Pacific Defender* had its No. 3 fuel tank holed by falling cargo. Continuing its trip into the lakes, the ocean vessel received subsequent repairs at Duluth.

Leaving Toronto in tow of the tugs *Glenside* and *Stormont* on the afternoon of April 30, the retired P. & H. Shipping steamer *Fernglen* arrived at Port Maitland, Ontario, the next day for scrapping. Built by the American Ship Building Company at Lorain, Ohio, in 1917, this vessel carried five names during its career and first entered Canadian registry with its purchase by Robert Pierson Holdings Ltd. in 1975. As such, it became the first vessel in the Soo River Company fleet, which renamed it *Judith M. Pierson*. Saved from demolition, this vessel's pilothouse remains intact, as of 2018, at Port Burwell, Ontario.

Sold through Gibson Shipbrokers to Batista E. Iramos Ltd. of Portugal earlier that year, the steamer *Lake Winnipeg* left Montreal on May 2 in tow of the tug *Irving Cedar*. Consequently, it became the first ship of the 730-foot class sold for dismantling.

Launched as the T2-SE-A1 tanker *Table Rock* by Kaiser Company Inc. at Portland, Oregon, in 1943, this vessel sailed on saltwater until purchased by Nipigon Transport Ltd. in 1961 for conversion into a Great Lakes bulk carrier. With this reconstruction performed by Blythswood Shipbuilding Company Ltd. at Glasgow, Scotland, the *Lake Winnipeg* arrived at Quebec City on September 1, 1962 after sailing across the Atlantic.

Following a visit to Davie Shipbuilding at Lauzon for additional work, in particular the cutting out of its cargo hatches not done in Scotland to provide additional strength for the ocean crossing, this vessel embarked upon its maiden voyage on September 18, 1962 when it cleared Sept-Iles, Quebec, with a load of iron ore for Cleveland, Ohio. Spanning just 21 years in length, the operational career of this lake vessel came to an untimely end due largely to a combination of high operating costs and tightening cargoes. Laid up for the final time on December 23, 1983 the *Lake Winnipeg* made it safely back across the Atlantic (this time with its hatches installed) to arrive at Lisbon, Portugal, on May 19, 1985, where scrapping began almost immediately.

Operated by a non-union crew, the U.S. flagged tug *R. W. Sesler* and its barge *USL 501* became targets of a work stoppage by the International Longshoremen's Association at Superior, Wisconsin, on May 3 when it attempted to take on a cargo of wheat at the Harvest States grain elevator. After this dispute was settled several days later, the tug/barge combination finished loading to pass downbound at Detroit on May 12 during its trip out of the lakes for an African port. Subsequently renamed *Invincible*, this episode did not end the tug's association with the Great Lakes as it returned in June of 2000 for pairing with the self-unloading barge *McKee Sons*.

Departing De Tour, Michigan, after being idled a few months into the 1984 season, the *Elton Hoyt 2nd* (2) passed upbound through the Soo Locks on May 5. Six days later, the *Indiana Harbor* worked its way down the Canadian side of the upper St. Marys River to the Algoma Steel Dock at Sault Ste. Marie, Ontario, which is located above the rapids in the river. Making this trial run in ballast, the thousand-footer became the largest vessel to have ever visited that facility up to that time.

While transiting the St. Lawrence Seaway on May 13, the combination Great Lakes/ocean bulker *Saskatchewan Pioneer* slammed hard into the upper approach wall at the Snell Lock. Although there was no reported damage to the 730-foot vessel, the impact knocked out a 40-foot section of the concrete barrier.

In early 1985, Federal Commerce & Navigation Ltd. (Fednav) of Montreal established a U.S. subsidiary named Fednav Lakes Services Inc. to operate a monthly RO/RO (Roll-On/Roll-Off) cargo service for the U.S. Department of Defense connecting Detroit, Milwaukee, and Toledo to ports in Europe. To this end, Fednav Lakes acquired the *Avon Forest*, a deep-sea vessel constructed by Port Weller Dry Docks Ltd. at St. Catharines, Ontario, in 1973, and placed it into American registry as the *Federal Lakes*. While inbound to the lakes on May 14, this 687-foot ship hit the Cote Ste. Catherine Lock after experiencing bow thruster problems. Passing through the Welland Canal two days later, the *Federal Lakes* continued to Toledo for a rechristening ceremony held on May 17. Surveyed at Hamburg, West Germany, that August for damages stemming from its May 14 accident, this vessel's first year of operation with Fednav Lakes Services proved anything but uneventful with three additional incidents

The steamer *Johnstown* (2) was the first U.S. flagged ship built during the postwar era to be sold for scrap.
(Photo by James Hoffman)

while transiting the Seaway, none of which resulted in any serious damage. These involved a pair of mishaps, one at the Snell Lock during mid-August and another at the St. Lambert Lock on September 19, before having its second run in with the Cote Ste. Catherine Lock that season on November 5.

Suffering its first accident since becoming a member of the P. & H. Shipping fleet the previous autumn, the *Elmglen* (2) went aground in Lake St. Francis near St. Zotique, Quebec, on May 12 while downbound with grain from Thunder Bay for Quebec City. With the tugs *Helen M. McAllister* and *Salvage Monarch* assisting, the steamer broke free of the bottom on May 15 after lightering 4,000 tons of cargo. Suffering no significant damage and allowed to depart shortly afterwards, the 33-year old vessel sailed to Quebec City to unload.

Purchased by Marine Salvage Ltd. the previous autumn, the *Pontiac* (2) had remained tied up at Ramey's Bend over the winter while awaiting its fate. Resold to Spanish ship breakers, the former Cleveland-Cliffs vessel passed downbound through the Welland Canal on May 16 in tow of the tugs *Glenevis*, *Argue Martin*, and *Stormont* bound for Quebec City.

Earlier that year, Marine Salvage Ltd. had purchased the steamer *Johnstown* (2) from the Bethlehem Steel Corporation, which it, too, resold for scrapping in Europe. As such, that vessel became the first U.S. flagged bulk carrier built during the postwar period to be sold for dismantling. Built by Bethlehem's Shipbuilding Division at Sparrows Point, Maryland, in 1952, the *Johnstown* (2) was one of three lake ships constructed by that yard due to a lack of available building berths at

Great Lakes shipyards during the early 1950s. The other members of this class were the *Sparrows Point* and *Elton Hoyt 2nd* (2), the latter of which went to the Interlake Steamship Company. Of the trio, the *Johnstown* (2) was the only one to remain a gearless bulk carrier with the other two units converted to self-unloaders during 1980 in reconstructions that undoubtedly extended their service lives. Outclassed by the three 1000-foot vessels commissioned by Bethlehem Steel between 1972 and 1980 and becoming a victim of the economic downturn of the early 1980s, this vessel last operated in 1981 when it entered an indefinite layup at Erie, Pennsylvania.

On May 18, the tugs *Helen M. McAllister* and *Salvage Monarch* towed the *Johnstown* (2) out of Erie, Pennsylvania, to begin its journey to join the *Pontiac* (2) at Quebec City for a tandem tow. Everything proceeded normally during the 65-mile trip across Lake Erie until high winds parted the towline at Port Colborne. The tugs managed to retrieve the 698-foot freighter but not before it nearly plowed into a pier at the Maple Leaf Mills grain elevator. With the tug *Daniel McAllister* joining the scrap tow, the steamer reached Quebec City without further incident.

Towed out of Quebec City on May 30 by the Polish tug *Koral*, the *Johnstown* (2) and *Pontiac* (2), both of which had spent their entire careers in their respective fleets, arrived at San Esteban de Pravia, Spain, on June 24. There, dismantling of the two former lake vessels began a short time later.

Engaged primarily in the movement of iron ore into the Algoma Steel mill at Sault Ste. Marie, Ontario, CSL's *Stadacona* (3) went aground near that facility on May 18. Caused by an engine failure, the 663-foot self-unloader apparently sustained no damage in the mishap.

After hitting the wall at the Iroquois Lock on May 22, the saltwater carrier *Sea Peony* suffered a second mishap the following day when it struck Lock 3 in the Welland Canal. Managing to complete its Great Lakes trip, this vessel underwent a subsequent survey at Antwerp, Belgium, during the middle of July for damage sustained in these two incidents.

Having languished at Sorel since being towed there from Montreal following its purchase by Marine Salvage Ltd. in 1982, the fire damaged tanker *Hudson Transport* arrived at the Ramey's Bend scrap yard in Port Colborne on May 28 in tow of the tugs *Glenevis* and *Argue Martin*. Despite the move, the scrap firm made no effort to dismantle the 23-year old vessel and it was to see subsequent service as a barge.

Retired from service with the pending arrival of its replacement, *Samuel Risley*, later that season, the Canadian Coast Guard icebreaking buoy tender *Alexander Henry* went to Kingston, Ontario, during the month May, where it was to function as a museum ship. Acquired by the Marine Museum of the Great Lakes, this 210-foot vessel served in that capacity until the sale of the museum's property in 2016 left its future in limbo. Saved from dismantling or intentional sinking as an artificial reef by an effort organized by the Lakehead Transportation Museum Society, the tug *Salvage Monarch* delivered the *Alexander Henry* to Thunder Bay in June of 2017 to await its eventual opening as a tourist attraction at that city.

At Port Arthur Shipbuilding, where it had remained since the end of the previous season undergoing a conversion to a combination ore/bulk/oil carrier, the motor vessel *Arctic* went aground for a short time at Thunder Bay on June 2 while being shifted between docks in strong winds. Three days later, another incident took place in the western waters of Lake Superior when the Greek bulker *Zenovia* spilled approximately 60 gallons of oil into Superior Harbor while loading grain at ConAgra's Elevator M.

On June 9, the Polish freighter *Ziemia Olsztynksa* sustained a 30-degree list when it touched bottom in the Saginaw River in an episode resulting in no reported damage. Just six days later, Interlake Steamship's *Mesabi Miner* became the first 1000-foot vessel to enter that waterway when it delivered a consignment of coal to the Consumers Power Company at Essexville, Michigan.

Made redundant following the acquisition of the *Cedarglen* near the end of the previous year, Goderich Elevators Ltd. sold the grain storage barge *Spruceglen* to Shearmet Recycling for scrapping at Thunder Bay. Towed by the tug *Thunder Cape*, the retired steamer left Goderich, Ontario, on June 15 bound for Lake Superior. Passing upbound through the Soo Locks the next day with the assistance of the locally based tug *W. J. Ivan Purvis*, the scrap tow arrived at Thunder Bay on June 18. Shearmet began cutting up the 603-foot vessel that August but went out of business a few months later, thereby leaving this process unfinished until finally completed on November 22, 1986 by the scrap firm's successor, the Lakehead Scrap Metal Company.

Emerging from Fraser Shipyards as a motor vessel following the completion of its repowering, USS Great Lakes Fleet's *George A. Sloan* sailed out of Duluth on June 17 with a load of taconite pellets for Lorain. This downbound voyage did not go smoothly, however, as the newly installed power plant caused problems for the "Maritime" class self-unloader while crossing Lake Superior and later on Lake Huron, the latter of which required a tow to De Tour by the tug *Chippewa*. Regardless of these early difficulties, the new diesel engine improved both the vessel's speed and its fuel efficiency.

With a new bulk carrier under construction at Collingwood Shipyards and plans to repower the *Comeaudoc* at the same yard over the 1985-86 winter layup, N. M. Paterson & Sons Ltd. retired the steamers *Quedoc* (2) and *Senator of Canada* in early 1985. Acquired by Marine Salvage Ltd. later that spring and subsequently resold for scrapping overseas, both vessels sailed from Toronto to Quebec City under their own power with the *Quedoc* (2) departing on June 20 followed by the *Senator of Canada* six days later.

Launched by Collingwood Shipyards Ltd. on May 30, 1957, the *Senator of Canada* measured 605' x 62' x 33' and had a maximum carrying capacity of 15,850 gross tons. Built by Davie Shipbuilding Limited at Lauzon in 1960, the *Quedoc* (2) shared these same overall dimensions but had a negligibly smaller carrying capacity 50 gross tons less than that of its fleet mate. Launched as the *New Quedoc*, this steamer received its final name in 1963 and became the first Great Lakes bulk carrier built during the 1960s sent to the scrap yard.

Clearing Quebec City in a tandem tow behind the tug *Captain Ioannis S.* on July 1, the *Quedoc* (2) and *Senator of Canada* arrived at Curacao, Netherlands Antilles, on July 18. With cutting beginning first on the *Senator of Canada*, scrapping of the two lake freighters continued well into 1986.

On June 22, vandals boarded the laid up Bethlehem Steel steamer *Arthur B. Homer* at Erie, Pennsylvania, and smashed several of the vessel's windows and portholes in addition to causing other damage. Sidelined since 1980, the 826-foot bulk carrier remained idle at that port until its tow to Port Colborne in December of 1986 for scrapping.

The maiden voyage of the *Paterson* (2)

closed out a long history of lake ship construction at Collingwood when the 736-foot gearless bulker sailed from that port on June 27 to load grain at Thunder Bay for Quebec City. Built to operate in the eastbound movement of grain from the Great Lakes through the Seaway to ports on the St. Lawrence River with backhauls of iron ore, it was not only the largest but also the last vessel ever constructed for the Paterson fleet.

On July 1, Gulf Canada Limited sold the tankers *Gulf Gatineau* and *Gulf Mackenzie* to Societe Sofati-Soconav, which renamed them *J. C. Phillips* and *L. Rochette* respectively. Having entered service during the 1976-77 timeframe, these two ships were among the newest tankers in service on the lakes at the time. This transaction closed out Gulf Canada's Great Lakes fleet operations, which dated back to its purchase and renaming of the tanker *B. A. Peerless* to *Gulf Canada* in 1969.

Sold to Marine Salvage Ltd. earlier in the year, the former Algoma Central steamer *E. B. Barber* left Toronto on July 6 in tow of the tugs *Helen M. McAllister* and *Salvage Monarch* for Quebec City following its resale for scrapping in Spain. Built by the Port Arthur Shipbuilding Company at Port Arthur, Ontario, in 1953, Algoma had this 574-foot lake freighter converted to a self-unloader and fitted with an 8-foot high trunk deck at Collingwood Shipyards in 1964. As such, it became that fleet's first self-unloading vessel. Operating primarily in the cement clinker and salt trades during its last season, the *Barber* laid up for the final time on November 29, 1984.

One day after the *E. B. Barber* cleared Toronto, the tugs *Glenevis*, *Argue Martin*, and *Princess No. 1* towed the *Saginaw Bay* out of Ramey's Bend and down the Welland Canal for delivery to Quebec City. Acquired by Marine Salvage the previous autumn, this motor vessel had arrived at the company's scrap yard on November 22, 1984 and remained untouched prior to its sale for dismantling overseas.

Having returned from taking the *Johnstown* (2) and *Pontiac* (2) across the Atlantic, the tug *Koral* towed the *E. B. Barber* and *Saginaw Bay* out of Quebec City on July 16 bound for Vigo, Spain. Arriving there on August 8, work on dismantling the two self-unloaders began the next day.

Columbia Transportation's *Wolverine* (2) suffered a minor mishap on July 6 when it lost steering and ran aground in the lower Detroit River. Sent down from Detroit, the tugs *Bantry Bay*, *Shannon*, and *Wicklow* managed to refloat the 11-year old self-unloader later in the day without damage.

The parade of scrap tows continued on July 15 with the departure of the ULS International steamers *R. Bruce Angus* and *Gordon C. Leitch* from Toronto for Quebec City in tow of the tugs *Glenada* and *Prescotont* respectively. Both of these ships last operated during the 1981 season with the *Leitch* entering its final layup on December 22 of that year followed by the *Angus* three days later. During their years of idleness at Toronto, Victory Soya Mills Ltd. had employed both vessels for grain storage.

Launched by the Port Arthur Shipbuilding Company at Port Arthur, Ontario, on November 18, 1950, the *R. Bruce Angus* began life as the tanker *Imperial Redwater*. Built to carry crude oil from the Lakehead Pipe Line Company terminal at Superior, Wisconsin, to the Imperial Oil refinery at Sarnia, Ontario, this vessel loaded its maiden cargo on May 15, 1951. When the completion of a pipeline made this trade route redundant, Imperial Oil sold this ship to the Upper Lakes & St. Lawrence Transportation Company Ltd. in late 1953 for conversion to a bulk carrier. This reconstruction took place at Collingwood Shipyards, with this steamer, now renamed *R. Bruce Angus*, loading its first grain cargo on June 23, 1954.

The *Gordon C. Leitch* was one of two ships built for the Upper Lakes & St. Lawrence Transportation Company Ltd. in 1952 that represented a significant departure from the established practices of that fleet in having always operated secondhand vessels since its founding in 1932. To fulfill its expansion plans, the company contracted the construction of this steamer along with that of a sister ship, *James Norris*, to the Midland Shipyards at Midland, Ontario. Launched on July 30, 1952, the *Leitch* began its maiden voyage on November 11 of that year by sailing from Midland to load wheat at Fort William, Ontario. At 663'6" in length and with carrying capacities in the 19,000 gross ton range, the *Gordon C. Leitch* and *James Norris* were two of the largest ships in service on the Great Lakes at the time of their commissioning.

Safely reaching Quebec City on their voyages off the lakes, the *R. Bruce Angus* and *Gordon C. Leitch* left that port on July 29 in tow of the tug *Irving Cedar*. Following a transatlantic crossing lasting three weeks, the two bulk freighters arrived at Setubal, Portugal, on August 20 for demolition.

Sold to Charpat Transportation Inc. and chartered to Windsor, Detroit Barge Line Ltd., the package freighter *Fort York* departed Hamilton on July 17 in tow of the tugs *Lac Como* and *Argue Martin*. Prior to leaving, the vessel had a rudimentary pushing notch cut into its stern to assist in its intended operation of carrying lumber. Angered by its employment as a barge, the Seafarers International Union (SIU) picketed the *Fort York* when it entered the Welland Canal on July 18, through which it cleared the next day.

Arriving at Windsor on the afternoon of July 21, the tugs *Argue Martin* and *Prescotont* took the *Fort York* up the Detroit River later that evening bound for Thunder Bay, where the SIU picketed it at the Keefer Terminal. Entering a temporary layup after making only three trips, it returned to service during late September towed by the tug *Tusker*.

Going aground at Montreal on July 18, a salvage operation involving the tugs *Donald P.*, *Leonard W.*, and *Pointe Sept-Iles* succeeded in refloating the saltwater bulker *Monty Python* after lightering about 2,000 tons cargo into the *P. S. Barge No. 1*. Having incurred no bottom damage in the mishap, the ocean freighter cleared Montreal on July 27. Sold for dismantling later that same year, this vessel had previously traded into the lakes as the *Monte Zalama*.

On July 20, the *Manitoulin* (5) struck the motor vessel *Arctic* at Thunder Bay. With both vessels receiving only minimal damage, this incident occurred just a few days before the latter sailed on its first trip following an extensive reconstruction at Port Arthur Shipbuilding, upon which it passed downbound through the Soo Locks on July 27. Two days later, the split hull dredge *Dodge Island* lost its starboard rudder when it struck a submerged log in Saginaw Bay near the mouth of the Saginaw River.

During the summer, Columbia Transportation entered into an agreement to sell the *W. W. Holloway* to Marine Salvage Ltd. for dismantling. Built by the American Ship Building Company at Cleveland in 1906 as the *Henry A. Hawgood*, this ship made its first passage through the Soo Locks on October 15 of that year bound for Two Harbors, Minnesota, on a voyage reported in the following day's edition of Sault Ste.

Shown here in better days, the bulk carrier *Leon Falk Jr.* sailed to Quebec City, Quebec, under its own power to await an overseas scrap tow. (Photo by James Hoffman)

Marie, Michigan's *The Evening News*. Renamed *C. Russell Hubbard* in 1912, this 552-foot lake freighter operated for a quarter of a century under that name until becoming *W. W. Holloway* in 1937.

Over its long career, this vessel received two significant reconstructions that allowed it to remain viable into the early 1980s, the first being its conversion to a self-unloader by the Christy Corporation at Sturgeon Bay, Wisconsin, in 1957. Five years later, over the 1962-63 winter layup, the American Ship Building Company's Lorain yard replaced the *Holloway*'s original 1,750 ihp triple-expansion steam engine with a new 2,250 bhp diesel power plant. Its small size a key attribute in serving customers with facilities requiring transits of restricted waterways or on high-frequency routes over short distances, the *W. W. Holloway* provided steadfast service until ending its operational career at Toledo on December 7, 1981. After its sale to Marine Salvage, the veteran laker remained at the northern Ohio port until towed to the breakers in August of the following year.

On August 2, the 767-foot steamer *Benson Ford* (3) became the largest ship to transit the Manistee River when it delivered coal to the Packaging Corporation of America Dock at Filer City, Michigan. The next day, the *Nanticoke* damaged seven hull plates when it hit an approach wall at the Canso Lock in the Strait of Canso. After stopping at nearby Mulgrave, Nova Scotia, for temporary patching, the CSL self-unloader sailed to Halifax for permanent repairs.

Three occupants of a pleasure boat that capsized near the mouth of the Detroit River on August 5 had the good fortune of being picked up by the *Canadian Olympic* in a rescue that elicited a letter of commendation from the U.S. Coast Guard.

Carrying a load of iron ore taken on at Quebec City, the motor vessel *Vandoc* (2) went aground while upbound in the St. Lawrence River on August 6 after venturing outside of the navigation channel near St. Zotique. Able to free itself from the bottom the following day, the 605-foot bulk carrier proceeded to Burns Harbor, Indiana, to unload before undergoing a damage inspection at Thunder Bay.

While sailing in Lake Michigan about 11 miles off the Wisconsin shore on August 12, the tug *Gregory J. Busch* radioed the U.S. Coast Guard station at Sturgeon Bay to report that one of the three barges it had in tow was taking on water. In response, the Coast Guard deployed a helicopter, a 41-foot utility boat, and the icebreaking tug *Mobile Bay* to render aid. Later that day, the stricken vessel capsized throwing four men into the water, two of which sustained minor injuries when the barge's load of construction equipment slid into the lake. Following the incident, the tug *John M. Selvick* delivered the overturned barge to the yard of its owner, Lakeshore Contractors Inc., at Muskegon, Michigan.

Destined for scrapping overseas following its sale to Corostel Trading Ltd., the *Menihek Lake* sailed from Hamilton on August 15 for Quebec City, where it arrived two days later. Built by Collingwood Shipyards in 1959, the 715'3" x 75'3" x 37'9" size of this ship made it one earliest vessels constructed to comply with the original maximum dimensions for operation on the St. Lawrence Seaway before an amendment to this policy raised the overall length restriction to 730 feet. Spending its entire career in the Carryore Limited fleet, this steamer's last active season came in 1984 when it operated for a brief period that summer before laying up at Hamilton on August 11 of that year.

Following four years of idleness, the *Leon Falk, Jr.* departed Ecorse under its own power on August 16 to join the *Menihek Lake* at Quebec City for a tandem scrap tow to Spain. Originally built as the T2-SE-A1 tanker *Winter Hill* by the Sun Shipbuilding & Dry Dock Company at Chester, Pennsylvania, in 1945, this ship underwent a conversion to a Great Lakes bulk carrier at Bethlehem Shipbuilding's Key Highway Shipyard at Baltimore, Maryland, in 1961. This reconstruction included the insertion of a 503-foot cargo section built by Schlieker-Werft at Hamburg, West Germany, that was towed across the Atlantic to Baltimore for joining to the bow and stern of the tanker. Retaining all of its original propulsion equipment, the converted vessel emerged from the shipyard with an overall length of 730 feet and a maximum carrying capacity of 24,250 gross tons. Renamed *Leon Falk, Jr.*, this ship conducted its sea trials on Chesapeake Bay in late June.

Entering service for the National Steel Corporation (Hanna Mining Co., mgr.), the lake carrier sailed from Baltimore on June 30, 1961 to load iron ore at Sept-Iles for Cleveland. Delivering this initial payload in its new configuration on July 8, 1961, this steamer remained committed to the movement of iron ore on the lakes until changing economic times and the service entry of newer vessels forced it into an early retirement on August 15, 1981. Ironically, the departure of the *Leon Falk, Jr.* for the scrap yard on August 16, 1985 came just one day after its sister ship, *Paul H. Carnahan*, laid up for the last time. Its Hanna Mining stack markings painted over but National Steel bow logos still in place, the *Leon Falk, Jr.* cleared the Welland Canal on August 17 to arrive at Quebec City two days later.

Leaving Quebec City on August 30 in tow of the tug *Captain Ioannis S.*, the *Leon Falk, Jr.* and *Menihek Lake* arrived off Vigo, Spain, on September 25, where that latter was taken into port the following day to be dismantled. Departing with the *Falk* in tow shortly afterwards, the same tug delivered the 730-foot bulk carrier to Gijon, Spain, on September 28 for scrapping.

Towing the *Outarde* (3) out of Toronto on August 16, the tugs *Atomic*, *James E. McGrath*, and *P. J. Murer* brought the retired steamer into Port Colborne the following day. Sold to ULS International earlier that year, dismantling of the 58-year old vessel began a few days later. During mid-September, a fire training exercise conducted by the Niagara Regional Fire Department gutted its forward cabins. Continuing into late autumn, the scrap yard finished breaking up the *Outarde* (3) that November.

Built by the American Ship Building Company at Lorain in 1927 as the *Robert Hobson*, the Interlake Steamship Company sold this 600-foot bulk carrier for scrap in August of 1975. It narrowly escaped the cutter's torch on this occasion, however, when acquired by the Quebec & Ontario Transportation Company just one month later. Renamed *Outarde* (3), the classic laker operated for another eight years until laying up for the final time on December 21, 1983.

While departing South Baymouth, Ontario, in high winds and limited visibility on the evening of August 18, the ferry *Chi-Cheemaun* went hard aground just outside the harbor entrance. With about one-third of its 300 passengers removed by lifeboats, the 365-foot motor vessel managed to refloat itself the next morning. After stopping at Tobermory, Ontario, to disembark its remaining passengers, the ferry sailed to Collingwood Shipyards for bottom repairs. These were completed quickly with the *Chi-Cheemaun* returning to service on August 21.

Just as it was about to pass beneath the raised Aerial Lift Bridge while leaving Duluth with a load of coal on September 2, the motor vessel *St. Clair* (2) lost power when a broken wire shut down its engines. As the captain used the bow and stern thrusters to avoid striking the entry piers, strong winds, with speeds reaching as high as 45 mph, began pushing the powerless vessel backwards through the canal. Rubbing against the edge of the channel, the self-unloader suffered a 35-foot long dent in its hull plating before floating back into the harbor. Towed to the Port Terminal, a subsequent dive inspection revealed damages to the extent of $50,000. Receiving temporary repairs, the 770-foot ship returned to service three days later.

As it proceeded outbound at Lorain during the evening hours of September 3, the *Philip R. Clarke* struck several boats at the Drawbridge Cove Marina after having trouble negotiating a bend in the Black River. With one yacht sunk and damage inflicted to ten other boats along with some of the marina's docks, the 767-foot lake freighter came to a stop just upstream of the Erie Avenue Bridge. Suffering no significant damage in the unfortunate mishap, the *Clarke* continued into Lake Erie after being released by the U.S. Coast Guard.

Mauled by a gale in the North Atlantic, the Yugoslav bulker *Solta* arrived at Montreal on September 6 with a cargo container hanging over its side and other storm related damage. Receiving the necessary inspection and repairs, the ocean freighter cleared port four days later bound for Cleveland.

The *Canadian Prospector* suffered light damage when it came together with the

Panamanian tanker *Norchem* in the St. Lawrence River near Montreal on September 8. Operating regularly between Valleyfield, Quebec, and Baltimore, Maryland, the saltwater vessel was somewhat less fortunate with the collision tearing open some hull plating near its port anchor that necessitated a stop at Montreal for repairs.

A broken oil line was the culprit of a crankcase explosion aboard the motor vessel *Paterson* (2) during its departure from Montreal on September 17 for Quebec City. Having entered service just three months earlier, four McAllister Towing tugs brought the stricken bulk carrier back into port for repairs prior to resuming its trip four days later.

While attempting to navigate the Calumet River on September 21, Interlake Steamship's *Elton Hoyt 2nd* (2) ran into the 95th Street Bridge at Chicago, Illinois. The impact knocked the bridge out of service for five hours and inflicted sufficient damage upon the steamer's bow and forward cabins to prompt a trip to Bay Shipbuilding for repairs the next day, where it remained until October 8.

Making too wide of a turn at Duluth on September 26, the Liberian bulker *Federal Rhine* rubbed up against the docked motor vessel *Belle River*. With both ships suffering superficial damage, the only harm to the thousand-footer was some dented hull plating on its forward port side. The next day, Halco's *Chemical Transport* underwent a survey at Montreal to assess a battering by ice while operating in Canada's Northwest Territories during late August and early September. In addition to hull plate and propeller damage, the 391-foot tanker also lost its port anchor at Igloolik on September 10.

As one of three vessels acquired in July of the previous year, the Hyman-Michaels Company had made no effort to begin dismantling the *August Ziesing* before its subsequent sale to Shearmet Recycling. Leaving Duluth on October 3, the tug *Thunder Cape* delivered the former U.S. Steel bulk carrier to Shearmet's scrap yard on the Mission River at Thunder Bay two days later with the assistance of the tug *Peninsula*. As future events would have it, however, the *Ziesing* was not to meet its fate at that port.

Less than three weeks following an engine failure at Montreal, the *Paterson* (2) ran into further trouble on the St. Lawrence River when it touched bottom near Cornwall Island on October 6. Having sustained some bottom damage in the incident, the bulk carrier remained in operation with the necessary repairs deferred until the upcoming winter layup.

While upbound in the Lake Huron Cut in tow of the tugs *Glenada* and *Tusker* on October 6, the barge *Fort York* took a sheer in high winds that sent a large sailboat onto the rocks near the Dunn Paper Company just north of the Blue Water Bridge at Port Huron, Michigan. With the strong currents present at the confluence of the lake and the St. Clair River contributing to the incident, the trio continued upbound. Swinging wildly once again just minutes later, however, the *Fort York* forced the downbound *Myron C. Taylor* out of the shipping channel near Buoys 7 and 8 without damage to either vessel.

Continuing upbound for Thunder Bay, the *Fort York* and its companions made it as far as Sault Ste. Marie, Michigan, before turning around following the cancellation of its lumber cargo. Returning down Lake Huron, the tugs secured the barge at the Canadian National Railway freight shed at Point Edward, Ontario. Its owner mired in financial and legal difficulties, the *Fort York* was

The *Savic* transits the Welland Canal while making its way off the Great Lakes. (Author's Collection)

seized on October 13.

After selling the *Edward B. Greene* and *Walter A. Sterling* near the end of the previous season, the Cleveland-Cliffs Steamship Company possessed a fleet consisting entirely of inactive carriers. On October 12, Cliffs took a significant step in ridding itself of these ships with the sale of the *Cliffs Victory* to the Hai International Corporation for scrapping overseas. Originally constructed for saltwater service, this steamer was one of the most distinctive lake freighters of the postwar era.

At the beginning of the 1950s, Cleveland-Cliffs faced an urgent need to expand the size of its fleet even as shipyards on the lakes were backlogged with orders brought about by the strong cargo demands of the Korean War and a booming economy. To work around this constraint, the shipping company purchased a Victory class cargo ship named *Norte Dame Victory* on December 10, 1950. Built by the Oregon Shipbuilding Corporation at Portland, Oregon, in 1945, it arrived at Bethlehem Shipbuilding's Key Highway Yard in Baltimore, Maryland, on January 2, 1951 to be converted to a Great Lakes bulk carrier. This reconstruction went quickly with the steamer leaving the shipyard in tow for the lakes on April 2 of that year. Renamed *Cliffs Victory*, it proceeded south along the East Coast and westward across the Gulf of Mexico before entering the Mississippi River. As the first large saltwater ship converted for Great Lakes service following the end of World War II, the black-hulled lake freighter became an object of considerable curiosity while making its way up the historic waterway.

Presenting a peculiar sight with its deckhouses and stack disassembled to provide bridge clearance, the 620-foot vessel reached Chicago after transiting the Illinois Waterway and Chicago Sanitary and Ship Canal. After making a remarkable passage through the downtown area of the sprawling metropolis on May 9, 1951, the *Cliffs Victory* arrived at the American Ship Building

Company's South Chicago yard later that same day. There, workers installed the vessel's deckhouses, propeller, and rudder in addition to removing two stern-mounted 120-foot floatation pontoons fitted at Baltimore to reduce draft in the rivers. This work completed, the *Cliffs Victory* entered service on June 4, 1951 when it sailed from South Chicago to load iron ore at Marquette, Michigan, for delivery to Cleveland.

Retaining its original 9,350 shp steam turbine that gave Victory class ships a high maximum speed (17 knots) to evade submarine attack, the *Cliffs Victory* was one of the fastest bulk freighters to have ever operated on the Great Lakes. During the early 1950s, this vessel was involved in a series of unofficial races with the C4 conversion bulk carrier *Charles M. White* with some of these results claiming the latter held a very slight speed advantage over its Cleveland-Cliffs competitor. Lengthened to 716'3" during a return visit to the South Chicago yard of the American Ship Building Company at the end of the 1956 season, the *Cliffs Victory* emerged from the shipyard the following spring as the longest ship on the Great Lakes. Gaining this distinction by a margin of just a few feet, it retained that title until the *Edmund Fitzgerald* entered service in 1958.

The *Cliffs Victory* remained one of Cleveland-Cliffs leading carriers until laying up at South Chicago in late 1981. Placed into Panamanian registry and renamed *Savic* following its sale to Hai International for $235,000 four years later, a Taiwanese crew boarded the idle steamer in preparation for a long ocean voyage to the Far East. Its departure delayed by boiler issues and traffic stoppages in the Welland Canal and St. Lawrence Seaway that autumn, the bulk carrier sailed from South Chicago under its own power on December 17. The voyage did not start out well, however, as a host of mechanical problems forced it to anchor off Milwaukee, Wisconsin, the next day. Having cancelled plans to take on a cargo of scrap due to the lateness of the season, the *Savic* passed Detroit for the final time on December 23. Transiting the Welland Canal on Christmas Day, it reached Montreal two days later.

Remaining at Montreal over the winter, the *Savic* later went to an anchorage near Lanoraie, Quebec. Resold and assigned a new crew, it finally got underway on September 11, 1986 bound for New York City to load containers for South Korea. Sailing out of that port on October 10, the steamer stopped at Honolulu, Hawaii, during mid-November after transiting the Panama Canal. On December 22, 1986, the long odyssey of this ship's final voyage finally came to an end when it arrived at Masan, South Korea, to be broken up. Of all of the lake freighters that have sailed upon the waters of the Great Lakes, few have been as distinctive as the *Cliffs Victory* while even fewer have endured such a torturous journey to the scrap yard.

Within the same timeframe that Cleveland-Cliffs disposed of the *Cliffs Victory*, the company also sold the "Maritime" class steamers *Cadillac* (4) and *Champlain* (3) to the Pai Marine Corporation of Jacksonville, Florida, for dismantling. With each of these ships belonging to one of the two separate design variants of that class of vessels built for the U.S. Government during World War II to bolster the lake fleet's carrying capacity to meet wartime demands, both had remained members of the Cliffs fleet throughout their entire careers.

During their construction, the U.S. Maritime Commission had assigned the sixteen members of the "Maritime" class names pending their acquisition and renaming by commercial operators. Launched as the *Lake Angelina* by the Great Lakes Engineering Works at River Rouge, Michigan, on October 31, 1942, the *Cadillac* (4) sailed on its maiden voyage on June 19, 1943. Built by the American Ship Building Company at Cleveland as the *Belle Isle*, the *Champlain* (3) followed its fleet mate into service when it cleared that port on July 11, 1943 bound for Superior, Wisconsin. Both ships operated steadily in the movement of raw materials around the lakes until entering indefinite layups at Toledo in September of 1981. Sold to the Pai Marine Corporation for $110,000 each, the retired steamers soon became the subject of prolonged legal litigation in U.S. District Court that delayed their tows to the scrap yard until August 1987.

Downbound in the St. Marys River on October 14 with the 290-foot barge *G.L.B. No. 2* in tow, the tug *Rod Mclean* sank after being run over by the loaded pulpwood barge near the Government Dock at Sault Ste. Marie, Ontario. The presence of an exceptionally strong current playing a prominent role in the accident, the tug's five crewmembers jumped into the river and were rescued by the Canadian Coast Guard vessel *Verendrye*, Seaway Towing's *Pilot Boat No. 6*, and a Purvis Marine workboat. A combined salvage operation involving J. W. Purvis Marine Ltd. and the tug's owner, A. B. McLean Ltd., raised the 78-foot vessel from the river bottom four days later.

Elsewhere on October 14, a major structural failure on the Welland Canal was to have an immediate economic impact upon the Great Lakes region. Downbound with a load of grain from Milwaukee for Alexandria, Egypt, the Liberian freighter *Furia* was preparing to exit Lock 7 at 10:25 a.m. when a large section of the lock's west wall collapsed at a point beginning about 12 feet above the low water level. With tons of concrete pinned between the port side of the ship's hull and the chamber's wall, officials refilled the lock later in the day to raise the saltwater vessel to the high water level so it could safely back out of the lock and secure to the upper approach wall.

Caused by a rupture in a penstock that carried water to the canal's electrical generating plant located at Lock 4, the accident put a halt to all traffic through the Welland Canal with a large number of ships going to anchor in Lake Erie and Lake Ontario while others began tying up at various ports around the lakes. Upbound below Lock 7 at the time of the collapse, the *Canadian Pioneer* backed down through the six locks in the canal necessary to reach Lake Ontario. Their trade patterns into the lakes blocked, ocean operators diverted some of their inbound cargoes to alternate destinations below the closed canal or anxiously awaited the reopening of the vital shipping artery.

Following the installation of steel bracing to minimize the possibility of a further collapse, engineers began dewatering Lock 7 on October 23 during which another sizable slab of concrete broke loose from the fractured lock wall. The next day, the Pitts Engineering Corporation started to remove the remnants of the broken wall section before beginning to fill in a hole measuring approximately 140 feet long and 40 feet high with new concrete. These repairs completed, the Welland Canal reopened at six o'clock in the morning of November 7 when the *Furia* reentered Lock 7 to resume its downbound journey. With over 130 vessels delayed by the 24-day closure, canal operators managed to clear the traffic backlog over the next six days.

Sold to the M&M Steel Company of Windsor for dismantling, two classic Amoco

Oil Company steam powered tankers went to the scrap yard during the month of October. Towed from its layup berth at Essexville, Michigan, by the tugs *Glenada* and *Mount McKay*, the *Amoco Wisconsin* became the first of this duo to make its final voyage when it arrived at Windsor on October 18. Built by the Manitowoc Shipbuilding Company at Manitowoc, Wisconsin, in 1930, this ship entered service for the Standard Oil Company (Indiana) in September of that same year as the *Edward G. Seubert*. Renamed *Amoco Wisconsin* following the transfer of its title to the American Oil Company (Amoco) in 1962, this ship operated until laying up for the final time on June 3, 1982.

Making a return trip to the Saginaw River, the tugs *Glenada* and *Mount McKay* pulled the *Amoco Illinois* out of Essexville on October 30. Unlike the preceding tow, however, this voyage did not pass without incident as the tugs experienced trouble controlling the retired tanker while downbound in the St. Clair River the following evening. Taking a sudden sheer toward shore, the *Amoco Illinois* demolished a covered boat hoist and approximately 25 feet of an adjacent dock before slamming into a seawall near St. Clair, Michigan. Led by the *Mount McKay*, the scrap tow continued downbound to arrive at Windsor on November 1 without further incident. Launched by the American Ship Building Company at Lorain on March 9, 1918 as the *William P. Cowan*, this ship received its final name in 1962. Finishing out a long career on the lakes, it entered a permanent layup on December 21, 1980.

Sold to Marine Salvage Ltd. for scrapping after sitting idle following its removal from service during the second half of the 1982 season, the sand sucker *Niagara* (2) left Erie, Pennsylvania, in tow of the tug *Glenside* on October 28. Assisted by the tug *Lac Manitoba*, the scrap tow arrived at Ramey's Bend the next day. Around this same time, a preservation group began a campaign to raise the necessary funds to purchase the former Erie Sand Steamship Company motor vessel and return it to Erie, Pennsylvania, for use as a floating museum. The initial phase of this endeavor having been successful, the *Niagara* (2) arrived back at Erie in tow of the tug *Glenbrook* on June 10, 1986. This restoration effort ultimately proved futile, however, with the elderly sand sucker remaining in limbo until sold to the Liberty Iron & Metal Company on November 21, 1997, which dismantled the 257-foot vessel at its layup berth over the next several months. Built by the F. W. Wheeler & Company at West Bay City, Michigan, in 1897, the *Niagara* (2) had retained the same name throughout its 100-year existence.

With the *Mesabi Miner* only going as far as the mouth of the Saginaw River in June, the 767-foot *Cason J. Callaway* became the largest vessel to make an actual transit of that river system when it ventured some 15 miles upstream to deliver a load of stone to Zilwaukee, Michigan, on October 29. That same day, a former fleet mate of the *Callaway* made its final journey when the *Eugene W. Pargny* arrived at the Azcon Metals scrap dock at Duluth for dismantling after a tow across the harbor from Superior, where it had been laid up since May 19, 1980. Built by the American Ship Building Company at Lorain in 1917, this 600-foot bulk carrier had its original triple-expansion steam engine replaced with a 3,000 bhp diesel engine at that same shipyard over the 1950-51 winter layup. Over an operational career spanning 63 years, this vessel had managed to avoid any major mishaps. Scrapping of the *Eugene W. Pargny* began at Duluth on September 7,

1987 and continued until July 1988.

Although hindered by a pair of traffic disruptions, the Canadian lake fleet received a significant boost with a strong demand for autumn grain movements. Prompted in part by a large sale of Canadian grain to the Soviet Union, the influx of available cargoes resulted in the reactivation of several vessels that had either not yet seen service during the season or had entered temporary layups. In addition, shippers were hard pressed to move as much grain through the Seaway as possible before the winter freeze up to make up for the time lost during the 24-day closure of the Welland Canal. Among those to benefit from the favorable market conditions was the Halco fleet, which after struggling to find work for its eight bulk carriers for most of the season managed to place all but one into service during autumn with the last returning to duty in December.

The bulk carrier *Golden Hind* returned to duty on the afternoon of November 6 when it departed Toronto bound for Midland to load grain for a St. Lawrence River port. By doing so, it became the only lake steamer of the former Quebec & Ontario Transportation Company to operate for Desgagnes Transport. Residing at Toronto in a state of idleness since December 18, 1983 and repainted in fleet colors earlier in the season, the Lock 7 wall collapse on the Welland Canal had delayed plans for this vessel to reenter service during mid-October. Operating throughout the balance of the season, the *Golden Hind* entered its final layup at Toronto on December 29.

Earlier in the year, the Inland Steel Company had sold the *Philip D. Block* to Marine Salvage Ltd. for dismantling. Leaving the familiar waters of Lake Michigan behind, the bulk carrier passed downbound

The *Philip D. Block* alongside the *Hudson Transport* at Ramey's Bend. (Photo by James Hoffman)

past Detroit on November 7 in tow of the tugs *Nebraska* and *Ohio*. Due to a heavy concentration of traffic resulting from the reopening of the Welland Canal following repairs to Lock 7, the scrap tow put in at Buffalo, New York, rather than continuing to Port Colborne. On November 14, the tugs *Glenevis*, *Lac Manitoba*, and *Ohio* delivered the 60-year old steamer to Ramey's Bend, where it was to remain until resold for scrapping overseas the following year.

Entering service for the Pioneer Steamship Company on April 11, 1925, the *Philip D. Block* operated as a member of that fleet until purchased by the Inland Steel Company in 1936. During the early 1950s, this vessel received two significant reconstructions that enabled it to remain a viable carrier until the early 1980s. This included a lengthening to 672' with the insertion of a 72-foot midsection in 1951 and a repowering with a 4,950 shp steam turbine in 1953, both of which took place at the American Ship Building Company's South Chicago yard. Remaining active in carrying raw materials into its owner's steel making facility at Indiana Harbor, this steamer laid up for the final time at that port on September 12, 1981.

The seemingly endless procession of lake vessels to the scrap yard continued on November 15 with the arrival of the *Alastair Guthrie* at Port Maitland in tow of the tugs *Glenside* and *Lac Manitoba*. Having operated as a barge for a brief period during the 1984 season, this ship had been laid up at Buffalo since September 17 of that year. Concentrating in the grain trade during the latter years of its career, the former Kinsman fleet steamer was broken up during 1986.

One of the oldest ships in service on the Great Lakes, the 1904-built cement carrier *J. B. Ford* finished its last voyage as a powered carrier when it laid up at Milwaukee on November 15. This was not the end for the 440-foot ship, however, as it found a second career as a cement storage vessel at both South Chicago and later Superior, Wisconsin, before its eventual sale for scrapping in 2015.

A storm with strong northeast winds gusting to 50 mph that generated 10-foot waves in western Lake Superior on the evening of November 18 pushed the 584-foot Liberian bulker *Socrates* hard aground off Park Point at a location about a mile southeast of the Duluth Entry. Coming to rest approximately 150 feet from shore in about 11 feet of water and lying parallel to the beach, the plight of the stranded ocean freighter quickly became a local spectacle as the waves continued their relentless assault. While drifting toward the beach, the bulker sustained two holes measuring about 2½ feet in diameter when a flailing anchor swung hard against its bow plating. This incident came three days after the *Socrates* had anchored off Duluth to await a loading berth at one of the port's grain elevators.

The poor weather conditions complicated early salvage efforts and led to the U.S. Coast Guard's decision to remove the ship's 24 crewmembers on November 19. Although early attempts to refloat the bulk carrier proved futile, tugs did manage to get its bow pointed toward the open lake over the next three days. After work crews had dredged tons of sand from alongside its hull, a fleet of six tugs finally pulled the *Socrates* free at 12:46 in the afternoon of November 24. With the two minor hull punctures representing the only significant damage suffered during its six-day encounter with the sandy lake bottom, repairs to the Greek freighter were completed two days later without the need for dry-docking. Loaded with 17,000 tons of wheat, the *Socrates* cleared Duluth on December 6 bound for Montreal to top off its

Great Lakes Shipping Log 1980-1989

The *Stadacona* (3) was towed to Thunder Bay, Ontario, after grounding at Stoneport, Michigan.
(Photo by James Hoffman)

grain cargo before sailing for an Italian port.

Another Greek freighter encountered problems while visiting the upper lakes when 80 mph winds pushed the *Cape Monterey* into a pier at Sault Ste. Marie, Michigan, during the early morning hours of November 21. Inflicting a 25-foot dent on its starboard side, this mishap did not prevent the ocean vessel from continuing to Duluth once the weather improved. That same day, the *Edgar B. Speer* arrived at Bay Shipbuilding after losing its starboard rudder while sailing on Lake Michigan.

On November 22, CSL's *Stadacona* (3) suffered severe stern damage in a grounding at Stoneport, Michigan. Freed the next day, the wounded self-unloader passed through the Soo Locks on November 24 in tow of the tugs *W. J. Ivan Purvis* and *Tug Malcolm* bound for Thunder Bay. Entering the dry dock at Port Arthur Shipbuilding later that month for repairs reportedly exceeding $1 million, work on the 663-foot vessel continued until January 24 of the following year.

A pair of mishaps involving saltwater vessels took place over a two-day period near the end of November. On November 26, the bulker *Argolikos* went aground in the lower St. Clair River near Harsens Island while upbound for Chicago in heavy fog. Closing the river to traffic for nearly four hours, the Panamanian vessel continued to its destination after extricating itself from the muddy bottom without damage. A similar incident took place two days later when the *Federal Elbe* grounded near Becancour, Quebec, while downbound in the St. Lawrence River with a cargo of zinc. After offloading about 2,200 tons of its cargo into the *P. S. Barge No. 1*, four tugs succeeding in refloating the ocean freighter on December 1. Suffering only minor damage, it went to reload at Becancour before sailing for Baie Comeau and finally Antwerp, Belgium.

On November 28, the tug *Amoco Michigan* and the barge *Amoco Great Lakes* were renamed *Michigan* and *Great Lakes* respectively with the operation of the tug-barge combination taken over by the Coastwise Trading Company of East Chicago, Indiana, that same season.

Three weeks following the completion of repairs to Lock 7 on the Welland Canal, another major traffic stoppage occurred on November 29 when the downbound Indian freighter *Jalagodavari* of the Scindia Steam Navigation Company hit the south side of the St. Louis de Gonzague Bridge that crosses the Beauharnois Canal near Valleyfield. The impact knocked a 60-foot section of the bridge and four vehicles into the water, the occupants of the latter surviving the ordeal without suffering any serious injuries.

With the St. Lawrence Seaway closed to traffic, investigators began the task of determining how the 535-foot vessel missed the raised bridge opening even as engineers assessed the stability of the severely damaged span. After the bridge received additional bracing, but with the *Jalagodavari* still in its unfortunate position, Seaway officials reopened the canal to upbound traffic on December 2 only to close it a few hours later due to high winds. Reopened once again to upbound traffic the following afternoon, the danger posed by the combination of a strong current and the wakes of passing ships prompted the decision to remove the stuck vessel to prevent further damage to the bridge. Moved from its precarious position by four tugs at 10:37 in the morning of December 5, the *Jalagodavari* went to a temporary anchorage in Lake St. Louis as the Seaway reopened to regular shipping traffic with 72 vessels awaiting passage. Detained by an avalanche of lawsuits stemming from the accident, the beleaguered ship spent the winter at Montreal before finally clearing that port on March 1, 1986.

While docked at Cleveland on December 1, a cook aboard the Polish bulker *Ziemia Lubelska* walked off the ship to seek political asylum in the United States. This proved successful with the 27-year old man's request granted 11 days later as his ship continued its voyage into the Great Lakes by sailing to Detroit and later Chicago.

On the evening of December 1, a strong winter storm ripped the *Stewart J. Cort* and *Edgar B. Speer* away from their moorings at Bay Shipbuilding. Working in blizzard conditions, the tugs *Baldy B.*, *Minnie Selvick*, and *Steven M. Selvick* arrived on the scene a short time later to begin an attempt to retrieve the two wandering thousand footers. Joined later by the U.S. Coast Guard's *Mobile Bay*, a shipyard tug, and a Roen Salvage tug along with crewmembers from the cutter *Acacia*, *Sparrows Point*, and the tug-barge unit *Great Lakes/Michigan*, this combined effort did not succeed in getting the *Cort* and *Speer* back to their berths until midday on December 3. Both ships suffered minor propeller and rudder damage during the episode.

The same high winds that created problems across the lake at Sturgeon Bay also caused the idle car ferry *Spartan* (2) to snap its lines and go aground in Pere Marquette Lake at Ludington, Michigan, on December 1. The 410-foot vessel remained stranded until refloated by the car ferry *City of Midland 41* and the Canonie Transportation tugs *Muskegon* and *South Haven* four days later.

At 11:45 in the morning of December 6, Collingwood Shipyards launched the Canadian Coast Guard icebreaker *Sir Wilfrid Laurier* at Collingwood. Completed at a cost of $50 million, this was to be the last ship ever built by the longstanding shipbuilder. With the repowering of the steamer *Comeaudoc* slated to begin over the upcoming winter representing the only other major project in its order queue and with no prospect of any new construction contracts, the shipyard closed in September 1986.

On December 7, the tugs *Chippewa* and *W. J. Ivan Purvis* towed the *Lakeshell* (3) to Sault Ste. Marie, Ontario, after the 399-foot tanker experienced engine trouble while upbound on Lake Huron. Two days later, its cargo was transferred into the *Eastern Shell* (2) for delivery to Thunder Bay.

The Finnish tanker *Kiisla* arrived on the lakes during the first half of December to begin working on charter to Sunoco in carrying cargoes from that company's refinery located at Sarnia to Chicago over the upcoming winter. Designed to operate in arctic conditions, the 428-foot ship nonetheless required the assistance of the U.S. Coast Guard's *Biscayne Bay* on January 9, 1986 after stopped by heavy ice during one of its early transits of the Straits of Mackinac.

During mid-December, Misener Shipping Limited returned the *Laketon* (2) to Nipigon Transport Limited following the end of that vessel's two-season charter agreement. The 14-year old gearless bulk carrier reverted to its former name, *Lake Nipigon*, at the beginning of the 1986 season.

Encountering rough seas while transiting Lake Ontario on the afternoon of December 15 during its last run of the season, the cement barge *Robert Koch* broke free of the tug *R. & L. No. 1* as the pair neared the harbor entrance to Oswego, New York. Although a crew put aboard the barge managed to drop its anchors, wave action pushed it onto a mud-covered reef about 900 feet off Sheldon's Point early the following morning.

Suffering severe structural damage and battered by 14-foot waves, the 240-foot barge settled on the bottom as water flooded into its cargo holds and engine room. To prevent an environmental disaster, the U.S. Coast Guard supervised the removal of nearly 4,000 gallons of fuel oil from the wreck on December 20. Left in place for the winter, the salvage of the *Robert Koch* and its subsequent disposition appears in the next chapter.

The Mercier Bridge at Montreal suffered several thousand dollars worth of damage on December 18 when struck by the saltwater bulker *Federal St. Laurent*, which itself sustained only some minor scuffing. Two days later, Fraser Shipyards completed dismantling the former Cleveland-Cliffs steamer *Frontenac* (2) at Superior, Wisconsin. The shipyard had purchased this vessel shortly after it suffered severe damage in a career ending grounding at Silver Bay on November 22, 1979.

Assisted through an icy Saginaw River by the tug *Barbara Ann*, the Pringle Transit Company's 630-foot *William R. Roesch* arrived at the Wirt Stone Dock at Bay City, Michigan, on December 23 with some ice-related bow damage. Working in subzero temperatures from the deck of the *Barbara Ann*, a repair crew managed to patch several small punctures in the hull of the self-unloader using steel plates brought some 150 miles north from Toledo. This completed, the *Roesch* cleared Bay City on December 25, the same day, incidentally, that its sister ship, *Paul Thayer*, sustained similar bow damage while moving through ice in western Lake Erie.

The Welland Canal closed to commercial traffic on the morning of December 30 just hours after the *Canadian Olympic* made the final official passage when it cleared downbound shortly before midnight the previous evening. Another ULS carrier, *Canadian Transport*, followed about ninety minutes later with coal from Port Colborne. As that vessel did not make a complete transit of the canal on this voyage, however, it did not receive recognition as being the last ship of the season. On December 31, the Canadian Coast Guard's *Griffon* and the U.S. Coast Guard's *Neah Bay* passed upbound through the canal.

Late in the evening of January 1, 1986, the *Algoport* became the last lake carrier to pass through the Soo Locks for the season when it locked upbound for Marquette. The locks recorded 4,439 cargo vessel transits of during the 1985 season, a figure representing a 41 percent decrease in such traffic compared to the 7,576 passages made in 1980.

Chapter Seven
The 1986 Shipping Season

The 1986 season started out on a positive note with shipments passing through the Soo Locks growing steadily throughout spring to reach a stable level for most of the summer before plummeting during August and September. Although recovering in October, tonnages slipped once again with movements faltering throughout the remainder of the season. With imported steel capturing approximately one-third of the domestic market, the iron ore float that season totaled only 51 million net tons, a figure that not only represented its lowest level since 1982 but also a loss of 7.4 million net tons in comparison to the 1985 season. Using the previous year as a benchmark, shipments of coal and grain remained relatively unchanged at 36.2 and 20.1 million net tons respectively while the stone trade increased by nearly nine percent to 27.2 million net tons.

Reflecting the growing dominance of self-unloading vessels in the U.S. fleet, the 1986 season marked the first time in which not a single U.S. flagged gearless bulk carrier operated solely in the iron ore trade. This resulted primarily from the idling of the Inland Steel steamer *Edward L. Ryerson*, which entered a long-term layup at Indiana Harbor, Indiana, on December 11, 1985. Although the *Ernest R. Breech* delivered several ore cargoes to Hamilton, Ontario, that season, the Rouge Steel vessel remained active in the movement of grain as did Interlake Steamship's *J. L. Mauthe*. Operated by Kinsman Lines, the only two other American straight deckers to see service that year were committed to the grain trade.

The *Chemical Transport* ran into some difficulty at the beginning of the year when it grounded in the Black Rock Channel at Buffalo, New York, while bound for Tonawanda, New York, with a load of gasoline from Sarnia, Ontario. Sustaining damage, but quickly refloated, the 391-foot tanker tied up at the Niagara Frontier Transportation Authority Dock at Buffalo on January 6 for repairs. Escorted through the ice by the tugs *Delaware* and *Kansas* along with the fireboat *Edward M. Cotter*, the *Chemical Transport* continued to its destination six days later.

On January 28, the Erie Sand Steamship Company entered into a charter agreement with the American Steamship Company to operate the self-unloader *Richard J. Reiss* (2). Having wintered at Erie, Pennsylvania, the "Maritime" class vessel was renamed *Richard Reiss* before entering service that spring by simply dropping its middle initial. Reportedly, this change took place due to the apparent reluctance on the part of Erie Sand's management to operate a ship with 13 letters in its name! Although given new stack markings, the *Reiss* was not repainted with the fleet's distinctive green hull color scheme like that applied to the *Consumers Power* (3) following that steamer's charter from the American Steamship Company in 1980.

On January 31, the Coastwise Trading Company sold the tanker *Amoco Indiana* to the Cement Transit Company (Medusa Cement) for conversion to a cement-carrying barge. Coming at a time of growth in the movement of cement on the lakes, Medusa awarded the Bay Shipbuilding Corporation a contract to perform this reconstruction at Sturgeon Bay, Wisconsin, where the 49-year old ship had been idle since December 20, 1982. In addition to removing the cabins and propulsion machinery, the transformation of this vessel also included the cutting down of its stern by 45'6" to produce an overall length of 419'9" and the installation of new cargo handling equipment. The latter included a belt conveyor system and a bow-mounted Webster bucket elevator with a 48-foot airflow boom conveyor to discharge cement. Work on this conversion was well underway by late November with the barge entering service during the summer of 1987 as the *Medusa Conquest*.

In 1986, the National Steel Corporation transferred its last operational vessel, the 1004-foot *George A. Stinson*, to the Skar-Ore Steamship Corporation. The M. A. Hanna Company of Cleveland, Ohio, retained its role as agent of the 8-year old vessel, which continued operating in the transportation of taconite from the upper lakes region to the lower lakes in particular to National Steel's Great Lakes Steel Division located on Zug Island in River Rouge, Michigan.

Escorted up the St. Marys River by the U.S. Coast Guard's *Katmai Bay*, the tanker *Kiisla* arrived at Sault Ste. Marie, Ontario, on February 15 before paying a return visit four days later to help alleviate a fuel shortage at the northern community. As related in the previous chapter, Sunoco had chartered the Finnish-flagged vessel to carry cargoes from its refinery at Sarnia to Chicago, Illinois, over the winter.

At 12:30 in the afternoon of March 7, a fire broke out aboard Algoma Central Marine's *Algosoo* (2) while that vessel was receiving some winter maintenance work at Port Colborne, Ontario. Igniting near the base of the loop conveyor belt and feeding on a combination of grease, oil, and wood, the blaze quickly spread throughout the stern of the self-unloader. Battling high winds and struggling within the confines of the smoke filled compartments, it took firefighters nearly eight hours to bring the flames under control. Causing considerable damage to the unloading system, the fire also gutted the vessel's aft accommodations. Although the engine room suffered heavy water damage from the firefighting operation, the two main engines and auxiliary equipment were, fortunately, repairable. Towed to Port Weller Dry Docks at St. Catharines, Ontario, on April 3 for repairs reportedly valued at $8 million, the *Algosoo* (2) returned to service on October 6 of that same year.

Spending the winter at the St. Lawrence Cement Company Dock in Duluth, Minnesota, after arriving there on December 14, 1985 with an unusual cargo of cement, the Kinsman Lines steamer *William A. McGonagle* was renamed *Henry Steinbrenner* (4) prior to entering service during late April. Another name change during the early months of the year took place within the Canadian fleet when Group Desgagnes (Desgagnes Transport) renamed the 349-foot motor vessel *New York News* (3) to *Stella Desgagnes*.

The various improvement projects over the winter layup period included the fitting of polymer liners into the cargo hold of the *Herbert C. Jackson* to decrease unloading times by improving the flow rates of cargoes such as fine coal. Elsewhere in the U.S. fleet, a 1,000 horsepower bow thruster unit removed from the *Enders M. Voorhees* was installed as a stern thruster in the *John G. Munson* (2).

Meanwhile, Collingwood Shipyards Ltd. made steady progress at repowering the N. M. Paterson & Sons bulk carrier *Comeaudoc* with a 8,158 bhp Krupp MaK diesel engine. Departing Collingwood, Ontario, during late April, the 26-year old ship sailed under its own power to Thunder Bay, Ontario, where it received final work before reentering service. Loaded with grain, the bulk carrier left that port on May 19 carrying its first cargo as a motor vessel.

The shipping season began at Cleveland on March 14 with the departure of the cement carrier *J. A. W. Iglehart* and the sailing of the *American Republic* a few days later to begin the ore shuttle between that city and Lorain, Ohio. In other early season activity, the *Arthur M. Anderson* cleared Milwaukee, Wisconsin, on March 23 to load iron ore at Escanaba, Michigan.

Arriving at Toronto, Ontario, on March 25 with a cargo of cement from Picton, Ontario, the *Stephen B. Roman* earned the honor of being the first ship of the season into that port for the third consecutive year. That same day, an early casualty took place when the *Richelieu* (3) struck a dock at Quebec City, Quebec. Although not seriously damaged, the Canada Steamship Lines (CSL) bulker went to Montreal, Quebec, to have some bow plates replaced during early April.

With Cargill Ltd. divesting itself of its stake in Nipigon Transport Ltd. the previous year, the M. A. Hanna Company entered into an agreement to sell the fleet to Algoma Central Marine in a deal finalized on March 27. This transaction involved the bulk carriers *Lake Manitoba*, *Lake Wabush*, and *Lake Nipigon*, the latter vessel having just returned from a two-year charter to Misener Shipping Ltd. during which it operated as the *Laketon* (2). All three vessels entered service for Algoma during the 1986 season in Nipigon colors prior to receiving new names the following year.

After spending the winter at the Algoma Steel Dock at Sault Ste. Marie, Ontario, the *Louis R. Desmarais* became the first commercial ship of the season to transit the Soo Locks when it locked downbound through the Poe Lock at 12:01 a.m. on April 1 while en route to Stoneport, Michigan. The shipping season on the St. Lawrence Seaway began on April 3 when Halco's *Frankcliffe Hall* (2) transited the St. Lambert Lock opposite Montreal even as its fleet mate *Island Transport* (2) opened the Welland Canal. Also passing through the Welland Canal that day was the tanker *Kiisla*, which was downbound after spending the winter operating out of Sarnia.

The newly renamed *Stella Desgagnes* encountered some difficulty on April 5 when it ran into a breakwater at Port Colborne. Two days later, the *Canadian Transport* had a fire start in its loop conveyor belt while at Hamilton. Docked at Dofasco's Dock #2 at the time of incident, the quick action of the vessel's crew managed to contain the blaze prior to the arrival of the Hamilton Fire Department thereby preventing any serious damage to the self-unloader.

The *Edgar B. Speer* arrived at Duluth on April 9 and tied up at the Port Terminal with starboard propeller damage. The necessary repairs completed, the thousand-footer left the next day to load taconite at Two Harbors, Minnesota.

Returning to the lakes to begin its second year of operating on monthly transatlantic voyages, the Fednav Lakes Services motor vessel *Federal Lakes* inflicted an estimated $100,000 in damage to a dock it hit at Toledo, Ohio, on April 17. The previous autumn,

The unmistakable motor vessel *Chicago Tribune* (2) laid up for the last time early in the 1986 shipping season. (Author's Collection)

that firm had announced its intention to expand its U.S. flagged RO/RO (Roll-On/Roll-Off) cargo service connecting selected U.S. ports on the Great Lakes to points in Europe to a biweekly schedule in 1986 with the addition of a second ship. Built by Port Weller Dry Docks Ltd. in 1972 as the *Laurentian Forest* for the Burnett Steamship Company Ltd. of Newcastle, England, a subsidiary of Montreal based Federal Commerce & Navigation Ltd., this ship was a sister ship to the *Federal Lakes*. Brought into U.S. registry and renamed *Federal Seaway* in addition to receiving a $3 million refit at Charleston, South Carolina, the 683-foot carrier arrived at Montreal on April 29 during its first trip into the lakes for Fednav Lakes Services.

Sidelined after grounding in the Trenton Channel of the Detroit River on May 5, 1980, the self-unloader *Sharon* departed its long-term layup berth at Monroe, Michigan, on April 18 in tow for Toledo. There, the 672-foot vessel joined the idle steamers *William G. Mather* (2) and *McKee Sons* to await its fate.

While inbound at Grand Haven, Michigan, with a cargo of salt on April 21, the motor vessel *Algoport* rammed a seawall near the city's downtown area. Although the impact demolished a 25 square foot section of walkway and an adjacent section of lawn, the self-unloader came away from the incident with no apparent damage. That same day, the 767-foot *Benson Ford* (3) delivered a load of limestone to the Sargent Docks and Terminal Company Dock at Saginaw, Michigan, thus becoming the largest ship to venture that far up the Saginaw River.

After completing one trip from Thunder Bay with grain, the *Chicago Tribune* (2) entered its final layup at Toronto on April 22. The idling of this 319-foot vessel resulted largely from the Canada Malting Company Ltd. awarding a contract for its grain movement requirements to the N. M. Paterson &

Sons Ltd. fleet. The size restrictions of the malting firm's grain elevator at Toronto dictated the use of smaller vessels that were uneconomical to operate on most other trade routes. To assist in fulfilling the terms of this agreement, Paterson sent its 355-foot bulk carrier *Ontadoc* (2) to the Port Arthur Shipbuilding Company at Thunder Bay for the installation of an additional cargo hold bulkhead to improve that vessel's ability to operate in this trade.

One final incident near the end of the month involved CSL's *Saguenay* (2), which grounded in the St. Lawrence River near Valleyfield, Quebec, on April 25. Spending part of the day aground, the self-unloader broke free of the bottom without any reported damage.

In early 1986, the National Gypsum Company sold its Huron Cement Division to the French cement firm Lafarge Coppee. This sale included the steamers *S. T. Crapo, E. M. Ford, J. B. Ford, Lewis G. Harriman, J. A. W. Iglehart,* and the motor vessel *Paul H. Townsend* all of which were sold to the Skaarup Lakes Shipping Corporation of Philadelphia, Pennsylvania, on April 29 to comply with federal laws prohibiting the foreign ownership of vessels engaged in domestic operations. This arrangement remained in effect until the subsequent transfer of these vessels to Inland Lakes Transportation Inc. of Alpena, Michigan, just before the beginning of the 1987 shipping season.

Shortly after entering service under its new name, the *Henry Steinbrenner* (4) was lined up to enter the Duluth Ship Canal on May 6 when the Aerial Lift Bridge suddenly jammed in a half-raised position. Unable to transit the canal, the 600-foot steamer broke off its approach and instead entered Duluth-Superior Harbor through the Superior Entry.

While attempting to depart Ashland, Wisconsin, on May 8, the *Indiana Harbor* knocked over a 30-foot section of railing on its port bow when strong winds forced it to scrape against the unused ore loading dock at that port. Having been idle since the previous spring due to poor economic conditions, the thousand-footer encountered no further difficulty on its return to service when it sailed into Lake Superior a few hours later. Two days after its much larger fleet mate's mishap at Ashland, the *American Mariner* lost steering while upbound in the Middle Neebish Channel of the St. Marys River. Going to anchor, the 730-foot self-unloader required a subsequent tow to the Carbide Dock at Sault Ste. Marie, Michigan, by the tugs *Vermont* and *Wisconsin* for repairs before continuing to Marquette, Michigan, the next day.

Making what was reportedly its first ever visit to Fairport, Ohio, on May 11, the *Canadian Transport* established a cargo record for that small port when it loaded 29,300 tons of salt for delivery to Montreal.

Just four weeks after the Duluth Convention Center Board approved its purchase for $110,000, the retired USS Great Lakes Fleet steamer *William A. Irvin* left its long-term layup berth at Duluth on May 12 in tow for Fraser Shipyards on the opposite side of the harbor. Having languished in a state of limbo since laying up at the end of the 1978 season, the 48-year old bulk carrier was put into the dry dock to begin its transformation into a floating attraction with a $210,000 renovation. Following the completion of this work, the North American Towing Company tugs *Dakota* and *Sioux* towed the *William A. Irvin* back to Duluth on June 17, where it opened to the public on June 28. Proving extremely popular, approximately 10,000 visitors toured the former United States Steel flagship during its first two weeks as a museum ship.

On May 13, the Liberian registered bulker *Polstar* collided with a yacht on the St. Lawrence River. Bound for Montreal when the accident occurred, the crew of the ocean freighter pulled the three occupants aboard the stricken craft to safety. Determining it posed a hazard to navigation, the U.S. Coast Guard later decided to sink the severely damaged yacht.

After operating a freight service between Thunder Bay and Windsor, Ontario, during the preceding two seasons, Jensen Shipping Ltd. found itself in an unfavorable position with its creditors. These financial difficulties resulted in the seizure of the company's package freighter *Jensen Star* by Greyhound Financial Inc. and its subsequent sale to the newly created Woodlands Marine Inc. of Thunder Bay. Renamed *Woodland*, the 25-year old motor vessel entered service for its new owners during the middle of May

Towed out of Milwaukee on May 25, where it had been laid up since December 18, 1981, the cement carrier *E. M. Ford* arrived at Sturgeon Bay the next day. Reentering service following a visit to Bay Shipbuilding's dry dock, the 88-year old steamer arrived at Alpena on June 3 to load its first cargo of the season.

The recent string of bad luck afflicting self-unloaders during the early part of the year continued on May 28 when Interlake Steamship's *Mesabi Miner* suffered a conveyor belt fire at Lorain. Inflicting some $3,000 in damage to the thousand-footer's unloading gear, this incident followed a similar mishap aboard the *Canadian Transport* just one month earlier and a considerably more serious blaze that ravaged the aft section of the *Algosoo* (2) during the first week of March.

During mid-1986, USS Great Lakes Fleet

The *William P. Snyder Jr.* was sold for dismantling at Port Colborne, Ontario, during the 1986 season.
(Author's Collection)

sold the *Leon Fraser* to Spitzer Great Lakes Ltd. for use in a project to redevelop the former American Ship Building Company yard at Lorain. Built by the Great Lakes Engineering Works at River Rouge as the first member of United States Steel's five unit "Super" class of steamers commissioned during 1942, the 639-foot bulk carrier had been idle at Lorain since December 20, 1981.

On June 3, the Toledo City Council purchased the *Willis B. Boyer* from the Cleveland-Cliffs Steamship Company for $120,000. Made obsolete by newer self-unloading lake freighters, the 617-foot bulk carrier had laid up for the final time on December 22, 1980. Constructed for the Shenango Furnace Company as the *Col. James M. Schoonmaker*, this vessel and its sister ship, *William P. Snyder, Jr.*, were the largest ships on the Great Lakes when they entered service in 1911 and 1912 respectively. Following an exhaustive restoration effort, the *Boyer* opened as a maritime museum at Toledo on July 4, 1987.

Proving to be somewhat less fortunate than its sister ship, Cleveland-Cliffs sold the *William P. Snyder, Jr.* to Port Colborne Marine Terminals Inc. for scrapping during this same timeframe, although it was to remain at Toledo until towed to Port Colborne the following summer. Acquired by that fleet in November 1970, this vessel remained a viable carrier throughout the balance of that decade with frequent trips up the Cuyahoga River at Cleveland with iron ore for the Republic Steel mills. As that important contract came to an end, the *William P. Snyder, Jr.* entered its final layup at Ashtabula, Ohio, on December 17, 1980. Built by the Great Lakes Engineering Works at Ecorse, this steamer had retained the same name throughout its entire 68-year operational career despite sailing for three different owners.

At 8:30 in the evening of June 3, the *American Republic* hit a submerged object while backing into the Erie Builders Concrete Company Dock at Erie, Pennsylvania, to deliver a cargo of stone. Shortly afterwards, the crew of the 634-foot vessel spotted a sunken automobile beneath its starboard propeller. Raised from the bottom of the slip just before midnight by the Erie County Sheriff Department, recovery personnel found several bone fragments inside the badly mangled vehicle. A more thorough search conducted the following morning that also included members of the Erie Fire Department and a U.S. Coast Guard patrol boat recovered additional human remains from the waters of Presque Isle Bay.

On April 18, ULS International sold the bulk carriers *Meldrum Bay*, *Frank A. Sherman*, *Red Wing*, and *Wheat King* through A. L. Burbank & Co. of New York for scrapping overseas. Two of these vessels, the *Red Wing* and *Frank A. Sherman*, cleared Toronto under their own power on June 10 for Quebec City. Almost immediately following their arrival at that port, both vessels were towed across the St. Lawrence River to Lauzon, Quebec, on June 13, from where they began their final journey to the scrap yard on October 27 in tow of the tug *Canadian Viking*. After a three-week long layover at Honolulu, Hawaii, beginning in mid-February of the following year necessitated by an encounter with heavy weather in the Pacific Ocean during which the *Red Wing* nearly sank, the scrap tow finally reached Kaohsiung, Taiwan, on April 30, 1987. There, work soon began on dismantling the two lake freighters.

Converted into a Great Lakes bulk carrier in 1960, the *Red Wing* had an interesting history that began with its construction as a T2 type tanker by the Sun Shipbuilding & Dry Dock Company at Chester, Pennsylvania, in

The *American Republic* struck a submerged automobile at Erie, Pennsylvania, on June 3, 1986.
(Author's Collection)

1944. Launched as the *Boundbrook* for the U.S. Maritime Commission, this vessel later sailed for Imperial Oil Company Ltd. as the *Imperial Edmonton* prior to its sale to St. Lawrence & Great Lakes Shipping Co. Ltd. (Upper Lakes Shipping Co. Ltd.) in late 1958. Taken to Port Weller Dry Docks Ltd. at St. Catharines the following summer for the previously noted reconstruction, the *Red Wing* began its maiden voyage as a lake freighter when it sailed from the shipyard on August 13, 1960 for Sandusky, Ohio, to load coal for delivery to Hamilton. Named after a professional hockey team based in Detroit, Michigan, this vessel operated until December 15, 1984 when it laid up at Toronto.

Launched by Port Weller Dry Docks Ltd. on May 31, 1958, the *Frank A. Sherman* was one of four new bulk freighters constructed for the Upper Lakes Shipping fleet during the 1950s, the others being the *Gordon C. Leitch*, *James Norris*, and *Seaway Queen*. This vessel's entry into service took place on July 12 of that year when it sailed from St. Catharines bound for Duluth to load iron ore for Hamilton. Remaining active in the bulk trades for the next two decades, the 681-foot steamer closed out its operational career when it entered an indefinite layup at Toronto on December 10, 1981.

The motor vessel *Calcite II* made its first ever visit to Goderich, Ontario, on June 13 when it arrived to load salt for Green Bay, Wisconsin. An equally uncommon call to that port by a USS Great Lakes Fleet carrier took place one month later when the *Cason J. Callaway* took on a partial cargo of salt on July 19. The 767-foot steamer then sailed across Lake Huron to Stoneport to top off with stone before delivering both cargoes to Duluth.

On June 20, the 630-foot *Wolverine* (2) suffered heavy rudder damage while backing into a slip at Marquette. Towed to Superior, Wisconsin, by the tug *Chippewa* sent from

Sault Ste. Marie, Michigan, the disabled self-unloader arrived at Fraser Shipyards three days later for repairs valued in excess of $200,000.

Acquired from Ingram Overseas Ltd. (Rowbotham Tankships Ltd.) the previous month by Societe Sofati-Soconav, the 274-foot British flagged tanker *Rudderman* arrived at Montreal on June 20. Built by Cochrane & Sons Limited at Selby, England, in 1968, this motor vessel was registered in Canada on July 1 as the *Henri Tellier*.

During the first half of 1986, the American Steamship Company sold the steamers *Detroit Edison* (2) and *Sharon* to Corostel Trading Ltd. of Montreal for dismantling. Towed out of Toledo, where it had been since mid-April following several years of idleness at Monroe, the *Sharon* reached Port Colborne on June 20 in tow of the tugs *Daniel McAllister*, *Helen M. McAllister*, and *Salvage Monarch*. Having returned up the lakes after delivering the *Sharon* to Quebec City, the *Salvage Monarch* towed the *Detroit Edison* (2) out of Sturgeon Bay on July 5. Later joined by the tugs *Cathy McAllister* and *Helen M. McAllister*, the scrap tow transited the St. Lawrence Seaway on July 13 en route to Quebec City.

Resold to Goldwils Inc. for scrapping at Brownsville, Texas, the two self-unloaders cleared Quebec City on July 16 in tow of the U.S. flagged tug *Prudent*. Although the *Sharon* was dismantled before the end of the year, work on its former fleet mate ran into a snag when vandals sank the *Detroit Edison* (2) on November 20. Raised from the bottom on January 16, 1987, the scrap yard began breaking up the 678-foot vessel the following month.

The *Sharon* dated back to its original construction by the Alabama Dry Dock and Shipbuilding Company at Mobile, Alabama, in 1945 as the T2 tanker *Archers Hope* for the U.S. Maritime Commission. Sold to Ships Inc. (Cities Service Oil Company) in 1948, this vessel operated on saltwater until acquired by the American Steamship Company in 1956 for conversion to a Great Lakes self-unloading bulk carrier. Reconstructed to an overall length of 588'10" with the addition of a new forward section by the Maryland Shipbuilding and Dry Dock Company at Baltimore, Maryland, in 1957, this ship entered the Great Lakes via the Mississippi River. Towed to the Manitowoc Shipbuilding Company at Manitowoc, Wisconsin, for the completion of its conversion, this steamer entered service that summer as the *Joseph S. Young*.

Lengthened to 672'10" by the American Ship Building Company at South Chicago, Illinois, with insertion of an 84' midsection in 1966, the American Steamship Company renamed this self-unloader *H. Lee White* three years later. Given the name *Sharon* in 1974 following the construction of a larger fleet mate, it operated in the coal, ore, sand, and stone trades until suffering a career ending grounding in the Trenton Channel of the Detroit River on May 5, 1980. As with several of the postwar saltwater conversions, this vessel experienced a busy, but all too brief, career on the Great Lakes.

Launched by the Manitowoc Shipbuilding Company at Manitowoc on September 9, 1954, the maiden voyage of the steamer *Detroit Edison* (2) began on April 15, 1955 when it sailed to load stone at Port Inland, Michigan, for Indiana Harbor. Lengthened to 678'3" by Fraser Shipyards at Superior, Wisconsin, in 1966, this vessel became the largest ship operated by the American Steamship Company until that firm began commissioning a new class of carriers built during the early 1970s as part of a major fleet modernization program. Having finished its last operational season, the *Detroit Edison* (2) entered its final layup at Sturgeon Bay on December 22, 1982.

On June 21, a strong summer thunderstorm wreaked havoc with several inactive ships at the Twin Ports. At Duluth, winds gusting to 86 mph ripped the USS Great Lakes Fleet "Super" class steamers *A. H. Ferbert* (2), *Irving S. Olds*, and *Enders M. Voorhees* from their moorings at Hallett Dock #5 and blew them, still lashed together, aground on the Superior side of St. Louis Bay. Despite demolishing some loading chutes on the Duluth, Missabe & Iron Range Railway #5 ore dock at the beginning of their unexpected foray, the three vessels suffered no appreciable damage. At the Azcon Corporation scrap yard, the *Joshua A. Hatfield* snapped its lines and went on a wild ride across the harbor basin before stranding on the sandy bottom off Minnesota Point.

On the opposite side of the harbor, the same gale force winds pushed the Interlake Steamship bulk carriers *Harry Coulby* (2) and *John Sherwin* (2) across their slip at Superior, Wisconsin, with enough force to pull out an anchor buried 10 feet deep. Despite the violence of their sudden breakaway, both steamers came away from the affair without any apparent damage.

Although tugs returned the three "Supers" to their layup berths the following day, the salvage effort to refloat the *Hatfield* presented a much more difficult proposition. Lodged firmly in the sand, the 600-foot bulk carrier remained hard aground until July 11 when a pair of tugs managed to free the steamer and moor it back at the scrap dock after favorable winds produced a sudden rise in the harbor's water level.

The Saint Vincent registered *Eglantine* suffered a minor grounding at Duluth on June 25. Although managing to free his vessel without requiring assistance, the captain of the ocean freighter apparently neglected to notify the U.S. Coast Guard of the incident before leaving the harbor. This omission brought about a special inspection of the 645-foot bulker upon reaching the Soo Locks.

Christened as the *St. Marys Cement* on May 24, the barge built at the Toledo Shipyard for St. Marys Holdings Inc. arrived at Ecorse on June 29 following a tow from Toledo by tugs belonging to The Great Lakes Towing Company. Paired with the *Triton*, a 3,950 horsepower tug brought into the lakes from the Gulf Coast specifically for this task, the 360-foot cement barge entered service a short time later with the duo passing upbound at Port Huron, Michigan, for the first time on July 3 while bound for Green Bay, Wisconsin.

During the summer, the American Steamship Company dissolved its Gartland Steamship Company and Reiss Steamship Company subsidiaries it had maintained since acquiring those fleets in 1969. Approved by the company's board of directors on July 1, this merger, which involved the motor vessels *Nicolet* and *Richard Reiss*, took place on July 23. At the time of this transition, the latter vessel was operating for the Erie Sand Steamship Company under a charter agreement.

After days of effort, the Cleveland Stevedore Company succeeded in removing the forward cabins and forecastle from the *John Dykstra* (2) on July 2 for use as a summer home on South Bass Island in western Lake Erie. Leaving Cleveland on July 10 in tow of the tugs *Glenbrook* and *Argue Martin*, the 612-foot bulk carrier arrived at Ramey's Bend for scrapping by Marine Salvage Ltd. two days later.

Launched by the Great Lakes Engineering

Works at River Rouge, Michigan, on April 26, 1924 as the *Benson Ford*, this ship was one of two bulk carriers built for the Ford Motor Company that year, the other being the *Henry Ford II*. Powered by 3,000 bhp Sun-Doxford diesel engines, this pair became the first large lake freighters equipped with diesel propulsion. Committed to the movement of raw materials to support the steel production requirements of Ford's massive River Rouge Complex at Dearborn, Michigan, throughout its entire career, this vessel last operated in December 1981. Renamed *John Dykstra* (2) the following year, it later passed into the ownership of Sullivan Marine for a planned conversion to self-unloading barge that never materialized.

The arrival of the *Calcite II* at Manistique, Michigan, with coal on July 8 did not escape the attention of the local press, which reported it as being the first large lake vessel to visit that port since the *John A. Kling* delivered a load of stone in 1973. That same day, tugs moved the *Hudson Transport* from Ramey's Bend to the Law Stone Dock at Port Colborne for the removal of its engines as work slowly progressed on converting the former Halco tanker into a petroleum products barge. With its cabins cut down before the move, the hull remained at that location for the next several months until returned to the scrap yard on December 1 of that year by the tugs *Glenada* and *Tusker*.

Losing power while outbound at Sandusky with 26,200 tons of coal for Montreal, CSL's *Manitoulin* (5) grounded off Cedar Point on the morning of July 15. Opening up a starboard ballast tank, it remained aground until freed late that evening with the assistance of a tug sent over from Cleveland. Following an inspection, the 730-foot self-unloader proceeded to Port Colborne for repairs.

A grounding in the St. Lawrence River resulted in the *Beechglen* going to Port Weller Dry Docks for repairs.
(Photo by James Hoffman)

Sold for scrapping after four and a half years of idleness, the *Wheat King* departed Toronto on July 15 in tow of the tugs *Glenevis*, *Glenside*, *Argue Martin*, and *Stormont*. Delivered to Lauzon eight days later, it remained there until finally beginning a transatlantic tow on November 24 behind the Polish tug *Jantar*. Arriving at Rotterdam, Netherlands, on January 23, 1987, the bulk carrier was used to store cattle feed under the name *Bulk Cat* until sold in mid-1989. Renamed *Brugse 1*, the retired laker cleared the Dutch port on August 22, 1989 in tow of the Soviet tug *Yasnyy* bound for dismantling at Chittagong, Bangladesh, where it arrived on October 11, 1989.

Launched as the tanker *Llandaff* by Lithgows Limited at Glasgow, Scotland, on June 26, 1952, this vessel saw considerable use in the movement of crude oil from the Mediterranean to ports in England until its sale to Upper Lakes Shipping in 1960. Sent to Port Weller Dry Docks Ltd. at St. Catharines for conversion to a bulk freighter, this vessel entered service as the *Wheat King* on April 17, 1961. Retaining its original 556'6" length and placed into Upper Lakes Shipping's Island Shipping Ltd. subsidiary, this ship was able to conduct both Great Lakes and ocean voyages. Restricted to lakes service following its lengthening to 728'11" at Port Weller Dry Docks in 1976, the *Wheat King* closed out its operational career at Toronto on December 11, 1981.

As iron ore shipments represent roughly 40 percent of the total bulk commerce moved on the lakes during any given season, it can be said that when the steel industry sneezes the Great Lakes shipping industry utters a nervous "bless you" and hopes for the best. Citing heavy losses in its energy and steel divisions, the LTV Corporation, parent of LTV Steel, filed for Chapter 11 bankruptcy protection on July 17. The result of a merger between LTV's Jones & Laughlin Steel Corporation subsidiary and the Republic Steel Corporation in 1984, LTV Steel was the second largest steel producer in the United States at the time. This filing quickly led to the closure of the Reserve Mining Company, of which LTV and Armco Steel both held an equal 50 percent stake, along with its associated ore loading dock at Silver Bay, Minnesota.

Its operations seriously impacted by the financial woes of one of its largest customers, Moore McCormack Resources Inc. reacted to the LTV bankruptcy by placing the Pickands Mather & Company and that firm's Interlake Steamship Company division up for sale. With Cleveland-Cliffs Inc. acquiring the Pickands Mather & Company in November, James R. Barker, having resigned from his post as chairman of Moore McCormack, brought the Interlake Steamship Company into private ownership in January of 1987.

The P. & H. Shipping steamer *Beechglen* went aground near St. Anicet, Quebec, on the morning of July 19 while downbound on Lake St. Francis in heavy fog with 15,400 tons of wheat for Trois-Rivieres, Quebec. Among the ship traffic delayed by this grounding was the *Wheat King* scrap tow, the four tugs of which joined in the effort to refloat the 680-foot bulk carrier. With six tugs assisting, the *Beechglen* was released on July 21 after lightering 1,100 tons of it cargo. Anchoring briefly off St. Zotique, Quebec, the veteran lake freighter went to Montreal for an inspection before proceeding to unload at Trois-Rivieres and then to Port Weller Dry Docks for repairs.

On July 24, McAllister Towing & Salvage Inc. succeeded in refloating the cement barge *Robert Koch*, which had wrecked off Oswego, New York, the previous December.

Following a stop at Kingston, Ontario, the hulk arrived at Sorel, Quebec, on July 27 in tow of the tugs *Daniel McAllister* and *Helen M. McAllister* before going to Contrecoeur, Quebec, during late August for dismantling by Gondel International. Leaving that port on October 16 in tow of the tug *Manic*, the partially dismantled vessel sat at Trois-Rivieres for the next four years until taken to Levis, Quebec, by the tug *Duga* on November 1, 1990, where the Davie Brothers shipyard completed the scrapping of the *Robert Koch*.

The last of the four bulk carriers sold by ULS International for scrapping earlier that year began its final journey on July 24 when the *Meldrum Bay* cleared Toronto in tow of the tugs *Glenevis*, *Glenside*, *Argue Martin*, and *Stormont*. Reported downbound in the Seaway three days later, the scrap tow arrived at Lauzon, where the 640-foot steamer remained until towed out by the Polish flagged tug *Jantar* on June 6, 1987 bound for scrapping at Lisbon, Portugal.

Launched by Midland Shipyards Ltd. at Midland, Ontario, on October 15, 1949 for Canada Steamship Lines as the *Coverdale*, this ship loaded its first cargo at Port Arthur, Ontario, on May 2 of the following year. Renamed *George Hindman* (4) with its sale to Hindman Transportation Co. Ltd. in 1973, this vessel operated in that fleet's trading patterns until sold to the Quebec & Ontario Transportation fleet in 1978. Given its final name before the beginning of the 1979 season, the *Meldrum Bay* loaded what proved to be its final cargo at Sarnia on December 18, 1983 before laying up at Toronto two days later. Passing into the ownership of Group Desgagnes in early 1984, this ship never operated for that company.

Having acquired the Nipigon Transport Ltd. fleet near the beginning of the year, Algoma Central Marine issued a press release on July 30 concerning its intent to purchase Carryore Ltd., the major shareholders of which included LTV Steel, M. A. Hanna Company, and the National Steel Corporation. With the sale of the *Menihek Lake* for scrapping the previous season, the fleet consisted only of the 715-foot bulk carrier *Carol Lake*.

A labor dispute involving the USX Corporation (formerly the United States Steel Corporation) and its 22,000 employees belonging to the United Steelworkers of America shut down the company's steel mills on August 1. With only four of its ore carriers in service due to weak demand, the work stoppage had an immediate impact upon the USS Great Lakes Fleet with the *Arthur M. Anderson*, *Cason J. Callaway*, *Edwin H. Gott*, and *Edgar B. Speer* laying up during the first week of August. Although the fleet's four active stone carriers were initially unaffected, the *Calcite II*, *John G. Munson* (2), *George A. Sloan*, and *Myron C. Taylor* all went to the wall in late September when negotiations failed to secure a new contract for the crews of those ships. Remaining idle throughout the balance of the year, the USX mills finally went back to work on February 1, 1987 when the union's membership approved a new four-year labor contract.

Decked out with a new coat of paint after being idle thus far in the season, Halco's *Maplecliffe Hall* was opened up for public tours at Montreal during early August. While inbound at Duluth on August 6, high winds nearly pushed CSL's *Murray Bay* (3) into the outbound thousand-footer *William J. De Lancey*. Although both ships avoided a collision by passing within 25 feet of one another near the outer entrance to the Duluth Ship Canal, the incident nonetheless prompted a Coast Guard investigation.

With no reasonable likelihood of their

Idle since the end of the 1983 season, the steamer *George M. Humphrey* (2) was sold for scrap in 1986. (Author's Collection)

return to service in the future, the National Steel Corporation sold the steamers *George M. Humphrey* (2) and *Paul H. Carnahan* to the Shiong Yek Steel Corporation for scrapping in Taiwan. Attesting to the good mechanical condition of these ships, both left the lakes under their own power. Operated by a crew made up of retired Hanna Mining Company sailors and executives, the *George M. Humphrey* (2) became the first of these bulk carriers to begin its final journey when it left Ecorse on August 13. Following a minor incident in the Welland Canal in which it struck an arrester cable at Lock 1, the 710-foot vessel arrived at Lauzon on August 16 to await the arrival of the *Carnahan* for a tandem ocean tow.

Built by the American Ship Building Company at Lorain in 1954, the *George M. Humphrey* (2) was the first vessel on the Great Lakes to feature a 75-foot beam. With a carrying capacity of 25,950 gross tons, this ship, along with several others built during the 1950s not converted into self-unloaders, became excess tonnage during the recession of the early 1980s. Operating under the management of the M. A. Hanna Company throughout its short career, this steamer laid up for the last time on December 31, 1983.

Untouched by Shearmet Recycling before that firm went out of business, ULS International acquired the former United States Steel bulk carrier *August Ziesing* for scrapping at Port Colborne. The 600-foot vessel left Thunder Bay on August 13 in tow of The Great Lakes Towing Company's tug *Ohio*, which handed it over to the Great Lakes Marine Contracting Ltd. tugs *Elmore M. Misner* and *Vac* off Long Point in Lake Erie four days later. Delivered to Port Colborne on August 18, the scrap yard wasted little time in going to work on the 68-year old steamer with its dismantling completed by mid-November.

While transiting the St. Clair River on the evening of August 20, the *Indiana Harbor* went aground when it lost steering near Marine City, Michigan. Lightering approximately 4,000 tons of coal into its fleet mate *St. Clair* (2) the following morning, the tugs *Barbara Ann*, *Nebraska*, and *Tug Malcolm* were able to refloat the thousand-foot vessel. Suffering no damage in the mishap, the *Indiana Harbor* proceeded to the nearby Detroit Edison St. Clair Power Plant Dock just north of Marine City to reload its lightered cargo.

Earlier that summer, the Rouge Steel Company sold its surplus bulk carriers *No. 266029* (ex-*William Clay Ford*) and *No. 265808* (ex-*Benson Ford* (2)) to the Erwin Robinson Company of Detroit for scrapping. On August 20, three Gaelic Tugboat Company tugs towed *No. 266029* from Ford basin on the Rouge River to the Detroit Marine Terminals Dock to have its pilothouse and chartroom removed for display at the Dossin Great Lakes Museum on Belle Isle before being moved to the Nicholson Terminal Slip at Ecorse on August 27. Joined by *No. 265808* the next day, both ships remained at that location until resold to Marine Salvage Ltd. later that autumn.

As it sailed northbound on Lake Michigan at 11:34 in the morning of August 20, the Yugoslav freighter *Jablanica* collided with the 30-foot fishing tug *Razel Brothers* seven miles off Whiskey Island at a position about 45 miles northwest of Charlevoix, Michigan. Taking place in good visibility and calm seas, the tug sank quickly in 50 feet of water with the loss of all three of its crewmembers. After U.S. Coast Guard investigators interviewed its crew at Sault Ste. Marie, Michigan, the 620-foot ocean vessel sailed for Duluth to take on a load of grain for Tunisia. Although the Charlevoix County prosecuting attorney charged the captain of the *Jablanica* with negligent homicide in early September, a Michigan judge later dismissed these criminal charges on November 20 of that same year.

Having remained at Toledo following its sale to Marine Salvage Ltd. the previous season, the *W. W. Holloway* arrived at Port Colborne on August 21 in tow of the tug *Salvage Monarch*. Leaving the 552-foot self-unloader at the West Street wharf, the *Salvage Monarch* towed the *Philip D. Block* out of Ramey's Bend the next day with the tugs *Glenevis* and *Stormont* assisting. Returning to Port Colborne after dropping off the former Inland Steel bulk carrier at Quebec City, the *Salvage Monarch* took the *Holloway* through the Welland Canal on August 30. Transiting the St. Lambert Lock near Montreal on September 1, the scrap tow arrived at Quebec City later that same day. The *W. W. Holloway* and *Philip D. Block* left that port on September 16 in tow of the tug *Jantar*, which delivered them to Recife, Brazil, on October 24 for dismantling.

Operated by the same crew that had taken the *George M. Humphrey* (2) on its last voyage as a powered vessel, the *Paul H. Carnahan* departed Ecorse on August 21. Following an uneventful passage through the Welland Canal and the St. Lawrence Seaway, the bulk carrier joined the *Humphrey* (2) at Lauzon three days later. Leaving in tow of the tug *Smit-Lloyd 109* on September 3, the two lake freighters arrived at Kaohsiung, Taiwan, for dismantling on December 10 following a three-month journey that took them halfway around the world.

Built as the T2-SE-A1 tanker *Honey Hill* by the Sun Shipbuilding & Dry Dock Company at Chester, Pennsylvania, in 1945, this vessel passed into the ownership of the Atlantic Refinery Company the following year. It operated for that firm as the *Atlantic Dealer* until taken out of service in 1958. Purchased by the Skar-Ore Steamship Corporation, a subsidiary of the M. A. Hanna Company, two years later, the American Ship Building Company converted this vessel into a 730-foot Great Lakes bulk carrier at its Lorain yard in a reconstruction involving the insertion of a 503-foot cargo section built by Schlieker-Werft at Hamburg, West Germany. Renamed *Paul H. Carnahan*, this steamer entered lakes service on October 15, 1961 when it cleared the shipyard bound to load iron ore at Superior, Wisconsin, for delivery to Cleveland. As one of two saltwater tanker conversions completed for the National Steel fleet (M. A. Hanna Company, mgr.) that year, the other being the nearly identical *Leon Falk, Jr.*, this ship last operated in 1985.

On August 22, Canadian Shipbuilding and Engineering Ltd. announced its merger with ULS International's Port Weller Dry Docks and the scheduled September 12 closure of Collingwood Shipyards. Citing the bleak outlook for future vessel construction in the Canadian fleet and the lack of a dry dock capable of handling large ships, the only remaining work at the historic yard at the time of this announcement was the sea trials of the Canadian Coast Guard icebreaker *Sir Wilfrid Laurier*.

The *Fred R. White, Jr.* made a rare voyage near the end of the month when it delivered stone to Washburn, Wisconsin, on August 26. Located on Chequamegon Bay in western Lake Superior, this arrival reportedly marked the first visit by a ship to that community since the 1979 season.

On September 1, Texaco Canada Inc. entered into a long-term lease agreement with Societe Sofati-Soconav concerning the operation of the tankers *Texaco Brave* (2) and *Texaco Chief* (2). Given new stack markings, both ships sailed under their original names until early November when the *Texaco Brave* (2) and *Texaco Chief* (2) became *Le Brave* and *A. G. Farquharson* respectively.

Towed out of Port McNicoll, Ontario, on September 2 by the tug *Glenside*, the retired Misener Shipping Ltd. steamer *John E. F. Misener* passed downbound at Port Huron three days later with the *Tug Malcolm* assisting. Headed for scrapping overseas after nearly four years of idleness, it transited the Welland Canal on September 8 in tow of the tugs *Glenside*, *Glenevis*, and *Stormont*. Making slow progress, the scrap tow continued eastward across Lake Ontario and downbound through the Seaway before finally arriving at Quebec City on September 18 after spending two days anchored for weather off Prescott, Ontario.

Built at St. Catharines in 1951 as the *Scott Misener* (2), this 654-foot vessel was both the largest lake carrier ever built in Canada up to that time and the first ship constructed by Port Weller Dry Docks Ltd. Renamed *John E. F. Misener* in 1954 to free up its original name for a larger newly commissioned fleet mate, this steamer worked steadily in grain and ore trades until laying up for the final time on December 15, 1982. At the time of its scrap sale, the 35-year old bulk carrier was not only the oldest vessel in the Misener fleet but also the smallest in terms of both size and carrying capacity.

Just as Canadian farmers were harvesting a record 52.4 million metric ton grain crop, 500 grain handlers walked off the job at the Saskatchewan Wheat Pool, the largest grain elevator operator at Thunder Bay, on September 3 after talks for a new contract broke down. In a show of solidarity, five other elevator companies locked out their 700 workers in a move that put an immediate halt to all grain shipments through the port.

The labor dispute at what was then Canada's largest grain port, along with a similar lockout of dockworkers at the Port of Quebec by the Maritime Employers Association, forced at least 30 Canadian vessels into layup by mid-September with that number continuing to grow daily as other ships finished their voyages.

As both the grain companies and the union representing the workers remained firm in their unwillingness to return to the bargaining table, grain from the prairies began moving east by rail to Montreal and ports on the St. Lawrence River to bypass the bottleneck at Thunder Bay. In addition to not being able to handle the volume normally carried by ship, however, this solution also increased the cost of transporting the grain to approximately $22 per metric ton compared to about $15 through the Seaway. In a desperate bid to resume shipments through the beleaguered port, a plan to load grain into vessels using equipment configured to handle coal and potash received serious consideration with Paterson's *Vandoc* (2) taking on a trial shipment using this method on September 30. With a tentative agreement hammered out on October 5 under the threat of federal back-to-work legislation, the union membership voted 57 percent in favor of the new contract four days later. As work began to clear up the 1.5 million metric ton backlog, there were 15 ships awaiting loading at Thunder Bay even as up to 30 others began heading to the port.

Clearing Toronto under its own power on September 9, the bulk carrier *Golden Hind* sailed to Quebec City in preparation for a tandem overseas scrap tow with the *John E. F. Misener*. Leaving on September 29 in tow of the ocean tug *Koral*, the two lake steamers arrived at Mamonal, Columbia, for dismantling on October 28.

Built by Collingwood Shipyards in 1952, the *Golden Hind* originally entered service for Imperial Oil Ltd. as the tanker *Imperial Woodbend* in carrying crude oil from Superior, Wisconsin, to Sarnia. Made redundant with the construction of a new pipeline, Mohawk Navigation Co. Ltd. purchased this vessel in 1954 and had it converted into a bulk carrier by E. B. McGee Ltd. at Port Colborne. Renamed *Golden Hind*, the 620-foot vessel entered service that summer in the grain trade. After Scott Misener Steamships Ltd. assumed the management of the Mohawk Navigation fleet in 1970, this ship operated for that concern until its sale to Trico Enterprises Ltd. (Quebec & Ontario Transportation Co. Ltd., mgr.) in 1973. Following the dissolution of that longstanding fleet ten years later, the *Golden Hind* passed into the ownership of Group Desgagnes in January 1984 for which it only made a few voyages during late 1985.

On September 12, tugs towed the *John Sherwin* (2) from its layup berth at Superior, Wisconsin, to the Cargill B1 Elevator at Duluth, where it loaded some 830,729 bushels of barley. Subsequently moved to the Cargill B2 Elevator three days later, the 806-foot bulk carrier, inactive since the 1981 season, held this government storage cargo until being unloaded over a four-day period beginning on February 22, 1988.

Taking a break from carrying raw materials into its owner's large steelmaking complex at Indiana Harbor, the Inland Steel steamer *Wilfred Sykes* paid a rare visit to the Detroit area on September 14 when it delivered a cargo of limestone to the Great Lakes Steel Dock on Zug Island.

While nearing the harbor entrance to Port Washington, Wisconsin, at 8:30 in the morning of September 15, a buildup of methane

The *Middletown* suffered a serious accident at Port Washington, Wisconsin, on September 15, 1986. (Photo by James Hoffman)

gas from a load of coal taken on at Conneaut, Ohio, exploded inside an electrical switch room aboard the steamer *Middletown*. Alerted to the accident by radio, the local fire and police departments along with the Ozaukee County Water Safety Patrol met the 730-foot self-unloader when it docked at the harbor minutes later. The blast and subsequent flash fire inflicted second and third degree burns to the vessel's chief engineer and assistant engineer, both whom were airlifted to the burn center at the St. Mary's Hospital in Milwaukee. Despite reports of considerable electrical damage, the *Middletown* began unloading at the Port Washington Power Plant late that evening before departing the following morning. Both of the critically burned men were to succumb to their injuries with the assistant engineer dying 16 days after the accident on October 1 and the chief engineer passing away over a year later on December 1, 1987.

Following a period of heavy rains, strong currents impeded shipping activity on the Saginaw River during mid-September with the *Louis R. Desmarais* and *Wolverine* (2) being trapped in the river for several days. On September 19, the *Charles E. Wilson* damaged a timber piling while passing through the I-75 drawbridge at Zilwaukee, Michigan, with this mishap followed by two similar incidents three days later involving the *Buffalo* (3) and *Wolverine* (2) that resulted in the destruction of three pilings. In the case of the *Buffalo* (3) accident, the cost to replace the pilings approached $150,000.

On September 21, the idle Canada Steamship Lines steamer *Nipigon Bay* suffered around $200,000 in smoke and water damage from a fire set by vandals in its forward cabins at Kingston. The Kingston Police Department subsequently apprehended two juveniles on October 16 and charged them with arson in connection with the blaze.

The rain-swollen Saginaw River claimed

another victim on September 24 when strong currents wedged the *Joseph H. Frantz* inside the open span of the Independence Bridge at Bay City, Michigan, as it attempted to pass upbound for the Wirt Stone Dock. Freed 36 hours later, the 61-year old self-unloader came away from the incident relatively unscathed. Contrary to initial reports, however, the drawbridge suffered heavy damage that led to the city filing a $1.5 million lawsuit against the Oglebay Norton Company the following year.

Blustery weather caused trouble at Duluth once again when the museum ship *William A. Irvin* broke free of its temporary mooring on September 26 in winds reaching 55 mph. Occurring just three months after first opening to the public, the 610-foot vessel dragged its anchor but suffered no damage. A few weeks later, on October 13, tugs moved the *Irvin* to a permanent home in the Minnesota Slip.

A pair of accidents involving three saltwater vessels took place on September 27, one of which occurred when the Spanish tanker *Bailen* scraped against Bridge 19 near Lock 8 in the Welland Canal. Elsewhere that same day, the downbound Yugoslavian bulker *Cvijeta Zuzoric* and the upbound *Federal Polaris* came together in the St. Clair River abreast St. Clair, Michigan. Both vessels were permitted to continue their respective voyages with the *Zuzoric* receiving a survey upon its arrival at Montreal on October 1 before clearing four days later with temporary patching. Continuing to Chicago, the *Federal Polaris* later spent most of October at Toledo undergoing bow repairs.

On September 30, the recently commissioned Canadian Coast Guard buoy tender *Caribou Isle* struck a rock near Blind River, Ontario, while searching for a missing person in Lake Huron's North Channel about 75 miles southeast of Sault Ste. Marie, Ontario. Taking on water through three hull punctures, the 75-foot tender was beached on Clara Island to prevent its sinking. Also in the area participating in the search, the icebreaker *Samuel Risley* arrived to render aid with its crew helping to install temporary patching before both vessels sailed for Parry Sound, Ontario. Following repairs, the *Caribou Isle* returned to its duty station at the Canadian Soo on November 8.

The settlement of the Thunder Bay grain handlers strike in early October not only brought out the ships sent into temporary layup but also the reactivation of nearly every member of the Canadian fleet during the late months of the year in a push to move the backlog of grain before the onset of winter halted navigation. This included six of the seven gearless bulkers in the Halco fleet, none of which had yet operated during the current season, with only the *Lawrencecliffe Hall* (2) not fitting out. In addition, Algoma Central's recently acquired *Carol Lake* and ULS International's *Canadian Hunter* returned to service for the first time in two years. Towed out of Toronto on October 13 for a dry dock survey at Port Weller Dry Docks after nearly five years of idleness, the *Seaway Queen* experienced boiler problems in the Welland Canal exactly one week later that necessitated a tow back the shipyard. With repairs completed quickly, the 717-foot steamer reentered the grain trade when it cleared St. Catharines for Thunder Bay on October 22.

The *Jean Parisien* encountered a minor mishap on October 10 when it brushed against a buoy in the East Outer Channel leading to the mouth of the Detroit River. Proceeding to the Ojibway Anchorage for an inspection, the self-unloader resumed its upbound voyage later in the day without any reported

The *Sewell Avery* became a dock face at Sault Ste. Marie, Ontario. (Author's Collection)

damage.

During the month of October, USS Great Lakes Fleet sold the bulk carrier *Sewell Avery* to A. B. McLean Ltd. for use as a dock facing at Sault Ste. Marie, Ontario. Laid up at Superior, Wisconsin, since September 3, 1981, the 620-foot vessel remained at the Twin Ports until towed across Lake Superior for use in this role the following spring. This steamer was one of three "Maritime" class vessels acquired by the Pittsburgh Steamship Company during the Second World War, the others being the *George A. Sloan* and *Robert C. Stanley*. Largely due to its conversion to a self-unloader in 1967, the *Sloan* remains active as of the 2019 season as the *Mississagi*.

On October 18, the *Murray Bay* (3) narrowly avoided hitting Bridge 11 in the Welland Canal when the vertical lift span failed to rise in time for its downbound passage. Dropping both anchors and with its engine at full astern, the 730-foot straight decker came to a stop crosswise in the channel about 30 feet from the bridge. Another CSL vessel ran into trouble that same day, when the *Manitoulin* (5) experienced engine problems and went aground while downbound on the St. Lawrence River. After the *P. S. Barge No. 1* lightered 2,300 tons of its wheat cargo, a trio of tugs refloated the big self-unloader two days later. Sailing to Montreal under its own power, the 20-year old ship cleared that port for Sept-Iles, Quebec, on October 23.

Making its first trip since receiving extensive repairs at Port Arthur Shipbuilding following a grounding at Stoneport the previous autumn, the *Stadacona* (3) departed Thunder Bay on October 21 with grain for Midland. That same day, the *Maplecliffe Hall* experienced mechanical difficulties shortly after departing Montreal that required a return to port for adjustments before sailing for Thunder Bay on October 25.

During the summer of 1986, the St. Lawrence Cement Company had acquired the 335-foot Saudi Arabian cement-carrying barge *Al Sayb-7* to replace the barge *Robert Koch* lost in a grounding accident at Oswego the previous December. To handle the barge in its new freshwater duties, Wakeham & Sons Ltd. purchased the 5,000 horsepower tug *Al Battal* from Arabian Bulk Trade Ltd., which it renamed *Petite Forte*. Given the name *Clarkson Carrier* while still in the Indian Ocean, the barge left the Middle East on September 11 in tow of the *Petite Forte*. Arriving at Montreal on October 22, the pair entered service between Clarkson, Ontario, and Oswego during late November.

Conducting a voyage prompted by the closure of Collingwood Shipyards, the ferry *Chi-Cheemaun* made an unusual passage through the Soo Locks on October 20 while bound for a 5-year survey at Thunder Bay. Two days later, the Panamanian freighter *Cervinia* suffered no damage when it struck a wall at the Snell Lock while downbound in the Seaway to load scrap at Montreal.

Following two years of layup at Superior, Wisconsin, due to economic conditions, Columbia Transportation's *Armco* reentered service when it left Fraser Shipyards to load iron ore at Duluth before sailing for Toledo on October 23.

A broken fuel line started a fire aboard Interlake Steamship's *James R. Barker* at 8:30 in the evening of October 27 while that vessel was upbound on lower Lake Huron for Escanaba. After evacuating the engine room, the crew extinguished the blaze with the ship's carbon dioxide (CO_2) fire fighting system. Maneuvering out of the shipping channel, the thousand-footer went to anchor approximately two miles north of Port Huron. Although there were no injuries, the incident left the *Barker* without engine power. Two days later, the *William J. De Lancey* arrived to tow its disabled fleet mate in a side-by-side arrangement to Bay Shipbuilding for repairs, where they arrived on November 2.

Since the beginning of the 1980s, Halco Inc. had experienced an extended period of financial hardship that culminated with its major creditor, the Royal Bank of Canada, seizing full control of the company in early 1986. On October 31, Navican Management Inc. of Montreal entered into an agreement to operate the fleet's eight bulk carriers pending their eventual sale. Concurrently, the bank sold Halco's six tankers to the newly formed Enerchem Transport Inc., also of Montreal. Following the transfer of ownership, Enerchem renamed the tankers in the following manner: *Chemical Transport* to *Enerchem Fusion*, *Doan Transport* to *Enerchem Catalyst*, *Gaspe Transport* to *Enerchem Avance*, *Industrial Transport* to *Enerchem Refiner*, *Island Transport* (2) to *Enerchem Laker*, and *James Transport* to *Enerchem Travailleur*.

Improperly secured with just three lines, the retired United States Steel steamer *B. F. Affleck* broke free from the Azcon Corporation scrap dock at Duluth during the early morning hours of October 31. In a near repeat of the unexpected foray by the *Joshua Hatfield* in June, winds reaching 30 mph pushed the 604-foot ship across the harbor until grounding a short distance from the U.S. Coast Guard Station on Minnesota Point. Unlike the previous instance involving the *Hatfield*, however, this refloating operation proved to be a much simpler affair with the two Great Lakes Towing Company tugs returning the *Affleck* to its berth later that same morning.

A few months prior to this incident, Azcon

The fire damaged *James R. Barker* (left) being towed to Sturgeon Bay, Wisconsin, by its slightly longer fleet mate *William J. De Lancey*. (Author's Collection)

had sold the *B. F. Affleck* to Port Colborne Marine Terminals Inc. for scrapping in Canada. On November 3, the tug *Thunder Cape* arrived at Duluth to retrieve the 59-year old lake freighter. Delayed by unfavorable weather conditions, the scrap tow cleared port three days later. Everything proceeded normally until six o'clock in the evening of November 8 when the *Thunder Cape* lost engine power while caught in 60 mph winds and 20-foot seas off the Keweenaw Peninsula. Left at the mercy of the waves, the crew of the tug had little choice but to cut the bulk carrier loose.

Upon receiving distress calls from the disabled tug, the U.S. Coast Guard's Station Portage at Hancock, Michigan, dispatched a 44-foot motor lifeboat to the scene. The icebreaker *Mackinaw*, which was on Lake Superior conducting a training mission, also took part in the rescue operation. Fearing the *B. F. Affleck* would capsize in the turbulent seas, the Coast Guard removed the two men who had been trying to anchor the wildly rolling freighter. After putting a line aboard, the tanker *Eastern Shell* (2) towed the *Thunder Cape* to Thunder Bay. Meanwhile, the Purvis Marine tug *Avenger IV* managed to take the *Affleck* in tow with the pair escorted across Lake Superior by the *Mackinaw* before arriving at Sault Ste. Marie, Ontario, on the morning of November 11.

Resuming its tow of the *B. F. Affleck* on November 21 following the completion of engine repairs, the *Thunder Cape* delivered the retired vessel to Port Colborne four days later without further incident. Banished to a mooring in a section of the old Welland

Canal for nearly a year, the *Thunder Cape* and *Michael D. Misner* moved the classic lake steamer to the scrap berth on October 17, 1987 to be broken up.

With much of its dredging requirements delegated to commercial contractors, the U.S. Army Corps of Engineers transferred the hopper dredges *Hains* and *Hoffman* to the U.S. Navy for use as naval gunnery targets. Having been laid up for four years, the *Hains* and *Hoffman* cleared Cleveland on November 4 in tow of The Great Lakes Towing Company tugs *Ohio* and *Superior* respectively. Transiting the Welland Canal the next day, the scrap tows reached Ogdensburg, New York, on November 7. Leaving the *Hoffman* behind, the *Ohio* and *Superior* delivered the *Hains* to Quebec City on November 9. Returning to Ogdensburg, the same tugs made a repeat trip down the Seaway with the *Hoffman*. Bound for Norfolk, Virginia, the rescue and salvage vessel USS *Grasp* towed both dredges out of Quebec City on November 17.

Sold for scrapping overseas after serving as a storage barge at Chicago for the past five years, the bulk carrier *Peter A. B. Widener* passed downbound in the Welland Canal on November 7 in tow of the tugs *Glenada* and *Tusker*. Arriving at Lauzon 11 days later, the 601-foot vessel remained there until leaving on July 9, 1987 behind the ocean tug *Jantar*. Making a successful crossing of the Atlantic, it reached Lisbon, Portugal, the following month for demolition.

Having reentered service just ten days earlier after sitting idle at Hamilton for two seasons, the *Scott Misener* (3) went aground in the St. Lawrence River on November 11 after losing its way in a blinding snow squall near Cornwall, Ontario. With the shipping channel blocked, five tugs converged on the scene to refloat the 684-foot vessel. In addition to the *Cathy McAllister* sent from Montreal, this small flotilla also included the tugs *Ohio* and *Superior* brought over from Ogdensburg while preparing to take the dredge *Hoffman* to Quebec City and the tugs *Glenada* and *Tusker* that were in the process of towing the *Peter A. B. Widener* to Lauzon. This effort proved successful with the bulk carrier coming off the bottom during the early hours of the following morning apparently undamaged.

Sold to Basic Marine Inc. after becoming surplus in the Inland Steel fleet, the 621-foot steamer *L. E. Block* arrived at Escanaba on November 11 in tow of the tugs *Daryl C. Hannah* and *Carla Anne Selvick*. Built by the American Ship Building Company at Lorain in 1927, the bulk carrier had been laid up at Milwaukee since October 30, 1981.

The *William J. De Lancey* suffered a minor mishap at Superior, Wisconsin, on November 17 when it went aground while loading coal at the Superior Midwest Energy Terminal. Discovered as the ship attempted to depart, a plan was soon developed to off-load a portion of its cargo into fleet mate *Charles M. Beeghly* that was in the Twin Ports unloading stone. Before this became necessary, however, the water level in the harbor rose a few inches thus allowing the 1013-foot vessel to float off the bottom and begin its voyage.

While tied up on the lower side of the St. Lambert Lock on November 19, Halco's *Frankcliffe Hall* (2) suffered bow damage when struck by the downbound saltwater bulker *Solta* in an accident that halted traffic in the Seaway's South Shore Canal for about six hours. An unusually unlucky fleet, another Halco vessel ran into trouble during November when the *Beavercliffe Hall* spent six days tied up at Thunder Bay undergoing repairs following an onboard fire.

It took five tugs to refloat the *Scott Misener* (3) following a grounding in the St. Lawrence River.
(Author's Collection)

The Coastal Canada Marine tanker *Coastal Canada* became the target of a labor dispute involving members of the Seafarers International Union (S.I.U.) on November 24 when part of its crew walked off the ship at Nanticoke, Ontario. Going into layup at Point Edward, Ontario, a few days later, the union picketed the steam-powered vessel until the signing of a three-year contract on December 6.

The saltwater bulker *Nata* sustained some bunker tank damage on November 25 when it struck an approach wall at the Iroquois Lock. Following a stop at Montreal, it sailed for an Indian port four days later.

Having returned to the lakes after delivering the *Peter A. B. Widener* to Lauzon, the tugs *Glenada* and *Tusker* towed *No. 265808* (ex -*Benson Ford* (2)) out of Ecorse on November 28 following that vessel's resale to Marine Salvage Ltd. of Port Colborne. Arriving at Ramey's Bend two days later, the former Ford Motor Company steamer left the scrap yard in late December when the tugs *Thunder Cape* and *Glenbrook* towed it to Thorold, Ontario, to take on a load of salt cake for storage over the winter.

Built by the Defoe Shipbuilding Company at Bay City in 1953 as the *Richard M. Marshall*, this ship served as flagship of the Great Lakes Steamship Company until that fleet ceased operation in 1957. Purchased by the Northwestern Mutual Life Insurance Company, it then moved into the Wilson Marine Transit Company under a charter agreement as the *Joseph S. Wood*. With a carrying capacity of 18,400 gross tons, however, the 644-foot steamer proved much too large for the needs of the Wilson fleet. As such, much of this charter was characterized by periods of extended idleness. This resulted in its sale to the Ford Motor Company on

153

February 14, 1966. Renamed *John Dykstra* and put to work delivering raw materials to the automaker's steel mill on the Rouge River in Dearborn, it later became *Benson Ford* (2) in 1982. The final years of its operation already described in the preceding chapters of this book, this bulk carrier laid up for the last time on December 16, 1984.

During the autumn of 1986, a corporate name change took place within the Canadian fleet when the Montreal based tanker operator Societe Sofati-Soconav became Socanav Inc. On November 30, that fleet's *L. Rochette* experienced an engine failure while on a voyage from Pointe Noire, Quebec, to Halifax, Nova Scotia. Sent to assist, the tug *Point Valiant* towed the disabled tanker into Halifax for repairs.

High winds on Lake Erie pushed the *Middletown* against a breakwater at Conneaut on December 3. Pulled free from its predicament by the tugs *Idaho* and *Minnesota*, the 730-foot self-unloader came away from the episode undamaged. The next day, the *American Republic* suffered a 5-foot gash in its starboard hull about 15 feet above the waterline when the same blustery conditions blew the motor vessel into a breakwater while entering Lorain.

On the morning of December 6, the CSL bulk carrier *Rimouski* suffered significant starboard bow damage when it rammed a wall while attempting to dock at the Prescott grain elevator located on the St. Lawrence River. Once unloaded, it received temporary repairs before sailing to Thunder Bay for the replacement of a 20' x 17' section of its shell plating and any affected internal structural members over the winter layup.

During early October, the Bethlehem Steel Corporation submitted a request to the U.S. Maritime Administration to sell the *Arthur B. Homer* to Port Colborne Marine Terminals Inc. for dismantling. With this approval granted, the 26-year old steamer left its long-term layup dock at Erie, Pennsylvania, on December 6 in tow of the tugs *Atomic*, *Elmore M. Misner*, and *Thunder Cape*. The *Homer* spent two days at anchor off Port Colborne due to high winds before arriving at the scrap dock on December 9. Beginning late the following month, work on breaking up the lake carrier continued until mid-October 1987.

Launched by the Great Lakes Engineering Works at River Rouge on November 7, 1959, the *Arthur B. Homer* began its maiden voyage when it sailed from Detroit on April 20, 1960 to load iron ore at Taconite Harbor, Minnesota. As the last ship built by that yard and one of the few U.S. lake freighters built from the keel up with a 730-foot length, this vessel had a maximum carrying capacity of 26,850 gross tons. Becoming Bethlehem's flagship, it remained the largest ship in that fleet until surpassed by the 1,000-foot *Stewart J. Cort* in 1972. Over the 1975-76 winter layup, Fraser Shipyards lengthened the *Homer* to 826' with the insertion of a 96-foot midsection that increased its carrying capacity to 32,150 gross tons. Unfortunately, this vessel was not converted to a self-unloader during this reconstruction. Consequently, it quickly became obsolete as the domestic ore trade increased its reliance on self-unloading carriers even as tonnages decreased in direct proportion to the significant downsizing of the steel industry during the early 1980s. No longer viable in the changing economic climate, this steamer entered an indefinite layup at Erie, Pennsylvania, on October 4, 1980.

Another 1950s built U.S. flagged bulk carrier also began its final voyage on December 6 when *No. 266029* (ex-*William Clay Ford*) left Ecorse in tow of the tugs

Glenada and *Tusker* bound for scrapping at Port Maitland, Ontario. Surviving a bout with heavy weather on Lake Erie, the scrap tow arrived at that port two days later, where scrapping of the former Ford Motor Company flagship took place the following year.

Built by the Great Lakes Engineering Works at River Rouge in 1953, this ship was the last unit of an eight-member class constructed by both that shipbuilder and the American Ship Building Company between 1952 and 1953 that all shared identical 647' x 70' x 36' dimensions. In the order of their entry into service, the other ships were *Philip R. Clarke*, *Edward B. Greene*, *Arthur M. Anderson*, *Cason J. Callaway*, *J. L. Mauthe*, *Reserve*, and *Armco*. In 1979, Fraser Shipyards lengthened the *William Clay Ford* to 767' with the insertion of a 120-foot mid-section at Superior, Wisconsin. This steamer remained active until the Rouge Steel Company purchased the *Edward B. Greene* and *Walter A. Sterling* from the Cleveland-Cliffs fleet in late 1984. Its short career at an end, the bulk carrier laid up for that last time at Dearborn on December 14, 1984.

Downbound with grain, the *Maplecliffe Hall* mangled some hull plating when it smacked into the approach wall at the Upper Beauharnois Lock in the St. Lawrence Seaway on December 8. Although requiring temporary patching, the 730-foot bulk carrier remained in operation throughout the rest of the season with Navican deferring permanent repairs until the upcoming winter layup.

Sailing in hazy conditions while downboud on the St. Lawrence River on the afternoon of December 8, the Polish bulker *Ziemia Olsztynska* suffered bow damage in a grounding on Hinckley Flats Shoal about three miles east of Cape Vincent, New York. Loaded with grain from Duluth and headed

A late season accident on the St. Lawrence Seaway left the bulk carrier *Maplecliffe Hall* with hull damage.
(Photo by Harold Fricke)

to Trois-Rivieres for topping off at the time of the mishap, the ocean carrier required lightering by the barge *Mapleheath* before the tugs *Cathy McAllister* and *Daniel McAllister* pulled it free three days later.

Arriving at Montreal on December 9, the Finnish flagged tanker *Kiisla* passed upbound through the Welland Canal three days later en route for its second winter of operating on the lakes.

Just two days after the *Maplecliffe Hall* mishap, the downbound Indian freighter *Jalagodavari* suffered some hull damage on December 10 when it also struck an approach wall at the Upper Beauharnois Lock. Interestingly, this incident came just one year after this ship caused a major traffic stoppage in the St. Lawrence Seaway when it rammed the St. Louis de Gonzague Bridge in the Beauharnois Canal on November 29, 1985. This latest mishap proved far less serious in nature, however, with the ocean vessel continuing to Montreal for temporary repairs.

Two accidents occurred in the Welland Canal on December 11, the first being a minor collision involving the saltwater vessels *Project Americas* and *World Palm* between Locks 2 and 3. A more serious episode took place aboard Halco's *Cartiercliffe Hall* that same day when a broken fuel line started a fire in the bulker's generator room shortly after exiting Lock 7 while downbound with grain. Although the Thorold Fire Department quickly brought the blaze under control, the 730-foot bulker remained tied up below the lock until sailing for Montreal two days later following the installation of a portable generator.

On the evening of December 12, the *Algosoo* (2) went aground near the east pier at Port Weller after losing engine power while attempting to enter the Welland Canal from Lake Ontario. Refloated the following morning by tugs *Glenevis* and *Stormont*, the 730-foot self-unloader had just returned to service two months earlier following extensive repairs from its fire in early March. Experiencing some flooding in the grounding, the Algoma Central vessel paid a subsequent visit to Port Weller Dry Docks.

Retired at Sarnia on December 13 during a ceremony organized by Imperial Oil Limited following its sale to Provmar Fuels Inc., the tanker *Imperial Sarnia* passed downbound in the Welland Canal the next day bound for Hamilton. Renamed *Provmar Terminal II*, the 408-foot vessel served as a fuel storage barge at that port until sold for scrapping at Port Colborne in 2012.

On December 16, ULS International had the *Canadian Ambassador* placed into Vanuatu registry and renamed *Ambassador* for operation by that company's Mar-Bulk Shipping Ltd. ocean subsidiary. Receiving new stack markings and a foreign crew, the 730-foot vessel cleared Sorel four days later for Savannah, Georgia.

One last incident took place just before the end of the season when a small fire broke out in the conveyor system aboard CSL's *Nanticoke* at Port Colborne on December 21. Quickly extinguished by its crew, the 6-year old self-unloader suffered no significant damage.

Commercial activity on the Welland Canal wound down for the season when the *Quebecois* made the final upbound transit on December 24 and the *Maplecliffe Hall* passed downbound the following day. The actual closure of the canal took place on December 26 when the Canadian Coast Guard icebreaker *Griffon* cleared for Midland. Continuing downbound, the *Maplecliffe Hall* closed the St. Lawrence Seaway on December 27.

The upbound passage of the crane vessel

Yankcanuck (2) through the Soo Locks on December 30 heralded the end of the shipping season on the upper lakes. Following the transit of a Canadian flagged tug, the locks closed the following day.

Due to the late season labor strife at Quebec City, the Halco bulkers *Beavercliffe Hall*, *Maplecliffe Hall*, and *Steelcliffe Hall* remained active in carrying grain from that port to Baie Comeau, Quebec, and Port Cartier, Quebec, until the early days of the following year. Upon the completion of these movements, the *Beavercliffe Hall* and *Maplecliffe Hall* went into winter layup at Montreal on January 8, 1987 with the *Steelcliffe Hall* leaving Quebec City the next day to join its fleet mates.

For the second year in a row, high water levels played a key role in a series of new cargo records. This included the *Lewis Wilson Foy* of the Bethlehem Steel fleet loading a 72,351 gross ton cargo of taconite at Escanaba for delivery to Indiana Harbor and American Steamship's *Indiana Harbor* carrying a 64,390 gross ton cargo of the same commodity through the Soo Locks. Meanwhile, the *Paterson* (2) established a new high point in the movement of iron ore through the St. Lawrence Seaway with a 28,502 gross ton payload. The western coal trade reached a new milestone when the *Columbia Star* carried a 70,706 net ton cargo from Superior, Wisconsin, to the Detroit Edison Company at St. Clair. In addition to its iron ore record, the *Indiana Harbor* also transported a record-setting 55,047 net tons of upbound coal from Toledo to Marquette. Proving the province of Canadian carriers, new records in the grain trade were represented by the *Prairie Harvest* taking on 1,241,082 bushels of barley and the *Canadian Navigator* establishing a new benchmark in the movement of mixed grain by carrying 854,699 bushels of barley and 183,051 bushels of wheat on a single voyage.

Chapter Eight
The 1987 Shipping Season

Although the annual parade of ships to the breakers continued to decline after reaching its peak for the decade in 1985, scrap sales nonetheless remained strong during the 1987 season with U.S. operators selling a dozen units for dismantling while their Canadian counterparts disposed of only two vessels. In addition, two former Cleveland-Cliffs steamers finally went to the breakers after legal entanglements delayed their voyages to the scrap yard for two years while another U.S. lake carrier went to the torch following several years in a non-transportation role.

A minor mishap took place barely two weeks into the year when a heating unit ignited some wood planking aboard Columbia Transportation's *Columbia Star* on January 11 while that vessel was in its winter quarters at Sturgeon Bay, Wisconsin. Causing no injuries, the fire inflicted only superficial damage to the thousand-footer.

Sold to Corostel Trading Ltd. of Montreal, Quebec, a period of exceptionally mild weather permitted an unusual winter scrap tow when the tugs *Glenada* and *Tusker* towed the *Clarence B. Randall* (2) out of Milwaukee, Wisconsin, on January 16. Resold to M&M Steel, the tugs delivered the 552-foot vessel to that firm's scrap yard at Windsor, Ontario, three days later for dismantling. Built by the American Ship Building Company at Cleveland, Ohio, in 1907, this ship had left the active lake fleet in 1976 upon its retirement by the Inland Steel Company. During its latter years, it had operated primarily in the movement of raw materials between the steelmaker's docks at Indiana Harbor, Indiana.

As mentioned in the previous chapter, James R. Barker resigned as chairman of Moore McCormack Resources Inc. following his acquisition of the Interlake Steamship Company in mid-January. The most obvious sign of this ownership change was the subsequent removal of the Pickands Mather & Co. logos from the bows of the fleet's ten vessels.

Endeavoring to downsize its pool of idle units, USS Great Lakes Fleet placed six vessels up for sale during February. This included the "Super" class bulk carriers *Benjamin F. Fairless*, *A. H. Ferbert* (2), *Irving S. Olds*, and *Enders M. Voorhees* along with the self-unloaders *T. W. Robinson* and *Rogers City*. With the exception of the *Benjamin F. Fairless* and *T. W. Robinson*, which last operated during the 1982 season, all of these ships had been inactive since 1981.

Faced with tightening market conditions in the Great Lakes/St. Lawrence Seaway petroleum trade, Shell Canadian Tankers Ltd. decided to split up its fleet by disposing of its last three large tankers while retaining three other units engaged in bunkering duties. To this end, it sold the motor vessels *Eastern Shell* (2), *Lakeshell* (3), and *Northern Shell* to Socanav Inc. during early 1987 while also entering into an agreement with the tanker operator to supply its bulk transportation needs for a 10-year period beginning on April 1.

During this same timeframe, another transaction took place within Canadian tanker fleet when Shediac Bulk Shipping Ltd. sold the *Seaway Trader* for off-lakes use. Renamed *Patricia II*, the 39-year old tanker entered service in the Gulf of Mexico later that spring.

Other than the ongoing conversion of the tanker *Amoco Indiana* to a cement-carrying barge for Medusa Cement at Bay Shipbuilding, the only other noteworthy project contracted to a U.S. shipyard outside of the usual general winter maintenance work involved the installation of a 1,000 horsepower stern thruster into the *Cason J. Callaway* by Fraser Shipyards at Superior, Wisconsin. Moved out of the dry dock on May 6, the 767-foot self-unloader remained idle until loading its first cargo of the season on July 12.

Preseason activity in the Canadian flagged fleet included the charter of Halco's *Frankcliffe Hall* (2) to Canada Steamship Lines (CSL). Remaining in Halco colors but flying the CSL fleet flag, the self-unloader spent part of the upcoming season operating on a sub-charter to ULS International. Continuing the process of renaming the motor vessels it acquired with the purchase of the Quebec & Ontario Transportation Company three years earlier, Group Desgagnes (Desgagnes Transport Inc.) renamed the 349-foot bulk carrier *Franquelin* (2) to *Eva Desgagnes* while that vessel was wintering at Toronto, Ontario.

Having purchased the Carryore Ltd. and

The *Enders M. Voorhees* was one of six freighters Great Lakes Fleet Inc. placed up for sale in early 1987.
(Author's Collection)

Nipigon Transport Ltd. fleets the previous season, Algoma Central Marine instituted a mass renaming of these recent acquisitions during the month of March in the following manner: *Carol Lake* to *Algocape*; *Lake Manitoba* to *Algomarine*; *Lake Nipigon* to *Algonorth*; and *Lake Wabush* to *Capt. Henry Jackman*. At the same time, the shipping company also renamed the bulk carriers *A. S. Glossbrenner* and *V. W. Scully* to *Algogulf* and *Algosound* respectively, both of which it had acquired from Labrador Steamship Company Ltd. in 1971.

A combination of diminishing stockpiles at Michigan steel mills and a mild winter allowed an early start to the shipping season when the *American Mariner* departed Toledo, Ohio, on March 2 to deliver its storage cargo of iron ore to the McLouth Steel Corporation at Trenton, Michigan. Continuing its early season activities on the lower lakes, the 730-foot self-unloader went on to open Sandusky, Ohio, on March 16 and later Calcite, Michigan, and Cedarville, Michigan, by taking on a split load at those stone two ports on March 23.

On March 3, voters at Muskegon, Michigan, turned down a proposed property tax increase to fund the operation of the car ferry *Viking* (2) in carrying automobile and passenger traffic between that city and Milwaukee during the summer months. With $9 million of the project's estimated $15.5 million cost already secured through state and local government funding, the rejection of the $6.5 million proposal effectively ended any hope of the 360-foot vessel returning to service in the Lake Michigan tourist trade.

During early March, the six former Huron Cement boats passed into the ownership of Inland Lakes Transportation Inc. of Alpena, Michigan, for operation by another newly created firm, Inland Lakes Management Inc. While retaining the same general Huron Cement fleet color scheme following this transition, the cement carriers had large red rectangular logos trimmed in black placed on each side of their bows that contained the initials "LIT" painted in white of which the letter "I" was larger than the two adjoining letters.

Anticipating a strong start in the movement of grain from Lake Superior to ports on the St. Lawrence River, the Halco bulk carrier *Lawrencecliffe Hall* (2) was dry-docked for a survey at the MIL Vickers Shipyard in Montreal on March 4. Laid up at that port since January 7, 1986, the 730-foot bulk carrier was the only unit in that fleet not to see service during the previous shipping season.

Beginning its earliest season since first entering service in 1974, the railcar ferry *Incan Superior* sailed from Thunder Bay, Ontario, on March 10 bound for Superior, Wisconsin. Completing its familiar journey across western Lake Superior, the 382-foot motor vessel opened the navigation season at the Twin Ports the following day.

No stranger to the challenges of early season navigation, the steamer *Medusa Challenger* left Milwaukee on March 12 with cement for delivery to Chicago, Illinois. The cement trade on Lake Ontario began one week later with the *Stephen B. Roman* opening Toronto on March 20 and the *English River* doing likewise at Hamilton, Ontario, the next day.

Its intended departure from Ecorse, Michigan, delayed due to ice conditions on the St. Clair River, the *George A. Stinson* made the first commercial passage through the Soo Locks when it locked upbound on March 23 to load ore at Superior, Wisconsin. That same day, the *John B. Aird* opened the season at Marquette, Michigan, when it loaded

21,825 tons of taconite for the Algoma Steel mill at Sault Ste. Marie, Ontario.

After spending an uncommon winter layup at Duluth, Minnesota, Misener Shipping's *John A. France* (2) sailed for Thunder Bay on March 28 after discharging a storage cargo of cement. At the latter port two days later, the *Algocen* (2) crashed into the United Grain Growers M Elevator after ice clogged its bow thruster. Leaving the dock with minor damage, the 730-foot bulk carrier came away from the mishap with a bent stem and a rip in its bow plating above the waterline that prompted a visit to Port Arthur Shipbuilding for repairs.

Following an unseasonably warm winter, a strong spring snowstorm deposited 16 inches of snow at Cleveland on March 31 while also blanketing much of central and southern Ontario with heavy snowfall amounts. At Hamilton, a thick layer of snow prevented the Burlington Canal Lift Bridge from rising thereby trapping a pair of ships inside the port while also preventing two others in Lake Ontario from entering until being cleared.

The St. Lawrence Seaway opened on March 31 when Pioneer Shipping's *Saskatchewan Pioneer* passed through the St. Lambert Lock with iron ore from Pointe Noire, Quebec, for Indiana Harbor. Just one day later, the Welland Canal recorded its first transits of the season with CSL's *Richelieu* (3) passing upbound and ULS International's *Canadian Century* downbound.

Preparing to conduct a very uncommon voyage, the motor vessel *Buffalo* (3) arrived at Huron, Ohio, on April 1 to load a cargo of grain for delivery to the Canada Starch plant at Port Colborne, Ontario. The next day, the U.S. Coast Guard's buoy tender *Mesquite* ripped a 3-foot hole in its hull and spilled a small amount of diesel oil when it brushed against a breakwater in Lake Charlevoix during a snowstorm.

After having its operations curtailed midway through the previous season by the USX steel strike, USS Great Lakes Fleet began putting its ships back to work. The *John G. Munson* (2) was one of these early departures when it left Fraser Shipyards on April 3 to load ore at Duluth for Gary, Indiana. On the other side of the border, a strong demand in the grain trade resulted in a large percentage of the Canadian fleet fitting out for a busy spring, including P. & H. Shipping's classic steamers *Birchglen* and *Oakglen*.

The *Algolake* experienced propulsion problems on April 4 while transiting the Straits of Mackinac with coal for Sault Ste. Marie, Ontario. Towed to De Tour, Michigan, by the tug *Avenger IV* for repairs, the self-unloader proceeded up the St. Marys River the following day to deliver its cargo.

While in tow of the tug *Walter R.* on Lake Michigan off Buffington Harbor, Indiana, at 12:15 a.m. on April 5, a barge owned by the C-Way Construction Company of Spring Lake, Michigan, began taking on water in 12-foot seas. Two men put aboard the wallowing craft lost their lives later that night when it capsized and plunged to the bottom. Following a 13-hour search of the 40-degree lake waters, the U.S. Coast Guard suspended the search for the two missing sailors. A dive team later located their bodies in wreckage of the sunken barge on April 10.

On April 8, the *Canadian Transport* delivered the first cargo to the newly opened Blue Water Aggregates Company Inc. Dock at Marysville, Michigan. Two days later, Rouge Steel's *Henry Ford II* paid a rare visit to Meldrum Bay, Ontario, to load stone for Cleveland.

A minor mishap took place on the St. Lawrence Seaway on April 12, when the

The steamer *Willowglen* suffered damage at the Soo Locks during late April. (Photo by James Hoffman)

Federal Seaway went aground near St. Zotique, Quebec, following a steering failure. The motor vessel went on to become the first U.S. flagged vessel to ever open the ocean shipping season at Toledo three days later.

As it was unloading wheat at Quebec City, Quebec, during mid-April, the *Algolake* had two of its cargo hold bulkheads collapse. The sudden shift of grain into another section of the cargo hold created a considerable amount of structural stress that damaged the vessel's spar deck. Coming less than two weeks after it had suffered engine difficulties in the Straits of Mackinac, the 730-foot carrier arrived at Montreal for repairs on April 17.

During the early morning hours of April 15, thieves using a cutting torch while attempting to steal navigational equipment from the pilothouse of the idle car ferry *Grand Rapids* at Muskegon started a fire that gutted the upper cabins of the 61-year old vessel. That same day, Halco's *Cartiercliffe Hall* hit a security gate at the St. Lambert Lock while downbound for Baie Comeau, Quebec. Although the bulk carrier suffered no damage, the incident delayed traffic through the Seaway for about 12 hours.

The downbound *Canadian Ranger* had a minor mishap in the lower section of the St. Clair River on April 17 when it struck a 17-foot fishing boat while meeting an upbound ship near Russell Island. The two occupants of the small craft along with another pair from a nearby boat all jumped into the water and were quickly picked up by other boaters in the area. With its anchor line catching on the bulk carrier's rudder, the small boat survived the encounter without suffering any damage despite being dragged a short distance downstream.

On April 25, the Greek bulker *Orestia* loaded the cargo of salt cake stored aboard

No. 265808 (ex-*Benson Ford* (2)) over the winter at Thorold, Ontario, for delivery to New Zealand. Also on that same date, the *Prairie Harvest* arrived at Port Weller Dry Docks for several weeks of hull work to repair ice damage sustained while operating in the Gulf of St. Lawrence.

Downbound from Lake Superior with grain on the afternoon of April 27, strong northwest winds pushed the *Willowglen* into the pier separating the MacArthur and Poe locks at Sault Ste. Marie, Michigan. Suffering some minor flooding through a 12-foot tear in its port bow near the waterline, the 620-foot steamer went to the Carbide Dock below the locks for temporary repairs before departing late the following evening. In a second unfortunate event on this particular voyage, Captain John Hartley became severely ill when his ship reached western Lake Erie on April 30. Taken ashore, he died later that day in Grace Hospital at Windsor.

The tanker *Etrema* grounded in Lake St. Pierre just west of Trois-Rivieres, Quebec, on May 2 while bound for Montreal with a load of naphtha. Lightered by the Socanav tanker *Hubert Gaucher*, which had been in a layup status at Sorel, Quebec, the tugs *Duga*, *Robert H.*, and *Capt. Ioannis S.* refloated the ocean ship the following day. Owned by the Shell Oil Company and registered in the Isle of Man, the 9-year old vessel resumed its voyage on May 4 following a brief stop at Trois-Rivieres.

Sold to Marine Salvage Ltd. for $150,000, the *T. W. Robinson* cleared its long-term layup berth at Calcite on May 2 in tow of the tugs *Glenada* and *Tusker* bound for Port Colborne. Delivered to Ramey's Bend three days later, the 62-year old self-unloader remained at the scrap yard until resold that summer to Siderurgica Aconorte S. A. for scrapping in Brazil. Taken in tow once again by the same pair of tugs on July 29, it arrived at Quebec City on August 2 to await a tandem scrap tow along with *No. 265808*.

Launched by the American Ship Building Company at Lorain, Ohio, on April 25, 1925, the *T. W. Robinson* entered service for the Bradley Transportation Company when it cleared the shipyard on July 11 of that year. At 588 feet in length, this steamer remained the largest ship in that fleet until the commissioning of the ill-fated *Carl D. Bradley* (2) two years later. As the first large lake vessel to feature turbo-electric propulsion, the *T. W. Robinson* remained active until entering its final layup on May 23, 1982.

Even as the *T. W. Robinson* headed for Port Colborne on its scrap tow, a former fleet mate, *George A. Sloan*, made an uncommon appearance on the Welland Canal when it transited downbound on May 3 for Oswego, New York.

Acquired by A. B. McLean Ltd. for use as a dock facing at Sault Ste. Marie, Ontario, the previous October, the *Sewell Avery* arrived at the Canadian Soo on May 4 in tow of the tugs *Avenger IV* and *Chippewa* following a three-day trip across Lake Superior from Duluth. Sunk in place on June 26 by filling its cargo holds with slag from the nearby Algoma Steel mill, a proposal to preserve the vessel's forward cabins on the grounds of Lake Superior State College across the river at Sault Ste. Marie, Michigan, ultimately failed due to cost considerations.

On May 5, the *Maplecliffe Hall* escaped serious harm when the explosion of a welder's acetylene tank started a small fire alongside the vessel at Montreal. The following day, Columbia Transportation's *Reserve* sailed for the first time since December 26, 1983 when it cleared Toledo for Superior, Wisconsin, to receive a 5-year inspection at Fraser Shipyards before loading its initial cargo of the season. While discharging a load of stone at Fairport, Ohio, on May 10, several cables holding the 250-foot unloading boom on the *Myron C. Taylor* suddenly snapped. Still partially loaded, the motor vessel went to Cleveland to have its damaged boom repaired. Departing that port on May 14, the *Taylor* sailed to top off at Port Colborne before returning to unload at Fairport.

The tug *Wilfred M. Cohen* cleared Marathon, Ontario, on May 10 with a raft of logs from Buchanan Forest Products consigned to Northern Wood Preservers Inc. at Thunder Bay, where the unusual tow arrived three days later. As the tug lost a good amount of the 9000-cord consignment during the 130-mile voyage across northern Lake Superior, warnings went out to small craft operators to be on the lookout for floating logs in the area. Once a common method of moving fresh cut timber to sawmills across the Great Lakes region, the *Cohen* repeated this trip during early July reportedly without the loss of any logs.

On May 16, Interlake Steamship's 806-foot *Charles M. Beeghly* became the largest ship to deliver a cargo up the Black River at Lorain when it discharged a load of stone near the head of navigation.

Struggling to maneuver in 50 mph winds during its approach to the Duluth, Missabe & Iron Range Railway ore dock at Duluth on May 18, the *William Clay Ford* (2) lost an anchor and approximately 360 feet of chain in St. Louis Bay. That same day, another mishap occurred when CSL's *Richelieu* (3) and the Panamanian bulker *Mountain Azalea* rubbed against each other in the Welland Canal with both vessels sustaining minor damage.

A ruptured compressed air line injured two crewmen working in the engine room of the

The *Medusa Challenger* delivered the first cargo to Medusa Cement's new facility at Toledo, Ohio, during the early part of the 1987 shipping season. (Author's Collection)

Edgar B. Speer on May 19 while that ship was fitting out for the season at the Cargill Elevator in Duluth. Shifting over to the Duluth, Missabe & Iron Range Railway Dock to load taconite two days later, the thousand-footer departed for Gary on May 22.

As part of a major investment program to improve its distribution network, Medusa Cement built a new terminal at Toledo to which the 81-year old *Medusa Challenger* delivered the first load of cement on May 21. The following morning, the *Charles M. Beeghly* suffered no damage when it passed through a severe thunderstorm while sailing on Lake Michigan despite encountering 114 mph winds.

Signifying the first visit by a USS Great Lakes Fleet vessel to the Superior Midwest Energy Terminal at Superior, Wisconsin, the *Philip R. Clarke* loaded a cargo of western coal at that facility on May 27 for delivery to Marquette.

A last minute deal reached between the Seafarers International Union (SIU) and the Canadian Lake Carriers' Association on May 29 to secure a new 3-year contract averted the possibility of a major labor strike in early June against 11 Canadian Great Lakes shipping companies. Slamming into the lower approach wall to the Snell Lock that same day while bound for Burns Harbor, Indiana, the Yugoslavian bulker *Malinska* tore open a 40' x 8' gash in its bow plating above the waterline. With the 729-foot vessel moved to a nearby mooring by the St. Lawrence Seaway Development Corporation tug *Robinson Bay*, the mishap delayed traffic through the lock for about nine hours.

The *Comeaudoc* encountered some difficulty on the evening of June 1 when it went hard aground in the St. Lawrence River west of St. Zotique while downbound with wheat from Thunder Bay for Quebec City. When a refloating effort by tugs failed the next day, the lighter *Mapleheath* was brought over from Valleyfield, Quebec, to assist in the salvage effort. Following several days of work, the 730-foot motor vessel finally came off the bottom on June 7 without any significant damage.

On June 9, the 1973-built *Presque Isle* (2) made its first appearance at Cleveland when it unloaded 52,350 gross tons of taconite at the C&P Dock. Loaded at the Burlington Northern ore dock at Superior, Wisconsin, to which this vessel had made its first visit on May 29, this was the inaugural cargo of several such voyages to Cleveland scheduled for that season.

While entering Duluth on June 11 to take on a grain cargo, a deck crane aboard the saltwater bulker *Atlantic Seaman* rubbed across the bottom of the Aerial Lift Bridge. Other than causing a few anxious moments, the incident inflicted no damage to either the 11-year old vessel or the bridge.

The tugs *Glenada* and *Tusker* pulled *No. 265808* out of Thorold on June 12 bound for Sorel, where the trio arrived five days later. There it remained until delivered to Quebec City by the same tugs on August 4. Paired with the *T. W. Robinson*, both vessels cleared that port on August 11 in tow of the Polish tug *Jantar*. Spending the next six weeks making its way south on the Atlantic, the scrap tow arrived at Recife, Brazil, on September 22, where both ships were dismantled.

Having remained at Toledo for a full year after its sale to Port Colborne Marine Terminals Inc. for scrapping, the former Cleveland-Cliffs steamer *William P. Snyder, Jr.* arrived at Port Colborne on June 17 in tow of the tugs *Michael D. Misner* and *Thunder Cape*. Dismantling of the 617-foot bulk carrier was completed the following year.

Built in 1976 for the primary purpose of

moving western coal from Superior, Wisconsin, to the lower lakes, the motor vessel *St. Clair* (2) remained a common visitor to the Detroit Edison Company dock at St. Clair, Michigan, throughout the 1980s. Arriving at that facility at the end of one such trip on June 21, this vessel tied up alongside the *Belle River*, which was already in the process of unloading. Likely the result of mechanical difficulties at the receiving dock or on the ship itself, this unusual procedure allowed the *St. Clair* (2) to offload its coal cargo into the thousand-footer for transfer ashore.

During the month of June, the U.S. Maritime Administration (MARAD) accepted an offer made by Fednav Lakes Services the previous summer to sell the motor vessels *Federal Lakes* and *Federal Seaway* for $29 million in order to discontinue that company's RO/RO (Roll-On/Roll-Off) service between the Great Lakes and Europe. Taking possession of the *Federal Lakes* and renaming it *Cape Lambert* a few months later, MARAD placed the 14-year old vessel into the James River Reserve Fleet on November 2, 1987. Meanwhile, the *Federal Seaway* finished out the season before joining its sister ship in the Ready Reserve Fleet on March 12, 1988 as the *Cape Lobos*.

Following a relatively quiet period in terms of accidents, the Liberian registered *Sunwind* went aground near the MIL Vickers Ltd. yard at Montreal on July 1 while bound for Contrecoeur, Quebec. Remaining stuck on the bottom overnight, the tug *Duga*, dispatched from Trois-Rivieres, along with four McAllister Towing & Salvage tugs managed to refloat the ocean carrier the next day. A second incident on the St. Lawrence River in

The *Presque Isle* (2) visited Cleveland, Ohio, for the first time during the summer of 1987.
(Photo by Duncan White)

less than a week took place on July 5 when the Socanav tanker *L. Rochette* spilled a significant amount of oil into the river below Quebec City.

Just one month after grounding in the St. Lawrence Seaway, the *Comeaudoc* encountered further difficulties on July 7 when a broken fuel line forced the 27-year old bulk carrier to anchor in the St. Marys River for repairs.

Reportedly purchased for off-lakes use in the Gulf of Mexico but subsequently resold to the Upper Lakes Towing Company after nearly six years of idleness at Calcite, the self-unloader *Rogers City* was towed into Menominee, Michigan, on July 10. Upon learning of a plan to convert the 64-year old steamer into a barge for Great Lakes service, however, its former owner, USS Great Lakes Fleet Inc., took legal action to prevent this reconstruction from going forward. As will be related later, this litigation proved successful for the shipping company with the veteran lake freighter being resold for scrapping overseas later in the year.

Its conversion from a powered tanker to a cement-carrying barge completed at Bay Shipbuilding, Medusa Cement's *Medusa Conquest* entered service during mid-July paired with the 4,000 horsepower tug *James A. Hannah*. Loading cement at Charlevoix, Michigan, the duo sailed across Lake Michigan to deliver this initial payload to Manitowoc, Wisconsin, on July 20.

While upbound at Sault Ste. Marie, Michigan, with a cargo of stone on the morning of July 16, Bethlehem Steel's *Sparrows Point* mangled some starboard bow plating when it slammed hard into the lower approach wall at the Poe Lock. With the impact also inflicting some minor damage to the pier, the steamer tied up at the locks for an inspection before resuming its voyage.

Having acquired the *Lakeshell* (3) from Shell Canadian Tankers Ltd. earlier that year as part of a deal involving three vessels, Socanav Inc. renamed the 399-foot tanker *W. M. Vacy Ash* at Montreal on July 18. While at the Burlington Northern ore dock at Superior, Wisconsin, that same day, the *Stewart J. Cort* loaded a record 56,251 gross tons of taconite in 3 hours and 35 minutes, thus beating its previous best time at that facility by 5 minutes.

Assisted by the tug *Glenada* during one of its regular trips to the Hazzard Marine Grain Terminal at Wallaceburg, Ontario, the *Eva Desgagnes* suffered rudder damage when it grounded near Johnson's Bend in the Chenal Ecarte on July 19. Managing to reach the dock late that evening with some difficulty, the 349-foot motor vessel remained there until towed to an anchorage in the St. Clair River just north of Port Lambton, Ontario, on July 24 by the tugs *Annie M. Dean* and *Glenada*. With the help of the latter tug, the *Stella Desgagnes* arrived at the Hazzard Dock the following day to load the 205,000 bushels of corn originally consigned to its sister ship in an operation that suffered a four-hour delay when the ship toppled the loading gear while being shifted. After the *Stella Desgagnes* cleared Wallaceburg on July 26, the *Annie M. Dean* and *Glenada* towed the *Eva Desgagnes* to the Government Dock at Sarnia, Ontario, for repairs.

On July 20, two mishaps involving three lake carriers occurred on the St. Marys River, the first of which took place shortly after three o'clock that morning when the 600-foot Kinsman Lines steamer *Henry Steinbrenner* (4) went aground near Six Mile Point. Suffering no damage from its unscheduled meeting with the muddy river bottom, the tugs *Avenger IV* and *Chippewa* pulled the 71-year old bulk carrier free about 11 hours later.

Within a few hours of the *Steinbrenner* (4) grounding, the *Reserve* and *Canadian Enterprise* sustained only superficial damage when they scraped sides at the western approach to the Soo Locks while maneuvering to lock downbound.

One further incident on July 20 involved the Cuban flagged general cargo ship *Pamit C.*, which ran aground in the St. Lawrence River about 20 miles above Quebec City while upbound for Montreal and Toronto. Freed the following day, hull damage kept it at Montreal until departing for the lakes on July 25. Placed under arrest upon returning to Montreal on August 3, however, the authorities briefly held the ocean carrier before releasing it the next day.

At 6:55 p.m. on July 22, a 4-inch crack about 200 feet in length opened up in the south wall of the Canadian Lock at Sault Ste. Marie, Ontario, with a loud bang. Upbound in the lock chamber at the time, the tour boat *Chief Shingwauk* was able to exit at the upper water level without incident. With the 92-year old lock put out of commission indefinitely, all of the recreational and tour boat traffic that normally transited the Canadian canal had to use the Soo Locks on the opposite side of the St. Marys River at Sault Ste. Marie, Michigan. The resulting congestion forced the U.S. Army Corps of Engineers to open the Davis Lock for daytime operation to minimize the impact upon commercial traffic. Over the next several years, a series of proposals to rebuild the damaged lock met with failure until work finally began on a $10.3 million project to construct a new lock inside the confines of the existing lock during the late 1990s. Nearly 11 years to the day of the original lock wall failure, the new lock opened to traffic on July 14, 1998 with the *Chief Shingwauk* making the first passage.

While upbound on the St. Lawrence River with a load of steel on July 27, the Cyprus registered *Andrew H.* lost steering and went aground off Cornwall Island. With some of its cargo lightered by the barge *Mapleheath*, tugs refloated the saltwater bulker on August 2. Suffering no serious damage, it went to Valleyfield to reload before continuing to Hamilton.

The *American Republic* made a rare passage down the Welland Canal on July 30 while bound to load iron ore at Contrecoeur for delivery to Cleveland. Making its first transit of the St. Lawrence Seaway the following day, the 634-foot motor vessel returned upbound through the system on August 2.

On August 1, Shell Canadian Tankers Ltd. transferred its last remaining vessels to Shell Canada Products Ltd., all of which were engaged in bunkering duties. In addition to the motor vessel *Rivershell* (4), this transaction also included the barges *Bayshell* (2) and *S. M. T. B. No. 7*. That same day, a burst pipeline created a 3,000-gallon diesel fuel spill at Taconite Harbor, Minnesota, during the refueling of Interlake Steamship's *James R. Barker*. With approximately 150 gallons of oil reaching the waters of Lake Superior, the spill prompted a 3-week cleanup operation.

Having departed Sault Ste. Marie, Michigan, the previous day, the tug *Chippewa* towed the *L. E. Block* out of Escanaba, Michigan, on August 3 bound for South Chicago, Illinois. Arriving there two days later, the retired bulk carrier began what was to be a short-lived career as a cement storage barge on Lake Calumet.

Arriving at Erie, Pennsylvania, on August 5, the *American Mariner* established a cargo record for that port when it delivered 31,700 tons of limestone taken on at Cedarville to the Erie Sand & Gravel Company. Two days later, the barge *STC 2004* flipped over in heavy seas on Lake Michigan about 10 miles south of Beaver Island while in tow of the tug *Gregory J. Busch*. Towed into St. James Harbor on the island, an accident while attempting to right the capsized barge seriously injured one man who later required a medical airlift to a hospital on the mainland. The *Busch* later took the *STC 2004* to the Twin City Drydock & Marine Inc. yard at Sault Ste. Marie, Michigan, on August 17 for repairs.

The *H. M. Griffith* became the first ship to use a newly installed hopper arrangement designed to accept deliveries by self-unloading vessels at the Robin Hood Elevator at Port Colborne when it unloaded a cargo of grain at that facility on August 11. A highly unusual cargo delivery took place in Lake Huron on August 13 when the *Calcite II* discharged 4,500 tons of limestone into the waters of Tawas Bay near East Tawas, Michigan, to form an artificial reef.

Following nearly two years of litigation, the U.S. District Court for the Northern District of Ohio approved the sale of the former Cleveland-Cliffs steamers *Cadillac* (4) and *Champlain* (3) to Corostel Trading Ltd. of Montreal for scrapping. Towed out of Toledo on August 17 by the tugs *Glenada* and *Elmore M. Misner*, the *Cadillac* (4) was the first of these two vessels to depart for the breakers. Reaching Port Colborne the next day, the 620-foot lake freighter cleared the Welland Canal on August 20 with the tug *Tusker* having replaced the *Elmore M. Misner*. Following a prolonged transit of the St. Lawrence Seaway plagued by several clearance inspections, high winds, and reportedly a near collision with another vessel above the Eisenhower Lock, the scrap tow finally arrived at Quebec City on August 31.

During late May, the Inland Steel Company sold the motor vessel *E. J. Block* to Marine Salvage Ltd. for dismantling. Towed out of its layup berth at Indiana Harbor by the tugs *Glenada* and *Tusker*, the 552-foot bulk carrier arrived at Ramey's Bend on August 18. Although Marine Salvage began breaking up the classic lake freighter the following January, this process was not completed until the closing months of 1991.

Built by the West Bay City Shipbuilding Company at West Bay City, Michigan, in 1908 as the *W. R. Woodford*, the Inland Steel Company purchased this steamer in 1911 and placed it into the newly formed Inland Steamship Company (Hutchinson & Company, mgr.). Renamed *N. F. Leopold* prior to the start of the 1912 shipping season, it later became *E. J. Block* in 1943. Three years later, the *Block* had its original reciprocating steam engine replaced by a pair of General Motors/Westinghouse diesel-electric engines as part of an extensive refurbishment performed by the American Ship Building Company's Lorain yard that provided nearly another 40 years of active service. Due to its limited carrying capacity of only 11,500 gross tons, Inland Steel used this ship primarily in the shuttling of raw materials at Indiana Harbor during the latter years of its career. After serving the steelmaker for 73 years, the *E. J. Block* laid up for the final time on August 4, 1984.

With the pace of scrap sales in the U.S. fleet continuing to gain momentum during late summer, two former members of the USS Great Lakes Fleet left Duluth on August 22 with the departure of the *Enders M. Voorhees* in tow of the tug *Avenger IV* followed by the *Thomas W. Lamont* later that day with the tug *Chippewa*. Their final voyages down the lakes and through the St. Lawrence Seaway proving uneventful, both ships arrived at Quebec City on September 3 in preparation for a transatlantic tow.

Launched by the Great Lakes Engineering

Works at River Rouge, Michigan, on April 11, 1942, the *Enders M. Voorhees* began its maiden voyage on July 29 of that year when it sailed from the shipyard to load iron ore at Duluth. Capable of carrying 19,150 gross tons of iron ore, the 639-foot straight decker remained one of U.S. Steel's premier units until the commissioning of three large carriers and the lengthening of four existing steamers during the 1972-80 timeframe. Its career cut short by the economic recession of the early 1980s, this vessel laid up for the last time on December 26, 1981.

Built by the Toledo Shipbuilding Company at Toledo in 1930, the *Thomas W. Lamont* entered service just as the onset of the Great Depression decimated the demand for iron ore. As such, the *Lamont* and the nearly identical *Eugene P. Thomas*, built that same year by the Great Lakes Engineering Works at River Rouge, became the last bulk carriers constructed on the Great Lakes until the Pittsburgh Steamship Company ordered the four members of the "Miller" class in 1937. While laid up at Superior, Wisconsin, during the winter of 1964-65, the Fraser-Nelson Shipbuilding and Dry Dock Company replaced the *Lamont*'s original 2,200 ihp triple-expansion steam engine with a 3,240 bhp Nordberg diesel engine. Nearing the end of its useful life by the beginning of the 1980s, the operational career of this 604-foot motor vessel came to a close when it entered an indefinite layup at Duluth on September 3, 1981.

Returning to the 1987 season, the *Thomas W. Lamont* and *Enders M. Voorhees* cleared Quebec City on September 15 in tow of the tug *Irving Cedar*. Having split up the tandem scrap tow after reaching Algeciras, Spain, on October 24, the Greek tug *Everest* departed with the *Lamont* on December 15 bound for Aliaga, Turkey, where the 57-year old bulk carrier arrived 12 days later for scrapping. After making its way back across the Mediterranean, the *Everest* towed the *Voorhees* out of Algeciras on January 13, 1988 to begin what was to be an eventful voyage to the scrap yard. Parting its towline while caught in a strong storm eleven days later while off the southern coast of Greece, the 639-foot steamer went ashore on Kythnos Island some 170 miles short of its intended destination. Subsequently breaking in two, the wrecked lake freighter remained stranded until being salvaged two summers later to finally arrive at Aliaga on August 23, 1989, nearly two years to the day it departed Duluth for the last time.

A nationwide railroad strike during late August not only shutdown the movement of grain from the Canadian prairies but also sent the railcar ferry *Incan Superior* into a temporary layup at Thunder Bay on August 23. After the Canadian government acted quickly to restore the rail transportation system with the passage of back to work legislation on August 28, the 382-foot vessel returned to service three days later.

Six years after carrying its final cargo, the *Champlain* (3) cleared Toledo on August 26 in tow of the tugs *Elmore M. Misner* and *Michael D. Misner*. After passing through the Welland Canal, the tug *Tusker* took over the scrap tow of the "Maritime" class steamer, which, unlike the troubled final voyage of *Cadillac* (4), made a routine Seaway transit before reaching Quebec City on September 6. Having remained inseparable throughout their entire careers, the *Cadillac* (4) and *Champlain* (3) cleared that port on September 8 in tow of the Dutch tug *Thomas De Gauwdief* for Aliaga, Turkey, where they arrived on October 30 for dismantling.

The growth of recreational traffic on the Cuyahoga River at Cleveland contributed to an early morning accident on August 31 in which the *Kinsman Independent* (2) struck two moored pleasure boats while downbound in the lower section of the river. Leaving a 27-foot catamaran in pieces, the 600-foot steamer also damaged another boat docked nearby with two people aboard the latter requiring treatment for minor injuries. That same day, the Soviet bulker *Zapolyarnyy* rescued two men that had been clinging to a capsized sailboat off Beaver Island in Lake Michigan for seven hours. With the crew of the ocean freighter also pulling the 17-foot craft from the water, the U.S. Coast Guard sent out a patrol boat from Charlevoix to return both the sailboat and its occupants to shore.

Having ceased operations the previous summer, the Reserve Mining Company sold a 60,000-ton stockpile of coal it originally acquired for power generation to the Cutler-Magner Corporation. This sale resulted in the barge *Buckeye* (2) and its companion tug *Olive L. Moore* making seven trips in western Lake Superior during late August and September moving the coal from Silver Bay, Minnesota, to Superior, Wisconsin.

Slamming into the Government Dock at Sault Ste. Marie, Ontario, on September 5, the Socanav tanker *Le Frene No. 1* inflicted approximately $100,000 in damage to the concrete pier while suffering no serious harm itself. Two days later, the Azcon Corporation began breaking up the *Eugene W. Pargny* at Duluth. Beginning nearly two years after it first arrived at the scrap yard, dismantling of the former U.S. Steel bulk carrier continued until July 1988.

On the afternoon of September 11, the barge *Fort York* suffered considerable damage when a fire ravaged its pilothouse and upper deck at Point Edward, Ontario. Assisted by the U.S. Coast Guard, it took firefighters over two hours to extinguish the smoky blaze. Suspected as being the work of vandals, this incident came just one month after a suspicious August 10 fire inflicted minor damage to the vessel's forecastle. Laid up just south of the Blue Water Bridge since ending its short stint as a lumber barge during the 1985 season, the former package freighter had become a sanctuary for vagrants in the months leading up to these incidents.

Less than 24 hours later, another mishap played out on the opposite side of the St. Clair River when at nine o'clock in the morning of September 12 the Yugoslavian bulker *Ruder Boskovic* ran into a seawall just downstream of the Blue Water Bridge at Port Huron, Michigan, while downbound in fog. Proceeding to an anchorage near St. Clair for an inspection, the ocean freighter suffered no significant damage in the incident while the cost to repair the seawall reached $180,000. A subsequent U.S. Coast Guard investigation blamed the accident on a language barrier between the U.S. pilot and the vessel's Yugoslavian wheelsman.

The protracted conversion of the *Hudson Transport* to a petroleum products barge entered a new phase on September 14 when the tugs *Elmore M. Misner* and *Michael D. Misner* moved the former Halco tanker into the small dry dock at Ramey's Bend to have its stern notched for operation with a tug. Other traffic on the Welland Canal that same day included the bunkering tanker *Marine Fuel Oil*, which passed downbound following its sale by the Marine Fueling Division of the Reiss Oil Terminal Corporation for off-lakes use. Upon reaching Oswego, the 116-foot motor vessel entered the New York State Barge Canal bound for its new duties at New Haven, Connecticut.

Acquired by Corostel Trading Ltd. for

Never operating during the 1980s, the steamer *Ashland* was sold for scrap in 1987. (Author's Collection)

scrapping overseas after nearly eight years of idleness, the former Columbia Transportation bulk carrier *Ashland* cleared Toledo on September 14 in tow of the tug *Tusker*. Later joined by the tug *Thunder Cape*, the scrap tow reached Montreal on September 22 before arriving at Lauzon, Quebec, the next day.

Built by the Great Lakes Engineering Works at Ashtabula, Ohio, as the *Clarence B. Randall*, this steamer entered service for the Pioneer Steamship Company (Hutchinson & Company, mgr.) on July 19, 1943 when it sailed for Two Harbors, Minnesota, to load iron ore. While in the process of winding down its operations, the Pioneer Steamship Company sold this vessel to Oglebay Norton's Columbia Transportation Division in May 1962 for $2 million. Renamed *Ashland* that same year, it became the first "Maritime" class bulk carrier acquired by Columbia Transportation although the fleet had operated a sister ship, *J. H. Hillman, Jr.*, since 1960 under a charter arrangement with the Wilson Marine Transit Company that was to continue until 1966. While downbound on Lake Superior with a load of iron ore from Silver Bay on December 10, 1979, an electrical failure left the 620-foot ship without engine power in 15-foot seas about 20 miles east of Copper Harbor, Michigan. Towed into Thunder Bay on December 12, 1979 by the tug *Peninsula*, it left the following day for Ashtabula. Sailing to Toledo after unloading this cargo, the *Ashland* entered its final layup on December 19, 1979.

Upon reaching the end of its useful life, nearly every lake vessel makes one last voyage to the scrap yard. While most will go to the breakers without much of a fuss, others seem far more reluctant to accept their fate as demonstrated by the scrap tow of the former USS Great Lakes Fleet steamer *A. H. Ferbert* (2). Destined for scrapping overseas following almost six years of inactivity, the retired vessel departed Duluth on September 15 in tow of the tug *Glenada*. Running into rough weather shortly afterwards, however, the pair required the assistance of the tug *W. J. Ivan Purvis* to complete the trip across Lake Superior. Reaching Sault Ste. Marie, Ontario, on September 19, the scrap tow went to anchor off De Tour two days later for an inspection after the "Super" class vessel broke free of its towline and rubbed the bottom of the St. Mary River. Sustaining some bottom damage, the U.S. Coast Guard ordered repairs before permitting the tow to continue. Following an uneventful passage down Lake Huron, the 639-foot ship suffered yet another mishap when shifting winds blew it hard aground in the St. Clair Cutoff Channel on September 24. In this instance, the 45-year old bulk carrier remained firmly lodged on the muddy bottom until pulled free two days later by a fleet of six tugs. Completing its journey off the lakes without further incident after spending a couple of days tied up in the Welland Canal due to unfavorable winds, the *A. H. Ferbert* (2) arrived at Lauzon on October 7 in tow of the tugs *Glenside* and *W. N. Twolan*.

Ordered by U.S. Steel's Pittsburgh Steamship Company before the United States entered World War II, the Great Lakes Engineering Works launched the *A. H. Ferbert* (2) at its River Rouge yard on May 22, 1942. Conducting its sea trials on Lake Erie on August 27, 1942, this ship had to return to the shipyard for repairs within days of entering service after running aground in the St. Marys River on its maiden voyage. Committed to the movement of raw materials for U.S. Steel throughout its entire career, it began making occasional voyages through the St. Lawrence Seaway during the early 1960s and later operated in the extended season navigation programs of the following decade before laying up for the final time on November 30, 1981.

Even as the *A. H. Ferbert* (2) began its troubled voyage from Duluth on September 15, the tug *W. N. Twolan* pulled the steamer *Samuel Mather* (6) away from its long-term layup dock at De Tour. Acquired by Marine Salvage Ltd. from the Interlake Steamship Company earlier that month and subsequently resold for scrapping overseas, the bulk carrier passed down the Welland Canal on September 19-20 with the tugs *Glenevis* and *Argue Martin* assisting. After the *Martin* dropped out with gearbox problems near Morrisburg, Ontario, on September 22, however, the tug *Glenbrook* joined the scrap tow, which arrived at Lauzon six days later.

Built by the Great Lakes Engineering Works at Ashtabula in 1943 for the U.S. Maritime Commission as the *Pilot Knob*, this ship was one of three "Maritime" class bulk carriers acquired by the Interlake Steamship Company during World War II. Renamed *Frank Armstrong* while in the final stages of construction, this vessel, like the *A. H. Ferbert* (2), suffered an accident on its maiden voyage when it collided with the steamer *Goderich* in the St. Marys River on June 5, 1943. Given the name *Samuel Mather* (6) in early 1976, this ship closed out the operation of "Maritime" class vessels by the Interlake Steamship Company when it entered an indefinite layup on November 23, 1981.

The *A. H. Ferbert* (2) and *Samuel Mather* (6) cleared Lauzon on December 3 in a tandem tow by the tug *Capt. Ioannis S.*, which delivered them to Sydney, Nova Scotia, six days later. Remaining there over the winter, the two lake freighters left Sydney on May 21, 1988 in tow of the tug *Irving Cedar* to arrive at Aliaga, Turkey, on June 20, 1988 for dismantling.

On the morning of September 23, the motor vessel *Canadian Enterprise* ran aground in the Amherstburg Channel of the Detroit River while upbound in heavy fog. Carrying a cargo of coal for delivery to the Lambton Generating Station at Courtright, Ontario, an initial attempt to refloat the stranded vessel by the Gaelic Tugboat Company tugs *Caroline Hoey*, *Susan Hoey*, and *Shannon* proved unsuccessful. After the tug *William A. Whitney* joined the salvage effort, the 730-foot self-unloader came off the bottom late that evening after offloading 1,840 tons of coal onto a barge brought alongside by the tug *Glenside*. Able to continue its voyage a short time later, the ULS International carrier paid a subsequent visit to the Port Arthur Shipbuilding yard at Thunder Bay for repairs.

The increased demand for iron ore during early autumn resulted in the reactivation of USS Great Lakes Fleet's *Roger Blough*, which had been laid up at Sturgeon Bay since September 12, 1981. Clearing Bay Shipbuilding on September 24, the uniquely sized 858-foot motor vessel sailed for Two Harbors, where it arrived three days later to load 43,603 gross tons of taconite pellets for the USX steel mill at Gary. The return of the *Blough* was significant in that all 29 Poe-class vessels in the U.S. fleet, defined as those restricted to the Poe Lock at Sault Ste. Marie, Michigan, due to their size, were in operation for the first time since 1981.

The 533-foot motor vessel *Nicolet* had a tough time in the Saginaw River on September 26 when it suffered propeller damage and went sideways in the channel before managing to extricate itself from this unpleasant situation without any further harm.

Having departed Montreal on August 8 for a stint in the Canadian Arctic, the package freighter *Woodland* returned to that port on September 27 for an overnight stay before clearing for Windsor.

A strike called by the Canadian Marine Officers Union on September 28 threatened several Canadian fleets during the busy fall grain rush. Proving somewhat ineffectual, however, ships continued operating with engineers that remained on the job or with replacement personnel until the union and ship owners reached an agreement during late October.

When the Reserve Mining Company shuttered its facilities following the LTV Steel bankruptcy, it had some 165,000 gross tons of taconite pellets awaiting shipment at company's Silver Bay loading facility. On September 30, the *Mesabi Miner* took on the first of three loads to reduce this stockpile with the last of it going out in a 4,937 gross ton shipment put aboard the CSL steamer *Stadacona* (3) near the end of October.

Encountering difficulty within days of reentering service following a three-month layup at Montreal, Halco's *Steelcliffe Hall* required a week's worth of bow repairs during early October following an altercation with a dock at Thunder Bay. Meanwhile, another Canadian bulker had its season interrupted when condenser problems sent the steamer *Canadian Hunter* to the wall in the Welland Canal on October 2 for lengthy repairs.

Following several days of delay at Port Colborne due to weather, the *Thomas Wilson* (2) passed downbound through the Welland Canal on October 4 in tow of the tugs *Thunder Cape* and *Tusker*. As the second bulk carrier sold by Columbia Transportation to Corostel Trading Ltd. for dismantling that season, it joined its former fleet mate,

The 1987 Shipping Season

Following a prolonged layup, USS Great Lakes Fleet's *Roger Blough* returned to service in September of 1987. (Photo by Tom Salvner)

Ashland, at Lauzon four days later to await a tandem scrap tow to Taiwan later in the year. In common with several of the six "Maritime" class steamers built by the American Ship Building Company during World War II that were powered by Lentz-Poppet double compound engines, the *Thomas Wilson* (2) experienced chronic reliability issues throughout its career. Saddled by its troublesome power plant and destined to become an early victim of changing economic conditions, the 620-foot vessel entered its final layup at Toledo on December 16, 1979.

As work on demolishing its former grain elevator at Kingston, Ontario, got underway to repurpose the property, CSL began the process of moving the *Hochelaga*, *T. R. McLagan*, *Metis*, and *Nipigon Bay* that had sat idle in the elevator's slip for several years to new layup berths at Toronto. Towed into the latter port on October 6, the 714-foot *T. R. McLagan* was the first of these vessels to make the westward trip across Lake Ontario followed by the cement carrier *Metis* on October 29. The *Nipigon Bay* reached Toronto on November 4 in tow of the tugs *Glenbrook*, *Glenevis*, and *Glenside* before the *Hochelaga* arrived six days later with the same set of tugs.

Operating in ocean service between ports in Europe, the *Atlantic Superior* suffered a grounding accident at Sines, Portugal, on October 5 that necessitated a dry-docking at Setubal, Portugal. Back on the lakes, three arson fires heavily damaged the cabins of the retired car ferry *Madison* at Muskegon on the evening of October 7. Interestingly, this incident came just six months after a similar blaze swept through its sister ship, *Grand Rapids*, also tied up at the Grand Trunk Dock as related earlier in this chapter. Both burned-out vessels were to remain at Muskegon until sold for dismantling in 1989.

While attempting to enter Ontonagon, Michigan, at 3:30 a.m. on October 8 to deliver

175

20,000 tons of coal, the *Charles E. Wilson* ran onto a sandbar near the harbor entrance. Managing to free itself early that afternoon, the 680-foot motor vessel sailed to Duluth to offload about 6,700 tons of coal before making an uneventful return to Ontonagon two days later.

A second mishap involving an American Steamship Company vessel on October 8 took place when strong westerly winds blew the *Indiana Harbor* aground near the outer breakwater at Lorain as it was backing into the harbor with a load of taconite for the Lorain Pellet Terminal. Sent over from Cleveland, the tugs *South Carolina* and *Superior* freed the thousand-footer early that evening without any damage to either the vessel or breakwater.

During early autumn, Imperial Oil Ltd. sold the *Imperial Quebec* to Coastal Shipping Ltd. (Woodward Marine, mgr.) of Goose Bay, Labrador, which took possession of the 30-year old tanker at Halifax, Nova Scotia, on October 9. Built by Collingwood Shipyards at Collingwood, Ontario, in 1957, this ship had made only rare appearances on the Great Lakes after the opening of the St. Lawrence Seaway two years later. While nearing the end of its career with Imperial Oil, however, the *Imperial Quebec* had taken a break from its regular duties on the east coast of Canada to operate out of Sarnia during the first few months of the 1987 shipping season. Renamed *Sibyl W.*, the 375-foot motor vessel visited Montreal for the first time under its new name on November 30 before departing for Oshawa, Ontario, on December 2.

The recent spate of grounding accidents claimed another victim on October 10 when P. & H. Shipping's *Willowglen* stranded off Ogden Island in the St. Lawrence River near Morrisburg while downbound with grain for Trois-Rivieres. Lightered by the *P. S. Barge No. 1*, the tugs *Glenside*, *Helen M. McAllister*, *Salvage Monarch*, *Sinmac*, *Thunder Cape*, and *Tusker* refloated the 620-foot bulk carrier three days later. With ballast tank No. 8 torn open, it continued to Trois-Rivieres to unload before sailing to Port Weller Dry Docks at St. Catharines, Ontario, for repairs.

Sold to International Marine Salvage of Port Colborne for dismantling, the former P. & H. Shipping steamer *Birchglen* passed downbound past Detroit on October 11 in tow of the tugs *Glenada* and *Michael D. Misner*. Granted a temporary reprieve from the cutting torch, it arrived at Toronto five days later for use as a grain storage barge. Built for the Interlake Steamship Company as the *William McLauchlan*, this 600-foot bulk carrier first entered service when it cleared Sandusky on March 31, 1927 with a load of coal for delivery to Superior, Wisconsin. Renamed *Samuel Mather* (5) in 1966, it became the *Joan M. McCullough* in 1976 following its sale to Robert Pierson Holdings Ltd. for service under the Canadian flag with the Soo River Company. Receiving its fourth and final name in late 1982 when P. & H. Shipping purchased the nine vessels of the bankrupt Soo River fleet, the *Birchglen* had sailed briefly at the beginning of the 1987 season before laying up at Midland, Ontario.

On October 12, the American Steamship Company fleet had its third grounding accident in less than a week when the motor vessel *Sam Laud* went aground in the Detroit River just above Belle Isle while bound for the Detroit Edison Company's Conners Creek Power Plant at Detroit, Michigan. After offloading part of its cargo into the *American Republic* the next day, the 634-foot self-unloader came off the bottom without any reported damage.

A fire of suspicious origin that broke out aboard the *James B. Lyons* on October 16 caused a reported $500,000 in damage to the 39-year old sand sucker at Lorain, where it had been out of service for an extended period.

An October 17 collision between Algoma Central's 730-foot *Algowood* and a small boat near Port Huron did surprisingly little harm to the latter vessel. A more serious mishap took place just two days later when the *George A. Sloan* went aground in the Amherstburg Channel of the Detroit River following a steering failure. Upbound with coal for Green Bay, Wisconsin, at the time of the accident, the 620-foot motor vessel came to stop less than 100 feet from the Bob-Lo Island amusement park ferry dock on Bois Blanc Island. Pulled free by the tugs *Carolyn Hoey*, *Susan Hoey*, and *Shannon* on October 20 after transferring its cargo to the *Calcite II*, the *Sloan* sailed to Toledo for extensive hull repairs. Entering the dry dock at the Toledo Shipyard that same day, this work proceeded quickly enough that the self-unloader returned to service later in the season.

Moored at Sault Ste. Marie, Ontario, while working the site of the new A. B. McLean Ltd. Dock just upstream of the Algoma Steel mill, the dredge *Canadian Argosy* suffered considerable damage on the evening of October 19 when a fire broke out in its machinery spaces. With the assistance of a U.S. Coast Guard 41-foot utility boat, the tug *Avenger IV*, and the pilot boat *Soo River Belle*, local firefighters brought the blaze under control without any injuries.

During the early morning hours of October 21, the West German captain of the Saint Vincent registered freighter *Sirius* went missing while his ship was northbound on Lake Michigan bound for Duluth. Unable to locate a body, the authorities suspected foul play but were unable rule out other possible causes such as accident or suicide to explain the disappearance of the 48-year old man. Following the arrival of a replacement captain flown in from Europe, the 579-foot *Sirius* cleared Duluth on October 29 with a load of grain for Italy.

In another incident involving an ocean visitor on October 21, the Polish flagged bulker *Ziemia Gnieznienska* found itself stuck on the bottom of Duluth Harbor while attempting to depart the Cargill B1 grain elevator. Loaded to a depth of 26 feet, soundings of the loading slip revealed some areas with only 24 feet of water. Refloated by the tugs *Arkansas*, *New Jersey*, and *Rhode Island*, the saltwater vessel departed the following day.

While downbound on the St. Lawrence River on the afternoon of October 22, the Yugoslav freighter *Danilovgrad* lost steering and went aground on the west end of Ogden Island in the same general vicinity as the *Willowglen* stranded earlier in the month. Loaded with 16,700 metric tons of soybeans, the ship remained hard aground for the next week before the *P. S. Barge No. 1* began lightering operations on October 29. Following the removal of about 2,500 metric tons of its cargo, the tugs *Duga*, *Leonard W.*, *Cathy McAllister*, *Helen M. McAllister*, and *Salvage Monarch* freed the bulker on October 31. Found to be undamaged, it proceeded down the Seaway after being reloaded by the *P. S. Barge No. 1* at the Wilson Hill Anchorage near Massena, New York.

Built by Collingwood Shipyards in 1958 as the second of five "Fort" class package freighters that entered the Canada Steamship Lines fleet over a 10-year period beginning in 1955, the *Fort York* went on to enjoy a routine operational career marred only by the minor mishaps common to all lake vessels. The same cannot be said, however, of this vessel's troubled departure from the lakes following its sale for scrapping overseas.

The *Fort York* had a tumultuous trip off the lakes. (Author's Collection)

On the afternoon of October 26, the Sandrin Brothers Ltd. tugs *Glenada* and *Tusker* pulled the *Fort York* away from its long-term layup berth at Point Edward with the intention of going into lower Lake Huron to turn around before heading downriver. Working against the strong current present in that area, the tow had not yet passed beneath the Blue Water Bridge when the 461-foot ship broke free of the tugs and began drifting sideways down the St. Clair River toward the Michigan shore. Dropping an anchor, the wayward vessel came to a stop before causing any major problems other than closing the river to traffic for 18 minutes.

With the *Fort York* returned safely to its dock, the *Tusker* spent the next day undergoing repairs from damage sustained in the incident. On the morning of October 28, the scrap tow resumed when the two tugs finally succeeded in getting the retired vessel turned around to proceed down the St. Clair River. About an hour later, however, the towline broke once again when the *Tusker* ran aground just north of downtown St. Clair after swerving to miss a small boat that strayed into the shipping channel. Managing to moor the *Fort York* a short distance away, the *Glenada* began working to refloat its stranded fleet mate. Even this effort proved troublesome with the *Glenada* getting a line tangled around its propeller before pulling the *Tusker* free at 3:12 a.m. on October 29. The inauspicious departure of the *Fort York*, prompted one Canadian Coast Guard official to comment, "I don't think it wants to leave Sarnia."

Clearing the Detroit River during the early hours of October 30, the scrap tow put in at Port Colborne the following day. Passing through the Welland Canal and St. Lawrence Seaway without incident, the tow encountered further difficulties on November 10 when the *Glenada* broke down with engine problems near Trois-Rivieres. The tug *Robert H.* having replaced the *Glenada*, the *Fort York* arrived at Lauzon on November 11. Still bearing the unmistakable scars of its September fire, the carrier left that port on December 13 in tow of the tug *Capt. Ioannis S.*, which delivered it to Sydney, Nova Scotia, three days later. Towed out of Sydney on July 22, 1988 by the tug *Phoceen*, the *Fort York* finally reached Recife, Brazil, on September 15, 1988 for scrapping.

On the afternoon of October 29, American Steamship's *Roger M. Kyes* closed out a month of several grounding casualties, and one that had proven particularly bad for that fleet, when it stranded on Gull Island Shoal about three miles north of Kelleys Island in Lake Erie. This mishap took place shortly after the motor vessel had left Sandusky with a load of coal for delivery to Detroit. Its forepeak and No. 1 starboard ballast tank flooded, the 680-foot self-unloader spent about 14 hours aground before managing to free itself early the following morning after offloading 3,000 tons of coal into the *American Republic*. Sailing to Sturgeon Bay after unloading at Detroit, the *Roger M. Kyes* spent three weeks in the dry dock at Bay Shipbuilding before returning to service on November 27.

Acquired earlier that season by the Durocher Dock & Dredge Company of Cheboygan, Michigan, the tug *General* lost engine power on Lake Ontario shortly after leaving Oswego with a pair of empty barges at 5:30 p.m. on October 29. As a U.S. Coast Guard 44 footer stood by to render assistance, the 70-foot vessel drifted for just over six hours before another tugboat arrived to tow it and the two barges back into port.

During the month of October, the Panoceanic Engineering Corporation of Alpena sold the crane-equipped sand sucker *Massey D.* to Catawba Transport for use on Lake Erie. Sailing under its own power to Port Clinton, Ohio, the 125-foot motor vessel operated briefly under the name *H. B. Cunningham* before being renamed *Steven H.* a short time later.

Late the previous year, USS Great Lakes Fleet had sold the bulk carriers *Robert C. Stanley* and *Ralph H. Watson* to Frederick Drontle of Cold Spring, Minnesota, who later resold them to Gordon Low of Calgary, Alberta. Subsequently acquired by Corostel Trading Ltd., both ships began making their way to the scrap heap during the second week of November.

Moved from its long-term layup berth at Hallett Dock #6A to the Port Terminal by the tugs *Arkansas* and *New Jersey*, the *Ralph H. Watson* cleared Duluth on November 10 in tow of the tugs *Avenger IV* and *Thunder Cape* to arrive at Sault Ste. Marie, Ontario, two days later. Resuming its trip down the lakes with the tugs *Elmore M. Misner* and *Thunder Cape* on November 14, the 611-foot carrier reached Port Colborne on November 22, where the tugs secured it in a section of the old Welland Canal near Ramey's Bend.

Meanwhile, the *Avenger IV* sailed back across Lake Superior to collect the *Robert C. Stanley*. Leaving Duluth on November 14, the tow spent some time anchored near Marquette after running into some heavy weather before finally making it to Sault Ste. Marie, Ontario, on November 19. Ten days later, the *Stanley* began the second leg of its journey when it departed in tow of the *W. J. Ivan Purvis* and *Thunder Cape*. Arriving at Port Colborne on December 4, by which time the *Elmore M. Misner* had replaced the *W. J. Ivan Purvis*, the late season scrap tow was reported downbound on Lake Ontario two days later. Encountering no problems while

No stranger to accidents, the *Roger M. Kyes* went aground on Gull Island Shoal in Lake Erie on October 29, 1987. (Author's Collection)

transiting the Seaway, the 620-foot steamer cleared the St. Lambert Lock on December 9 before reaching Sorel the next day.

Having returned to Port Colborne, the *Elmore M. Misner* and *Thunder Cape* took the *Ralph H. Watson* down the Welland Canal on December 13. Joining the *Robert C. Stanley* at Sorel six days later, both vessels remained there for the next 17 months until leaving in a tandem tow with the tug *Fairplay IX* on May 16, 1989. Crossing the unfamiliar waters of the Atlantic and Mediterranean, the two steamers arrived at Aliaga, Turkey, for dismantling on June 19, 1989.

Built by the Great Lakes Engineering Works at River Rouge in 1938, the *Ralph H. Watson* had remained active in the ore trade until laying up for the final time at Duluth on May 16, 1980. As one of four "Miller" class steamers built for the Pittsburgh Steamship Company during the late 1930s, it was one of the first ships in that fleet to feature one-piece hatch covers. Constructed by the same shipyard, the "Maritime" class bulk carrier *Robert C. Stanley* suffered a serious incident within a few months of entering service when a large crack developed across its spar deck on November 10, 1943 while upbound in heavy weather on Lake Superior. With cables ran between its fore and aft winches to prevent the crack from worsening, the lake freighter made a cautious return to Sault Ste. Marie, Michigan, for temporary patching. Remarkably, it operated for another month in this condition due to wartime production demands. Having become redundant in an era of larger self-unloading vessels, the *Robert C. Stanley* closed out its relatively brief operational career when it entered a permanent layup at Superior, Wisconsin, on November 25, 1981.

During the autumn, McKeil Work Boats

Ltd. of Winona, Ontario, purchased the barge *Wittransport II*, which had resided at Deseronto, Ontario, since arriving there from Kingston in May of 1984. Towed across Lake Ontario, the tug *Stormont* delivered the barge to Hamilton on November 15. It was within this same timeframe that the company also acquired the canal-sized crane ship *Condarrell* from Marine Salvage Ltd. Subsequently moved from Toronto to Hamilton, McKeil renamed the 259-foot motor vessel *D. C. Everest* in 1988, thereby reviving its original name when built in 1953.

Spending a good part of the year operating off the lakes, the tug-barge combo *Great Lakes/Michigan* ran aground on November 15 while attempting to dock at Island Park, New York, during a loaded voyage from Linden, New Jersey. Occurring near the westernmost section of Long Island, the accident left the tug *Michigan* with propeller and rudder damage.

Downbound at Sault Ste. Marie, Michigan, on November 16 with a load of coal for the lower lakes, the *William J. De Lancey* came away from a minor incident at the Soo Locks apparently unscathed when it rubbed the bottom while entering the Poe Lock. Another mishap on the St. Marys River took place just three days later when the downbound *Edwin H. Gott* sliced open some starboard bow plating when it struck the edge of the channel near the entrance to the Rock Cut. Taking on 30 inches of water in its forepeak tank, the thousand-footer went to an anchorage in Munuscong Lake with the assistance of the tug *Chippewa* for a damage inspection. After an air compressor unit was put aboard to control the flooding, it continued downbound to anchor off De Tour on November 20 before clearing the next day for Gary. Dry-docked at Bay Shipbuilding on November 26, the shipyard completed the necessary repairs quickly with the 1004-foot self-unloader returning to service on December 7.

The crane vessel *Yankcanuck* (2) made an unusual appearance at Marquette on November 19 when it arrived to take on a cargo of taconite pellets. Two days later, a small fire broke out aboard the Liberian registered *Dimitrios* while downbound on the St. Marys River just below Mission Point. Quickly extinguished by its crew, the blaze inflicted only minor damage to the saltwater vessel.

Sold to Corostel Trading Ltd. for dismantling overseas after USS Great Lakes Fleet Inc. pursued legal action to halt its conversion to a barge, the steamer *Rogers City* cleared Menominee on November 23 in tow of the tug *Avenger IV*. With the tugs *Glenbrook* and *W. N. Twolan* taking over the tow after it passed through the Welland Canal on December 2, the 552-foot self-unloader arrived at Lauzon on December 7. Departing on December 15 with the ocean tug *Phoceen*, the scrap tow put in at Sydney, Nova Scotia, four days later, where the *Rogers City* spent the winter. Collected by the *Phoceen* several months later, it finally arrived at Recife, Brazil, on June 23, 1988 for scrapping.

Built by the American Ship Building Company at Lorain in 1923 as the *B. H. Taylor*, this vessel was later renamed *Rogers City* in 1957. Laying up for the final time on December 17, 1981, it had avoided any significant accidents during its long career other than the collapse of the A-frame structure holding its self-unloading boom at Carrollton, Michigan, on October 26, 1971.

Just six weeks after catching fire at Lorain, the sand sucker *James B. Lyons* arrived at Erie, Pennsylvania, on November 24 following its purchase by Presque Isle Sand & Gravel Inc., a subsidiary of the Erie Builders Concrete Company. The next day, the tugs *Princess No. 1* and *R. & L. No. 1* towed the hull of the former Halco tanker *Hudson Transport* down the Welland Canal from Ramey's Bend to Port Weller Dry Docks for dry-docking prior to its service entry as a barge. Renamed *Scurry* and operated by Bocadon Marine Transport Inc. of Toronto, its first voyage in this configuration took the 360-foot barge to the Shell Canada Ltd. refinery at Corunna, Ontario, where it arrived on December 6 in tow of the McKeil tugs *Glenevis* and *Stormont*.

On November 26, the Yugoslavian flagged freighter *Split* hit the port bow of Misener Shipping's *Canada Marquis* as the latter sat at anchor off Pointe des Ormes in the St. Lawrence River near Trois-Rivieres. With both vessels sustaining only light damage, the ocean carrier arrived at Montreal later that same day.

Normally ending its voyages to Lake Erie at Conneaut, Ohio, USS Great Lakes Fleet's *Edgar B. Speer* arrived at Lorain on November 27 with a load of taconite pellets. Met by the 767-foot *Philip R. Clarke* inside the lower harbor, the thousand-footer began transferring its cargo into the smaller ship, which then carried it up the Black River to the USX steel mill. In total, the *Clarke* made three such trips before the *Speer* was finished unloading.

Making its now common late season appearance, the Finnish tanker *Kiisla* arrived at Montreal on November 28 en route to begin its third consecutive winter operating between ports on the lakes. Two days later, the *Canadian Pioneer* suffered electrical damage when a fire broke out in its engine room while unloading at Nanticoke, Ontario. Proceeding to the Welland Canal, the 730-foot self-unloader tied up at the Welland Dock on December 2 for repairs.

USS Great Lakes Fleet's *Edgar B. Speer* made a pair of unusual trips to Lorain, Ohio, with taconite pellets during the late months of the 1987 season. (Photo by Tom Salvner)

In another late autumn transaction, Socanav Inc. sold the tanker *Northern Shell* to Ridgeway Maritime Inc. of Greece. As one of the three vessels included in the acquisition of the Shell Canadian Tankers Ltd. fleet earlier that year, it had never operated for Socanav. Renamed *Leon*, the 550-foot tanker departed Toronto on December 10 bound for its new duties on saltwater.

Around this same time, Socanav also entered into an agreement with Master Securities Ltd. of the Bahamas to sell the tanker *Le Cedre No. 1* for $2.5 million. Remaining in operation under the Canadian flag until near the end of the year, the 14-year old vessel arrived at Halifax, Nova Scotia, on December 17. Renamed *Cam Etinde*, it sailed for an overseas port on December 23.

A minor mishap occurred shortly after midnight on December 10 when the *Enerchem Catalyst* went aground in the Detroit River. Called to assist, a pair of Gaelic Tugboat Company tugs refloated the tanker about four hours later without damage. That same day, Rouge Steel's *Henry Ford II* ran into some difficulty while transiting the Saginaw River when it became stuck for about an hour inside the open span of the I-75 drawbridge at Zilwaukee, Michigan.

Closing out its 120-year history of Great Lakes vessel ownership, the Cleveland-Cliffs Steamship Company donated the steamer *William G. Mather* (2) to the Great Lakes Historical Society of Vermilion, Ohio, on December 10 for preservation as a museum ship. Idle at Toledo since December 21, 1980, the 618-foot bulk carrier remained there until departing for Cleveland on October 7, 1988 in tow of the tugs *Alabama* and *Wyoming*. Delivered to the G. & W. Industries Dock on the Cuyahoga River the next day, it later went to the Mid-Continent Coal & Coke Company Dock as volunteers worked to complete the restoration effort. Moved to the East 9th Street Pier on October 16, 1990 by the tugs *Delaware* and *Idaho*, the *William G. Mather* (2) opened to the public in May of 1991.

On December 11, the tug *Ohio* towed the *Merle M. McCurdy* out of Buffalo, New York, bound for scrapping by Triad Salvage Inc. at Ashtabula. After spending two days anchored off Presque Isle due to weather, the tow arrived at Ashtabula on the morning of December 14. Battling low water levels and damaging two boat docks in the process, it took the tugs *Iowa* and *Minnesota* about six hours to move the 601-foot bulk carrier up the Ashtabula River to the scrap yard. Environmental concerns over the removal of asbestos, however, forced the scrap company to resell the *McCurdy* to International Marine Salvage for dismantling in Canada the following year. Towed out of Ashtabula on the morning of June 10, 1988 by the tugs *Glenevis* and *Michael D. Misner*, it arrived at Port Colborne later that same day, where it was broken up over the next 12 months.

Launched in 1910 as the *William B. Dickson*, this vessel was one of three steamers built by the Great Lakes Engineering Works at Ecorse that year for the Pittsburgh Steamship Company. Idle at Lorain after the 1960 season, it returned to service in 1969 as the *Merle M. McCurdy* following its acquisition by the Kinsman Marine Transit Company. Concentrating on the movement of grain during its final years, the classic lake freighter operated until laying up at Buffalo on November 19, 1985.

Scheduled for saltwater duties during the upcoming winter, the package freighter *Woodland* made a rare appearance at Toronto on December 12 when it arrived to load a 135-ton self-unloading unit consigned to the

The motor vessel *Henry Ford II* encountered a minor delay at Zilwaukee, Michigan, in early December 1987. (Photo by James Hoffman)

Verolme Shipyard at Angra dos Reis, Brazil. Strapped to the deck of the 404-foot motor vessel for the 6,500-mile journey, this unit was slated for use in the conversion of CSL's Panamax bulk carrier *Atlantic Huron* to a self-unloader (subsequently rechristened *CSL Innovator* on April 19, 1988).

Making another unusual visit to Lorain with ore that season, the *Edgar B. Speer* entered the harbor on December 13 and tied up alongside the *Cason J. Callaway* at the Lorain Pellet Terminal. Equipped with a shuttle boom that has an outboard reach of only 52 feet, the *Speer* unloaded its cargo into the *Callaway*, which then used its own 250-foot boom to reach the storage area on the dock.

A blizzard packing 72 mph winds that blanketed much of southeast Wisconsin with 13 inches of snow on December 15 also tore the Greek bulker *Capetan Yiannis* from its moorings at Milwaukee. Slammed repeatedly between two piers by 10-foot waves for the next four hours, the ocean carrier suffered hull, propeller, and rudder damage before finally being secured by three tugs after the wind changed direction. Left disabled by the incident, it required temporary patching in preparation for a tow to Lauzon for repairs. Towed out of Milwaukee on December 19 by the tugs *John Purves*, *Carl William Selvick*, and *Minnie Selvick*, this ship's exit from the lakes was to play a prominent role in that season's closing of the St. Lawrence Seaway.

On December 16, the Liberian tug *Rembertiturm* moved the steamers *Ashland* and *Thomas Wilson* (2) from their berths at Lauzon to make the short trip across the St. Lawrence River to Quebec City. Picked up by another Liberian tug, *Osa Ravensturm*, both vessels left on December 21 bound for scrapping in Taiwan with the *Rembertiturm* assisting until the tandem scrap tow reached Les Escoumins, Quebec. Venturing into the North Atlantic during one of the most inopportune times of the year, all proceeded normally until the *Thomas Wilson* (2) broke its towline while caught in heavy seas on December 30. Battered by the waves, the former lake freighter foundered early the following morning at a position approximately 220 miles northeast of Bermuda.

Having sustained heavy storm damage while chasing the *Thomas Wilson* (2), the *Osa Ravensturm* set course for Bermuda only to have the *Ashland* break free of its towline a few hours later. Tracked by the U.S. Coast Guard, the bulk carrier wallowed in the storm-tossed waters until retrieved by the *Rembertiturm* on January 2, 1988. Towed to an anchorage near St. George's, Bermuda, a subsequent storm on January 16, 1988 pushed the *Ashland* onto the Pigeon Rocks in Bailey's Bay. Refloated four days later with severe bottom damage, the poor condition of the 45-year old vessel precluded any further consideration of continuing the tow to Taiwan. Resold for scrapping at Mamonal, Columbia, it arrived at that South American port on February 5, 1988 following a brief stop in the Dominican Republic.

Sidelined since suffering a fire at Nanticoke on November 30, the *Canadian Pioneer* returned to service on December 16. Arriving at Sorel two days later, ULS International transferred this ship into Vanuatu registry for use in the company's Mar-Bulk Shipping saltwater subsidiary in much the same manner as it had done with the *Canadian Ambassador* in late 1986. Renamed *Pioneer*, the self-unloader cleared Sorel on December 21 bound for Trois-Rivieres before continuing to Savannah, Georgia.

Reportedly making its first trip into Cleveland in 10 years, Rouge Steel's *Ernest R. Breech* delivered a cargo of iron ore to the C&P Dock on December 19. The *Roger Blough* experienced a minor mechanical issue after loading taconite at Two Harbors on December 21 when a faulty hydraulic motor caused its hatch crane to break down. Sailing to Duluth with open cargo hatches, the 858-foot carrier tied up at the Port Terminal to have its hatch covers put in place by the dock's container crane before departing for the lower lakes the next day.

One final incident just before the end of the year took place on Christmas Day when the 1898-built tug *Frederick T. Kellers* spilled a small amount of fuel oil into the Saginaw River. Owned by the American Tug & Transit Company of Bay City, Michigan, the 85-foot tugboat lasted until its dismantling in 1994.

Handed over to the tugs *Duga*, *Helen M. McAllister*, and *Salvage Monarch* upon reaching Port Colborne on December 24, the tow of the *Capetan Yiannis* continued its journey off the lakes during the final week of December with the *Cathy McAllister* joining to assist in the Seaway. In a passage that came five days past the official closing date of the St. Lawrence Seaway, the disabled Greek freighter became the last commercial vessel through the system for the season when it cleared the St. Lambert Lock on December 29. Taken to Lauzon, the ocean freighter entered the MIL Davie dry dock for repairs on January 4, 1988.

Meanwhile, shipping continued on the upper lakes with a combination of favorable winter weather and a strong demand for iron ore resulting in the U.S. Army Corps of Engineers extending the navigation season at the Soo Locks. While arriving at Superior, Wisconsin, on January 4, 1988 to load one of these late season ore shipments, the *H. Lee White* (2) experienced engine problems and went instead to Fraser Shipyards for winter layup with its cargo rescheduled for the *American Mariner*, which was due to arrive a few days later. The Soo Locks closed for season on January 15, 1988 with the downbound passage of the *Edgar B. Speer* with iron ore for Gary. As the only iron ore loading port on the lakes located below the locks, shipments through Escanaba continued until January 23, 1988 when the *Roger Blough* loaded the final cargo of the season.

Totaling 61.7 million net tons, iron ore shipments on the Great Lakes during 1987 increased by a remarkable 10.6 million net tons, or 21 percent, in comparison to the previous year. As such, it represented the best year for that commodity since the 1984 season. Also experiencing a significant increase in demand, stone shipments grew by 22 percent to 33.1 million net tons. Meanwhile, the movement of grain rose by nearly 11 percent from 20.1 million net tons in 1986 to 22.3 million net tons in 1987. Of the four major dry bulk commodities moved on the Great Lakes during the season, only the coal trade recorded a single digit increase with shipments totaling 37.7 million net tons, a level representing just a four percent improvement from the year before. Overall, bulk commerce on the lakes grew by 13 percent to 171.9 million net tons.

Due to receding water levels brought about by an extended period of record low precipitation and high evaporation rates during the summer months, lake carriers established only one new cargo record during the 1987 season. This occurred on August 6 when Interlake Steamship's *James R. Barker* loaded 58,959 net tons of coal at Conneaut for delivery to Muskegon, thus beating the previous record for this commodity originating from a lower lakes port by 3,912 net tons.

Chapter Nine
The 1988 Shipping Season

Coming off a year of strengthening tonnages and with the demand for steel remaining high, the Great Lakes shipping industry could look toward the 1988 season with a sense of measured optimism. Within days of the previous season ending, however, came some news that cast serious doubt upon the future of the region's icebreaking capability. Citing a $105 million budget cut in a January 26 statement, the U.S. Coast Guard announced its intention to remove the icebreaker *Mackinaw* (WAGB-83) from service that spring as part of a planned drawback affecting 52 facilities and ships nationwide. As the largest and most powerful icebreaker ever built for Great Lakes service, this vessel had remained a critical asset in opening up navigation channels and assisting icebound ships during the winter and early spring ever since its commissioning nearly a half century earlier in 1944. Responding to considerable political pressure, Congress managed to avert the mothballing of the *Mackinaw* when it passed a new spending bill later that spring to restore the necessary funding.

With the dry bulk fleet laid up by late January, commercial navigation on the lakes continued with the usual pattern of winter tanker traffic. In addition to the Finnish flagged *Kiisla*, other vessels involved in these movements included the *Enerchem Avance*, *Gemini*, *Jupiter*, and the tug-barge combo *Great Lakes/Michigan*.

Early in the year, the Royal Bank of Canada wrapped up its effort to dispose of the last eight vessels remaining in the Halco Inc. fleet with Canada Steamship Lines Inc. (CSL) and N. M. Paterson & Sons Ltd. each acquiring three while Misener Shipping took the other two. This series of transactions involved seven gearless bulk carriers and one self-unloader, all of which received new names prior to entering service that season. As such, the *Cartiercliffe Hall*, *Frankcliffe Hall* (2), and *Maplecliffe Hall* passed into CSL ownership to become the *Winnipeg* (3), *Halifax*, and *Lemoyne* (2) respectively. As CSL had with two of its carriers, Paterson revived some former fleet names by renaming its acquisitions in the following manner: *Beavercliffe Hall* to *Quedoc* (3), *Montcliffe Hall* to *Cartierdoc* (2), and *Steelcliffe Hall* to *Windoc* (2). Lastly, Misener named the *Lawrencecliffe Hall* (2) and *Ottercliffe Hall* for a pair of executives serving within that family run organization at the time with the former becoming the *David K. Gardiner* and the latter *Peter Misener*.

Arriving at St. Romuald, Quebec, on the foggy morning of February 1, Socanav Inc.'s *L'Orme No. 1* ran hard into a pier while attempting to dock at the Ultramar Refinery located across the St. Lawrence River from Quebec City, Quebec. The impact ruptured a pipeline used for loading ships, which triggered a fire that quickly engulfed both the dock and the bow of the tanker. With the flames threatening to spread to the fully laden *Enerchem Travailleur* moored at the same dock, that vessel was able to get underway for the safety of the river in just a matter of minutes. Reacting with equal swiftness to the unfolding crisis, the crew of the *L'Orme No. 1* soon had the blaze extinguished but not before it left the tanker with a scorched bow and the dock out of commission for nearly two weeks. Bearing the unmistakable scars of its fiery encounter, the 14-year old ship arrived at Montreal, Quebec, on February 5 where it remained until returning to service on March 2 following the completion of repairs.

Slated for a return to service that spring after sitting out the previous season, Columbia Transportation's *Joseph H. Frantz* suffered some minor smoke damage from a galley fire at Toledo, Ohio, on February 19. Around the same time, another incident at Toledo involving a member of that fleet sent two workers to a local hospital after they lost consciousness inside of a fuel tank aboard the *Courtney Burton*.

On February 22, the Cargill B2 grain elevator at Duluth, Minnesota, began unloading the 830,729 bushels of barley that had been stored aboard Interlake Steamship's *John Sherwin* (2) since September of 1986. Completed four days later, the operation triggered a dispute between local longshoremen and Cargill when the latter brought in outside personnel to perform the actual work.

Bustling with activity during the early months of the year, Fraser Shipyards Inc. at Superior, Wisconsin, completed two noteworthy contracts in addition to the usual assortment of routine winter maintenance work. The first was the dry-docking of the cement carrier *J. A. W. Iglehart* for some $2 million worth of hull repairs followed by the 767-foot self-unloader *Philip R. Clarke* for the installation of a stern thruster. Another vessel modernization within the U.S. fleet during the winter layup period involved Rouge Steel's *William Clay Ford* (2), which had its electrical system converted from DC to AC power by the Bay Shipbuilding Corporation at Sturgeon Bay, Wisconsin.

Like their American counterparts, Canadian ship owners also undertook a series of upgrades to their existing vessels within this same timeframe. At Thunder Bay, Ontario, the Port Arthur Shipbuilding Company completed one such project when it fitted the 640-foot *Algorail* (2) with a stern thruster using a unit salvaged during the dismantling of the *William Clay Ford*. Other shipyard activity included the conversion of two 730-foot self-unloaders to "Caribbean" class standards with Algoma Central's *Algobay* having this work performed by Port Weller Dry Docks at St. Catharines, Ontario, while CSL's *Nanticoke* went to Halifax, Nova Scotia, during mid-January for its modifications. Receiving additional hull strengthening during this process, the operational footprint of these vessels grew to include limited ocean service along the east coasts of Canada and the United States down to the Gulf of Mexico and into the Caribbean.

At Hamilton, Ontario, Canadian Shipbuilding & Engineering Ltd. performed an unusual reconstruction that winter with the installation of a bow-mounted self-unloading apparatus aboard ULS International's *Canadian Ranger*. Incorporating a 160-foot boom and a traveling unloading leg that accessed the holds through the cargo hatches, this unorthodox system was limited to handling grain with the unloading of other commodities still performed by shoreside equipment as is done with conventional straight deck bulk carriers. This conversion allowed deliveries to grain elevators equipped with specialized unloading hoppers without reducing the volume capacity of the vessel's six cargo holds—an important factor in the efficient transportation of grain.

Early in the year, ownership of the thousand-footer *George A. Stinson* was transferred from the Skar-Ore Steamship Corporation to Stinson Inc. with the M. A. Hanna Company of Cleveland, Ohio, still acting as agent for the vessel.

During one of its regular runs between Detroit, Michigan, and Windsor, Ontario, on the afternoon of March 2, the tug *R. G. Cassidy* experienced a steering failure while crossing the Detroit River with a loaded railcar barge. Slamming into the Windsor shore moments later, the pair ripped up a 65-foot section of a walkway belonging to the Holiday Inn hotel located at the water's edge but apparently came away from the incident unscathed themselves.

A powerful snowstorm packing 70 mph winds that swept across northeastern Minnesota during the night of March 11-12 tore the museum ship *William A. Irvin* away from its moorings in the Minnesota Slip at Duluth. Pushed some 50 feet along the dock, it was not until later that afternoon that Duluth Arena-Auditorium personnel managed to secure the retired steamer. Although wrecking two gangplanks, the episode caused no serious damage to the *Irvin*.

The American Steamship Company's *American Republic* kicked off the 1988 shipping season with its departure from Cleveland on March 15 for nearby Lorain, Ohio, to begin the ore shuttle between those two Lake Erie ports. Sailing from Toledo two days later, the steamer *S. T. Crapo* made one of its typical early season debuts when it headed north to load cement at Alpena, Michigan.

With voluntary restraint agreements (VRAs) in effect with 19 steel producing nations and the European Community (EC) restricting steel imports, the American steel industry remained busy during the early months of the year. The favorable market conditions had domestic mills operating at 88 percent of capacity in January with this utilization rate growing to 92 percent of capacity by late March. It was against this setting that the Soo Locks at Sault Ste. Marie, Michigan, opened for the season on March 22 when the *Algowest* locked upbound through the Poe Lock for Thunder Bay. There was no shortage of Algoma Central Marine (ACM) vessels at the locks that day with *Algocape* and *Algomarine* also passing upbound while the *Algowood* made the first downbound commercial transit of the season.

An early season casualty took place on March 23 when the tug *Olive L. Moore* lost its rudder after running into heavy ice on Green Bay shortly after clearing Menominee, Michigan, with the barge *Buckeye* (2). Leaving the 524-foot barge anchored in the bay, the tug was towed to Sturgeon Bay for repairs. These same ice conditions claimed a second victim the next day when the *St. Clair* (2) tore open some hull plating after leaving Bay Shipbuilding. Continuing to Escanaba, Michigan, a subsequent damage survey instigated a return trip to the shipyard.

The navigation season at the Soo Locks was barely two days old when the upbound tanker *Enerchem Refiner* was instructed to tie up at the upper end of the center pier for a U.S. Coast Guard inspection on March 24. Found to be overloaded, the 391-foot vessel went across the St. Marys River to Sault Ste. Marie, Ontario, to offload 400 tons of cargo at the Algoma Steel mill before resuming its voyage to Taconite Harbor, Minnesota.

A strong demand for iron ore prompted the reactivation of the Inland Steel Company's 730-foot gearless bulk carrier *Edward L. Ryerson*, which sailed from Indiana

During early April 1988, the *Black Bay* lost steering and went aground in the St. Lawrence River.
(Photo by Kenneth Bonnell)

Harbor, Indiana, on March 26 bound for Escanaba following two years of idleness. This ship was the first of four U.S. flagged vessels that returned to service by the middle of May after being laid up for extended periods, the others being the *Irvin L. Clymer*, *E. M. Ford*, and the *Joseph H. Frantz*.

The St. Lawrence Seaway opened for commercial traffic on March 29 when Misener Shipping's *John A. France* (2) passed upbound through St. Lambert Lock with a cargo of iron ore. Later in the day, an accident took place in the Pointe-aux-Trembles Anchorage in the St. Lawrence River when the anchored CSL bulk carrier *Simcoe* (2) sustained significant stern damage when struck from behind by the container ship *Castano*. Following temporary patching at Montreal, the 730-foot motor vessel received permanent repairs at Thunder Bay.

During late March, the Rouge Steel Company self-unloaders *Benson Ford* (3) and *Henry Ford II* made rare appearances at Lorain to load taconite pellets for delivery to Dearborn, Michigan. A minor mishap occurred on March 31 when the 1000-foot *Indiana Harbor* rubbed the bottom of the St. Marys River at Stribling Point. Going to the Carbide Dock at Sault Ste. Marie, Michigan, a subsequent inspection revealed no damage.

The string of early season incidents persisted well into April with no less than four taking place during the first full week of the month. The first of these happened on April

5 when CSL's *Black Bay* went aground after experiencing a steering failure in the Brockville Narrows section of the St. Lawrence River while upbound with iron ore from Pointe Noire, Quebec. Proving somewhat reluctant to come off the bottom, the *P. S. Barge No. 1* lightered 2,200 tons of its cargo two days later as part of a salvage operation that also included the shifting of an additional 250 tons of ore from the No. 1 to No. 3 cargo hold. Released on April 8 by the tugs *Helen M. McAllister* and *Salvage Monarch*, the 730-foot steamer went to Thunder Bay for repairs after discharging its cargo at Hamilton.

Encountering a combination of heavy vessel traffic, ice, and fog in the lower St. Marys River on April 6, the motor vessel *Quedoc* (3) snagged a submerged power cable running between De Tour, Michigan, and Drummond Island while going to anchor near Frying Pan Island in the De Tour Passage. Having just entered service for N. M. Paterson & Sons Ltd., the 730-foot bulk carrier continued upbound to load grain at Superior, Wisconsin, after having its anchor chain cut. Foggy weather also played a role in an accident on the St. Lawrence River that same day when the upbound Liberian bulker *Handymariner* grounded in Lake St. Francis near St. Anicet, Quebec. After offloading some 1,000 tons of steel coils onto the barge *Genmar 130*, the tugs *James Battle*, *Cathy McAllister*, and *Daniel McAllister* pulled the ocean carrier free on April 10. Reloaded at Valleyfield, Quebec, it continued to Cleveland and Sault Ste. Marie, Ontario, before going to Bay Shipbuilding for bow repairs.

On the evening of April 7, the *Richelieu* (3) became the third CSL bulker to sustain damage in nine days when it struck an underwater obstruction while departing Saskatchewan Pool No. 6 at Thunder Bay with a load of grain. Opening up a hole in its forward port side, the 729-foot lake freighter cleared port with temporary repairs before going to Port Weller Dry Docks for drydocking later that month.

In a casualty blamed partly on low water levels, the bad luck plaguing the CSL fleet that spring claimed yet another victim on April 10 when the recently acquired *Winnipeg* (3) went aground at Thunder Bay. Although able to free itself, the mishap left the bulk carrier with some hull damage. That same day, a gunman fired as many as 18 rifle shots at the steamer *Beechglen* as it sailed downbound in the St. Lawrence Seaway near Massena, New York. Although the crew found bullet holes in the captain's office, dining room, fuel tanks, and stack, there were no injuries. It was not until January 21 of the following year that the New York State Police arrested a 22-year old man from Rooseveltown, New York, on first-degree reckless endangerment charges in connection with this incident.

Following a tow from Sandusky, Ohio, that began earlier that day, the tug *William A. Whitney* delivered the retired sidewheel steamer *G. A. Boeckling* to the Toledo Shipyard on April 13 to begin the next phase of its ongoing restoration. Going into the dry dock on May 16, the former Cedar Point ferry remained at the shipyard until being moved to the Hocking Valley Slip that autumn.

While upbound at Sault Ste. Marie, Michigan, on April 17, high winds and ice pushed the *Edwin H. Gott* against the south wall of the Poe Lock. Coming away from the impact with a 12-foot tear in its port bow, 1004-foot vessel sailed to Duluth for the necessary repairs before continuing on to Two Harbors, Minnesota, on April 21.

Nearing the end of its career with the American Steamship Company (ASC), the idle self-unloader *Adam E. Cornelius* (3) made the short trip from the Frog Pond on the Toledo lakefront to the Toledo Shipyard in tow of the tugs *Galway Bay* and *Patricia Hoey* on April 18. After spending two days in the dry dock, the 29-year old steamer was returned to the Frog Pond.

During this same timeframe, ASC disposed of two other idle vessels with the sale of the *John T. Hutchinson* and *Consumers Power* (3) to Corostel Trading Ltd. of Montreal for scrapping overseas. After being laid up for over six years, the *John T. Hutchinson* cleared Toledo on April 18 in tow of the tug *W. N. Twolan*. Joined by the tug *Glenside* at Port Colborne, Ontario, the scrap tow passed down the Welland Canal on April 22 before transiting the U.S. section of the St. Lawrence Seaway two days later. After delivering the *Hutchinson* to Lauzon, Quebec, on April 27, the tugs returned to the lakes with *W. N. Twolan* going to Erie, Pennsylvania, to retrieve the *Consumers Power* (3).

Launched on May 1, 1943, the *John T. Hutchinson* was one of two "Maritime" class vessels built by the American Ship Building Company at Cleveland that year the other being the *Belle Isle* (*Champlain* (3)). Entering service for the Buckeye Steamship Company (Hutchinson & Co., mgr.) on July 29, 1943, this ship served as that fleet's flagship until its sale to the American Steamship Company in late 1963. Converted to a self-unloader over the following winter by the Fraser-Nelson Shipbuilding & Dry Dock Company at Superior, Wisconsin, this vessel remained active until entering its final layup at Cleveland on December 18, 1981. A little

The steamer *John T. Hutchinson* on its tow off the lakes. (Photo by Jeff Cameron)

more than a year and a half later, the tug *Ohio* towed the *Hutchinson* to Toledo on August 4, 1983.

After spending the winter serving as a grain storage barge, the former P. & H. Shipping steamer *Birchglen* left Toronto, Ontario, on April 21, in tow of the tugs *Atomic* and *Elmore M. Misner* bound for scrapping in Nova Scotia. With the *Atomic* replaced by the tug *Thunder Cape* for the Seaway transit, the tow proceeded normally until the *Birchglen* took a sudden sheer and struck the port bow of the upbound *Quedoc* (3) near Buoy 2A in Lake St. Louis on the afternoon of April 23. Going aground immediately after the collision, the latter vessel suffered heavy damage to 350 feet of its bottom. Refloated two days later, the *Quedoc* (3) went to Port Weller Dry Docks for repairs lasting until early June.

Meanwhile, the *Birchglen* scrap tow continued down the St. Lawrence River until reaching an anchorage just downstream from Quebec City on April 24. The 600-foot bulk carrier departed two days later in tow of the tug *Orion Expeditor*, which delivered it to Point Edward, Nova Scotia, for dismantling by Universal Metal Co. Ltd.

On April 25, the N. M. Paterson & Sons bulk freighter *Kingdoc* (2) passed downbound through the Welland Canal with grain for Sorel, Quebec. En route to saltwater service for the company's Polaris Navigation Ltd. subsidiary, it arrived at that port three days later. Transferred to Bahamas registry and renamed *Norstar*, the 315-foot motor vessel sailed for Genoa, Italy, on May 1 with a load of pig iron.

Rounding out that month's roster of accidents, the upbound Indian bulker *Soren Toubro* ran aground near Buoy 61 in the St. Marys River on April 27. Freed by the tug *Chippewa*, the ocean carrier stopped at the Carbide Dock at Sault Ste. Marie, Michigan, for an inspection before continuing its voyage.

With springtime stone shipments experiencing volumes 14 percent higher in comparison to the same period of the previous year, USS Great Lakes Fleet reactivated its 71-year old *Irvin L. Clymer* following two season of idleness at Superior, Wisconsin. Departing Duluth on April 28, the 552-foot self-unloader sailed to Lorain to deliver a load of iron ore before reentering the stone trade.

Having just completed the *Birchglen* scrap tow, the tugs *Elmore M. Misner* and *Thunder Cape* towed the sludge barge *Isle Royale* up the Welland Canal on April 29 bound for scrapping by Marine Salvage Ltd. at Ramey's Bend. This vessel dated back to its 1947 construction by Canadian Vickers Ltd. at Montreal as the canal-sized bulk carrier *Southcliffe Hall* for the Hall Corporation of Canada Ltd. fleet. Lengthened to 341 feet during its conversion to a self-unloader in 1959, it was renamed *Orefax* two years later. Remaining active until the end of the 1970 season, it was sold late the following year for use as a sludge barge in a major deepening project in the St. Lawrence River to provide deep draft vessels access to Quebec City. Renamed *Isle Royale* to serve in this role, it had sat unused at Whitby, Ontario, for several years prior to its sale for dismantling.

En route to join the *John T. Hutchinson* for an ocean voyage to the scrap yard, the *Consumers Power* (3) left Erie, Pennsylvania, on the evening of May 2 in tow of the tug *W. N. Twolan*. Transiting the Welland Canal on May 5, the scrap tow reached Lauzon four days later following an uneventful passage through the Seaway.

Spanning nearly 60 years, the *Consumers Power* (3) owed its lengthy operational career

Following an eventful career, the *Consumers Power* (3) was sent to the scrap yard during the first half of 1988. (Photo by James Hoffman)

to one of the most audacious salvage operations ever carried out on the Great Lakes. Built by the American Ship Building Company at Lorain, this 605-foot vessel entered service for the Kinsman Transit Company in 1927 as the *George M. Humphrey*. While bound for South Chicago, Illinois, with 13,992 gross tons of iron ore on June 15, 1943, it sank in the Straits of Mackinac without loss of life following a collision with the steamer *D. M. Clemson* (2). Consequently, it gained the unfortunate distinction as becoming the first member of the 600-foot class to be declared a total loss.

Resting in 80 feet of water, the wreck was located in the middle of a busy shipping lane. It removal imperative, the U.S. Army Corps of Engineers accepted a bid from Captain John Roen of Sturgeon Bay to either raise the sunken vessel or clear it to a depth of 35 feet. With only the tips of the *Humphrey*'s masts breaking the surface of the water, Roen set out to accomplish what many thought was impossible. Beginning that September, the salvage effort continued until the onset of winter before resuming the following May. Refloated on September 11, 1944, the salvaged bulk carrier received extensive refurbishing over the following winter at Roen's Sturgeon Bay shipyard.

Reentering service for the Roen Transportation Company as the *Captain John Roen* in 1945, it operated under charter agreements for the next two seasons until being sold to the American Steamship Company in early 1947. Converted to a self-unloader by the Manitowoc Shipbuilding Company at Manitowoc, Wisconsin, and renamed *Adam E. Cornelius* (2) in 1948, this vessel became the *Consumers Power* (3) with the launching of a larger company steamer in 1958. Chartered to the Erie Sand Steamship Company in 1980, it remained active in the bulk trades until laying up for the final time on December 6, 1985.

Destined for scrapping in Asia, the *Consumers Power* (3) and *John T. Hutchinson* departed Lauzon on June 14, 1988 in tow of the Panamanian tug *Omega 809*. Temporarily splitting up the two retired lake freighters upon reaching the Panama Canal, the *Omega 809* made a southbound transit with the *Consumers Power* (3) on July 12 followed two days later by an identical passage with the *John T. Hutchinson*. Rejoined, the tandem scrap tow continued westward across the vast expanse of the Pacific Ocean. Delivered to Kaohsiung, Taiwan, on October 2, Li Chong Steel & Iron Works Co. Ltd. wasted little time in dismantling both vessels with work beginning by the middle of the month.

After delivering some 11,000 tons of steel coils to Chicago, Illinois, the Cyprus flagged bulk carrier *Pontokratis* began making its way through the Calumet River toward Lake Michigan on the evening of May 6 with the tugs *Florida* and *South Carolina* assisting. While passing through the open draw of the Baltimore & Ohio Railroad (CSX) bascule bridge at 8:08 pm, however, the port bridge wing of the ocean freighter snagged the raised 235-foot long bridge leaf. Coming to a stop after traveling approximately another 50 feet with the bridge leaf collapsed upon its wheelhouse, the immobilized ship blocked all shipping traffic through that stretch of the river. After salvage crews had cleared away most of the wreckage but with pieces of the bridge still entangled in its superstructure, tugs moved the *Pontokratis* out of the bridge opening on May 16. With permanent repairs deferred until reaching an off-lakes shipyard, the 7-year old vessel cleared the Seaway on June 28 after loading grain at Duluth.

A far less serious incident involving a bridge took place in Duluth-Superior Harbor on May 7 when the *Philip R. Clarke* knocked over a dolphin put in place to protect the Richard I. Bong Memorial Bridge. That same day, CSL's 714-foot bulk carrier *T. R. McLagan*, inactive since 1984, left Toronto in tow for a survey at Port Weller Dry Docks before reentering service on May 19. While the steamer remained in CSL fleet colors, it actually operated for P. & H. Shipping under the terms of a two-year charter agreement with the intention of the latter company obtaining full ownership of the vessel at the end of that period.

On May 8, the steamer *Benson Ford* (3) and tanker *L'Orme No. 1* came across the auto ferry *Saguenay* adrift on the Detroit River. Catching up to the wandering vessel, which had been brought to the area to serve as the basis for a proposed floating apartment complex on the Windsor waterfront, the tug *R. G. Cassidy* had it quickly secured to a dock with the assistance of the Coast Guard. Just two days later, the tanker *Imperial Bedford* suffered some slight bow damage when it hit the south guard wall at the lower end of the Eisenhower Lock while on a loaded voyage from Montreal to Sarnia, Ontario.

Its return to service indicative of a significant improvement in the construction market, the 90-year old cement carrier *E. M. Ford* arrived at Alpena on May 14 to load its first cargo after sitting out the previous season at Milwaukee, Wisconsin.

While being mended by the locally based ship repairer Sandrin Brothers Ltd. on the morning of May 16, sparks from a cutting torch ignited a fire inside of a cargo tank aboard the Socanav Inc. tanker *Eastern Shell* (2) at Sarnia's Government Dock. With the workers scrambling to safety through a hole already cut in the side of the hull during the removal of some damaged plating, it took the vessel's crew and the Sarnia Fire Department about 30 minutes to extinguish the blaze. Although suffering roughly $100,000 in damage, repairs proceeded quickly with the 356-foot tanker returning to service within a few weeks.

Following a temporary lull in grounding casualties, two such accidents took place over a two-day period during the third week of May. On May 20, the *George A. Sloan* went aground at Port Huron, Michigan, after losing its way on a fog shrouded St. Clair River. Arriving to assist, the Malcolm Marine tug *Barbara Ann* had little difficulty pulling the 620-foot "Maritime" class vessel free of the soft river bottom. The next day, Algoma Central Marine's *Algocape* grounded in Lake St. Louis while downbound with grain for Baie Comeau, Quebec. Lightered by the *P. S. Barge No. 1*, a group of tugs managed to refloat the 715-foot bulk carrier on May 23. After reloading at nearby Montreal, the steamer resumed its voyage two days later.

Its final cargo being a load of grain delivered to Quebec City, P. & H. Shipping's *Oakglen* arrived at Sorel on June 3 to await an overseas scrap tow. Entering service in 1923 as the *William H. Warner*, the classic 600-foot steamer had sailed under five different names over its 65-year career on the lakes. Built by the American Ship Building Company at Lorain for G. A. Tomlinson's Panda Steamship Company this ship passed into the ownership of the International Harvester Company in 1933, which renamed it *The International* early the following year. Acquired by Envirodyne Inc. and renamed *Maxine* when International Harvester sold its Wisconsin Steel Division in 1977, this vessel remained active primarily in the movement of iron ore into that company's steel mill located on the Calumet River at South Chicago. Having no prior experience in the steel industry, however, Envirodyne fared badly in this venture with Wisconsin Steel going bankrupt and closing in 1980. As previously related in Chapter 2, the Triad Salvage Company of Ashtabula, Ohio, purchased the *Maxine* the following year before reselling it to the Soo River Company for service under the Canadian flag. Renamed *J. F. Vaughn*, it operated only briefly for Soo River before that firm went into receivership in August of 1982. When Parrish & Heimbecker Ltd. purchased the ships of the defunct fleet to form its P. & H. Shipping Division just weeks later, that firm gave the aging bulk carrier one final name change by renaming it *Oakglen*.

The Cyprus flagged *Mitera Vassiliki* encountered some trouble on June 4 when it struck a pier at the Soo Locks while downbound from Lake Superior after having spent a month at Thunder Bay for unspecified reasons. Ripping a small hole in its port side, the saltwater vessel went to the Carbide Dock for temporary repairs before continuing to Toledo.

Also on June 4, the tug *Salvage Monarch* towed the *Irving S. Olds* out of Duluth with the help of the tug *New Jersey* following that vessel's sale to Marine Salvage Ltd. for scrapping overseas earlier that spring along with its sister ship *Benjamin F. Fairless*. The disposal of its last two remaining "Super" class steamers represented the final vessel sales made by the USS Great Lakes Fleet during the 1980s. Passing downbound at Sault Ste. Marie, Michigan, on June 7, the *Irving S. Olds* scrap tow began making its way down the Welland Canal four days later. Upon reaching Port Weller, Ontario, the *Salvage Monarch* handed the retired lake freighter over to the tug *Helen M. McAllister*, which had assisted during the canal transit, before heading back up the lakes to fetch the *Fairless*. With the *Cathy McAllister* having joined the scrap tow, the *Olds* arrived at Montreal on June 14 to await a tow to Quebec City.

Built by the American Ship Building Company at Lorain, the launch of the *Irving S. Olds* along with that of its sister ship *A. H. Ferbert* (2) by the Great Lakes Engineering Works at River Rouge, Michigan, on May 22, 1942 coincided with several such shipyard launches across the United States that day in observance of National Maritime Day. Beginning its maiden voyage on October 6, 1942, the *Irving S. Olds* was the last of the five "Super" class vessels built for U.S. Steel's Pittsburgh Steamship Company to enter service. Remaining active in the bulk trades for the next 39 years, the 639-foot bulk carrier entered its final layup at Duluth on December 3, 1981.

While it was at Duluth to pick up the *Irving S. Olds*, the tug *Salvage Monarch* assisted in moving the former USS steamer *Joshua A. Hatfield* to the scrapping berth at the Azcon scrap yard on June 4. Work on stripping out its cabins began almost immediately with the cutting up of the 600-foot vessel continuing until November of the following year.

Venturing outside of its usual trade routes, Inland Lake Transportation's *Paul H. Townsend* made an uncommon appearance at Montreal on June 7 when it arrived to load cement for delivery to Buffalo and Oswego, New York. The 447-foot motor vessel followed up this voyage with a repeat trip through the Seaway during early July. Inactive since August of 1986 due to a lack of demand, Interlake Steamship's *Elton Hoyt 2nd* (2) cleared its layup berth at De Tour on June 11 and proceeded upbound through the Soo Locks bound for Superior, Wisconsin, to load iron ore.

While transiting the northernmost section of the St. Clair River on June 12, the barge *Hannah 2903* slammed into a seawall at Port Huron after breaking free of the tug *Ohio* just below the Blue Water Bridge. Causing an estimated $80,000 in damage to the seawall, the incident delayed vessel traffic in the river for about an hour while the *Ohio* regained control of its runaway barge. Loaded with fuel oil for Duluth, the 264-foot *Hannah 2903* underwent an inspection the next day when the pair reached Sault Ste. Marie, Michigan.

A major accident took place on the lower St. Lawrence River on the morning of June 15 when the downbound motor vessel *Algowest* and the small upbound coastal freighter *Coudres de L'ile* came together in heavy fog near Les Escoumins, Quebec. Carrying a load of scrap metal for delivery to Montreal, the 200-foot *Coudres de L'ile* sank in 100 feet of water almost immediately with the loss of one life. Sustaining only minor damage in the collision, the *Algowest* rescued the nine other crewmembers of the sunken vessel. After unloading its grain cargo at Baie Comeau, the 730-foot bulk carrier went to Welland, Ontario, for repairs.

Assisted once again by the tug *New Jersey*, the *Salvage Monarch* cleared Duluth on June 17 with the *Benjamin F. Fairless*. Reaching the Soo Locks two days later, the scrap tow transited the Welland Canal on June 23 with the tug *Helen M. McAllister* assisting. Following a passage through the Seaway marred only by a parted towline near the Eisenhower Lock, which resulted in no damage or significant traffic disruption, the *Fairless* arrived at Quebec City in tow of the tugs *Cathy McAllister* and *Helen M. McAllister* on June 28.

Launched by the American Ship Building Company's Lorain yard on April 25, 1942, the *Benjamin F. Fairless* entered service for the

The former *Ernest R. Breech* after being renamed *Kinsman Independent* (3). (Author's Collection)

Pittsburgh Steamship Company on September 15 of that year when it sailed for Duluth. With trips through the Seaway becoming common during the early 1960s, this steamer later participated in U.S. Steel's extended navigation season experiments during the 1970s. Having become increasingly active in the movement of grain during its later years of service, the *Fairless* closed the final chapter of gearless bulk carrier operations by the USS Great Lakes Fleet when it laid up at Duluth on October 4, 1982.

After helping deliver the *Benjamin F. Fairless* to Quebec City, the *Helen M. McAllister* assisted the *Salvage Monarch* with another scrap tow before both tugs sailed for Montreal to collect the *Irving S. Olds*. The *Olds* arrived at Quebec City on July 2, where the two "Super" class steamers remained until leaving on July 9 in tow of the ocean tug *Osa Ravensturm*. Following a four-month journey that included a transit of the Panama Canal, the two retired lake freighters arrived at Kaohsiung, Taiwan, on November 8 for dismantling.

Exactly one month following its minor stranding at Port Huron, the *George A. Sloan* required a tow into Calcite, Michigan, by the tug *Chippewa* on June 20 after experiencing reduction gear problems. That same day, the USX Corporation announced plans to sell its transportation businesses to Blackstone Capital Partners of New York City. In addition to all of the steelmaker's railroads, the $500 million deal also included the Pittsburgh & Conneaut Dock Company and USS Great Lakes Fleet Inc. With USX retaining a 40 percent stake in these properties, Blackstone placed them into a joint venture named Transtar Inc. based out of Monroeville, Pennsylvania. Continuing to operate from its headquarters in Duluth, the

USS Great Lakes Fleet was largely unaffected by this transaction.

Back on the lakes after working on saltwater over the previous winter, the package freighter *Woodland* arrived at Milwaukee on June 22 to perform one of the most unusual assignments of its career. Taking on a load of consumer goods, the 404-foot vessel was opened to the public during June 24-26 when it hosted a sales event organized by a regional retailer named American TV & Appliance.

On June 23, Kinsman Lines Inc. announced its purchase of the *Harry Coulby* (2) from the Interlake Steamship Company and the *Ernest R. Breech* from the Rouge Steel Company (some sources claim the latter had been sold to Marine Salvage Ltd. before being acquired by Kinsman but this is contradicted by the 1988 Annual Report of the Lake Carriers' Association). While the *Harry Coulby* (2) remained idle at Superior, Wisconsin, until returning to service the following summer as the *Kinsman Enterprise* (2), the *Ernest R. Breech* sailed on its first trip for Kinsman on June 24 when it cleared the Rouge River after being renamed *Kinsman Independent* (3).

Concurrent with its acquisition of the aforementioned vessels, Kinsman Lines sold the *Kinsman Independent* (2) to Marine Salvage Ltd. for scrapping. Leaving Toledo in tow of the tug *Salvage Monarch* on June 26, it passed through the Welland Canal the next day. Later met by the tug *Helen M. McAllister*, which had just finished taking the *Benjamin F. Fairless* to Quebec City, the scrap tow transited the Seaway on June 30. Reaching Sorel on July 1, the two tugs tied up the 600-foot steamer alongside the *Oakglen*, which had arrived there under its own power on June 3.

Both of these ships had been constructed by the American Ship Building Company's Lorain yard in 1923 with the *Kinsman Independent* (2) being launched as the *Richard V. Lindabury* on February 24 of that year barely two months before the *Oakglen* slid down the ways as the *William H. Warner* on April 21. Built for the Pittsburgh Steamship Company, the *Richard V. Lindabury* served the raw material transportation needs of the U.S. Steel Corporation until its sale to the S. & E. Shipping Corporation (Kinsman Lines) in February of 1978. Renamed *Kinsman Independent* (2), it spent most of its remaining career in the grain trade before laying up for the final time on December 11, 1987.

Beginning their final journey, the tug *Fairplay XIV* towed the *Kinsman Independent* (2) and *Oakglen* out of Sorel on August 10. Following a voyage lasting nearly five weeks, the virtually identical lake carriers arrived at Aliaga, Turkey, on September 11 for dismantling.

On June 26, the motor vessel *Manitoulin* (5) had a minor mishap at Sault Ste. Marie, Ontario, when it caught a cable in its wheel at the Algoma Steel Mill. Resulting in no damage to the large self-unloader, divers freed the tangled wire shortly afterwards. The next day, a more serious accident took place at Ludington, Michigan, when the barge *Hannah 2901* grounded on some uncharted rocks as it was leaving the harbor in tow of the tug *Betty Gale*. The mishap apparently took place when the pair moved over in the channel while meeting the inbound car ferry *City of Midland 41*. Although suffering a 30-foot tear in its hull, the barge did not spill any of its sodium chloride cargo. The *Hannah 2901* remained aground until refloated on June 29 after lightering into another barge.

Four years after its sale to United Metals, the dismantling of the former CSL package freighter *Fort Henry* finally began at

Hamilton during the spring of 1988. Although earlier preservation efforts had failed, arrangements were made to have its pilothouse removed intact to serve as a visitor center near Lock 3 on the Welland Canal. Arriving at that location aboard a barge towed by the tugs *Paul E. No. 1* and *Stormont*, the pilothouse opened to the public on July 14. Built by Collingwood Shipyards at Collingwood, Ontario, in 1955 the *Fort Henry* was the lead unit of CSL's five-member strong "Fort" class of package freighters commissioned over a 10-year period ending in 1965. In addition to being the only one to feature fore and aft cabins, it also became the first of these ships to be removed from service upon entering layup for the last time during the autumn of 1979. Vandalized on numerous occasions, this ship's pilothouse lasted until being broken up for scrap in 2002.

In the second incident of the month involving a saltwater vessel at the Soo Locks, the Polish flagged bulker *Ziemia Tarnowska* hit a lock wall on June 30. Damaged above the waterline, it anchored in the St. Marys River for an inspection before receiving permission to continue upbound.

Having last operated in 1962, the passenger steamer *Aquarama* cleared Muskegon, Michigan, on July 6 in tow of the tugs *Glenada* and *Tusker*. The only C4 class cargo ship ever converted for passenger service on the Great Lakes, it arrived at Sarnia on July 10. Purchased by a group of investors the previous year for conversion into a hotel and convention center, plans were to have some initial work done at Sarnia while awaiting the completion of the dredging required at Port Stanley, Ontario, to accommodate the 520-foot vessel. Just before its departure from Muskegon, the *Aquarama* was opened to the public during that community's Great Lumbertown Music Festival. Proving extremely popular with some 16,000 tickets sold, the owners repeated this event at Sarnia that August during which another 25,000 visitors toured the unique steamship.

Just after 3:00 am on July 9, the upbound *Henry Steinbrenner* (4) and the downbound *Mesabi Miner* came together in a glancing collision near Pt. Louise in the upper St. Marys River. Blamed on heavy fog, neither vessel suffered any structural damage in the incident.

On July 10, the *Canadian Enterprise* became the first Canadian flagged vessel to load at the Superior Midwest Energy Terminal at Superior, Wisconsin, when it took on 28,354 net tons of western coal for delivery to Thunder Bay. The next day, the 826-foot *William Clay Ford* (2) arrived at Ashland, Wisconsin, with a load of coal for the C. Reiss Coal Company, thereby becoming the largest ship to unload at that Lake Superior port.

A pair of minor mishaps occurred at Port Weller Dry Docks on July 13 when a small fire broke out in a ballast tank aboard the *Hon. Paul Martin* and the *Enerchem Travailleur* rammed an abutment while backing out of the shipyard. More trouble occurred in the Welland Canal the following day when the *Federal Hudson* brought traffic to a standstill for several hours after losing power below Lock 2.

After becoming the first vessel from the People's Republic of China to transit the Welland Canal, the *Ju Yong Guan* delivered 4,904 tons of talc at Cleveland on July 20. Paying a subsequent visit to Detroit, it loaded a shipment of equipment formerly used by the Chrysler Corporation's Trenton Engine Plant at Trenton, Michigan, bound for Changchun, China, to establish the manufacture of engines for that nation's domestic automobile industry.

The *Sam Laud* encountered an unusual problem while preparing to moor at the Bay Aggregate Inc. Dock at Bay City, Michigan, on July 21 when its lines snagged a pleasure boat that attempted to pass between the 634-foot self-unloader and the dock.

Also on July 21, the cement carrier *Badger State (3)* arrived at Manitowoc for dismantling following a tow across Lake Michigan from Ferrysburg, Michigan. Built in 1943 by the Lancaster Iron Works at Perryville, Maryland, as the tanker *Spindletop*, this 221-foot ship operated as a water carrier and later in the coastal tanker trades as the *Lake Charles* prior to being converted into a cement carrier and renamed *Atlas Traveler* in 1962. Purchased by the Erie Sand Steamship Company in 1976, it entered service in the Lake Ontario cement trade later that year. Renamed *Loc Bay* in 1977, Erie Sand sold this motor vessel to the Cement Transit Company (Medusa Cement) near the end of the 1979 season. Although renamed *Badger State* (3) early the following year, Medusa subsequently abandoned plans to employ the small cement carrier on the short run across Lake Michigan between its manufacturing plant at Charlevoix, Michigan, and its terminal at Manitowoc. Consequently, it remained idle at Erie, Pennsylvania, until leaving in tow of the tug *Barbara Andrie* on December 21, 1983. After spending the winter at Port Huron, the *Badger State* (3) arrived at Ferrysburg in May of 1984 for use as a cement storage barge.

On July 22, the explosion of a circuit breaker seriously injured a crewman aboard the *Canadian Century* as it was taking on coal at Sandusky. That same day, Algoma Central Marine's *Algomarine* cleared Thunder Bay with an unusual load of tree bark for Detroit. After discharging this cargo, the bulk carrier sailed to Port Weller Dry Docks to undergo a $16 million reconstruction into a self-unloader.

Looking somewhat decrepit with most of its superstructure stripped away, the tugs *Cheyenne* and *Mohawk* towed the excursion steamer *Canadiana* out of Buffalo on July 23. The tow arrived at the Marsh Engineering Dock at Ramey's Bend the same day, where the nonprofit Friends of the Canadiana Inc. intended to begin the next phase of an ambitious restoration project to return the 78-year old vessel to service on Lake Erie. Faced with costs in excess of $4 million, however, the owning organization, which later reorganized as the S. S. Canadiana Preservation Society Inc. in 1993, ultimately failed in this endeavor with the hull remaining at Ramey's Bend in a steadily deteriorating condition until being scrapped in 2004.

With a severe drought producing historically low water levels on the Mississippi River, grain shipments through the Twin Ports remained strong during much of the summer with many Canadian lake freighters loading for ports on the St. Lawrence River. Plaguing farmers on both sides of the border, the extremely dry summer combined with a growing percentage of Canadian shipments going through west coast ports pushed the season's movement of grain to its lowest level in 19 years.

The *Courtney Burton* mangled its propeller when it grounded at Taconite Harbor on August 4. With three propeller blades bent, it sailed to Superior, Wisconsin, to have one of the blades replaced at Fraser Shipyards the next day. Shifting across the harbor to load iron ore, the 690-foot steamer cleared Duluth on August 6 for Toledo, where it was to have the other two blades replaced.

Acquired by the Gaelic Tugboat Company after five years of idleness, the former Erie Sand Steamship Company self-unloading sand sucker *Lakewood* (2) cleared Erie, Pennsylvania, on August 4 in tow of the tug *William Hoey*. Tied up in the Nicholson Slip at Ecorse, Michigan, the next day, work on converting the 390-foot vessel to a barge began shortly afterwards with its 1,650 horsepower General Motors diesel engine being removed during late September followed by a tow to Toledo at the end of October for dry-docking.

Reflecting the continued strength of domestic steel production rates, Interlake Steamship's *J. L. Mauthe* took a break from its usual grain hauling duties to carry a handful of iron ore cargoes during the second half of the season, the first being loaded on August 7 at Superior, Wisconsin, for delivery to Cleveland. Just one day later, another of the few straight deck bulk carriers operating in the American fleet made an equally noteworthy departure from its regular trade routes when the Inland Steel Company's *Edward L. Ryerson* loaded stone at Stoneport, Michigan.

After spending a few days at Fraser Shipyards for hull and self-unloading gear repairs, USS Great Lakes Fleet's *Irvin L. Clymer* loaded coal at the Superior Midwest Energy Terminal on August 8. Shortly after clearing the Duluth Entry later in the day, however, it suffered an engine failure approximately two miles offshore. After power was restored less than an hour later, the 552-foot steamer continued to Marquette, Michigan.

Deviating from its established pattern of returning to saltwater at the beginning of spring, the Finnish tanker *Kiisla* remained in operation on the Great Lakes throughout the entire year. Paying a visit to Sturgeon Bay during late summer, the 428-foot vessel was in the dry dock at Bay Shipbuilding from August 8 to August 20.

On the morning of August 9, the *Canadian Transport* lost power and went aground in

The motor vessel *Lemoyne* (2) had fire break out in its engine room during late summer. (Photo by Jim Bearman)

the upper St. Marys River while downbound with coal for Nanticoke, Ontario. After lightering 900 tons of its cargo into fleet mate *Canadian Enterprise,* the 730-foot self-unloader came off the bottom the next day with the assistance of the tugs *Anglian Lady, Avenger IV,* and *Wilfred M. Cohen.* Holed at the bow, the *Canadian Transport* went to Thunder Bay later in the month for repairs during which it suffered a minor fire on August 23.

While moored at the Welland Dock on August 10, the motor vessel *Lemoyne* (2) suffered an engine room fire. Ignited by a worker's torch, a large contingent of firefighters called in from Welland, Ontario, managed to extinguish the blaze before it spread to other areas of the ship. An early report estimating the damage at being somewhere between $75,000 and $100,000 may have been in error, however, as the 730-foot vessel was back in service within a few weeks.

Having proven itself no stranger to establishing new records in the grain trade since its 1985 construction, the *Paterson* (2) loaded 29,000 metric tons of winter wheat at Sarnia on August 12, the largest single cargo of that particular crop ever shipped through that port up to that time.

On August 17, the *Fred R. White, Jr.* came across two men amongst the wreckage of a 19-foot boat floating in Lake Erie about eight miles off Ashtabula. Pulled to safety, the pair remained aboard the 636-foot carrier until a U.S. Coast Guard crew arrived from Fairport, Ohio, to retrieve them. While outbound from the Twin Ports that same day, a mix of high winds and a strong current pushed the Yugoslavian freighter *Bijelo Polje* into the north pier of the Duluth Ship Canal near the Aerial Lift Bridge. Although the saltwater vessel suffered no appreciable damage in the incident, the pier required some $100,000 worth of repairs.

In other happenings on August 17, the Michigan Department of Transportation announced its intention to place the car ferry *Chief Wawatam* up for sale. On October 26, the Michigan Transportation Commission rejected several lower offers to either preserve or scrap the historic vessel when it voted 4-1 in favor of accepting the high bid of $110,000 from Purvis Marine Ltd. for its use as a barge. Four years after crossing the Straits of Mackinac for the final time under its own power, the *Chief Wawatam* cleared Mackinaw City, Michigan, on December 15 in tow of the tug *Anglian Lady* for Sault Ste. Marie, Ontario, where it arrived the following afternoon. Making its first trip as a barge in mid-1990, the former car ferry lasted in this service until being broken up for scrap by Purvis Marine at the Canadian Soo in 2009.

Having recently experienced some type of unspecified mechanical or marine casualty, the *Edgar B. Speer* arrived at Sturgeon Bay on August 19 to enter the Bay Shipbuilding yard for the replacement of a lost rudder. Two days later, the *Roger M. Kyes* went aground on a sandbar while entering Fairport in a stiff northeast wind. Freeing itself later in the day, the self-unloader proceeded to the Morton Salt Dock for an inspection.

In the third such occurrence to affect a Canadian vessel that month, the *Algomarine* had a fire break out in its bow thruster tunnel while at Port Weller Dry Docks on August 26. Although burning for nearly five hours and sending two firefighters to the hospital, the 730-foot vessel sustained nothing more serious than some minor plate buckling. Clearing the dry dock on August 30, it went to the Welland Dock for repairs and other work by Herb Fraser & Associates before returning to the shipyard on October 7 to begin its conversion to a self-unloader.

In another mishap involving a Canadian lake freighter during August, the *Canadian Hunter* came away from an altercation with the east abutment of Bridge 10 in the Welland Canal with considerable damage to its port bow. Requiring a substantial amount of replacement plating near the anchor pocket, the steamer went to Hamilton for repairs.

Targeted for retirement by the U.S. Coast Guard earlier in the season due to budgetary constraints, the icebreaker *Mackinaw* began receiving some $150,000 worth of engine work at Cheboygan, Michigan, during the summer. Remaining idle for the balance of the year, the 290-foot vessel returned to service on March 12, 1989.

The beginning of September proved particularly unlucky for the Socanav fleet with two of its tankers having grounding accidents, the first of which involved the *Hubert Gaucher* in the lower St. Lawrence River on September 1. Refloated by three tugs, it went to Quebec City for repairs. Just one day later, the *L'Orme No. 1* also stranded in the St. Lawrence but managed to break free of the bottom at high tide after lightering into another vessel.

While attempting to moor at Cleveland on September 2, the Polish flagged *Ziemia Tarnowska* lost maneuvering power and slammed hard into Dock 24 North. Coming just two months after its unfortunate encounter with a lock wall at Sault Ste. Marie, Michigan, at the end of June, the bulker inflicted some $175,000 in damage to the pier while suffering little harm itself.

The 1000-foot *Indiana Harbor* established a new benchmark in the upbound movement of coal on September 3 when it loaded a 59,058 net ton payload at Sandusky for delivery to Marquette. This bested the former record of 58,959 net tons set the previous season by Interlake Steamship's *James R. Barker*.

On September 6, a failed oil pump left the *Cason J. Callaway* with turbine damage at the Soo Locks. Tying up at the Carbide Dock for repairs, the 767-foot steamer remained at Sault Ste. Marie, Michigan, until sailing for Lorain on September 18.

Making one of its regular visits to the Morton Salt Dock at Fairport on September 9, the *Irvin L. Clymer* loaded salt for Ogdensburg, New York. This particular voyage is likely the first time the venerable vessel had ever ventured east of the Welland Canal.

While delivering a load of steel to South Chicago on September 12, Misener Shipping's *Canada Marquis* suffered some hatch coaming and tank top damage when a crane moving a payloader into a cargo hold collapsed down upon its deck. Following a two-day cleanup, the 730-foot bulk carrier finished unloading and then sailed to Thunder Bay for repairs.

A second incident on September 12 took place on northern Lake Superior when the tug *Annis Lee* ran into a strong storm while towing two 60-foot diameter storage tanks sold to a Hamilton scrap dealer during the dismantling of the Husky Oil terminal at Thunder Bay. After one of the tanks broke free in the eight-foot seas, the tug's captain ordered the other cut loose before seeking shelter behind Moss Island. Once the weather improved, the tug retrieved both tanks from where they went aground off Longcroft Island and towed them to Rossport, Ontario. The *Annis Lee* later passed through the Soo Locks on October 6 with one of the tanks while the second remained in the Rossport area until the same tug returned it to Thunder Bay for scrapping the following July.

In addition to those taken out by the *Annis Lee*, two other former Husky Oil storage tanks left Thunder Bay aboard the motor vessel *Woodland*. Carried as deck cargo, the tanks extended high above the vessel's superstructure while their width obstructed much of its pilothouse. Locking through the Soo Locks on September 15, the package freighter delivered its unusual payload to Hamilton following an uneventful trip down the lakes.

While proceeding outbound at Milwaukee with the assistance of the tug *Bonnie G. Selvick* on the morning of September 16, the *E. M. Ford* developed bow thruster problems. With the thruster unit jammed in the operating position, the cement carrier wrecked a dock and damaged three pleasure boats when it swung across the narrow channel near the Broadway Street Bridge. Brought back under control, the steamer went to an anchorage in the outer harbor to await a clearance from the U.S. Coast Guard.

Carrying a load of gasoline from Sarnia, the Canadian tanker *Sibyl W.* went hard aground off Fighting Island North Light in the Detroit River on September 18. After initial salvage efforts proved unsuccessful, the 375-foot vessel offloaded 8,600 gallons of gasoline into a barge. Refloated on September 20 by the Gaelic Tugboat Company's *Bantry Bay*, *Carolyn Hoey*, and *Susan Hoey*, it left for Montreal later in the day after reloading.

Another unusual cargo originating from a Lake Superior port that month involved the *Canadian Leader*. After taking on grain at Superior, Wisconsin, it moved across the harbor to Duluth's Port Terminal on September 19 to load a pair of 120-ton crusher shafts formerly used by the Reserve Mining Company in the production of taconite at Babbitt, Minnesota. With the two units welded to its deck, the 730-foot steamer sailed for Quebec City on September 25.

On September 23, the tug *James E. McGrath* capsized and sank in the Welland Canal after getting caught in the prop wash of CSL's *Hon. Paul Martin*. The accident occurred while the tug was assisting the much larger self-unloader away from the fit out wall at Port Weller Dry Docks. All four crewmembers aboard the *McGrath* were able to reach safety. Refloated two days later, the 77-foot tug returned to duty at the shipyard following repairs.

The September 27 arrival of the *Ashley Lykes* at Duluth marked the first time a U.S. flagged ocean vessel had visited the Twin Ports in two years. Loading 5,800 tons of grain for Ethiopia, the bulker made a subsequent stop at Milwaukee before returning to saltwater.

A raised cargo crane caused the Indian flagged freighter *Soren Toubro* to veer away from entering the Duluth Ship Canal on September 30 when it became clear the boom would not clear the Aerial Lift Bridge. After completing a wide circle in Lake Superior to give the crew time to lower the crane, it made a normal entry into the harbor. This could have easily become this vessel's second accident of the season following its earlier grounding in the St. Marys River near the end of April.

During early autumn, Presque Isle Sand & Gravel Inc. renamed the former National Sand and Gravel Company sand sucker *James B. Lyons* to *Emmett J. Carey*. Earlier in the year, the 114-foot motor vessel had been fitted with a new pilothouse and painted in a color scheme consisting of a red hull and gray trim.

While departing the Twin Ports on October

5 with a load of grain, the Cyprus flagged *Maria Angelicoussi* rubbed up against the north pier of the Duluth Ship Canal very near the same spot hit by the *Bijelo Polje* on August 17. Blamed on a strong current, the mishap inflicted no damage to either the vessel or the pier.

Near ten o'clock in the evening of October 5, the *Enerchem Refiner* ran into the East Outer Channel Light No. 1 in western Lake Erie. Its bow badly crushed, the 391-foot tanker sailed to Lauzon for repairs. Entering the dry dock on October 13, it was back in service by late November.

The early autumn capsizing of a Hannah Marine Corporation tank barge in northern Lake Huron brought about a protracted salvage operation. This episode began on October 9 when the barge *OLS-30* began taking on water north of Rogers City, Michigan, while in tow of the tug *Kristin Lee* on a voyage from Ludington to Bay City with 850,000 gallons of liquid calcium chloride. Intentionally ran aground near Forty Mile Point, the 275-foot barge capsized and partially sank with its stern coming to rest in 135 of water and its bow protruding above the surface.

With the salvage of the sunken barge requiring specialized equipment and expertise, a contract was awarded to McAllister Towing & Salvage Inc. of Montreal shortly after the accident. In addition to the challenging nature of the wreck, this effort encountered a legal challenge brought forth by two Michigan sport fishing associations during late October after government regulators approved the release of the barge's cargo into the lake. This resulted in a subsequent agreement to pump the calcium chloride solution to another barge. A further setback took place on December 3 when the salvage barge *McAllister 252* broke free of its anchorage and went aground in 60 mph winds. Refloated by four tugs exactly one week later, a subsequent inspection of the *McAllister 252* revealed a 3-foot tear in its hull that necessitated a trip to Sturgeon Bay for dry-docking. Battling frigid weather conditions and a series of mechanical breakdowns, the salvors had little choice but to seal up the *OLS-30* for the winter before suspending operations on December 14 pending the resumption of work the following spring.

Having reached the end of its use as a cement storage barge at South Chicago, the tugs *Chippewa* and *Eddie B.* towed the retired steamer *L. E. Block* out of Lake Calumet on the morning of October 12. Following a short weather delay, the tow cleared Calumet Harbor the next day bound for Escanaba. Delivered to the Basic Marine Inc. yard, the 621-foot ship remained there in a steadily deteriorating condition until being sold for dismantling in 2006.

Arriving at Fraser Shipyards on October 13 with bow thruster problems, Interlake Steamship's *Herbert C. Jackson* received a 1,000 horsepower bow thruster engine removed from its long idle fleet mate *John Sherwin* (2). This accomplished, the *Jackson* sailed from the shipyard two days later only to make a return visit on November 7 for shell plating repairs on its starboard side.

The *T. R. McLagan* made an unscheduled stop at Port Colborne on October 15 after snagging a sunken automobile with its port anchor in the Welland Canal while upbound between the Welland Dock and Ramey's Bend in high winds. Once the twisted wreckage was removed, the steamer resumed its trip to Thunder Bay.

A steering failure caused the second major accident of the season for the Paterson fleet's *Quedoc* (3) when the bulk carrier slammed into and dragged along the breakwater at Burns Harbor, Indiana, during the early hours of October 26. A subsequent dive inspection revealed a considerable amount of ripped open shell plating and bent frames on the starboard side. The severity of the damage required the ship be taken to the nearest available dry dock, which in this case was at Sturgeon Bay. Arriving at Bay Shipbuilding in tow of Selvick Marine Towing tugs on November 7, the lengthy repair job kept the 730-foot motor vessel at the shipyard over the upcoming winter.

Sent to the wall during early June, Misener Shipping's *Scott Misener* (3) left Hamilton on October 30 in tow for Toronto, where it was to be used to store soybeans for Victory Soya Mills. With grain shipments on the lakes continuing their downward trend, it was to remain in this service throughout the following year and was in fact only to sail for a few months at the beginning of the 1990 season before being retired.

On November 2, the motor vessel *Peter Misener* hit a shoal while upbound on the Saguenay River with a load of petroleum coke from South Chicago for Port Alfred, Quebec. Although the violent impact smashed its bulbous bow and opened up the No. 1 port ballast tank, there were no injuries among the vessel's crew. Continuing to Port Alfred with significant bow damage extending from the forefoot up to the 20-foot draft mark, it went to Montreal after unloading. Repaired by Montreal Tanker Repairs Inc., the 730-foot bulk carrier resumed trading on December 17 when it sailed to load grain at Thunder Bay.

Earlier in the year, the Bay Shipbuilding Corporation had secured a $19.8 million United States Maritime Administration (MARAD) contract to convert the former

The *Peter Misener* suffered considerable damage on the Saguenay River at the beginning of November. (Author's Collection)

After being laid up at Midland, Ontario, for several years, the steamer *Sir James Dunn* was towed to Toronto, Ontario, during the autumn of 1988. (Author's Collection)

Moore-McCormack Lines cargo freighter *Mormactide* into a maritime training ship for the State University of New York Maritime College. Scheduled to take a full year to complete, this major reconstruction included the enlargement of the living quarters to accommodate up to 800 officers and cadets in addition to providing expanded classrooms, laboratories, and maintenance shops. Pulled from the James River Reserve Fleet, the *Mormactide* cleared Norfolk, Virginia, on October 27 in tow of the tug *Shelia Moran*. Arriving at Montreal on November 7, the tow was upbound in the St. Lawrence Seaway the next day with the Great Lakes Towing Company tugs *Ohio* and *Superior* assisting. Although arriving off Sturgeon Bay on November 15, poor weather delayed the docking of the *Mormactide* at the Bay Shipbuilding yard for another two days.

Barely a week after the *Peter Misener* accident, misfortune befell another Misener Shipping vessel when the *David K. Gardiner* had an ore bucket fall into its No. 5 cargo hold at Quebec City on November 10. Heading back up the lakes, the lake freighter received the necessary internal repairs at Thunder Bay.

While upbound in the Seaway for the first time, the Panamanian tanker *Arcturus* went aground in Lake St. Louis on November 11. Although not refloated until the following day, it suffered no serious damage in the late season mishap.

On November 12, the *Woodland* arrived at Port Weller Dry Docks to deliver a disassembled crane and other equipment brought down the lakes from the closed Collingwood Shipyards yard at Collingwood. The next day, the tugs *W. N. Twolan* and *Glenbrook* encountered heavy weather on Lake Erie while towing the idle CSL steamer *Sir James*

Dunn from Midland, Ontario, to Toronto. Finding refuge in the calmer waters of Presque Isle Bay off Erie, Pennsylvania, the tow passed through the Welland Canal on November 15 after the weather cleared. The 36-year old bulk carrier reached Toronto on November 18, where it, like the *Scott Misener* (3), was to serve as a soybean storage hull for Victory Soya Mills.

Bound for use as a museum ship at Buffalo after being displayed at Groton, Connecticut, for the past ten years, the World War II era Gato class submarine USS *Croaker* arrived at Montreal in tow of the tug *Judy Moran* on November 16. Handed over to the tugs *Ohio* and *Superior*, the submarine transited the St. Lawrence Seaway on November 19. After passing upbound through the Welland Canal on November 21, it joined the guided missile cruiser USS *Little Rock* and destroyer USS *The Sullivans* at the Buffalo Naval and Servicemen's Park (later becoming the Buffalo and Erie County Naval & Military Park).

Running aground while entering Taconite Harbor, the *Mesabi Miner* opened up a 150-foot tear in its bottom on November 19. Departing without loading, the thousand-footer sailed to Sturgeon Bay for repairs. Arriving at Bay Shipbuilding on November 22, it remained in the shipyard until December 1.

As it moved upbound in the Seaway for Kingston, Ontario, on November 21, steering gear difficulties delayed the saltwater tanker *Astorga* at the Eisenhower Lock. Some 400 miles to the west on that same date, the 604-foot *Canadoc* (2) went aground off Port Huron in the St. Clair River. Freed just a few hours later, the motor vessel apparently suffered no damage from its encounter with the river bottom.

On November 22, the small Danish freighter *Soren TH* ran aground near Lame Squaw Island in the St. Lawrence River while upbound with general cargo for Cleveland. With the accident occurring about three miles downstream from the Ogdensburg-Prescott International Bridge, the ocean carrier was freed on November 25 by the tugs *Cathy McAllister*, *Helen M. McAllister*, and *Robinson Bay* after offloading some of its bunker fuel.

Sold to Keystone Navigation Inc. for use under Canadian registry in the Nova Scotia salt trade, the former American Steamship Company steamer *Adam E. Cornelius* (3) cleared Toledo on November 24 in tow of the tug *Barbara Ann*. Continuing its journey off the lakes, the 29-year old vessel arrived at Montreal after passing through the St. Lawrence Seaway on November 29 with the tugs *Cathy McAllister*, *Daniel McAllister*, and *Helen M. McAllister*. Resold to Keybulk Transportation Inc. early the following year, it remained there until being towed out by the tug/supply vessel *Triumph Sea* on January 23, 1989 bound for Halifax, Nova Scotia. Converted to a self-unloading barge by Halifax Dartmouth Industries Ltd., it entered service as the *Capt. Edward V. Smith* during the summer of the 1989. Although there initially appeared little likelihood of this vessel ever making a return to Great Lakes trading, it did just that during spring of 1995 under the name *Sea Barge One*. Renamed *Sarah Spencer* in 1996, the barge remained active through the 2008 season and was later sold for scrapping in 2019.

Returning to 1988, the notoriously bad November weather brought about the usual late season traffic disruptions with one such instance involving the oldest gearless bulk carrier operating on the Great Lakes. Carrying a load of wheat from Superior, Wisconsin, the 72-year old *Henry Steinbrenner*

(4) ran into a stiff gale off Silver Bay, Wisconsin, while downbound on Lake Superior during the morning of November 26. Buffeted by 14-foot waves, the 600-foot steamer returned to the Twin Ports, where it remained until resuming its voyage down the lakes the following day.

Acquired at the beginning of the year as part of its purchase of the CSL subsidiary Quebec Tugs Ltd., Groupe Ocean Ltd. sold the self-propelled bunkering barge *Sillery* to Provmar Fuels Inc. of Hamilton. Having served in bunkering duties at Quebec City for many years, the 175-foot barge passed through the St. Lawrence Seaway in tow of the tug *Glenbrook* on November 27 bound for Hamilton.

Also on November 27, the Polish bulker *Ziemia Gnieznienska* hit the lower wall at the Snell Lock while inbound for Cleveland with a load of steel. Causing no significant damage, the incident did little more than create a brief traffic stoppage in the Seaway.

Less than a week after the *Henry Steinbrenner* (4) beat a hasty retreat back to port, rough weather on Lake Superior created problems for another of the few active straight deck bulk carriers in the U.S. fleet. With a fall storm whipping up heavy seas out on the open lake, the *Edward L. Ryerson* went to anchor off Isle Royale after departing Duluth with a load of taconite on December 2. Returning to Duluth to refuel, the 730-foot steamer began its downbound voyage for the second time a few days later in much calmer weather.

In an incident remarkably similar to that suffered by its former fleet mate *Fort York* at Point Edward, Ontario, the previous year, a fire broke out aboard the idle CSL package freighter *Fort Chambly* at Windsor just after daybreak on December 6. As thick smoke billowed into the sky above the Detroit River, the flames spread to engulf the crew quarters and pilothouse. Hindered by security measures put in place to deter the activities of vandals and vagrants such as welded shut doors and barbed wire wrapped around mooring lines, firefighters fought the blaze throughout the morning hours before finally extinguishing it that afternoon. Like the *Fort York*, the *Fort Chambly* remained afloat despite taking on a considerable amount of water during the firefighting operation. Laid up at Windsor since the end of the 1981 season, the fire left its superstructure little more than a burned-out shell with long scorch marks emanating from nearly every opening. Later ruled the work of an arsonist by an official investigation, this casualty ended all consideration of the 463-foot ship becoming a combination museum and restaurant at Collingwood.

Having returned to saltwater following its refit at Port Weller Dry Docks that summer, the 736-foot *Hon. Paul Martin* was renamed *Atlantic Erie* at Savannah, Georgia, during early December. This followed a naming convention began by the CSL fleet with the construction the company's first Seaway-sized self-unloading vessel specifically designed for both Great Lakes and ocean service, the *Atlantic Superior*, in 1982.

It was during this same timeframe that Enerchem Transport Inc. renamed the 414-foot tanker *Asfamarine* to *Enerchem Asphalt*. Purchased earlier that fall, it had carried the fleet's stack and hull markings since mid-October. Built by the Oskarshamns Shipyard at Varv, Sweden, in 1972, this was the first vessel acquired by Enerchem since its establishment two years earlier with the purchase of six tankers from the Halco fleet.

On December 9, the Greek freighter *Arc Minos* caused a minor traffic disruption in the Seaway when it struck the lower gate of the Iroquois Lock. That same day, the Pringle Transit Company's *Paul Thayer* went aground near Long Tail Point in Green Bay. Refloated nine hours later, the 630-foot motor vessel was able to continue to the C. Reiss Coal Company Dock at Green Bay, Wisconsin, to unload.

While upbound in the Amherstburg Channel of the Detroit River on the evening of December 11, the 730-foot *Canadian Progress* went aground after going out of the navigation channel to avoid a collision with the tug *Princess No. 1* and its barge. With low water levels complicating the salvage operation, it soon became evident that the stranded vessel would require lightering. After offloading 3,500 tons of its coal cargo into the Gaelic Tugboat Company's recently acquired *Lakewood* (2) on December 13, a fleet of eight tugs freed the *Canadian Progress* the following day. Suffering no serious damage in the grounding, it continued upbound later in the day to unload at the Lambton Generating Station located on the St. Clair River at Courtright, Ontario. Meanwhile, the *Lakewood* (2) delivered the lightered coal to Windsor, arriving there on December 16 in tow of the tugs *Carolyn Hoey* and *Shannon*.

One final scrap sale took place before the end of the year when Desgagnes Transport Inc. sold the 58-year old *Chicago Tribune* (2) to International Marine Salvage. Towed out of Toronto on the afternoon of December 13, it passed up the Welland Canal the following day with the tugs *Michael D. Misner* and *Thunder Cape*. Delivered to Port Colborne, scrapping of the 319-foot vessel began on January 14, 1989.

Built by Earles Shipbuilding & Engineering Ltd. at Hull, England, as the motor vessel *Thorold*, this ship entered service for the Ontario Transportation & Pulp Company Ltd. fleet in March 1930. This came just two years before the company reorganized as the Quebec & Ontario Transportation Company Ltd. Renamed *Chicago Tribune* (2) in 1933, the design of this canal-sized freighter incorporated a unique trunk deck to maximize its cubic capacity for the carriage of newsprint. This resulted in a distinctive profile easily recognizable from a considerable distance. Repowered in 1958 with a 1,880 bhp Fairbanks, Morse & Co. diesel engine, this ship was later lengthened from 258'6" to 319' by Port Weller Dry Docks Ltd. at St. Catharines in 1962. Purchased by Group Desgagnes in 1984, the *Chicago Tribune* (2) remained in active service until laying up for the last time at Toronto on April 22, 1986 after making only a single trip that season.

An unusual mishap took place at the Soo Locks on December 18 when the *Columbia Star* snagged a raised cable boom with its pilothouse while upbound in the Poe Lock. Although the boom, which had moved out of its upright position after being taken out of service prior to the accident, was a total loss, the thousand-footer sustained only light damage.

In another transaction near the end of the year, N. M. Paterson & Sons Ltd. sold the 315-foot motor vessel *Labradoc* (2) to Genav Maritime Co. Ltd. for off-lakes use. Renamed *Falcon Crest* during mid-December and transferred to Maltese registry, it left Montreal on January 8, 1989 to load at Sorel before sailing for the Atlantic. Built by Davie Shipbuilding Ltd. at Lauzon in 1966, this ship is probably best remembered for nearly foundering in a storm on Lake Erie on April 6, 1979. Towed to safety and repaired, the *Labradoc* (2) last operated for the Paterson fleet when it laid up at Montreal on September 22, 1988.

Arriving at the Twin Ports on December 22, the steamer *Wilfred Sykes* loaded the final

Shown at Port Stanley, Ontario, in 1986, the *Labradoc (2)* was sold for off-lakes use in late 1988. (Photo by Brad Jolliliffe)

iron ore cargo shipped from Duluth that season. Following the departure of this vessel two days later, the Duluth, Missabe & Iron Range Railway routed its remaining cargoes through the company's loading dock at Two Harbors as ice began building up on western Lake Superior with the onset of winter.

Meanwhile, commercial shipping through the St. Lawrence Seaway for the 1988 season ended on the afternoon of December 23 with the downbound passage of the Liberian tanker *Chippewa* through the St. Lambert Lock. On December 24, the upbound *Enerchem Travailleur* and downbound *J. W. McGiffin* were the final vessels to clear the Welland Canal although some traffic continued moving within the canal through Christmas Day.

Slamming into the ore dock at Two Harbors while arriving to load on Christmas Eve in a strong easterly wind, the *James R. Barker* ripped open a 6-foot gash in its hull just ahead of the starboard anchor pocket. Its cargo cancelled, the big self-unloader sailed to Duluth the next day for repairs and winter layup.

One of the most senior members of the U.S. fleet reached the end of its operational career on December 28 when the motor vessel *Henry Ford II* laid up for the last time at Dearborn. Just as the year drew to a close three days later, ULS International Inc. changed its corporate name to ULS Corporation on December 31.

Shipping continued at a reduced level into the early weeks of the following year with the *Wilfred Sykes* closed Escanaba on January 7, 1989 when it sailed for Indiana Harbor after loading taconite. Arriving at Superior, Wisconsin, that same day, the *American*

Mariner tied up at the Burlington Northern ore dock to load the last cargo of the season from that facility. Bad weather delayed the loading, however, and the 730-foot carrier did not clear port until January 10, 1989.

For the second year in a row, USS Great Lake Fleet's *Edgar B. Speer* closed the commercial navigation season at the Soo Locks when it locked downbound through the Poe Lock on January 15, 1989 bound for Gary, Indiana. Incidentally, the *Speer* carried the largest single cargo through the locks that season with a 67,056 net ton payload of iron ore loaded at Two Harbors for delivery to a lower lakes port.

As is common practice, the movement of iron ore on Lake Superior from Marquette to Sault Ste. Marie, Ontario, continued for brief period after the Soo Locks shut down for the winter. Having loaded at Marquette the previous day, CSL's *Frontenac* (5) delivered the last such cargo to Algoma Steel on January 18, 1989.

Peaking at 68.3 million net tons, iron ore shipments for the season represented a nearly 11 percent improvement over those of the previous year. Largely driven by U.S. exports to Ontario Hydro power plants reaching record levels, the movement of coal recorded its best season since 1984 with a seven percent growth to 40.5 million net tons. Growing by seven percent to 35.5 million net tons, the stone trade reached its best seasonal total since 1979. The cement trade also had a good year with a nine percent increase in loadings to 4.1 million net tons. Impacted heavily by the severe drought that troubled U.S. and Canadian farmers during the summer months, however, the grain trade tumbled by over 14 percent to only 19.1 million net tons. Despite the poor performance of the grain sector, sizable gains in ore, coal, stone, and cement shipments along with stability in the potash and petroleum trades pushed the total movement of bulk cargoes on the lakes during the 1988 season upward by five percent to 181.2 million net tons.

Chapter Ten
The 1989 Shipping Season

By the beginning of 1989, the remarkable downsizing of the Great Lakes fleet that characterized the challenges faced by the shipping industry during the decade had nearly reached its conclusion. For the first time since 1982, a season would pass without a U.S. shipping company sending any of its ships to the breakers. While the size of the U.S. lake fleet remained stable, Canadian operators sold five of their carriers for demolition and another for off-lakes use during this same period. In addition to these sales, three former vessels from the U.S fleet and one from the Canadian fleet originally retired during the 1970s went to the scrap yard.

Beginning a year that was to witness several mishaps involving Canadian tankers, the *Enerchem Asphalt* ran aground at Oswego, New York, on January 10 while inbound for the Niagara Mohawk Power Corporation's power plant with 35,000 barrels of oil. Freed by the tug *Apalachee* within a few hours, the 414-foot vessel suffered no appreciable damage in the incident. Just three days later, another member of the Enerchem Transport fleet ran into trouble when the *Enerchem Catalyst* grounded near Round Island in the Straits of Mackinac. Bound from Sarnia, Ontario, to Chicago, Illinois, with a cargo of sodium hydroxide, the tanker came to a rest in 22 feet of water. When four tugs failed to refloat the stranded vessel, the *Enerchem Avance* was called to the scene from Sarnia to assist in the lightering operation. After off-loading over 400,000 gallons of the caustic soda into its fleet mate, the *Enerchem Catalyst* came off the bottom on January 17. Following an inspection by a commercial diver, it reloaded before clearing for Chicago that same day.

The Bay Shipbuilding Corporation yard at Sturgeon Bay, Wisconsin, remained busy during the early months of the year with the *Quedoc* (3) in for bottom repairs, the ongoing conversion of the *Mormactide* into a training ship, and an assortment of winter layup work. One of the latter projects involved Bethlehem Steel's *Stewart J. Cort*, which required starboard propeller repairs after rubbing the bottom at Mission Point in the St. Marys River near the end of the 1988 season. In addition, the 60-year old *Myron C. Taylor* had some of its cargo hold steel renewed while the *Benson Ford* (3) received a partial conversion from DC to AC power. In other shipyard activity within the U.S. fleet, the *Arthur M. Anderson* had a stern thruster installed by Fraser Shipyards at Superior, Wisconsin.

On January 30, the Ontario Ministry of Transportation purchased the 333-foot Norwegian ferry *Skudenes* for $10 million. The purpose of this acquisition was to add a second ferry to operate alongside the *Chi-Cheemaun* between the Bruce Peninsula and Manitoulin Island on Lake Huron. Given the name *Ontario No. 1* (2) for the delivery trip to the lakes, it required dry-docking at Shelburne, Nova Scotia, after suffering weather damage during the Atlantic crossing. After reaching Toronto, Ontario, on May 9, the ferry continued on to Owen Sound, Ontario, for further work. Renamed *Nindawayma* following a public naming contest, it entered service for the Ontario Northland Transportation Commission on June 29.

As is normally the case, the movement of cement began prior to the opening of the Soo Locks at Sault Ste. Marie, Michigan, when the *Paul H. Townsend* cleared Detroit, Michigan, on March 11 for Alpena, Michigan. Escorted through the ice-clogged St. Clair River and lower Lake Huron by the *Tug Malcolm*, it arrived at Alpena the following day. The 447-foot motor vessel went on to open the shipping season at Cleveland, Ohio, on March 20.

Conducting its first operational assignment for McKeil Marine Ltd., the crane vessel *D. C. Everest* began shifting cargo aboard the laid up Misener Shipping steamer *John A. France* (2) at Hamilton, Ontario, on March 12. That same day, the U.S. Coast Guard icebreaker *Mackinaw* (WAGB-83) was placed back into commission following the completion of engine repairs that began the previous summer. Sailing from Cheboygan, Michigan, it passed upbound through the Soo Locks on March 14 to begin icebreaking operations on Whitefish Bay in preparation for the start of the shipping season.

On March 13, the Rouge Steel Company announced the sale of its marine operations to Lakes Shipping Company Inc., a newly established affiliate of the Interlake Steamship Company. Involving the steamers *Benson Ford* (3), *William Clay Ford* (2), and the motor vessel *Henry Ford II*, this transaction ended the Ford Motor Company's long history of lake freighter ownership stretching back to the 1920s. All three vessels received new names in the following manner: *Benson Ford* (3) to *Kaye E. Barker*, *Henry Ford II* to *Samuel Mather* (7), and *William Clay Ford* (2) to *Lee A. Tregurtha*. As part of the sales agreement, Rouge Steel also awarded the shipping company a long-term contract to deliver raw materials to its steel mill located on the Rouge River at Dearborn, Michigan.

Making its familiar early start in the Lake Ontario cement trade, the *Stephen B. Roman* arrived at Toronto on March 14, thus opening the navigation season at that port for the sixth consecutive year.

Due to the depletion of stockpiles on the lower lakes, the U.S. Army Corps of Engineers began allowing special transits through the Poe Lock at Sault Ste. Marie, Michigan, on March 15 prior to the official opening of the Soo Locks on March 21. As one of the vessels approved for an early passage, USS Great Lakes Fleet's *Edgar B. Speer* cleared Milwaukee, Wisconsin, on March 13 to load iron ore at Two Harbors, Minnesota. Escorted by the U.S. Coast Guard's *Katmai Bay* and *Mackinaw*, the thousand-footer became the first commercial vessel to pass through the locks on March 15. Meanwhile, the *Edwin H. Gott* had sailed from Duluth, Minnesota, on March 14 to Two Harbors following a short delay caused by engine problems. Carrying a load of iron ore for delivery to Gary, Indiana, it became the first downbound vessel of the season to reach the Soo Locks on March 16. The movement of western coal from Lake Superior began on March 19 with the departure of the *Belle River* from the Superior Midwest Energy Terminal (SMET) at Superior, Wisconsin, for a Michigan power plant.

The healthy state of the dry bulk material trades allowed the Oglebay Norton Company put two self-unloaders in its Columbia Transportation Division fleet back into operation following lengthy layups.

The *J. Burton Ayers* returned to service in 1989 following a lengthy layup. (Photo by James Hoffman)

These were the "Maritime" class steamers *Crispin Oglebay* (2) and *J. Burton Ayers*, which had been idle at Toledo, Ohio, since 1981 and 1985 respectively. Moved to the Toledo Shipyard on March 17 for dry-docking by Merce Industries Inc., the *Ayers* became the first of the pair to begin the process of returning to service.

Among the first Canadian vessels to leave their winter layup berths that season, the ULS Corporation's *Canadian Enterprise* and *Canadian Olympic* began the movement of coal to the Ontario Hydro power plants located at Courtright, Ontario, and Nanticoke, Ontario, during mid-March.

Reflecting the recent agreement between the Rouge Steel Company and the Interlake Steamship Company, the *Herbert C. Jackson* opened the navigation season at Toledo on March 20 when it arrived to load coal for Dearborn. With the *Charles M. Beeghly* and *Elton Hoyt 2nd* (2) also employed on this route, the Interlake fleet was to deliver at least five coal cargoes to the steel mill by April 15.

The *Medusa Challenger* became the first ship of the season into Grand Haven, Michigan, on March 21. This came after the 83-year old cement carrier struggled with heavy ice while southbound on Lake Michigan, including one 40-mile stretch between Charlevoix, Michigan, and the Manitou Islands that took two days to traverse.

The season at Marquette, Michigan, began at a brisk pace with three American Steamship Company (ASC) vessels arriving off the upper harbor on March 23. After pushing its way through the ice field on Lake Superior, the *H. Lee White* (2) was the first to tie up at the Lake Superior & Ishpeming Railroad iron ore loading dock followed by the *Buffalo* (3) and *Charles E. Wilson*.

The Twin Ports welcomed its first arrival from the lower lakes on March 25 when the

George A. Stinson docked at Superior, Wisconsin, to load 39,196 gross tons of taconite pellets at Burlington Northern for Detroit. That same day, the tanker *W. M. Vacy Ash* opened the season at Thunder Bay, Ontario, with a load of gasoline.

The Duluth waterfront was the scene of a mysterious incident on the morning of March 27 when employees arriving for work at the Great Lakes Towing Company found the 81-foot tugs *Arkansas* and *Louisiana* slowly sinking at their moorings. Just after eight o'clock that morning, one member of a U.S. Coast Guard crew attempting to start pumps on board the *Arkansas* nearly drowned when the stern of the tug suddenly dipped toward the bottom. With the door to the engine room pinned shut by the inrushing water, the guardsman scrambled to safety by squeezing through a porthole. Efforts to keep the two foundering vessels afloat ultimately failed, however, with both settling to the bottom a short time later. A subsequent salvage operation raised the *Arkansas* on April 15 and the *Louisiana* four days later. Clearing Duluth on May 8 in tow of the tug *Ohio*, the tugs went to Cleveland for repairs. In the end, investigators were unable to determine what caused the unusual double sinking.

On March 27 a buildup of ice apparently factored into the *Mesabi Miner* going aground after making too wide of a turn near Johnson Point in the St. Marys River while downbound from Taconite Harbor, Minnesota, with taconite pellets for Lorain, Ohio. At the time of the mishap, the Middle Neebish Channel was open to two-way traffic as the West Neebish Channel normally used by downbound vessels on the opposite side of Neebish Island had not yet opened for the season. Opening up a one-foot square hole that flooded its forepeak tank, the grounded thousand-footer brought a halt to all traffic in the river. Refloated by three tugs on March 29, it went to an anchorage off Lime Island as the eleven ships delayed by the accident began moving once again. A subsequent underwater inspection revealed no further damage other than that sustained on the port bow. Ballasted to keep the hull breach above the waterline, the *Mesabi Miner* received the necessary repairs upon reaching Lorain.

Another early season casualty involved the *Herbert C. Jackson*, which came away from an altercation with heavy ice conditions at Stoneport, Michigan, on March 29 with considerable propeller damage. With one blade missing and another bent, the 690-foot steamer limped to the Torco Dock at Toledo to have both blades replaced after delivering its stone cargo to a dock on the Rouge River.

During the early morning hours of March 29, the barge *Scurry* went aground just above the Detroit River Light while in tow of the tugs *Glenada* and *Tusker* on a loaded voyage from Toledo to Sarnia. Joined by the Great Lakes Towing Company's *Indiana*, the tugs refloated the barge about 12 hours later. At about one o'clock the next morning, however, the upbound tow experienced further trouble when an electrical failure caused the *Tusker* to lose power a short distance upstream of Belle Isle in the upper Detroit River. Caught in the strong current, the *Scurry* ran aground for the second time on this particular trip when it wandered out of the navigation channel near Buoy G113. Apparently suffering no serious harm in either of these incidents, the barge was pulled free by the Malcolm Marine tug *Barbara Ann* a short time later.

Winter showed little sign of releasing its hold on Lake Superior during late March with ice reported as being between 27 and 38 inches thick over much of the lake and windrows in some places reaching 15 to 20 feet in height. At the western end of the lake, these harsh conditions prevented the railcar ferry *Incan Superior* from beginning its season until some three weeks later in the year than usual. Finally departing winter layup at Thunder Bay, it reached the Twin Ports on April 6.

The St. Lawrence Seaway opened on March 30 with the Finnish tanker *Kihu* locking upbound through the St. Lambert Lock en route to Toronto for a cargo of vegetable oil. Meanwhile, Misener Shipping's 730-foot bulk carrier *J. N. McWatters* (2) led the movement of downbound traffic when it passed through the Iroquois Lock that same day bound to load iron ore at Pointe Noire, Quebec. Commercial traffic through the Welland Canal began the following day with the *J. W. McGiffin* being the first upbounder and the *Canadian Progress* the first downbounder.

Its $16 million conversion to a self-unloader completed, the *Algomarine* left Port Weller Dry Docks at St. Catharines, Ontario, on April 1. Sailing the short distance to Hamilton, the motor vessel took on its first cargo in this configuration when it loaded slag for Detroit.

The April 1 arrival of Algoma Central's *Capt. Henry Jackman* heralded the beginning of the grain season at Duluth. This came just four days before the first ocean vessel reached the Twin Ports when the Polish bulker *Pomorze Zachodnie* entered the harbor to load grain at both Cargill in Duluth and Harvest States in Superior, Wisconsin.

Following an extended period of idleness, the 339-foot U.S. Army Corps of Engineers hopper suction dredge *Markham* left Cleveland on April 4 in tow of the Gaelic Tugboat Company tugs *Kinsale*, *William A. Whitney*, and *Wicklow*. Delivered to the Toledo Shipyard, the 29-year old vessel underwent a $217,000 refit in preparation of assuming new duties in England. Departing the lakes during early August, the *Markham* lasted until being sunk as an artificial reef off the coast of North Carolina in 1994.

Having run into some difficulty with ice on its first trip of the season, the steamer *Reserve* tied up at the Port Terminal in Duluth on April 5 for propeller repairs. That same day, the *Canadian Leader* also arrived at the Port Terminal after slamming into the Peavey Company's Connors Point Elevator Dock at Superior, Wisconsin, while attempting to moor in heavy ice. With damage limited to some bent plating and opened seams above the waterline on its starboard bow, a repair crew from Fraser Shipyards soon had the 730-foot carrier back in service.

The navigation season at Oshawa, Ontario, began on a rather inauspicious note on April 6 when the tug *Michael D. Misner* collided with the inbound Liberian tanker *Stolt Castle*. Its hull punctured, the tanker spilled about 900 gallons of fuel oil into the harbor that was quickly contained.

The *Philip R. Clarke* made an unscheduled stop at Sault Ste. Marie, Michigan, on April 7 after rubbing the bottom of the St. Marys River. An inspection at the Carbide Dock prompted a trip to Fraser Shipyards at Superior, Wisconsin, for repairs. In a separate occurrence on April 7, engine problems forced the Polish flagged *Ziemia Krakowska* to seek shelter off Keweenaw Point in Lake Superior. After sitting at anchor for a few days, the 18-year old ocean vessel continued on to Duluth.

The *William J. De Lancey* inaugurated a new trade route in the movement of western coal on April 8 when it departed the Superior Midwest Energy Terminal at Superior, Wisconsin, bound for Muskegon, Michigan. Destined for the Consumers Power

Company's B. C. Cobb Power Plant, this 57,745 net ton shipment was the first of many brought down from Lake Superior to that facility until its closure in 2016.

The aftereffects of winter caused problems for mariners on the upper lakes well into April with some 1,000-foot vessels requiring about four hours to complete downbound passages through the Soo Locks due to large buildups of slush ice. In addition, several periods of poor visibility also slowed or stopped traffic on the St. Marys River during the early days of the month. At the same time, U.S. Coast Guard icebreaking operations in the region were under tremendous pressure with three of the four 140-foot icebreaking tugs assigned to work the spring breakout experiencing a variety of mechanical failures.

Meanwhile, heavy ice also remained a concern at the Twin Ports with several cargo vessels encountering delays. Unable to use the ice-clogged Superior Entry, the *Stewart J. Cort* made an uncommon passage through the Duluth Entry on April 9 while en route to the Burlington Northern ore dock at Superior, Wisconsin. In a testament to the severe ice conditions present in the harbor, the thousand-footer struggled for five hours to cover the six miles to the loading dock.

In its second incident in less than a week, the tanker *Stolt Castle* spilled a small amount of styrene into the St. Clair River while at Sarnia on April 12. Detected by a monitoring station located downstream near Courtright, the discharge did not put local drinking water supplies at risk. The minor nature of the spill notwithstanding, government regulators wasted little time in filing pollution charges against the vessel's owner and charging its captain for failing to report the spill.

Early in the season, some Canada Steamship Lines (CSL) self-unloaders began making trips into the Twin Ports with unusual inbound shipments of oats for General Mills, the first of which arrived aboard the *Tadoussac* (2) on April 14. With the *Stadacona* (3) bringing in a few of these loads during early May, the *Manitoulin* (5) made at least one trip in this trade during the upcoming summer.

The Cyprus flagged bulker *Arosa* arrived at the St. Lambert Lock opposite Montreal, Quebec, on April 15 after sustaining ice-related bow damage in the Gulf of St. Lawrence. Able to continue up the Seaway for Cleveland, it stopped at Port Colborne, Ontario, two days later for repairs.

The navigation season on the St. Marys River was barely a month old when the *Enerchem Avance* found the bottom while nearing the Government Dock at Sault Ste. Marie, Ontario, with a load of diesel oil on April 18. Pulled free seven hours later by the tug *Avenger IV*, there were no reports of any serious damage or cargo spillage.

Returning to service for the first time in nearly three and a half years, the *J. Burton Ayers* cleared Toledo on April 23. Passing Detroit the next day, the "Maritime" class steamer continued upbound to load stone for delivery to LTV Steel at Cleveland.

The most serious accident thus far in the season took place on April 24 when the Philippine bulk carrier *General Vargas* crushed and sank the tug *Minnie Selvick* in the Fox River at Green Bay, Wisconsin. The accident happened as the ill-fated tug and fleet mate *Steven M. Selvick* were towing the ocean freighter to the Leicht Transfer & Storage Company's north dock. Pushed hard against the wooden pilings protecting the Green Bay & Western Railroad Bridge, the *Minnie Selvick* sank almost immediately with the *Steven M. Selvick* rescuing two of its three crewmembers while the third scrambled onto a piling. Coming to a rest in shallow water on the east side of the shipping channel with just the top half of its pilothouse protruding above the surface, the wreck did not interfere with vessel traffic on the Fox River. Raised from the bottom on May 10 by Kadinger Marine Service, the *Minnie Selvick* was towed to Sturgeon Bay for dry-docking a few days later before being taken to Kewaunee, Wisconsin, on November 2 for scrapping.

Towed out of the dry dock at Fraser Shipyards in its new Lakes Shipping Company colors on April 25, the *Lee A. Tregurtha* sailed across the harbor from Superior, Wisconsin, to Duluth one day later to load iron ore for Dearborn. Following the *Tregurtha*'s departure, the tugs *Illinois* and *Rhode Island* moved the long idle *Harry Coulby* (2) into the dry dock in preparation of that steamer entering service for Kinsman Lines that summer.

Its springtime icebreaking duties on the upper lakes completed for the season, the U.S. Coast Guard's *Mackinaw* made a rare passage down the Welland Canal on April 26. One of the stops made during its visit to Lake Ontario was Toronto, where the well-known vessel hosted public tours.

On April 27, the Singapore-registered tanker *Tove Cob* spilled approximately 20,000 gallons of animal tallow into Lake Ontario off Clarkson, Ontario. The leak was discovered while the vessel was at the Petro-Canada Dock to load gasoline after coming from the Darling & Company Ltd. Dock in nearby Toronto. Although largely contained and consisting of a sticky non-toxic substance, the spill nonetheless created a foul-

The J. B. Ford was towed to South Chicago, Illinois, near the beginning of the 1989 season for cement storage and transfer duties. (Photo by James Hoffman)

smelling mess along the local shoreline.

Located in the small community of Thessalon, Ontario, on the north shore of Lake Huron, the newly opened Smelter Bay Aggregates loading dock shipped its first cargo on April 28 when Algoma Central's *Agawa Canyon* loaded 10,000 tons of concrete sand. Equipped with a single stationary belt conveyor, the configuration of the dock permitted the loading of ships measuring up to 730 feet in length at a rate of 2,500 tons per hour.

The idle cement carrier *J. B. Ford* was towed from Milwaukee to South Chicago, Illinois, early in the season to serve in the cement storage and transfer role at a Lafarge Corporation terminal located on the Calumet River. Elsewhere within the Inland Lakes Transportation fleet, the *E. M. Ford* made what was reportedly its first trip to the Twin Ports in at least a decade when it arrived on May 1 with a load of cement. While unloading, the venerable steamer had some starboard bow repairs done by a work crew sent over from Fraser Shipyards.

On May 5, the icebreaker *Mackinaw* stuck the Norfolk & Western Railroad Bridge at Toledo while towing the buoy tender *Mariposa* to the Toledo Shipyard. Damage amounted to a 9-foot gash on the starboard bow above the waterline with repairs deferred until the 290-foot vessel returned to Cheboygan. This mishap followed an earlier incident on the Maumee River that spring in which the barge *Medusa Conquest* swung into some pilings when the CSX Transportation Bridge failed to open in time for its passage.

Salvage efforts to recover the partially sunken barge *OLS-30* in northern Lake Huron resumed during early May. Since capsizing the previous October, drifting ice had moved the barge about two and one-half miles southeast from its original position. The primary contractors for this operation were McAllister Towing & Salvage Inc. of Montreal and the New Jersey based Donjon Marine Company. Over a four-hour period on May 14, the salvage barge *McAllister 252* succeeded in raising the barge with steel cables. Left floating upside down, the tugs *Patricia B. McAllister*, *Carl William Selvick*, and *Venture* towed the *OLS-30* to Calcite, Michigan. A subsequent inspection found the barge contained only a small portion of the calcium chloride it was carrying at the time of the accident with the balance having seeped into the lake during the winter. On May 16, the salvage team began transferring what remained of the cargo to the barge *Hannah 2901*. Once emptied, the *OLS-30* was towed out to deep water and righted. Clearing Calcite on May 24 in tow for Sturgeon Bay, it arrived at Bay Shipbuilding two days later for dry-docking and repairs.

After losing a propeller blade on Lake Superior, the *Elton Hoyt 2nd* (2) reached Sault Ste. Marie, Michigan, on May 7. After assisting with the passage through the Soo Locks, the Wellington Towing tug *Chippewa* escorted the steamer down the St. Marys River and into northern Lake Michigan.

A pair of minor groundings claimed two Canadian vessels during the second week of May, the first of which involved the *Algorail* (2) at Grand Haven on May 7. Having just loaded sand, the 640-foot self-unloader managed to free itself within a few hours apparently undamaged. The next day, the *Mantadoc* (2) went aground off Sarnia while upbound on the St. Clair River with iron ore for Burns Harbor, Indiana. Able to break free of the bottom without requiring tug assistance, the bulk carrier resumed its voyage without any reports of damage.

Sold to International Marine Salvage for dismantling, the former Shell Oil of Canada

The *Prairie Harvest* was converted to a self-unloader at Port Weller Dry Docks during the 1989 season.
(Photo by Mike Cleary)

Ltd. tanker *Fuel Marketer* (2) left Toronto on May 9 in tow of the tug *Stormont*. Last operating in 1977, it had served as a training school for commercial divers at Toronto since the early 1980s. Arriving at Port Colborne the following day, the scrap yard wasted little time in cutting up the 259-foot vessel with this work completed by that November.

Earlier that year, the Pilot Oceanways Corporation of Panama finalized an agreement with Shell Canada Products Ltd. to acquire the 209-foot self-propelled bunkering barge *Bayshell* (2) for off-lakes use. Towed out of Toronto by the tug *Glenevis* on May 10 after nearly six years of inactivity, the barge reached Montreal two days later. Renamed *Petropan I*, it cleared that port on May 22 in tow of the U.S. flagged tug *Neptune* bound for Panama.

Towed over from Toronto after remaining idle thus far in the season, the bulk carrier *Senneville* arrived at Port Weller Dry Docks during the second week of May for an extensive hull renewal project. Requiring a five-month stay at the shipyard, this involved a considerable amount of steel work to correct the negative consequences of normal operational wear and tear upon the vessel's light construction. Although returned to a layup status at Toronto on October 11, it managed to make a few runs late in the year after returning to service during early November.

Taking a break from its usual work in the grain and ore trades, Misener Shipping's *Ralph Misener* delivered a load of wood chips at the Detroit Marine Terminals Dock #1 on May 17. Two days later, the U.S. flagged cargo ship *Jean Lykes* went into the dry dock at Fraser Shipyards in Superior, Wisconsin, for painting and general hull work. Making a rare visit for a saltwater ship of any flag, it spent less than a week at the shipyard before departing the Twin Ports on May 25.

After plans for a move to Port Stanley, Ontario, stalled, the Sarnia City Council grew concerned about the continued presence of the *Aquarama* on the city's waterfront and issued a deadline for it to leave by the end of May. With that date fast approaching, the tugs *Barbara Ann* and *Tug Malcolm* towed the 520-foot vessel the short distance downriver to Marysville, Michigan, on May 24. This move did not go without incident, however, as two members of the crew working at the bow of the retired passenger steamer were injured when a cable snapped during the departure from Sarnia. The *Aquarama* remained at Marysville for only a short time, leaving on June 1 when the same pair of tugs towed it to the Russell Street Slip at Windsor, Ontario.

During May 24-25, a storm system disrupted shipping operations at the Twin Ports with high winds and heavy downpours. Battling 74 mph winds on May 24, the thousand-footer *Lewis Wilson Foy* experienced some severe rolling while turning around on a turbulent Lake Superior off the Superior Entry. Even as the *Foy* took its wild ride out on the lake, debris blown off the Burlington Northern ore dock pelted the CSL self-unloader *Frontenac* (5) as that vessel was loading taconite pellets. While departing the Cargill B1 Elevator in Duluth the next day, strong gusts nearly pushed the motor vessel *Silver Isle* aground at Park Point. With a safe passage through the Duluth Ship Canal out of the question, the bulk carrier went across the shared harbor to leave via the Superior Entry.

Blustery spring weather also figured in a May 25 mishap that left a 21-foot pleasure boat wrecked at Cleveland when high winds pushed the *Nicolet* into a dock at Shooters Restaurant on the Cuyahoga River. The next day, the *Enerchem Travailleur* suffered an engine failure while making its way between Locks 7 and 8 on the Welland Canal. Spending the night tied up in the canal for repairs, the tanker resumed its transit on May 27.

Venturing farther north than is usual for a ship operated by the Erie Sand Steamship Company, the *Richard Reiss* made a rare appearance at Sault Ste. Marie, Michigan, when it locked upbound through the Soo Locks on May 27. After delivering sand loaded at Drummond Island to Sault Ste. Marie, Ontario, it took on a cargo of slag before returning downbound through the locks the next day bound for Cleveland.

The first voyage of the Cuban freighter *Bahia de La Habana* into the St. Lawrence Seaway proved unpleasantly eventful on May 28 when gusting winds slammed the three-year old vessel into an approach wall at Beauharnois, Quebec. Lightly damaged, it proceeded inbound for Toronto following an inspection at the Lower Beauharnois Lock. That same day, CSL's *Prairie Harvest* entered the dry dock at Port Weller Dry Docks for a $20 million conversion to a self-unloader.

Purchased by Socanav Inc., the former British registered tanker *New Orleans* arrived at Quebec City, Quebec, on May 31. Built at Lodose, Sweden, in 1967, the company acquired this 344-foot motor vessel primarily to serve customers located in shallow draft ports. Renamed *Nancy Orr Gaucher*, it arrived at Montreal on June 17 and went up the Seaway four days later en route to Hamilton.

Near the beginning of summer, CSL put four of its idle ships up for sale. These were the bulk carriers *Sir James Dunn*, *Georgian Bay*, and *Nipigon Bay* along with the fire damaged package freighter *Fort Chambly*. All of these vessels had been idle for several years with the *Fort Chambly* having entered an indefinite layup in 1981 while the other three last operated during the 1982 season. Corostel Trading of Montreal acquired all four for scrapping overseas a short time later with their departures from the lakes taking place between July and August.

For the second time that season, the U.S. Coast Guard's *Mackinaw* delivered a buoy tender to the Toledo Shipyard when it towed the *Bramble* from Detroit to Toledo in early June for a comprehensive overhaul that included the installation of a new pair of engines, two new boilers, and two new generators. Unlike its previous trip to the shipyard to deliver the *Mariposa*, however, the icebreaker's voyage into the Maumee River proved uneventful on this particular occasion.

A pair of saltwater ships encountered minor difficulties on the St. Lawrence River during the early days of June. On June 2, the Liberian freighter *Shimone* caused a short traffic disruption when a hawser fouled its propeller near Linda Island in the Thousand Islands while downbound with a load of steel destined for an Italian port. Just three days later, the discovery of hatch coaming damage delayed the *Federal Inger* for a short time at the Eisenhower Lock while upbound with steel coils for Burns Harbor.

Arriving at the Lower Lake Dock Company's Dock No. 3 in Sandusky, Ohio, on June 8 to load coal for delivery to Iceland, the Philippine bulker *Freenes* became the first saltwater vessel to visit that port in several years.

The Interlake Steamship Company's last operating straight decker *J. L. Mauthe* took a temporary hiatus from hauling grain when shipments in that trade receded during the summer. Shifted to the movement of iron ore, the 647-foot steamer cleared Superior, Wisconsin, on June 10 after loading at the Burlington Northern Dock for Cleveland.

Returning to service after nearly eight years of idleness, the *Crispin Oglebay* (2) departed Toledo on June 11 to load stone at Stoneport for LTV Steel in Cleveland. Just one day later, the other recently reactivated Columbia Transportation "Maritime" class self-unloader, *J. Burton Ayers*, went aground at Ferrysburg, Michigan, while attempting to turn around after unloading. Freed with the help of the tug *Carol Ann*, there were no reports of the steamer sustaining any damage.

Due to the size constraints of the Lake Superior & Ishpeming Railroad ore dock, thousand-foot vessels rarely load at Marquette. One member of that class capable of doing so, the tug/barge combination *Presque Isle* (2), had one of its infrequent visits to take on iron ore interrupted by unloading gear problems that kept it in port from June 12 to June 17.

While attempting to moor with tugboat assistance, strong winds pushed CSL's *Black Bay* into the Burlington Northern Dock in Superior, Wisconsin, on June 13. Although its port bow damaged the dock's No. 27 shuttle conveyor, damage to the 730-foot steamer amounted to only some minor scuffing.

Granted an extraordinary reversal of fortune with its sale to Kinsman Lines after several years of inactivity, the former *Harry Coulby* (2) cleared Fraser Shipyards on June 13 as the *Kinsman Enterprise* (2). Towed to the Peavey Company's Connors Point Elevator in Superior, Wisconsin, the 631-foot steamer loaded 533,000 bushels of wheat before going to the Port Terminal in Duluth for final fit out work. Clearing the Twin Ports late in the evening of June 18, it only made one more round trip before entering a temporary layup at Buffalo, New York, that lasted until early September.

During a ceremony held at Buffalo on June 15, the American Steamship Company renamed the motor vessel *Roger M. Kyes* to *Adam E. Cornelius* (4). This renaming carried on a tradition in that fleet dating back to 1908 of having one vessel thus named and another named John J. Boland to honor the company's two founding partners.

The largest U.S. flagged tanker operating on the Great Lakes made a rare trip through the Seaway on June 20 when the Cleveland Tankers fleet's *Gemini* passed downbound for Montreal. The C&P Dock in Cleveland received a pair of unusual visits by members of the USS Great Lakes Fleet during the third week of June with the *John G. Munson* (2) arriving to unload iron ore on June 20 followed the next day by the *Cason J. Callaway* with a second load.

At 2:15 a.m. on June 21, a fire broke out aboard the former Cedar Point ferry *G. A. Boeckling* as it sat moored in the Hocking Valley Slip at Toledo. In addition to destroying the wooden upper works, the intense heat generated by the blaze also buckled the vessel's main deck and hull. The extensive nature of the damage put an immediate end to the long running restoration effort coordinated by the non-profit group Friends of the Boeckling with the burned-out hull subsequently sold for scrap. An investigation into this incident resulted in the arrest of a 26-year old local man on September 8. Having started the fire by burning cardboard for illumination while trespassing on the vessel, a jury found him guilty of arson on December 22 of the same year.

The *American Mariner* carried an uncommon split cargo out of Superior, Wisconsin, at the beginning of summer when it took on a partial load of coal at the Superior Midwest Energy Terminal before shifting over to the Harvest States Elevator on June 21 to load grain. After delivering the coal to Marquette, it sailed down the lakes to discharge the grain at Windsor. The 730-foot self-unloader repeated this voyage two months later when it cleared the Twin Ports on August 22 with a second split load of coal and grain.

Renamed *Samuel Mather* (7), the former *Henry Ford II* cleared its Rouge River layup berth on June 23 in tow of the tug *Shannon*. The *Shannon* delivered the self-unloader to the Hocking Valley Slip at Toledo with the assistance of the tug *Galway Bay*, where it remained until moved to that port's Frog Pond on November 7. Identified only by having its new name painted on the stern, this ship never operated for the Lakes Shipping Company before being sold for scrap five years later.

Towed by the tugs *Delaware* and *Ohio*, the former passenger and package freight ferry *Normac* passed upbound through the Welland Canal on June 24. It should be recalled that this vessel had rested on the bottom of Toronto Harbor for five years after being sunk by the ferry *Trillium* during the summer of 1981. Extensively rebuilt over the winter of 1988-89, the tugs delivered the *Normac* to Cleveland where it was operated as Captain John's Seafood floating restaurant.

Rechristened *Capt. Edward V. Smith* and paired with the tug *Irving Miami*, the former American Steamship Company steamer *Adam E. Cornelius* (3) delivered its first cargo as a self-unloading barge when it arrived at Rimouski, Quebec, on July 3 with road salt from Pugwash, Nova Scotia.

Departing Toronto on July 7, the *Nipigon Bay* became the first of the four CSL ships sold for demolition to begin its journey to the breakers. Passing through the Snell Lock

Moved to other ports on two occasions after laying up for the final time at Montreal in December of 1982, the steamer *Nipigon Bay* left the lakes during the summer of 1989. (Photo Tom Salvner)

three days later with the McKeil Marine tugs *Glenbrook*, *Glenevis*, *Lac Como*, and *Stormont*, the bulk carrier arrived at Sorel, Quebec, on July 12 to await the arrival of the *Fort Chambly*.

Built by Collingwood Shipyards Ltd. at Collingwood, Ontario, in 1951 as the tanker *Imperial Leduc*, this vessel operated for Pipeline Tankers Ltd. (Imperial Oil Company Ltd., mgr.) until purchased by Canada Steamship Lines in 1954. Renamed *Nipigon Bay* the following year, service in the tanker trades continued until it went to the Port Arthur Shipbuilding Company yard at Port Arthur, Ontario, at the end of the 1957 shipping season for conversion to a bulk carrier. Lengthened from 620' to 692' during this reconstruction, a return visit to that shipyard during the winter of 1980-81 resulted in the installation of a five-foot high trunk deck that increased its cubic carrying capacity by nearly 20 percent. Unfortunately, changing economic times put an early end to this vessel's operational career just a few years later when it laid up for the last time at Montreal on December 2, 1982.

On July 8, the British container ship *Canadian Explorer*, not to be confused with a bulk carrier of that same name operated by ULS Corporation, ran aground off Vercheres, Quebec, in the St. Lawrence River while outbound for the Atlantic. The tug *Cathy McAllister* made short work of freeing the stranded carrier by refloating it just four hours later.

Its dilapidated condition after seven years of layup at the head of Lake Superior far removed from its glory days as an active carrier in the Canada Steamship Lines fleet, the steamer *Georgian Bay* cleared Thunder

Bay on July 11 in tow of the tugs *Anglian Lady* and *Avenger IV*. Locking downbound at the Soo Locks two days later, the tow transited the Welland Canal on July 16 with the *Avenger IV* now joined by the tug *Glenevis*. During this segment of the trip, the *Glenevis* hit the arrestor cable at Lock 3 thereby creating an 11-hour traffic delay in the canal. Once clear of the Welland Canal, the tow stopped at Hamilton on July 17 to have the remaining bunker fuel still aboard the *Georgian Bay* removed. Towed out of that port three days later by the *Glenevis*, the retired bulk carrier made one final passage through the St. Lawrence Seaway with the tugs *Glenbrook* and *Stormont* assisting before ending up at Sorel on July 24 in preparation for an overseas scrap tow.

Originally laid down as a tanker at Collingwood Shipyards but sold to Canada Steamship Lines while still on the ways and completed as a bulk carrier, the *Georgian Bay* first entered service in May of 1954. Destined to remain in the CSL fleet throughout its entire carrier, the 620-foot steamer remained particularly active in the movement of grain on an annual basis until entering an indefinite layup at Thunder Bay on December 9, 1982.

The Socanav tanker *Le Frene No. 1* resumed trading on July 14 after being at Sorel since March 15 undergoing a refit to address engine problems. In other activity on July 14, the motor vessel *Soodoc* (2) visited Montreal for the first time since having its registry transferred to the Bahamas late the previous year. Reflagged Canadian to deliver supplies to the Arctic, it returned to Bahamian registry in mid-November.

The *Fort Chambly* left Windsor on July 13 in tow of the tugs *Lac Manitoba* and *Argue Martin* bound for Port Colborne, where it arrived two days later. After passing down the Welland Canal on July 16, the retired package freighter reached Sorel three days later with the tugs *Glenbrook* and *Stormont*.

Declared a total loss following a fire at Windsor in December of 1988, the *Fort Chambly* was one of three "Fort" class package freighters built by Collingwood Shipyards for Canada Steamship Lines between 1955 and 1961. Entering service for that fleet in early 1961, this ship had an interesting, although brief, career that included both Great Lakes and ocean service. Outfitted with deck cranes by Eriksbergs Mekaniska Verkstads Aktiebolaget at Gothenburg, Sweden, in 1976, it traded on saltwater under the Bermuda flag as the *Chambly Era* until reverting to its original name after returning to Canadian registry in 1978. Remaining active during the waning days of CSL's package freight service, the *Fort Chambly* last operated when it tied up at Windsor on December 23, 1981.

Their fates sealed, the *Fort Chambly* and *Nipigon Bay* cleared Sorel on August 9 in a tandem tow by the ocean tug *Fairplay IX*. Following an uneventful transatlantic voyage, the two carriers reached Aliaga, Turkey, for dismantling on September 19.

A minor incident on July 22 caused a short delay for traffic transiting the Seaway when the Spanish tanker *Mar Caterina* struck a fender boom while downbound at the Snell Lock.

Less than two months after it had entered the Socanav fleet, an explosion aboard the *Nancy Orr Gaucher* at Hamilton on July 25 left one crewmember with minor burns. The accident happened when a pressure build-up in a cargo tank led to an uncontrollable release of asphalt as the vessel was unloading. Bursting through a deck valve, the violent discharge spewed about 250 metric tons of liquid asphalt dozens of feet into the air before subsiding a half hour later. Much of the sticky mess showered down upon the tanker's deck and the front of its superstructure, while a smaller amount spilled into the harbor. Maintained at a temperature of approximately 300 degrees Fahrenheit, the asphalt that went overboard quickly solidified. This not only confined the footprint of the spill but also simplified the subsequent cleanup operation.

The *Nancy Orr Gaucher* remained at Hamilton until departing on August 8 for Montreal, still carrying what remained of its 30,000-barrel cargo after the consignee refused to accept delivery. While arriving at Socanav's yard in Sorel for repairs on September 2, however, the 344-foot tanker suffered a further mishap when one of its anchors snagged several telephone cables in the Richelieu River. Leaving some 5,000 customers without phone service for a week, this incident reportedly caused $2 million in damage to the cables. Its repairs completed, the *Gaucher* sailed from the repair yard on October 15 for Bronte, Ontario.

A second accident at the Snell Lock in just four days took place at 5:15 a.m. on July 26 when the Singapore registered chemical tanker *Lake Anne* hit a lock wall while downbound from Sarnia. Holed, the vessel spilled some 3,000 gallons of xylene that was contained within the lock. Due to the flammability of its cargo, Seaway officials ordered the 27 members of the crew off the ship and closed off the surrounding area during the 11-hour cleanup operation.

Columbia Transportation's *Crispin Oglebay* (2) made an uncommon excursion into the upper St. Marys River on July 26 to load slag at Sault Ste. Marie, Ontario. Finally loaded after spending several hours at anchor, the 620-foot steamer went aground while backing away from the A. B. McLean Dock.

Easily refloated by the tugs *Vermont* and *Wisconsin* sent over from the American Soo, it stopped at the Carbide Dock for a Coast Guard inspection after passing downbound through the locks.

Purchased by the Texas based Marine Specialty Company through a federal court sale of seized assets, the unfinished tug originally started by the Upper Peninsula Shipbuilding Company nine years earlier began its trip off the lakes during the last week of July. Having sat at Sault Ste. Marie, Michigan, since the previous autumn, the tug left the Carbide Dock on July 26 in tow of the ocean tug *Thunder*. Assisted down the lakes to Montreal by the tug *Iroquois*, the tow continued down the eastern seaboard of the United States and across the Gulf of Mexico to reach Houston, Texas, on August 19. The same company also acquired the partially built barge still at Ontonagon, Michigan, with that unit heading to Texas near the end of the 1990 shipping season.

The oldest vessel in the American Steamship Company fleet, the 84-year old *Nicolet*, remained busy on Lake Erie during the summer months delivering corn to Port Colborne and returning westward with stone for Cleveland. During this same period, the *Edward L. Ryerson* operated outside of the ore trade to carry limestone out of Port Inland, Michigan, with deliveries split between Burns Harbor and Indiana Harbor, Indiana.

On August 3, the *Sir James Dunn* was towed from Toronto to Hamilton for the removal of its bunkers. Passing outbound through the Seaway in tow of the tugs *Glenbrook*, *Glenevis*, *Lac Como*, and *Stormont* on August 10, the former CSL bulker joined the *Georgian Bay* at Sorel the next day. Configured for a tandem overseas scrap tow, both cleared that port on August 26 with the Panamanian tug *M. C. Thunder*. The transatlantic journey encountered problems five weeks later, however, when the *Sir James Dunn* broke free from the tow during a storm on October 3 about 230 miles south of Ponta Delgada in the Azores. After leaving the *Georgian Bay* at Ponta Delgada, the *M. C. Thunder* went out in search of the drifting lake freighter. The *Dunn* was later located 300 miles southwest of the Azores by the Panamanian tug *Dalmar Servant*, which towed it to Ponta Delgada. Experiencing no further difficulties, the *M. C. Thunder* delivered the *Georgian Bay* and *Sir James Dunn* to Aliaga, Turkey, on November 16 to be broken up.

The *Sir James Dunn* dated back to its construction by the Port Arthur Shipbuilding Company at Port Arthur, Ontario, in 1952. At 663'4" in length, this steamer was one of the largest vessels on the lakes at the time of its commissioning. Soon surpassed by several larger carriers designed for service on the St. Lawrence Seaway, the *Dunn* remained active until laying up at Midland, Ontario, on December 22, 1982.

On August 5, Kinsman's straight deck bulk carrier *Henry Steinbrenner* (4) paid a rare visit to Marquette to load an even rarer cargo of natural iron ore. Taken down the lakes to the C&P Dock at Cleveland, the ore was not destined for steel production but rather for use in the cosmetics industry.

The *Ontadoc* (2) arrived at Montreal on August 8 for the installation of two cargo cranes by Mount-Royal/Walsh Inc., each with a lifting capacity of 15 tons. Upon the completion of this work, the newly converted crane vessel sailed for the Canadian Arctic on August 25.

In its second mishap in as many months, the *Black Bay* went aground near Buoy 20 in the lower St. Marys River on the morning of August 11 while downbound with iron ore for Hamilton. Lightered by the barge *PML Salvager*, the tugs *Anglian Lady* and *Avenger IV* freed the Canada Steamship Lines carrier the next day. Having suffered significant bottom damage, it sailed to Hamilton to unload before going to Fraser Shipyards at Superior, Wisconsin, for repairs. Arriving at the shipyard on August 29 for dry-docking, the steamer did not return to service until October 8 when it loaded taconite pellets at the Burlington Northern Dock. Requiring further work, it anchored off the Twin Ports later in the day to be met by a workboat from Fraser Shipyards before finally departing for Hamilton on October 11.

While sailing on Lake Ontario bound for Oswego on the foggy morning of August 13, the barge *Clarkson Carrier* and tug *Petite Forte* hit a charter fishing boat about three miles off Mississauga, Ontario. Flung into the lake by the force of the collision, all five occupants of the small craft were pulled from the water by a nearly boat. This incident led to the captain of the *Petite Forte* being cited for not posting a proper lookout for the prevailing conditions.

In a separate incident on August 13, the *Enerchem Asphalt* suffered an engine room fire while loading liquid asphalt at the Ultramar Refinery in St. Romuald, Quebec. Towed across the St. Lawrence River to Quebec City to have the fire extinguished, the 17-year old vessel sustained heavy damage in the incident. Leaving that port on August 21 in tow of the *Cathy McAllister* and *Salvage Monarch*, it arrived at Montreal the next day for repairs by Mount-Royal/Walsh Inc. During a trial run up the St. Lawrence River on September 24, the *Enerchem Asphalt* encountered further problems when an engine failed while returning from Sorel. Limping back to Montreal for further work with one of its two engines out of

The *Edward L. Ryerson* made a pair of rare trips to the Great Lakes Steel Dock on the Detroit River during the second half of the 1989 season. (Author's Collection)

commission, the tanker reentered regular service on October 3.

When a labor strike interrupted salt shipments from the Magdalen Islands in the Gulf of St. Lawrence during early spring, Algoma Central's *Sauniere* came into lakes for use in the freshwater salt trade. Making a number of rare appearances at a various inland ports, the 642-foot self-unloader made what is likely to be its first ever visit to Grand Haven on August 16.

Returning from a trip to the Canadian Arctic to deliver gasoline with ice-related propeller damage, the Socanav tanker *Eastern Shell* (2) went into the company's yard at Sorel during mid-August for repairs.

As U.S. flagged saltwater vessels are a rarity on the Great Lakes, it is noteworthy that two such visitors, the *Jean Lykes* and *Marjorie Lykes*, were both at the Twin Ports on August 18. Just two days later, the Canada Steamship Lines bulk carrier *Simcoe* (2) made an unusual visit to the Superior Midwest Energy Terminal at Superior, Wisconsin, to load coal.

At about 2:30 a.m. on August 22, the tanker *L'Orme No. 1* had its main generator fail while entering Lock 3 on the Welland Canal. After backing out of the lock, it tied up below Bridge 5 for repairs. That same day, Inland Steel's *Edward L. Ryerson* made its first visit to the Detroit area when it arrived at the Great Lakes Steel Dock on Zug Island to load mill scale. Sailing for Indiana Harbor on August 26, the 730-foot bulk carrier made a repeat voyage to Detroit during mid-November.

A cargo transfer involving two American Steamship Company vessels took place at the Torco Dock in Toledo on August 26 when the *St. Clair* (2) offloaded coal into its smaller fleet mate *American Republic*. The *St. Clair* (2) then finished unloading at Monroe, Michigan, while the *American Republic* went to Detroit Edison's Trenton Channel Power Plant at Trenton, Michigan, with its cargo.

Purchased by Marine Salvage Ltd. for dismantling following a 10-year stint as a storage barge at Port Huron, Michigan, the *Kinsman Enterprise* left the Port Huron Terminal Company Dock on August 26 in tow of the tugs *Barbara Ann* and *Tug Malcolm*. This vessel is not to be confused with a steamer bearing the same name that had just entered service for Kinsman Lines during mid-June. Delivered to Port Colborne, the tugs *Elmore M. Misner* and *Salvage Monarch* towed the 601-foot vessel down the Welland Canal on August 28. Passing through the Seaway with the tugs *Helen M. McAllister* and *Salvage Monarch*, it spent some time in the St. Zotique Anchorage due to high winds before reaching Sorel on September 1. Towed out of Sorel on September 6 by the Polish tug *Jantar*, the retired steamer arrived at Aliaga, Turkey, on October 10 for scrapping.

Built by the Chicago Shipbuilding Company at Chicago in 1906 for the Pittsburgh Steamship Company as the *Norman B. Ream*, this ship was active in the movement of raw materials for the United States Steel Corporation until late 1960. Acquired by the Kinsman Marine Transit Company in 1965 following five years of idleness, it sailed as the *Kinsman Enterprise* until laying up at Toledo at the end of the 1978 season. Sold to the Economic Development Corporation of Port Huron the following spring, the tugs *Barbara Ann* and *Tug Malcolm* towed it to that city on August 23, 1979. Unofficially renamed *Hull No. 1*, the Port Huron Terminal Company used the old vessel for the storage of agricultural commodities such as corn and sugar beets.

Towing the former Dunbar & Sullivan Dredging Company's 135-foot dredge *Niagara*, the tug *William J. Dugan* locked upbound at Sault Ste. Marie, Michigan, on August 28. While crossing Lake Superior the following night, however, the tow ran into a summer storm packing 30-40 knot winds. Wallowing in 12-foot seas, the *Niagara* began taking on water. When it became obvious the unmanned dredge could not be saved, the tug's crew cut the towline shortly before it sank at seven o'clock in the morning of August 30 about 13 miles north of Grand Island Light in 700 feet of water. At the time of it loss, the 76-year old *Niagara* was reportedly en route to Duluth for use as a floating restaurant.

During the month of August, the Osborne Materials Company acquired the former Presque Isle Sand & Gravel Inc. sand sucker *Emmett J. Carey*. Operating on Lake Erie out of Fairport, Ohio, while owned by this company, the 114-foot motor vessel lasted until being scrapped in 2016.

On September 1, the sailing yacht *Francy* suffered an engine room explosion and fire at Grand Haven. At the time of the accident, Interlake Steamship's *Elton Hoyt 2nd* (2) was in port unloading coal. Called upon to assist local firefighters, members of the steamer's crew used a utility boat to move emergency equipment across the Grand River to the burning vessel.

Restricted to ore loading docks equipped with belt conveyors due to the small size of its cargo hatches, Bethlehem Steel's *Stewart J. Cort* visited Taconite Harbor for the first time in seven years on September 6 when it loaded taconite pellets for Burns Harbor.

Also on September 6, two former Grand Trunk-Milwaukee Car Ferry Company car ferries began making their way to the breakers when the *Grand Rapids* and *Madison* left their layup berths at Muskegon. Having spent their entire operational careers on Lake Michigan, both vessels had passed to the Bultema Dock & Dredge Company during the last half of the 1970s with the *Grand Rapids* sold in 1975 and the *Madison* in 1979. Clearing Muskegon in tow of the tugs *Anglian Lady* and *Princess No. 1*, the *Grand Rapids* reached Port Maitland, Ontario, on September 11. The *Madison* arrived at Port Colborne the same day with the tugs *Chippewa* and *Thunder Cape* but was found to have too deep of draft to make it into the Marine Salvage Ltd. scrap yard at Ramey's Bend. This led to a subsequent tow that afternoon to join its former fleet mate at Port Maitland, where scrapping of the two car ferries did not begin until 1994.

On September 11, the bulk carrier *Windoc* (2) went aground at Thunder Bay while shifting between the Manitoba Pool No. 3 and United Grain Growers "A" grain elevators. Freed by the tug *W. J. Ivan Purvis* within a few hours, the 730-foot vessel suffered no serious damage and was able to load its scheduled cargo. Another incident at that port happened just two days later when the *Richelieu* (3) suffered an engine failure while departing the United Grain Growers "A" grain elevator after loading 25,600 metric tons of wheat. Moved to the Keefer Terminal by the *W. J. Purvis*, it spent the next couple of days tied up at the dock before clearing for a St. Lawrence River port on September 15.

In a repeat performance of a cargo transfer operation conducted by the American Steamship Company during late August, the *Indiana Harbor* met the *H. Lee White* (2) at the Torco Dock in Toledo on September 19. Carrying western coal for the Detroit Edison power plant at Trenton, but far too large to navigate the channel in the Detroit River leading to the dock, the thousand-footer offloaded into the 704-foot *H. Lee White* (2) so that vessel could make the final delivery.

The Cyprus flagged cargo ship *Lady II* hit an approach wall at the Iroquois Lock while outbound in the Seaway on September 23. Holed at the bow above the waterline, the ocean carrier went to Montreal for temporary patching. While in the St. Marys River that same day, the *J. Burton Ayers* suffered its second grounding accident of the season. The resultant damage required the steamer be dry-docked at the Toledo Shipyard for repairs from September 27 to October 15.

Sold to the Mexican firm Navisur S. A. de C. M. for off-lakes use, the former Desgagnes Transport 349-foot motor vessel *Eva Desgagnes* cleared Toronto on September 23. Renamed *Telchac* and arriving at Sorel two days later, it sailed for Mexico on September 30. Built by Port Weller Dry Docks Ltd. in 1955 as the *Griffon*, the small size of this carrier allowed it to operate in specialized trades that were impractical for larger ships. One of three new vessels ordered by Beaconsfield Steamships Ltd. during the 1950s, its ownership moved to Mohawk Navigation Company Ltd. in 1963 and later to Quebec & Ontario Transportation Company Ltd. in 1967. As related in Chapter 5, Group Desgagnes acquired the vessels of the latter fleet in early 1984 after that firm ceased operating at the end of the 1983 season. Having sailed as the *Franquelin* (2) since 1967, this ship retained that name until being renamed *Eva Desgagnes* in 1987.

The *Cecilia Desgagnes* tied up at Montreal on September 27 after returning from a voyage to the Arctic with heavy bow damage. Following repairs, the crane-equipped bulk carrier returned to service on October 11 when it sailed for Becancour, Quebec.

A conveyor belt fire that broke out aboard

The *H. M. Griffith* was damaged by a conveyor belt fire while transiting the Welland Canal in September of 1989. (Author's Collection)

the *H. M. Griffith* at Lock 8 in the Welland Canal just after five o'clock in the afternoon of September 27 proved difficult to extinguish and stopped traffic in the canal for four hours. With the smoky fire burning in the unloading tunnel, the tug *Argue Martin* assisted the 730-foot self-unloader to a dock at Port Colborne, where firefighters finally brought the blaze under control. Downbound with coal for Hamilton at the time of the incident, it remained at Port Colborne undergoing repairs until the end of October.

Leaving its homeport of Cheboygan on October 8, the U.S. Coast Guard's *Mackinaw* sailed to Sturgeon Bay. Arriving at the Bay Shipbuilding Corporation yard, the icebreaker went into the dry dock for a $1.1 million improvement project that included starboard shaft repairs and work on five of its six main diesel generators.

During the month of September, Canadian fleets had nearly every one of their vessels in service for the fall grain rush. Grain movements remained steady until grain elevators on the St. Lawrence River became filled to capacity as overseas shipments dried up. Without available cargoes the laying up of ships grew to such an extent that by the middle of October the roster of carriers idle up at Thunder Bay included the *Algocen* (2), *Baie St. Paul*, *J. N. McWatters* (2), *Murray Bay* (3), *Quedoc* (3), *Whitefish Bay*, and *Windoc* (2). Several of the idled carriers, including all of those noted as being at Thunder Bay, did return to operation later in the fall following a major export grain sale.

Its days as a gearless bulk carrier at an end, Algoma Central Marine's *Algogulf* arrived at Port Weller Dry Docks in St. Catharines on October 11 for a $15.7 million conversion to a self-unloader. Put in the dry dock the next day, this reconstruction continued over the coming winter with the 730-foot motor vessel making its first voyage as a self-unloader during the spring of 1990 after being renamed *Algosteel* (2).

During autumn, the Cyprus Minerals

Company began restarting the former operations of the defunct Reserve Mining Company through its Cyprus Northshore Mining Corporation subsidiary. As a direct result, Interlake Steamship's *Kaye E. Barker* delivered 5,000 tons of coal loaded at Superior, Wisconsin, to Silver Bay, Minnesota, on October 13. It should be recalled that the Reserve Mining Company had shut down following the 1986 LTV Steel bankruptcy. The first shipment of taconite pellets through the reopened loading dock at Silver Bay took place the following April.

Beset by reduction gear problems, the *Myron C. Taylor* was towed into Calcite on October 15 by fleet mate *George A. Sloan*. Helped to the dock by the tug *Chippewa*, the stricken self-unloader transferred its cargo to another vessel. Following repairs, the *Myron C. Taylor* resumed trading to finish out its season on Christmas Day. Interestingly, this affair closely resembled a similar episode that occurred the previous season in which reduction gear problems also resulted in the *George A. Sloan* requiring a tow into Calcite for repairs.

Approximately $1 million worth of new Ford Motor Company cars and trucks were lost or damaged in an early morning fire that swept through four automotive railcars aboard a barge at Windsor on October 20. The incident began when two of the railcars burst into flames shortly after being loaded on the barge. As the burning railcars were behind another row of railcars, the Windsor Fire Department had difficulty reaching the blaze. Assisted by the Detroit fireboat *Curtis Randolph*, however, the firefighters managed to extinguish the fire in about an hour's time. Without causing any injuries, the incident left 60 vehicles destroyed and another 40 damaged in adjacent railcars.

Sold by Spitzer Great Lakes Ltd. to Fraser Shipyards Inc. after being idle at Lorain since 1981, the *Leon Fraser* was towed past Detroit on October 22 by the tugs *Superior* and *Tug Malcolm*. Locking upbound through the Soo Locks three days later, the tow arrived off the Twin Ports on the afternoon of October 27 but had to anchor due to unfavorable winds. Brought into the harbor through the Duluth Entry late that evening, the former USS Great Lakes Fleet steamer arrived at Fraser Shipyards in Superior, Wisconsin, to be rebuilt as a cement carrier. Shortened from 639'6" to 519'6" in length and fitted with self-unloading equipment during this conversion, it entered service in the cement trade for Inland Lakes Transportation during the summer of 1991 as the *Alpena* (2).

A regular Seaway caller ran into trouble on October 26 when the *Ziemia Krakowska* struck Berth 15 at Trois-Rivieres, Quebec, while attempting to moor at Berth 16 with two tugs assisting. Despite inflicting significant damage to the pier, the Polish bulker only suffered a few superficial scratches.

A close call on the St. Clair River caused a few anxious moments at Port Huron on October 29 when Bethlehem Steel's *Lewis Wilson Foy* was just about to pass beneath the Blue Water Bridge to enter Lake Huron. Forced toward the Michigan shore to avoid two pleasure boats that failed to move out of the navigation channel, the thousand-footer came within a few dozen feet of coming up against the seawall running along the Thomas Edison Parkway. After successfully maneuvering away from the shore, it continued into the lake without further incident.

On October 31, the *Cason J. Callaway* made a rare visit to Ludington, Michigan, with a load of stone for the Dow Chemical Company. At the end of October, the *Roger Blough* sailed on its first trip since entering the Bay Shipbuilding yard at Sturgeon Bay on July 8 for a 5-year survey and temporary layup. Returning to service after the *Edwin H. Gott* experienced engine problems, the big carrier put in at the Port Terminal in Duluth on November 8 for repairs to a newly installed propeller.

By the close of October, iron ore shipments were running 2.4 percent over the same period of the previous season. Using this same comparison, the movement of stone also remained strong with nearly a four percent increase. Although both trades continued their modest growth during early November, a series of storm delays and the onset of brutally cold weather that brought about the early closure of the Soo Locks were to erase these gains by the end of the year.

Renamed *Nordic* at Gothenburg, Sweden, in early October, the newest addition to the Enerchem Transport fleet passed upbound in the St. Lawrence Seaway for the first time under that name on November 3. Built by the Hayashikane Shipbuilding & Engineering Company Ltd. at Shimonoseki, Japan, as the *Nordic Sun*, the 505-foot chemical tanker had been a regular visitor to the Great Lakes since its construction in 1981. Entering the Enerchem fleet through a charter agreement signed earlier that autumn and given the company's stack markings, the *Nordic* remained under the Liberian flag during this arrangement.

As the navigation season on the St. Lawrence Seaway entered its final weeks, a trio of saltwater ships suffered mishaps on the lakes over a one-week period in mid-November. The first involved the Panamanian flagged *Baltic Trader*, which lost power and hit the upper tie-up wall at Lock 1 on the Welland Canal on November 12. Just three days later, another engine casualty left the cargo ship *Lydia* adrift on Lake Ontario. The third happened on November 18 when the inbound Panamanian bulker *Star I* rubbed against some rocks near the harbor breakwater at Holland, Michigan, in strong winds. Sustaining some bottom damage, it made a subsequent trip across Lake Michigan to the Bay Shipbuilding yard at Sturgeon Bay on November 23 for repairs.

Demanding higher wages, the 2,200 unionized members of the Canadian Coast Guard walked off their jobs on November 14. Although the strikers pledged to return to work in emergencies, the walkout not only disrupted the maintenance of buoys but also halted icebreaking operations on the St. Lawrence River as winter set in. Combined with record-breaking cold weather, the strike was to be a significant factor in the development of a major traffic jam in Canadian waters at the end of the season.

On November 19, six Polish sailors seeking political asylum left the *Ziemia Tarnowska* as it was downbound at Lock 2 in the Welland Canal with a load of wheat from Duluth. With one of the crewmen having a change of heart and rejoining the ship at Montreal, the other five began the process of applying for refugee status in Canada.

Following a routine loading at the Burlington Northern ore dock, the Canada Steamship Lines steamer *Halifax* had some engine problems while departing Superior, Wisconsin, on November 23. Sailing to Thunder Bay for repairs, the self-unloader required further work for propulsion related issues at Port Colborne during mid-December.

The Socanav tanker *J. C. Phillips* had its downbound transit of the Seaway interrupted on November 24 by a grounding accident in the Beauharnois Canal near Valleyfield, Quebec. Freed by the tug *Patricia B. McAllister* later in the day, it went to Valleyfield for an initial damage survey.

Near the end of the 1989 season, the *Sparrows Point* suffered serious damage in a grounding on Lake Michigan. (Author's Collection)

Escorted by the tug *Salvage Monarch*, the 432-foot motor vessel left for Quebec City on November 26 to undergo a further inspection.

Deeply laden with taconite pellets from Escanaba, Michigan, for Indiana Harbor, Bethlehem Steel's *Sparrows Point* ran hard aground in the Porte des Morts Passage (otherwise known as the Death's Door Passage) connecting Green Bay and Lake Michigan on November 30. After offloading about 4,000 tons of pellets to a pair of barges, the 698-foot self-unloader was refloated the following day by Selvick Marine Towing tugs. The steamer went down the lake to unload before arriving at Sturgeon Bay on December 7, where entered the dry dock at Bay Shipbuilding four days later for temporary hull repairs. Refloated on December 29, the *Sparrows Point* required a second dry-docking for additional bottom work before reentering service during the spring of 1990.

Renamed *Atlantic Huron* to reflect its ability to operate in both Great Lakes and ocean service, the former *Prairie Harvest* cleared Port Weller Dry Docks at St. Catharines on November 30 following the completion of its conversion to a self-unloader. Heading up the Welland Canal, it went to load the first of two trial loads of coal at Sandusky for delivery to Hamilton before sailing for saltwater.

The movement of iron ore into Cleveland continued at a brisk pace during late November and early December with many deliveries going to the C&P Dock. This traffic included several loads brought in by Canadian straight deck bulk carriers to be unloaded by the dock's Hulett machines. The Lorain to Cleveland ore shuttle also remained busy with the majority of these trips made by the American Steamship Company's purpose built *American Republic* and Columbia Transportation's *Wolverine* (2).

By early December, the Canadian Coast Guard strike was beginning to hinder vessel traffic on the St. Lawrence River. Due to the lack of winter buoy maintenance, navigation between Quebec City and Les Escoumins, Quebec, was suspended from December 1 until December 4 when restricted daylight operations resumed. Meanwhile, movements between Quebec City and Montreal operated with upbound and downbound transits conducted on an alternating day schedule. The work stoppage lasted until the Canadian Parliament passed back-to-work legislation on December 15.

Even as efforts continued to keep vessels moving, a late season mishap shut down the Seaway on December 3 when the *Enerchem Asphalt* hit the upper gates at the St. Lambert Lock. Holed at the bow, the tanker inflicted some $1 million in damage to a lock gate. Repair crews worked around the clock in frigid temperatures to replace the smashed gate with traffic remaining at a standstill until the system reopened on December 6.

In one of the most unusual episodes of the decade, a December 4 accident on Lake Superior ended the career of a U.S. Coast Guard cutter. While conducting buoy maintenance duties usually performed by the *Sundew* based out of Duluth, the buoy tender *Mesquite* ran onto a reef about one-half mile southeast of Keweenaw Point. Resulting from a sequence of navigation errors, the grounding occurred at 2:10 in the morning just after the retrieval of Keweenaw Light Buoy LB1. Stranding in 12 feet of water, the resultant flooding from breaches in the hull became progressively worse over the next few hours as four-foot seas worked the 180-foot vessel on the rocky ledge. Provided with few alternatives as the situation continued to deteriorate, the commanding officer gave the order to abandon ship shortly after six o'clock that morning. The Indian freighter *Mangal Desai* picked up all 53 members of the crew, three of which were later airlifted to Hancock, Michigan, for treatment of non-life threatening injuries.

After receiving a formal request from the U.S. Coast Guard later that morning, the U.S. Navy's Naval Sea Systems Command (NAVSEA) contracted the civilian salvage company Donjon Marine Co. Inc. to perform a damage survey and develop a salvage plan to recover the *Mesquite*. Mobilizing its resources, that firm had sufficient personnel in Traverse City, Michigan, to begin operations within 18 hours of the accident. Although the salvors developed a salvage plan following an initial damage survey, a powerful storm with strong winds and 10-foot waves pummeled the stranded cutter on December 8-9. This inflicted a considerable amount of additional damage and prompted an after-storm survey on December 10 that preceded an underwater video inspection two days later. A detailed analysis of the data collected by these examinations resulted in the termination of any further salvage operations that year. Declared a total loss but possessing only minimal scrap value, work began the following spring to prepare the wrecked buoy tender for its intentional sinking in what later became the Keweenaw Underwater Preserve. That event took place on July 14, 1990 when the barge *Weeks 297* lifted the *Mesquite* off the reef before moving it about a mile away to be lowered to a designated spot on the bottom of Keystone Bay in 110 feet of water.

A buildup of silt created by recent storm activity caused some problems for the *Paul*

H. Townsend while entering St. Joseph, Michigan, on December 5 when the cement carrier spent some time on a sandbar before freeing itself and continuing to unload at the Lafarge Corporation Dock. In a separate mishap the same day, the Cyprus flagged *Clipper Atlantic* ran aground at Port Colborne. Reported downbound in the Welland Canal on December 8, the ocean carrier grounded for the second time while bound for the Atlantic when it stranded in the St. Lawrence River near St.-Pierre-les-Becquets, Quebec, on December 21. Refloated on December 26 with the assistance of the tugs *Duga* and *Capt. Ioannis S.*, a subsequent inspection at nearby Trois-Rivieres revealed no evidence of any serious damage.

On December 7, the Vanuatu registered *Capitaine Torres* vanished during a fierce storm in the Gulf of St. Lawrence. Outbound from the lakes with a cargo of machinery from Burns Harbor for delivery to Taiwan at the time of its disappearance, a search turned up no trace of the vessel's 23 crewmembers other than a pair of empty life rafts. The same storm also sank the 270-foot Panamanian freighter *Johanna B.* with the loss of 16 lives and the fishing trawler *Johnny and Sisters II* with all eight of its crew. In addition to these losses, the barge *Capt. Edward V. Smith* (the former *Adam E. Cornelius* (3)) broke free of the tug *Arctic Nanook* off the Gaspe Peninsula on December 8 while bound for the Magdalen Islands to load salt. Carrying roughly 50,000 gallons of diesel oil to power its unloading equipment, the wayward barge created a considerable amount of concern for those living along the rocky coast of Cape Breton Island. After its anchors finally caught the bottom about six miles off Cheticamp, Nova Scotia, on December 13, the *Capt. Edward V. Smith* was towed to Georgetown, Prince Edward Island, the following evening for repairs.

The tug *Carl William Selvick* encountered heavy weather on Lake Michigan while towing the tug *James Harris* and three barges to Milwaukee on December 9. Buffeted by 40 mph winds and five-foot waves, the tow sought shelter at Sheboygan, Wisconsin. While entering the harbor, however, the gusting winds pushed the 41-foot *James Harris* and one of the barges into the north breakwater with both sinking in 14 feet of water without any injuries. Refloated shortly afterwards, the tug and barge went to Chicago to be surveyed.

More than a year after coming into the Great Lakes for conversion to a school ship at Bay Shipbuilding, the former *Mormactide* cleared Sturgeon Bay on December 9 as the *Empire State VI*. Forced to put in at Ogdensburg, New York, on December 14 with engine problems, it ran onto a sandbar just a few hundred feet off the dock while departing the next day. Refloated two days later by the tugs *Angus M.*, *Glenbrook*, and *Evans McKeil*, the *Empire State VI* cleared Montreal on December 24 bound for New York City.

Compounded by the absence of Canadian icebreakers, the formation of heavy ice slowed traffic on the St. Lawrence Seaway throughout early December. The congestion grew to include as many as 100 ships with several having their inbound trips cancelled. On December 7, the Liberian bulk carrier *Pacific Trader* became the last upbound saltwater vessel to enter the system for the season. Bound for Detroit it reversed course in Lake St. Louis when the prevailing conditions ruled out a return trip before the closing date of the Seaway.

The brutally cold winter weather also interfered with shipping operations on the

The last trip of the 1989 season for the steamer *Elmglen* (2) was marred by an incident in the St. Marys River. (Author's Collection)

St. Marys River with some lower sections of the river becoming covered by six to eight inches of ice. This situation developed even as the U.S. Coast Guard had its icebreaking capabilities reduced with the *Mackinaw* being in the dry dock at Sturgeon Bay until the end of December. Meanwhile, ice measuring up to 10 inches thick at the Twin Ports sent the *Incan Superior* into an early winter layup at Thunder Bay on December 14.

After spending much of the season on the iron ore run between Marquette and Sault Ste. Marie, Ontario, CSL's *Stadacona* (3) arrived at Calcite during mid-December to load stone. Before it could load, however, the 663-foot self-unloader sustained serious structural and electrical damage when approximately 5,000 tons of ice formed inside its cargo holds while the crew was using high-pressure water hoses to remove iron ore residue. Laying up for the winter at Windsor on December 15, the vessel received repairs before beginning what became its last operational season the following spring.

Having been laid up at Halifax, Nova Scotia, since January, the former Coastal Canada Marine Inc. tanker *Coastal Canada* was renamed *Coastal I* and reregistered in St. Vincent during the autumn. This was done in preparation of the 548-foot steamer going overseas for dismantling with that trip beginning on December 19 in tow of the Soviet tug *Gigant*. Following a three-month journey, it arrived at Alang, India, on March 22, 1990 to be broken up.

While downbound on the St. Marys River with a cargo of wheat on December 21, the *Elmglen* (2) was diverted to the Middle Neebish Channel due to an ice blockage in the West Neebish Channel. Encountering severe ice conditions and poor visibility later that evening, the steamer ran out of the navigation channel and rubbed the bottom near Johnson Point. Slicing open a ballast tank, the grounding went unnoticed by the crew until the vessel took on a slight list to starboard. Brought back to an even keel through pumping and counter flooding, it went to Goderich, Ontario, for winter layup and temporary patching. This proved to be a career-ending accident as P. & H. Shipping decided against permanent repairs and disposed of the bulk carrier after a brief period of service the following spring.

As winter tightened its relentless grip on the upper lakes, shipping operations began winding down on Lake Superior. The *Indiana Harbor* closed the season at the Twin Ports on December 22 when it sailed from Superior, Wisconsin, with taconite pellets for Ashtabula, Ohio. The next day, Two Harbors shipped its final ore cargo with the departure of the *Edgar B. Speer*.

On December 22, the *Seaway Queen* made the last downbound passage through the Welland Canal for the season while en route to Toronto followed by the *Enerchem Avance* making the final upbound transit the next day on its way to Sarnia. With these passages completed, the canal closed on December 24.

Following a flurry of activity during its final weeks of operation, the navigation season on the St. Lawrence Seaway ended when the *Saskatchewan Pioneer* locked through the St. Lambert Lock bound for the Netherlands with grain on December 23. Later in the day, the Canadian Coast Guard icebreaker *J. E. Bernier* made the final transit of the system.

Coming nearly three weeks earlier than planned by the growing impassability of the navigation channels, the commercial navigation season at the Soo Locks ended on December 27 when the *American Republic* locked downbound for Ashtabula. This preceded the canal's official closing at midnight on December 28. Recording 4,875 cargo vessel passages during its 289 days of operation, the locks recorded their third lowest traffic volume of the decade in 1989. The Lake Carriers' Association reported that the early closure of the Soo Locks left about 1.6 million net tons of iron ore awaiting shipment at Lake Superior ports.

The year closed with one final accident when the tanker *Kiisla* ran aground on December 29 while inbound at Buffalo during a snow squall with 1.7 million gallons of xylene and toluene for the Noco Dock in Tonawanda, New York. Refloated a few hours later, tugs moved it to the Burnette Trucking Dock for an inspection. Although divers found a 47"x 5" gash in the number one ballast tank, the tanker's double hull construction prevented any cargo leakage. The increased draft caused by the flooded ballast tank, however, ruled out any possibility of reaching the Noco Dock. Escorted by the Canadian Coast Guard icebreaker *Griffon* to minimize the risk of further damage by ice while crossing Lake Erie, the *Kiisla* cleared Buffalo on January 2, 1990 bound for Sarnia to unload. Arriving there the next day, it sailed for dry-docking at Sturgeon Bay on January 6, 1990.

Unaffected by the closing of the Soo Locks, USS Great Lakes Fleet's *Arthur M. Anderson*, *Roger Blough*, and *Philip R. Clarke* remained active in the Lake Michigan iron ore trade with loadings at Escanaba continuing well into mid-January. The last of these went out on January 19, 1990 when the *Clarke* took on 23,151 gross tons of taconite pellets for delivery to South Chicago.

The movement of dry bulk commerce on the Great Lakes during the 1989 season amounted to 162.1 million net tons or a decrease of four percent in comparison to the

169.2 million net tons carried the previous year. Despite the season beginning with the U.S. Army Corps of Engineers allowing early transits through the Soo Locks to replenish stockpiles at lower lakes ports, the iron ore trade slid slightly from 68.3 million net tons to 66.7 million net tons. Had those same locks remained open until the middle of January, however, it is likely the total ore float would have met or slightly exceeded that of the prior season.

Meanwhile, a double-digit increase in coal shipments from both Lake Superior and South Chicago was offset by a labor strike at a major eastern coal producer that translated into a sharp drop in loadings at Lake Erie ports. Together, these factors resulted in that commodity slipping from 40.5 million net tons to 39.4 million net tons. Curtailed by adverse weather conditions near the end of the season, the movement of stone nonetheless had its second best season of the decade by ending the year with just in excess of 35 million net tons shipped. While grain carried by U.S. vessels grew by 76 percent to 1.3 million net tons, shipments originating at Thunder Bay dropped by a remarkable 41 percent to 6.8 million net tons. The latter figured heavily in the grain trade falling to its lowest level of the decade at only 15 million net tons, a figure less than half that carried on the lakes during the 1980 season.

Chapter Eleven
Conclusion

When the *Philip R. Clarke* tied up for the winter at Milwaukee, Wisconsin, on January 21, 1990, it closed out a decade that had witnessed some of the most significant changes in the Great Lakes shipping industry since the end of the Second World War. Over this span of time, the movement of commerce on the Great Lakes had fallen by 16.2 percent from 206.7 million net tons in 1980 to 173.2 million net tons in 1989. Although easily retaining its position as the single largest commodity moved by the lake fleet, the iron ore float had dropped from 81.7 million net tons to only 66.7 million net tons during this same period. Contributing to this reduced level of demand were efficiency measures implemented by domestic steelmakers to remain competitive, which had the effect of requiring less iron ore for every ton of steel produced.

A comparison of the 1980 and 1989 seasons reveals the movement of stone had increased by 25.2 percent while that of coal and cement remained relatively unchanged. Suffering heavy losses after the 1984 season, however, the most significant decline during this period took place in the grain trade. Throughout the first five seasons of the decade, the carriage of grain averaged 29.0 million net tons on an annual basis with this figure plummeting during the second half of the decade to an average of 19.3 million net tons. As only a small portion of the U.S. fleet operated in the movement of grain, this 33.4 percent decrease in available cargoes had a far more significant impact upon Canadian ship owners. In fact, the 15.0 million net tons carried on the lakes in 1989 was the worst year for this commodity since the 1960 shipping season.

The continued decline of the grain trade was a major factor in the formation of some pooling agreements involving several major Canadian fleets during the early 1990s. Near the end of the 1989 season, Algoma Central Marine and the ULS Corporation announced the creation of a new partnership named Seaway Bulk Carriers. Taking effect on January 1, 1990, this arrangement combined the traffic functions of six gearless bulk carriers in the Algoma fleet and ten in the ULS fleet in the transportation of grain for the Canadian Wheat Board and the westbound movement of iron ore on the St. Lawrence. Each fleet retained direct ownership of its respective vessels. This preceded a similar arrangement to combine the straight deckers owned by Canada Steamship Lines, Misener Holdings Ltd., and Pioneer Shipping Ltd. into Great Lakes Bulk Carriers during the winter of 1990-1991. In 1993, Algoma and ULS expanded their collaborative efforts when they placed their self-unloading vessels into an alliance known as Seaway Self-Unloaders.

A shrinking cargo base translated into a remarkable, but inevitable, downsizing of the Great Lakes fleet during the 1980s. In 1980, the combined fleet of powered vessels under American and Canadian registry on the

Great Lakes numbered 325 vessels. By 1985, this figure had fallen to 276 units and finally to only 205 ships at the beginning of the 1990 shipping season. Likewise, the single trip carrying capacity of the dry bulk fleet in the iron ore, coal, stone, and grain trades fell from 5.5 million gross tons in 1980 to 4.4 million gross tons at the end of 1989. Nowhere was this reduction more apparent than in the number of gearless bulk carriers in the U.S. fleet, which had fallen from 79 units in 1980 to just seven carriers at the end of the decade while at the same time the number of self-unloaders had grown from 50 to 55 vessels. Although self-unloaders had come to dominate operations within the U.S. fleet, straight deck bulk carriers retained a prominent position in the Canadian fleet due to its commitment to the movement of grain through the St. Lawrence Seaway. As such, the number of gearless vessels under the Canadian flag at the end of the 1989 stood at 55 in comparison to 34 self-unloaders.

Despite the challenging business climate, several shipping companies nonetheless invested in modernizing their fleets with the construction of 21 new ships and the conversion of 15 bulk carriers to self-unloaders during the 1980s. In addition, Canadian ship owners also rebuilt three existing bulk freighters along with converting a package freighter to a cement carrier. During this same period, five former saltwater tankers joined the Canadian lake fleet.

In addition to new tonnage and conversions, the process of modernization carried out over the decade also included the incorporation of what was then the latest in computer technology. In one such example during the 1989 season, the American

Entering service in 1985, the *Paterson* (2) remained the last powered vessel added to the dry bulk fleet for the next twenty-six years. (Author's Collection)

Steamship Company installed loading computers aboard the *American Mariner, American Republic, Buffalo* (3), *Adam E. Cornelius* (4), *Sam Laud, H. Lee White* (2), and *Charles E. Wilson*. Approved by the U.S. Coast Guard and the American Bureau of Shipping, these computers increased efficiency by analyzing the loading sequence. That same year, USS Great Lakes Fleet Inc. invested in similar installations for the *John G. Munson* (2) and *George A. Sloan*.

The changing dynamics of the steel industry ruled out any need to replicate the extended navigation season operations conducted during the 1970s. Despite this, the U.S. Army Corps of Engineers did make an effort to push back the closing date of the Soo Locks into January as requested to meet the needs of commerce. Although the dry bulk trade ground to halt shortly after the closing of the locks, tankers routinely operated year-round on the lakes throughout the decade.

By 1989, the paring down of vessels on both sides of the border had reduced the Great Lakes fleet to a size sufficient to meet the prevailing demand. As such, U.S. shipping companies operated 65 of the 69 units enrolled in the Lake Carriers' Association during that season while only four members of the Canadian fleet remained idle. This utilization rate not only reflected a continuation of strong tonnage demands in comparison to some earlier seasons of the decade but also the significantly reduced size of the Great Lakes fleet as a whole with only a few serviceable units held in reserve.

Although managing to survive the decade, the Canada Steamship Lines bulk carrier *Whitefish Bay* and the venerable Kinsman Lines steamer *Henry Steinbrenner* (4) both sailed their last during the closing days of 1989. The natural progression of phasing out surplus carriers continued into the following decade with the straight deckers *Canadoc* (2), *Elmglen* (2) and *Scott Misener* (3) all being retired during the 1990 shipping season.

Reliant upon the transportation markets it serves, the Great Lakes shipping industry emerged from the 1980s with a vastly reduced, but more efficient and robust, fleet of carriers.

APPENDICES

Appendices

Appendix A

The Republic Steel C4 Conversions

On December 31, 1950, the Nicholson-Universal Steamship Company, in which the Republic Steel Corporation had acquired a 70-percent stake, purchased three C4 saltwater cargo transports from the U.S. Maritime Administration for conversion into Great Lakes bulk carriers. Intended for use in delivering iron ore to Republic's docks located on restricted waterways in Cleveland, Ohio, and South Chicago, Illinois, these vessels were rebuilt to 600'3" x 71'6" x 35' by the Maryland Drydock Company at Baltimore, Maryland, using new forward hull sections built at Pascagoula, Mississippi. Arriving on the lakes via the Mississippi River and the Chicago Sanitary and Ship Canal during the second half of 1951, all three went to the American Ship Building Company's yard at South Chicago for final work. These reconstructions proceeded quickly with one of these steamers making its maiden voyage that same year and the other two entering service at the start of the 1952 shipping season.

The T. H. Browning Steamship Company of Detroit, Michigan, managed the three converted freighters for Nicholson-Universal (later Nicholson-Universal Steamship Division, Republic Steel Corporation) until they passed into the management of the Wilson Marine Transit Company in 1957. Renowned for their high top speeds, large forward deckhouses, and bright orange Republic Steel stacks, the latter of which were retained until the Cleveland-Cliffs Steamship Company took over the steelmaker's iron ore hauling contract in 1972, the three sister ships had a carrying capacity of 15,500 gross tons.

Tom M. Girdler – Built: 1946 – Kaiser Company, Inc., Vancouver, Washington, as C4-S-A4 type cargo ship *Louis McHenry Howe*. Renamed *Tom M. Girdler* in 1951. Maiden voyage as Great Lakes carrier: October 22, 1951. Official Number: 249104.

Troy H. Browning (3) – Built: 1946 – Kaiser Company, Inc., Vancouver, Washington, as C4-S-A4 type cargo ship *Scott E. Land*. Renamed *Troy H. Browning* (3) in 1951. First cargo loaded as a Great Lakes carrier: April 18, 1952. Renamed *Thomas F. Patton* in 1955. Official Number: 249354.

Charles M. White – Built: 1946 – Kaiser Company, Inc., Vancouver, Washington, as C4-S-A4 type cargo ship *Mount Mansfield*. Renamed *Charles M. White* in 1951. Commissioned for Great Lakes Service: April 22, 1952. Official Number: 249263.

Appendix B

	Bulk Commerce on the Great Lakes 1980-1989							
Season	Iron Ore (Net Tons)	Coal (Net Tons)	Stone (Net Tons)	Cement (Net Tons)	Potash (Net Tons)	Grain (Net Tons)	Petroleum (Net Tons)	Total (Net Tons)
1980	81,723,442	41,306,125	28,011,339	4,213,053	891,171	31,509,534	19,028,847	**206,683,511**
1981	83,893,203	39,096,577	24,586,743	3,706,778	1,593,556	28,235,436	15,667,667	**196,779,960**
1982	43,134,081	36,759,518	15,076,245	3,021,696	1,813,142	28,283,271	14,351,287	**142,439,240**
1983	58,335,209	36,578,742	18,418,662	3,284,106	1,599,778	28,846,648	14,964,244	**162,027,389**
1984	64,136,610	43,134,292	23,156,860	3,408,621	2,032,470	28,152,658	14,961,876	**178,983,387**
1985	58,431,773	36,334,525	24,992,777	3,398,789	1,857,561	20,055,902	12,883,941	**157,955,268**
1986	51,017,057	36,266,922	27,225,922	4,082,975	1,629,493	20,155,541	11,987,025	**152,364,935**
1987	61,702,505	37,731,742	33,163,539	3,805,799	1,702,174	22,338,366	11,521,158	**171,965,283**
1988	68,306,193	40,521,133	35,501,484	4,162,954	1,684,293	19,101,760	11,972,621	**181,250,438**
1989	66,710,045	39,469,501	35,075,213	4,479,295	1,402,811	15,007,810	11,104,592	**173,249,267**

This chart illustrates the general decline in the movement of bulk cargoes on the Great Lakes during the period of 1980 to 1989. Over a period ten years, commerce on the lakes fell by 16.2 percent from 206.7 million net tons in 1980 to 173.2 million net tons in 1989. The most significant losses took place in the ore, grain, and petroleum trades while coal and cement remained relatively stable. Although experiencing some dismal seasons, the movement of stone ended the decade with a 25 percent increase in volume.

Powered Dry Bulk Cargo Vessels 1980-1990

	1980			1985			1990	
Type & Flag	Number of Ships	Single Trip Carrying Capacity*	Type & Flag	Number of Ships	Single Trip Carrying Capacity*	Type & Flag	Number of Ships	Single Trip Carrying Capacity*
Bulk Carriers			**Bulk Carriers**			**Bulk Carriers**		
Canadian Fleet	88	1,771,510	Canadian Fleet	74	1,727,395	Canadian Fleet	52	1,325,705
United States Fleet	81	1,453,340	United States Fleet	41	781,475	United States Fleet	10	226,625
Subtotal	**169**	**3,224,850**	Subtotal	**115**	**2,508,870**	Subtotal	**62**	**1,552,330**
Self-Unloaders			**Self-Unloaders**			**Self-Unloaders**		
Canadian Fleet	33	855,220	Canadian Fleet	34	1,013,950	Canadian Fleet	34	1,018,450
United States Fleet	51	1,506,375	United States Fleet	60	1,942,675	United States Fleet	52	1,813,750
Subtotal	**84**	**2,361,595**	Subtotal	**94**	**2,956,625**	Subtotal	**86**	**2,832,200**
Cement Carriers			**Cement Carriers**			**Cement Carriers**		
Canadian Fleet	3	14,850	Canadian Fleet	3	20,850	Canadian Fleet	3	20,850
United States Fleet	8	61,200	United States Fleet	8	61,200	United States Fleet	7	59,750
Subtotal	**11**	**76,050**	Subtotal	**11**	**82,050**	Subtotal	**10**	**80,600**
Grand Total			**Grand Total**			**Grand Total**		
Canadian Fleet	124	2,641,580	Canadian Fleet	111	2,762,195	Canadian Fleet	89	2,365,005
United States Fleet	140	3,020,915	United States Fleet	109	2,785,350	United States Fleet	69	2,100,125
Grand Total	**264**	**5,662,495**	Grand Total	**220**	**5,547,545**	Grand Total	**158**	**4,465,130**

*=Carrying Capacity in Gross Tons at Mid-Summer Draft

Receding cargo volumes along with new construction and the modernization of existing vessels precipitated a considerable downsizing of the Great Lakes fleet during the 1980s. This table takes into consideration the status of the dry cargo lake fleet as of April 1 for each of the specified years. During this period, the number of powered dry bulk vessels shrank from 264 units in 1980 to only 158 units at the beginning of the 1990 shipping season. Notable in this reduction is the virtual elimination of straight deck bulk carriers in the U.S. fleet. These figures show that while the fleet shrank in size by 40 percent its single trip carrying capacity fell by only 21 percent. This reflects the lake fleet transitioning to a smaller number of efficient carriers during a time of falling demand.

Appendix C

New Vessel Construction, Self-Unloader Conversions, and Reconstructions
1980 to 1989
(Self-Propelled Vessels)

New Construction

1980　American Mariner
　　　Burns Harbor
　　　Nanticoke
　　　Edgar B. Speer

1981　Algowood
　　　American Republic
　　　Canadian Pioneer
　　　Columbia Star
　　　William J. De Lancey
　　　Lake Wabush

1982　Algowest
　　　Atlantic Superior
　　　L'Earble No. 1 (2)

1983　John B. Aird
　　　Canada Marquis
　　　Canadian Ambassador
　　　Saskatchewan Pioneer
　　　Selkirk Settler

1984　Prairie Harvest

1985　Hon. Paul Martin
　　　Paterson (2)

Self-Unloader Conversions

1980　Frankcliffe Hall (2)
　　　Elton Hoyt 2nd (2)
　　　Sparrows Point

1981　Charles M. Beeghly
　　　Courtney Burton
　　　Edward B. Greene
　　　James Norris

Self-Unloader Conversions (cont'd)

1982　Arthur M. Anderson
　　　Armco
　　　Cason J. Callaway
　　　Philip R. Clarke
　　　Middletown

1983　Reserve

1988　Canadian Ranger (grain only)

1989　Algomarine
　　　Atlantic Huron

Reconstructions

1980　Canadian Navigator (lengthened 82'10" with new forebody)

1981　James Transport (lengthened 40')
　　　Nipigon Bay (deepened 5')
　　　Northern Shell (lengthened 87')

1983　Canadian Explorer (forward section of steamer Northern Venture grafted to stern of motor vessel Cabot)
　　　Stephen B. Roman (package freighter Fort William to a cement carrier)
　　　Whitefish Bay (steamer Quetico to a gearless bulk carrier)

1984　Canadian Ranger (forward section of steamer Hilda Marjanne grafted to stern of motor vessel Chimo)

Appendices

Appendix D

Powered Vessels Removed from the Great Lakes Fleet 1980-1989

Year: 1980

Vessel	Disposition
American	Non-Transportation
Brookdale (2)	Scrap
Eugene J. Buffington	Scrap
D. M. Clemson (2)	Scrap
Thomas F. Cole	Scrap
Alva C. Dinkey	Scrap
Tom M. Girdler	Scrap
Governor Miller	Scrap
D. G. Kerr (2)	Scrap
Lac Des Iles[1]	Scrap
Marlhill[2]	Non-Transportation
C. H. McCullough Jr.	Scrap
J. P. Morgan Jr.	Scrap
Thomas F. Patton	Scrap
Pierson Independent	Scrap
Raymond H. Reiss	Scrap
J. F. Schoellkopf Jr.	Scrap
Charles M. White	Scrap
Peter A. B. Widener[3]	Barge Conversion

1=Resold for non-transportation use and sunk while in tow to Mexico.
2=Sank while in tow to Mexico.
3=Subsequently sold for scrap in 1986.

Year: 1981

Vessel	Disposition
Canso Transport[4]	Off-Lakes Use
Coastal Transport[4]	Off-Lakes Use
Hallfax	Off-Lakes Use
H. C. Heimbecker	Scrap

4=Not known to have operated on the lakes while part of the Halco fleet.

Year: 1982

Vessel	Disposition
Hudson Transport[5]	Total Loss
L'Erable No. 1	Off-Lakes Use
Lakespan Ontario	Off-Lakes Use
Pointe Noire	Scrap
Prindoc (3)	Off-Lakes Use
Spruceglen	Non-Transportation

5=Later converted to a tank barge.

Year: 1983

Vessel	Disposition
Baie Comeau II	Off-Lakes Use
Cape Breton Miner	Off-Lakes Use
City of Milwuakee	Museum

Year: 1983 (cont'd)

Vessel	Disposition
Conallison	Scrap
John Dykstra (2)[6]	Barge Conversion
John Hulst	Scrap
Horace Johnson	Scrap
Leadale (2)	Scrap
Hilda Marjanne[7]	Scrap
Nordale	Scrap
Northern Venture[7]	Scrap
Ontario Power	Off-Lakes Use
Sylvania	Scrap
Troisdoc (3)	Off-Lakes Use

6=Subsequently sold for scrap in 1986.
7=Forward hull section reused.

Year: 1984

Vessel	Disposition
B. F. Affleck	Scrap
C. L. Austin	Scrap
George M. Carl	Scrap
Cedarglen	Non-Transportation
Frank R. Denton	Scrap
Elmglen	Scrap
Erindale	Scrap
Fernglen	Scrap
Fort Henry	Scrap
Fort York[8]	Scrap
E. G. Grace	Scrap
Joshua A. Hatfield	Scrap
Lawrendoc	Off-Lakes Use
Paterson	Scrap
Pineglen	Scrap
Pontiac (2)	Scrap
Saginaw Bay	Scrap
Silverdale	Scrap
Texaco Warrior	Off-Lakes Use
Eugene P. Thomas	Scrap
Homer D. Williams	Scrap
St. Lawrence (3)	Scrap
Ungava Transport	Non-Transportation
August Ziesing	Scrap

8=Later sold for use as a barge and scrapped in 1988.

Year: 1985

Vessel	Disposition
Amoco Illinois	Scrap
Amoco Wisconsin	Scrap
R. Bruce Angus	Scrap
E. B. Barber	Scrap

Appendices

Year: 1985 (cont'd)

Vessel	Disposition
Philip D. Block	Scrap
Cadillac (4)	Scrap
Champlain (3)	Scrap
Cliffs Victory	Scrap
Leon Falk Jr.	Scrap
Alastair Guthrie	Scrap
Johnstown (2)	Scrap
Lac Ste. Anne	Scrap
Lake Winnipeg	Scrap
Gordon C. Leitch	Scrap
Meldrum Bay	Scrap
Menihek Lake	Scrap
Niagara (2)[9]	Scrap
Outarde (3)	Scrap
Eugene W. Pargny	Scrap
Quedoc (2)	Scrap
Senator of Canada	Scrap
W. W. Holloway	Scrap

9=Resold for failed preservation project and scrapped in 1997.

Year: 1986

Vessel	Disposition
Amoco Indiana	Barge Conversion
Sewell Avery	Non-Transportation
Willis B. Boyer	Museum
Canadian Ambassador	Off-Lakes Use
Paul H. Carnahan	Scrap
Detroit Edison (2)	Scrap
No. 265808[10]	Scrap
No. 266029[11]	Scrap
Golden Hind	Scrap
Arthur B. Homer	Scrap
George M. Humphrey (2)	Scrap
William A. Irvin	Museum
Robert Koch	Scrap
John E. F. Misener	Scrap
Red Wing	Scrap
Sharon	Scrap
Frank A. Sherman	Scrap
William P. Snyder Jr.	Scrap
Wheat King	Scrap

10=Formerly Benson Ford (2).
11=Formerly William Clay Ford.

Year: 1987

Vessel	Disposition
Ashland	Scrap
Birchglen	Scrap
E. J. Block	Scrap
Canadian Pioneer	Off-Lakes Use
A. H. Ferbert (2)	Scrap
Imperial Quebec	Off-Lakes Use

Year: 1987 (cont'd)

Vessel	Disposition
Thomas W. Lamont	Scrap
Le Cedre No. 1	Off-Lakes Use
Samuel Mather (6)	Scrap
William G. Mather (2)	Museum
Merle M. McCurdy	Scrap
Northern Shell	Off-Lakes Use
T. W. Robinson	Scrap
Rogers City	Scrap
Seaway Trader	Off-Lakes Use
Robert C. Stanley	Scrap
Enders M. Voorhees	Scrap
Ralph H. Watson	Scrap
Thomas Wilson (2)	Scrap

Year: 1988

Vessel	Disposition
Badger State	Scrap
Chicago Tribune (2)	Scrap
Consumers Power (3)	Scrap
Benjamin Fairless	Scrap
John T. Hutchinson	Scrap
Kingdoc (2)	Off-Lakes Use
Kinsman Independent (2)	Scrap
Labradoc (2)	Off-Lakes Use
Oakglen	Scrap
Irving S. Olds	Scrap

Year: 1989

Vessel	Disposition
Coastal Canada	Scrap
Eva Desgagnes	Off-Lakes Use
Sir James Dunn	Scrap
Fort Chambly	Scrap
Georgian Bay	Scrap
Nipigon Bay	Scrap

Appendix E

Soo Locks Passages

The following are a few lists recording the passage of vessels through the Soo Locks at Sault Ste. Marie, Michigan, on the specified dates. While several of these ships remain in service today, many others are no longer trading on the Great Lakes.

August 29, 1984

Upbound
- J. N. McWatters (2) .... 12:40 a.m.
- Black Bay .... 2:55 a.m.
- Chicago Tribune (2) .... 9:39 a.m.
- Benson Ford (2) .... 1:29 p.m.
- Edward B. Greene .... 1:29 p.m.
- Laketon (2) .... 1:38 p.m.
- Belle River .... 4:11 p.m.
- Comeaudoc .... 6:26 p.m.
- A. S. Glossbrenner .... 7:14 p.m.
- Jensen Star .... 8:12 p.m.
- George A. Stinson .... 9:28 p.m.
- Frontenac (5) .... 11:00 p.m.
- Birchglen .... 11:23 p.m.

Downbound
- Melody .... 1:36 a.m.
- Canadian Transport .... 3:36 a.m.
- Tarantau .... 6:25 a.m.
- Tadoussac (2) .... 8:27 a.m.
- Lawrencecliffe Hall (2) .... 1:33 p.m.
- Kingdoc (2) .... 2:15 p.m.
- Canada Marquis .... 3:03 p.m.
- American Mariner .... 3:36 p.m.
- John G. Munson (2) .... 3:58 p.m.
- Stewart J. Cort .... 4:29 p.m.
- T. R. McLagan .... 4:58 p.m.
- Jean Parisien .... 5:33 p.m.
- Vissani .... 9:47 p.m.
- Edward L. Ryerson .... 10:45 p.m.

October 11, 1985

Upbound
- H. Lee White (2) .... 6:25 a.m.
- William Clay Ford (2) .... 12:52 p.m.
- Elton Hoyt 2nd (2) .... 4:05 p.m.
- Jade Kim .... 4:49 p.m.

Downbound
- St. Clair (2) .... 1:19 a.m.
- Kinsman Independent (2) .... 4:30 a.m.
- Algolake .... 6:28 a.m.
- Jean Parisien .... 8:28 a.m.
- Kingdoc (2) .... 9:49 a.m.
- American Mariner .... 11:28 a.m.
- Yankcanuck (2) .... 2:46 p.m.
- Stadacona (3) .... 5:31 p.m.
- Oakglen .... 9:50 p.m.
- Mesabi Miner .... 11:07 p.m.
- Black Bay .... 11:25 p.m.

June 12, 1987

Upbound
- St. Clair (2) .... 4:02 a.m.
- Enerchem Avance .... 10:10 a.m.
- Canadian Leader .... 10:19 a.m.
- Agawa Canyon .... 11:16 a.m.
- Algogulf .... 11:26 a.m.
- Columbia Star .... 5:26 p.m.
- Canadian Enterprise .... 7:47 p.m.
- H. Lee White (2) .... 8:43 p.m.
- Mesabi Miner .... 10:07 p.m.

Downbound
- Armco .... 8:21 a.m.
- William Clay Ford (2) .... 2:56 p.m.
- Woodland .... 3:39 p.m.
- Galassia .... 3:56 p.m.
- Ralph Misener .... 4:57 p.m.
- Sam Laud .... 8:30 p.m.
- Wolverine (2) .... 10:01 p.m.
- J. L. Mauthe .... 11:25 p.m.

Vessel Index

A. G. Farquharson, 145
A. H. Ferbert (2), 29, 139, 158, 173, 197
A. S. Glossbrenner, 30, 34, 80, 160
Acacia, buoy tender, 127
Adam E. Cornelius (2), 194
Adam E. Cornelius (3), 25, 39, 51, 192, 209, 225, 238
Adam E. Cornelius (4), 225, 244
Adrieene B., 21
Aegis Hispanic, 93
Agawa Canyon, 25, 68, 221
Agia Trias, 77
Akranes, 103
Al Battal, tug, 150
Al Sayb-7, barge, 150
Alabama, tug, 183
Alastair Guthrie, 7, 76, 93, 103, 125
Alexander Henry, buoy tender, 112
Algobay, 10-11, 35, 47, 65, 72, 82, 188
Algocape, 160, 189, 196
Algocen (2), 15, 34, 70, 161, 233
Algogulf, 160, 233
Algolake, 77, 107, 161-162
Algomarine, 160, 189, 201, 203, 218
Algonorth, 160
Algoport, 129, 133
Algorail (2), 62, 188, 221
Algosea, 45, 52
Algosoo (2), 47, 131, 135, 156
Algosound, 160
Algosteel (2), 233
Algoway (2), 22, 30
Algowest, 15, 54, 82, 107, 189, 197
Algowood, 18, 26, 66, 100, 109, 177, 189
Alka, 48
Alpena (2), 234
Alva C. Dinkey, 11
American Century, 29
American Mariner, 4, 134, 160, 168, 186, 225, 244
American Republic, 12-13, 28-29, 59, 132, 136, 154, 168, 176, 179, 189, 230-231, 237, 240, 244
American Viking, tug, 69

American, dredge, 62
Amilla, 100
Amoco Great Lakes, barge, 46, 85, 127
Amoco Illinois, 51, 123
Amoco Indiana, 53-54, 131, 159
Amoco Michigan, tug, 46, 85, 127
Amoco Wisconsin, 19, 51, 54, 63, 123
Anangel Spirit, 79
Andrew H., 168
Anglian Lady, tug, 203, 227, 229, 232
Angus M., tug, 238
Annie M. Dean, tug, 167
Annis Lee, tug, 204-205
April T. Beker, tug, 57
Aquarama, 200, 223
Arc Minos, 210
Archers Hope, 138
Arctic Nanook, tug, 238
Arctic Trader, 66
Arctic, 112, 115
Arcturus, 208
Argolikos, 126
Argue Martin, tug, 111-112, 114-115, 139, 141-142, 173, 227, 233
Arkansas, tug, 77, 177, 179, 217
Armco, 17, 36, 51, 150, 155
Armonia, 34
Arosa, 219
Arthur B. Homer, 5, 17, 22, 113, 154
Arthur K. Atkinson, 17, 89
Arthur M. Anderson, 1, 23, 32, 57, 68, 132, 142, 155, 214, 240
Arthur Simard, 23, 44
Asean Knowledge, 32
Asfamarine, 210
Ashland, 22, 172, 175, 184-185
Ashley Lykes, 205
Ashtabula, barge, 57
Astorga, 209
Atlantic Dealer, 145
Atlantic Erie, 210
Atlantic Hawk, 68
Atlantic Huron, 236
Atlantic Huron, Panamax carrier, 184

253

Index

Atlantic Seaman, 165
Atlantic Superior, 39, 49, 58-59, 95, 175, 210
Atlas Traveler, 201
Atomic, tug, 98, 101, 108, 118, 154, 193
August Ziesing, 95, 119, 143
Avenger IV, tug, 151, 161, 163, 167, 169, 177, 179, 181, 203, 219, 227, 229
Avon Forest, 110
Axel Heiberg, 24

B. A. Peerless, 94, 114
B. F. Affleck, 1, 95, 150-151
B. H. Taylor, 181
Badger (2), 44, 73
Badger State (3), 1, 201
Bagotville, tug, 35, 76
Bahia de La Habana, 223
Baie Comeau II, 77
Baie St. Paul, 62, 96, 233
Bailen, 148
Baldy B., tug, 127
Baltic Trader, 235
Bantry Bay, tug, 87, 89, 96-97, 114, 205
Barbara Ann, tug, 26-27, 31, 51, 53, 60, 66, 87, 96-98, 128, 144, 196, 209, 217, 223, 231
Bayshell (2), 66, 168, 222
Beavercliffe Hall, 152, 157, 187
Beechglen, 56, 74, 141, 191
Belle Isle, 122, 192
Belle River, 55, 82, 105, 109, 119, 166, 215
Benjamin Fairless, 18, 47, 50, 57, 61, 158, 196-199
Benson Ford, 13-14, 60, 72, 140
Benson Ford (2), 60, 74, 89, 93, 100-101, 103, 144, 153-154, 163
Benson Ford (3), 101, 105, 109, 116, 133, 190, 195, 214-215
Beograd, 103
Betty Gale, tug, 199
Beverly Anderson, tug, 57
Bijelo Polje, 203, 206
Birchglen, 56, 72, 161, 176, 193
Biscayne Bay, icebreaking tug, 87, 128
Black Bay, 81, 106, 191, 224, 229
Bonnie G. Selvick, tug, 95, 205
Boundbrook, 137
Bramble, buoy tender, 87, 224
Bristol Bay, icebreaking tug, 41, 87
Brookdale (2), 10, 13, 20, 45
Brugse 1, 141

Buckeye (2), barge, 27, 59, 171, 189
Buffalo (3), 20, 147, 161, 216, 244
Bulk Cat, 141
Burns Harbor, 2, 4, 8, 17, 70, 88

C. H. McCullough, Jr., 7-8
C. L. Austin, 59-60, 96, 102
C. Russell Hubbard, 116
C.T.C. No. 1, 49
Cabot, 64, 70-71, 76
Cadillac (4), 34, 41, 62, 121-122, 169-170
Calcite II, 1, 55, 75, 89, 137, 140, 142, 169, 177
Cam Etinde, 183
Canada Marquis, 31, 70, 73, 76, 106, 182, 204
Canadian Ambassador, 37, 61, 72, 78, 156, 185
Canadian Argosy, dredge, 177
Canadian Century, 161, 201
Canadian Enterprise, 168, 174, 200, 203, 216
Canadian Explorer, 71, 76, 226
Canadian Hunter, 30, 148, 174, 204
Canadian Leader, 59, 66, 205, 218
Canadian Mariner, 42
Canadian Navigator, 5, 32, 62, 157
Canadian Olympic, 28, 117, 128, 216
Canadian Pioneer, 29, 37, 48, 61, 72, 122, 182, 185
Canadian Progress, 87, 109, 211, 218
Canadian Prospector, 4, 26, 51, 118
Canadian Ranger, 76, 90, 162, 188
Canadian Transport, 72, 129, 132, 134-135, 161, 202-203
Canadian Viking, tug, 136
Canadiana, 46, 69-70, 201
Canadoc (2), 209, 244
Canso Transport, 25
Cape Breton Miner, 12, 16, 24, 65
Cape Monterey, 126
Cape Transport, 37
Capetan Yiannis, 184-185
Capitaine Torres, 238
Capt. Edward V. Smith, barge, 209, 225, 238
Capt. Henry Jackman, 160, 218
Captain Ioannis S., 17, 42, 46, 106, 113, 118, 163, 173, 179, 238
Captain John Roen, 194
Captain Panapagos D. P., 52
Caribbean Prince, 95
Caribbean Trailer, 80, 89
Caribou Isle, buoy tender, 148
Carl D. Bradley (2), 163

Carl William Selvick, 184, 221, 238
Carla Anne Selvick, 152
Carlos Manuel De Cespedes, 7
Carol Ann, tug, 224
Carol Lake, 142, 148, 160
Caroline Hoey, tug, 174
Cartiercliffe Hall, 6, 10, 25, 156, 162, 187
Cartierdoc (2), 187
Cason J. Callaway, 1, 22-23, 31-32, 50, 85, 123, 137, 142, 155, 159, 184, 204, 225, 234
Castano, 190
Catherine Desgagnes, 106
Cathy B., tug, 11
Cathy McAllister, tug, 6, 17, 74, 138, 152, 156, 177, 185, 191, 197, 209, 226, 229
Cecilia Desgagnes, 106, 232
Cedarglen, 56, 58, 102-103, 113
Cervinia, 150
Chambly Era, 227
Champlain (3), 41, 62, 121-122, 169-170, 192
Charles E. Wilson, 147, 176, 216, 244
Charles M. Beeghly, 10, 90, 152, 164-165, 216
Charles M. White, 5, 15, 121
Chemical Transport, 23, 48, 119, 130, 150
Cheyenne, tug, 201
Chicago Tribune (2), 26-27, 73, 80, 84, 96, 133, 211
Chi-Cheemaun, 31, 118, 150, 214
Chief Shingwauk, 168
Chief Wawatam, 19, 58, 76, 97, 203
Chimo, 64, 76, 90
Chippewa, tanker, 212
Chippewa, tug, 53, 56, 66, 74, 81, 113, 128, 137, 163, 167-169, 181, 193, 198, 206, 221, 232, 234
Christine E., tug, 36, 58
City of Midland 41, 73, 127, 199
City of Milwaukee, 80
Clarence B. Randall, 172
Clarence B. Randall (2), 2, 158
Clarkson Carrier, barge, 150, 229
Cliffs Victory, 27, 38, 120-121
Clipper Atlantic, 238
Coastal Canada, 94, 153, 239
Coastal I, 239
Coastal Transport, 25
Col. James M. Schoonmaker, 136
Columbia Star, 3, 19, 29, 82, 105, 157-158, 211
Comanche, tug, 51
Comeaudoc, 113, 128, 132, 165, 167

Company, 2
Conallison, 31, 35, 39, 59, 78, 96-97
Condarrell, 20, 31, 59, 78, 181
Congar (3), 9, 59
Constructor, tug, 57
Consumers Power (3), 3, 130, 192-195
Coudres de L'ile, 197
Courtney Burton, 17, 29, 188, 201
Coverdale, 142
Crispin Oglebay (2), 9, 29, 216, 224, 228
CSL Innovator, 184
Curtis Randolph, fireboat, 234
Cvijeta Zuzoric, 148

D. B. Weldon (2), 29, 68
D. C. Everest, 20, 181, 215
D. D. S. Salvager, barge, 34, 229
D. G. Kerr (2), 11-12
D. M. Clemson (2), 11, 194
Dakota, tug, 134
Daldean, ferry, 87
Dalmar Servant, tug, 229
Daniel McAllister, tug, 17, 26, 36-37, 58, 68, 70, 92, 109, 112, 138, 142, 156, 191, 209
Danilovgrad, 177
Daryl C. Hanna, tug, 11, 31, 57, 152
David K. Gardiner, 187, 208
Defiance, tug, 57
Delaware, tug, 130, 183, 225
Demeterton, 5
Des Groseilliers, icebreaker, 46, 87
Detroit Edison (2), 21, 47, 63, 138-139
Dimitrios, 181
Doan Transport, 150
Dodge Island, dredge, 115
Donald P., tug, 115
Donegal, tug, 34
Dredge Primrose, 98
Duga, tug, 142, 163, 166, 177, 185, 238

E. B. Barber, 34, 103, 114
E. G. Grace, 85-86, 98, 102
E. J. Block, 14, 103, 169
E. J. Newberry, 32, 48, 55-56
E. M. Ford, 1, 3, 14, 134-135, 190, 195, 205, 221
Eastern Shell (2), 128, 151, 158, 195, 230
Eddie B., tug, 206
Edgar B. Speer, 4, 6, 126-127, 132, 142, 165, 182, 184, 186, 203, 213, 215, 240
Edmund Fitzgerald, 121

Index

Edna G., tug, 9, 27
Edouard Simard, 23, 44
Edward B. Greene, 16, 52, 55, 65-66, 93, 100-101, 120, 155
Edward G. Seubert, 123
Edward L. Ryerson, 130, 189, 202, 210, 228, 230
Edward M. Cotter, fireboat, 130
Edwin H. Gott, 22, 55, 81, 142, 181, 191, 215, 235
Eglantine, 139
Elmglen, 56, 63, 92
Elmglen (2), 100, 111, 239, 244
Elmore M. Misner, tug, 102, 108, 143, 154, 169-171, 179-180, 193, 231
Elton Hoyt 2nd (2), 10, 19, 65, 80, 110, 112, 119, 197, 216, 221, 231
Emmett J. Carey, 205, 231
Empire State VI, 238
Enders M. Voorhees, 18, 33, 57, 132, 139, 158, 169-170
Enerchem Asphalt, 210, 214, 229, 237
Enerchem Avance, 150, 187, 214, 219, 240
Enerchem Catalyst, 150, 183, 214
Enerchem Fusion, 150
Enerchem Laker, 150
Enerchem Refiner, 150, 189, 206
Enerchem Travailleur, 150, 187, 200, 212, 223
Erindale, 35, 68, 74, 79, 84, 102
Ernest R. Breech, 33, 51, 62, 74, 89, 93, 130, 189, 199
Erol Beker, barge, 57
Eskimo, 9
Ethel Everard, 91
Etrema, 163
Eugene J. Buffington, 11
Eugene P. Thomas, 1, 7, 31, 102, 170
Eugene W. Pargny, 1, 7, 123, 171
Eva Desgagnes, 159, 167, 232
Evans McKeil, tug, 238
Everest, tug, 170

Fairplay IX, tug, 15, 180, 229
Fairplay XIV, tug, 199
Falcon Crest, 211
Favorite, salvage tug, 74
Federal 6, tug, 12
Federal Danube, 103
Federal Elbe, 126
Federal Hudson, 200
Federal Inger, 224

Federal Lakes, 110, 132-133, 166
Federal Maas, 89
Federal Pioneer, 106
Federal Polaris, 148
Federal Rhine, 119
Federal Schelde, 96
Federal Seaway, 133, 162, 166
Federal St. Laurent, 128
Fernglen, 56, 59, 63, 92, 109
Florida, 195
Fort Chambly, 17, 42, 210, 223-224, 226-227
Fort Henry, 22, 42, 91, 93-94, 199-200
Fort St. Louis, 42
Fort William, 42, 60, 62
Fort York, 4, 42, 91, 93-94, 115, 119, 171, 177-179, 210
Francy, yacht, 231
Frank A. Sherman, 20, 28, 136-137
Frank Armstrong, 173
Frank R. Denton, 12, 63, 102
Frankcliffe Hall (2), 13, 23, 48, 73, 132, 152, 159, 187
Franquelin (2), 53, 80, 84, 159, 232
Fred R. White, Jr., 145, 203
Frederick T. Kellers, tug, 185
Freenes, 224
French River, 25, 89
Frobisher Transport, 24
Frontenac (2), 27, 128
Frontenac (5), 36, 66, 100, 213, 223
Fuel Marketer (2), 222
Furia, 122

G. A. Boeckling, 52, 191, 225
G. W. Falcon, tug, 95
G. W. Rogers, tug, 76
G.L.B. No. 2, barge, 122
G.L.M. 507, barge, 39
Galway Bay, tug, 97, 192, 225
Gaspe Transport, 42, 150
Gaucho Taura, 99
Gemini, 187, 225
Gemini Pioneer, 39
General, tug, 179
General Vargas, 219
Genmar 130, barge, 191
George A. Sloan, 1, 105, 113, 142, 149, 163, 177, 196, 198, 234, 244
George A. Stinson, 25, 68, 87-88, 131, 160, 189, 217

George D. Goble, 2
George Hindman (4), 142
George L., 18
George M. Carl (2), 32, 83, 96-97, 100
George M. Humphrey, 194
George M. Humphrey (2), 143-144
Georgian Bay, 63, 223, 226-229
Gerdt Oldendorff, 48
Gigant, tug, 239
Glenada, tug, 15, 53, 58, 114, 119, 123, 140, 152-153, 155, 158, 163, 165, 167, 169, 173, 176, 178-179, 200, 217
Glenbrook, tug, 123, 139, 153, 173, 175, 181, 208, 210, 226-228, 238
Glenevis, tug, 58, 62, 68, 78, 86, 92, 94, 96, 98, 111-112, 114, 125, 141-142, 144-145, 156, 173, 175, 182-183, 222, 226-228
Glenside, tug, 54, 76, 86, 92, 94, 96, 98, 109, 123, 125, 141-142, 145, 173-176, 192
Goderich, 173
Goderich (2), 5
Golden Hind, 54, 56, 80, 84, 94, 124, 146
Gordon C. Leitch, 11, 15, 28, 45, 114-115, 137
Gotham, tug, 95
Governor Miller, 11
Grand Rapids, 162, 175, 231-232
Great Lakes, barge, 127, 181, 187
Gregory J. Busch, tug, 117, 169
Griffon, 232
Griffon, icebreaker, 87, 129, 156, 240
Grigorousa, 59-60
Guardian Carrier, 91
Gulf Canada, 18, 24, 94, 114
Gulf Commander, tug, 36
Gulf Gatineau, 72, 114
Gulf MacKenzie, 114

H. C. Heimbecker, 37, 49
H. Lee White, 138
H. Lee White (2), 186, 216, 232, 244
H. M. Griffith, 3, 21, 169, 233
Hains, dredge, 26, 62, 152
Halifax, 187, 235
Hallfax, 20
Hamilton Energy, 107
Handymariner, 191
Hankey, 47
Hannah 2901, barge, 199, 221
Hannah 2903, barge, 197
Hanseat, tug, 7, 15

Harry Coulby (2), 139, 199, 220, 224
Helen Evans, 17
Helen M. McAllister, tug, 6, 15, 58, 60, 74, 91, 111-112, 114, 138, 142, 176-177, 185, 191, 196-199, 209, 231
Hellas in Eternity, 41
Henri Tellier, 138
Henry A. Hawgood, 115
Henry Ford II, 3, 13, 60, 65-66, 85, 107, 140, 161, 183, 190, 212, 215, 225
Henry Steinbrenner (4), 131, 134, 167-168, 200, 209-210, 229, 244
Herbert C. Jackson, 19, 88, 96, 131, 206, 216-217
Hilda Marjanne, 28, 64-65, 76, 90
Hochelaga, 5, 35, 45, 91, 175
Hoffman, dredge, 62, 152
Homer D. Williams, 1, 7, 102
Hon. Paul Martin, 101, 108, 200, 205, 210
Honey Hill, 144
Horace Johnson, 1, 79
Howard F. Andrews, 55
Hubert Gaucher, 61, 70, 163, 204
Hudson Transport, 41-42, 54, 112, 140, 171, 182
Hull No. 1, storage barge, 231
Huron, barge, 41

Idaho, tug, 154, 183
Illinois, tug, 220
Imperial Acadia, 53
Imperial Bedford, 195
Imperial Collingwood, 45
Imperial Edmonton, 137
Imperial Leduc, 94, 226
Imperial London, 9
Imperial Quebec, 176
Imperial Redwater, 94, 114
Imperial Sarnia, 21, 156
Imperial St. Clair, 20
Imperial Woodbend, 94, 146
Incan Superior, 65, 89, 160, 170, 218, 239
Indiana Harbor, 55, 57, 62, 79, 109-110, 134, 144, 157, 176, 190, 204, 232, 240
Industrial Transport, 150
Inland Transport, 11
Interspirit, 31
Invincible, tug, 110
Iowa, tug, 103, 183
Irene Diamond, 41
Irvin L. Clymer, 17, 27-28, 33, 55, 190, 193, 202, 204

Index

Irving Cedar, tug, 109, 115, 170, 173
Irving Miami, tug, 225
Irving S. Olds, 18, 139, 158, 196-198
Island Transport (2), 132, 150
Isle Royale, 193, 210

J. A. W. Iglehart, 132, 134, 188
J. B. Ford, 97, 125, 134, 221
J. Burton Ayers, 27, 41, 216, 219, 224, 232
J. C. Phillips, 114, 235
J. E. Bernier, icebreaker, 240
J. F. Schoellkopf, Jr., 3, 5-6
J. F. Vaughn, 37, 49, 55-56, 196
J. G. II, tug, 95
J. H. Hillman, Jr., 172
J. L. Mauthe, 19, 61, 108-109, 130, 155, 202, 224
J. N. McWatters (2), 27, 218, 233
J. P. Morgan, Jr., 11
J. R. Sensibar, 9, 31
Jablanica, 144
Jacques Desgagnes, 69
Jalagodavari, 59, 127, 156
Jalatapi, 79
James A. Farrell, 2
James A. Hannah, tug, 51, 107, 167
James B. Lyons, 176, 181, 205
James Battle, tug, 191
James E. McGrath, tug, 70, 72, 76, 103, 108, 118, 205
James Harris, tug, 238
James Nasmyth, barge, 92
James Norris, 1, 24, 28, 45, 80, 109, 115, 137
James R. Barker, 5, 57, 77, 93, 150, 168, 186, 204, 212
James Transport, 23, 40, 45-46, 48, 150
Jantar, tug, 141-142, 144, 152, 165, 231
Jean Lykes, 222, 230
Jean Parisien, 15, 35-36, 50, 66, 80, 85, 148
Jensen Star, 25, 89, 107, 135
Jiggs, tug, 69
Joan M. McCullough, 55-56, 176
Johanna B., 238
John A. France (2), 42, 161, 190, 215
John A. Kling, 20, 140
John B. Aird, 59, 67, 71, 107, 160
John Dykstra, 33, 60, 154
John Dykstra (2), 60, 72, 103, 139-140
John E. F. Misener, 63, 92, 145-146
John G. Munson (2), 23, 55, 65, 70, 85, 132, 142, 161, 225, 244

John Hulst, 1, 79
John J. Boland (3), 9, 93
John M. Selvick, tug, 3, 49, 53, 76, 85, 117
John McLean, tug, 56, 62, 67
John O. McKellar (2), 45, 100
John Purves, tug, 27, 36, 184
John Roen V, tug, 20
John Sherwin (2), 40, 139, 146, 188, 206
John T. Hutchinson, 74, 192-193, 195
Johnny and Sisters II, fishing trawler, 238
Johnstown (2), 111-112, 114
Jos. Simard, 44
Joseph H. Frantz, 148, 188, 190
Joseph H. Thompson, 9, 103
Joseph L. Block, 30
Joseph S. Wood, 153
Joseph S. Young, 138
Joseph X. Robert, 25, 45, 55-56
Joshua A. Hatfield, 95, 139, 150, 197
Ju Yong Guan, 200
Judith M. Pierson, 56, 59, 109
Judy Moran, tug, 209
Jupiter, 96, 187

Kansas, tug, 102, 130
Kasos, 96
Kathrine Sif, 54
Katmai Bay, icebreaking tug, 17, 81, 87, 131, 215
Kaye E. Barker, 215, 234
Kentucky, tug, 103
Kihu, 218
Kiisla, 128, 131-132, 156, 182, 187, 202, 240
Kingdoc (2), 20, 193
Kinsale, tug, 6, 34, 38, 218
Kinsman Enterprise, 231
Kinsman Enterprise (2), 199, 224
Kinsman Independent (2), 87, 171, 199
Kinsman Independent (3), 199
Koba, 67
Komsomolets Latvii, 106
Koral, tug, 96, 112, 114, 146
Kristin Lee, tug, 206

L. E. Block, 14, 31, 152, 168, 206
L. Rochette, 114, 154, 167
L'Erable No. 1, 44
L'Erable No. 1 (2), 3, 40, 55, 61
L'Orme No. 1, 44, 187-188, 195, 204, 230
La Liberte, 89
Labradoc (2), 211

Lac Como, tug, 115, 226, 228
Lac Des Iles, 4, 18, 26
Lac Manitoba, tug, 123, 125, 227
Lac Ste. Anne, 13, 80, 84, 108
Lake Angelina, 122
Lake Anne, 228
Lake Charles, 201
Lake Manitoba, 49, 132, 160
Lake Nipigon, 70, 83, 128, 132, 160
Lake Wabush, 26, 82, 132, 160
Lake Winnipeg, 8, 11, 13, 109-110
Lakeshell (3), 19, 21, 47, 128, 158, 167
Lakespan Ontario, ferry, 32, 48
Laketon (2), 83, 95, 128, 132
Lakewood (2), 19, 69, 202, 211
Lauren Castle, tug, 3, 19
Laurentian Forest, 133
Lawrencecliffe Hall (2), 13, 95, 148, 160, 187
Lawrendoc (2), 93
Le Brave, 145
Le Cedre No. 1, 44, 83, 183
Le Chene No. 1, 44
Le Frene No. 1, 44, 171, 227
Le Saule No. 1, 44
Leadale (2), 21, 26, 32, 61-62, 68
Lee A. Tregurtha, 215, 220
Lehigh (3), 24
Lekeitio, 51
Lemoyne (2), 187, 203
Lenny B., 21
Leon, 183
Leon Falk, Jr., 27, 117-118, 145
Leon Fraser, 136, 234
Leon Simard, 37, 44
Leonard W., tug, 74, 115, 177
Lewis G. Harriman, 9, 134
Lewis Wilson Foy, 34, 53, 105, 157, 223, 234
Lionel Parsons, 68
Llandaff, 141
Loc Bay, 1, 201
London Earl, 40
Louis R. Desmarais, 36, 50, 132, 147
Louisiana, tug, 217
Ludger Simard, 44
Lydia, 235
Lyman, dredge, 62

M. C. Thunder, tug, 228-229
Mackinaw, icebreaker, 47, 81, 85, 87, 107-108, 151, 187, 204, 215, 220-221, 224, 233, 239

Madison, car ferry, 175, 231-232
Maine, tug, 6
Maitland No. 1, barge, 20
Malinska, 165
Manco, tug, 41, 95
Mangal Desai, 237
Manic, tug, 142
Manitoulin (5), 50, 115, 140, 149, 199, 219
Mantadoc (2), 221
Maplebranch (2), 44
Maplecliffe Hall, 101, 142, 149, 155-157, 163, 187
Mapleheath, barge, 58, 68, 74, 156, 165, 168
Maria Angelicoussi, 206
Marine Fuel Oil, 171
Marinsal, 3, 7
Mariposa, buoy tender, 221, 224
Marjorie Lykes, 70, 79, 230
Markham, dredge, 62, 218
Marko Marulic, 77
Marlhill, 3, 26
Martha Envoy, 78
Mary Turner, barge, 57
Maryland, tug, 6
Mataafa, 92
Mathilda Desgagnes, 9, 45
Matthew Andrews (2), 83
Maxine, 3, 37, 196
Mazahua, 65
McAllister 252, barge, 206, 221
McKee Sons, 110, 133
Medicine Man, yacht, 37
Medusa Challenger, 160, 165, 216
Medusa Conquest, barge, 131, 167, 221
Megalohari II, 18
Mel William Selvick, barge, 27, 36
Meldrum Bay, 19, 36, 80, 84, 108, 136, 142
Menihek Lake, 3, 45, 103, 117-118, 142
Merle M. McCurdy, 9, 97, 183
Mesabi Miner, 4, 113, 123, 135, 174, 200, 209, 217
Mesquite, buoy tender, 161, 237
Metis, 65, 73, 175
Metro Sun, 107
Michael D. Misner, tug, 152, 165, 170-171, 176, 183, 211, 218
Michigan, tug, 127, 181, 187
Middletown, 17, 36, 51, 147, 154
Minnesota, tug, 154, 183
Minnie Selvick, tug, 49, 127, 184, 219-220

Index

Miseford, tug, 26, 49
Mississagi, 149
Mitera Vassiliki, 196
Mobile Bay, icebreaking tug, 85, 89, 117, 127
Mohawk, tug, 201
Montana, tug, 69
Montcliffe Hall, 23, 187
Monte Zalama, 38, 115
Montrealais, 10-11, 74, 80
Monty Python, 115
Mormaclynx, 49
Mormactide, 208, 214, 238
Mount McKay, 123
Mountain Azalea, 164
Murray Bay (3), 87, 142, 149, 233
Muskegon, tug, 127
Myron C. Taylor, 1, 55, 75, 119, 142, 164, 214, 234

N. F. Leopold, 169
Nacional Aveiro, 51
Nancy Orr Gaucher, 223, 227-228
Nanticoke, 8-9, 50, 66, 97, 107, 116, 156, 188
Nata, 153
Neah Bay, icebreaking tug, 87, 129
Nebraska, tug, 97, 125, 144
Neglen, 98
Neptune, tug, 222
New Jersey, tug, 177, 179, 196-197
New Orleans, 223
New Quedoc, 113
New York News (3), 57, 80, 84, 89, 102, 131
Newcastle, tug, 97
Newfie Queen, tug, 57
Niagara, dredge, 231
Niagara (2), 57, 123
Niagara II, 84
Nicolet, 1, 9, 25, 41, 95, 139, 174, 223, 228
Nindawayma, ferry, 215
Nipigon Bay, 18, 30, 63, 91, 94, 147, 175, 223, 225-227
No. 73, scow, 100
No. 134, scow, 100
No. 153 scow, 100
Norchem, 119
Nordale, 26, 38, 72
Nordic, 235
Nordic Sun, 235
Normac, 29, 225
Norman B. Ream, 231

Norstar, 193
Norte Dame Victory, 120
North Dakota, tug, 31
Northcliffe Hall, 37
Northern Shell, 24, 158, 183
Northern Venture, 64-65, 70-71
Nosira Madeleine, 72

Oakglen, 56, 161, 196, 199
Oceanport, barge, 36
Ohio, tug, 17-19, 69, 74, 78, 93, 96, 102-103, 125, 143, 152, 183, 193, 197, 208-209, 217, 225
Olau Syd, 24
Olive L. Moore, tug, 26-27, 59, 87, 97, 171, 189
OLS-30, barge, 206, 221
Omega 809, tug, 195
Ontadoc (2), 229
Ontario No. 1 (2), ferry, 214
Ontario Power, 27, 65
Orestia, 162
Orion Expeditor, 193
Osa Ravensturm, tug, 184-185, 198
Ottercliffe Hall, 26, 75, 83, 103, 187
Outarde (3), 70, 80, 84, 108, 118

P. J. Murer, 118
P.S. Barge No. 1, 115, 126, 149, 176-177, 191, 196
Pacific Defender, 109
Pacific Trader, 238
Pamit C., 168
Panoil (2), 34
Paterson, 63, 100
Paterson (2), 93, 105, 109, 113, 119, 157, 203
Patricia B. McAllister, tug, 221, 235
Patricia Hoey, tug, 192
Patricia II, 159
Paul E. No. 1, tug, 200
Paul H. Carnahan, 88, 107, 117, 143-145
Paul H. Townsend, 134, 197, 215, 238
Paul Thayer, 14, 128, 211
Paulina C., 78
Pegasus, 77
Peninsula, tug, 119, 172
Pennsylvania, tug, 69
Peter A. B. Widener, 11, 18, 27, 152-153
Peter Misener, 103, 187, 207-208
Peter Robertson (2), 3, 7
Petite Forte, tug, 150, 229

Index

Petropan I, 222
Philip D. Block, 14, 124-125, 144
Philip R. Clarke, 1, 23, 32, 55, 75, 80, 85, 96, 118, 155, 165, 182, 188, 195, 218, 240, 242
Philippe L. D., 96
Phoceen, tug, 179, 181
Pic R., 92
Pic River, 92
Pierson Daughters, 55-56
Pierson Independent, 2
Pilot Boat No. 6, 122
Pilot Knob, 173
Pineglen, 56, 63, 92, 98
Pioneer (3), 39
Point Carroll, tug, 72
Point Valiant, tug, 20, 154
Pointe Noire, 58, 63
Pointe Sept-Iles, tug, 115
Pola Dyo, 58
Polstar, 135
Pomorze Zachodnie, 218
Pontiac (2), 98, 102, 111-112, 114
Pontokratis, 195
Prairie Harvest, 73, 77, 86, 101, 157, 163, 223, 236
Prescotont tug, 95, 114-115
Presque Isle (2), 165, 224
Princess No. 1, tug, 114, 182, 211, 232
Prindoc (3), 47
Project Americas, 156
Provmar Terminal, 103
Provmar Terminal II, 156
Prudent, tug, 138

Quebecois, 57, 59, 156
Quedoc (2), 18, 103, 113
Quedoc (3), 187, 191, 193, 206, 214, 233
Quetico, 62

R. & L. No. 1, tug, 58, 70-72, 76, 91, 103, 108, 128, 182
R. Bruce Angus, 94, 114-115
R. G. Cassidy, tug, 189, 195
R. G. Sanderson, 68
R. W. Sesler, 110
Ralph H. Watson, 1, 7, 179-180
Ralph Misener, 16, 25, 85, 222
Ramdas, 39
Ramona, fish tug, 30
Raymond H. Reiss, 21, 105

Razel Brothers, fish tug, 144
Rea, 34
Red Wing, 28, 103, 136-137
Reiss Brothers, 2
Rembertiturm, tug, 184-185
Reserve, 17, 53, 76, 155, 163, 168, 218
Rhode Island, tug, 177, 220
Rhone, 18
Richard J. Reiss (2), 9, 13, 47, 85, 97, 130
Richard M. Marshall, 153
Richard Reiss, 130, 139, 223
Richard V. Lindabury, 199
Richelieu (3), 25, 65, 132, 161, 164, 191, 232
Rimba Balau, 54
Rimouski, 62, 154
Rival, tug, 91
Rivershell (3), 66, 92
Rivershell (4), 168
Robert C. Norton (2), 7
Robert C. Stanley, 1, 7, 28, 149, 179-180
Robert H., tug, 163, 179
Robert Hobson, 118
Robert Koch, 35, 91, 128, 141-142, 150
Robert S. Pierson, 2, 55-56
Robinson Bay, tug, 32, 36, 58, 68, 74, 109, 165, 209
Rod McLean, tug, 56, 122
Roger Blough, 22, 34, 174, 185-186, 234, 240
Roger M. Kyes, 20, 73, 81, 97, 179, 203, 225
Rogers City, 1, 158, 167, 181
Roland Desgagnes, 7, 37, 51
Roy A. Jodrey, 18, 36
Royal Clipper, 58
Royalton, 7
Royalton (2), 75, 95, 103
Rudderman, 138
Ruder Boskovic, 73, 171

S. M. T. B. No. 7, barge, 168
S. T. Crapo, 107, 134, 189
Saginaw Bay, 17, 45, 102, 114
Saguenay, ferry, 195
Saguenay (2), 134
Saint Vincent, 92
Sainte Marie II, 17
Salamis, 48
Salvage Monarch, tug, 7, 15, 58, 60, 68, 70, 91, 109, 111-112, 114, 138, 144, 176-177, 185, 191, 196-199, 229, 231, 236
Sam Laud, 39, 76, 176, 201, 244

Index

Samuel Mather (5), 176
Samuel Mather (6), 9, 29-31, 40, 57, 173
Samuel Mather (7), 215, 225
Samuel Risley, icebreaker, 112, 148
Sandgate, 33
Sarah Spencer, barge, 209
Saronis, 35
Saskatchewan Pioneer, 31, 73, 76, 110, 161, 240
Savic, 121
Scan Crusader, 15
Scotia II, barge, 49
Scott Misener (2), 145
Scott Misener (3), 152, 207, 209, 244
Scurry, barge, 182, 217
Sea Barge One, barge, 209
Sea Peony, 112
Seatransport, 98
Seaway Queen, 4, 9, 137, 148, 240
Seaway Trader, 45, 61, 73, 159
Selkirk Settler, 31, 70, 76, 106
Senator of Canada, 103, 113
Seneca, tug, 53
Senneville, 22, 30, 74, 222
Sewell Avery, 1, 7, 34, 149, 163
Shannon, tug, 6, 38, 51, 73, 97, 114, 174, 177, 211, 225
Sharon, 6, 9, 22, 133, 138
Shelia Moran, tug, 208
Shell Scientist, 107
Shelter Bay, 29
Shimone, 224
Shirley Lykes, 98
Sibyl W., 176, 205
Sifnos, 99
Silver Isle, 22, 92, 223
Silver Leader, 102
Silver Magpie, 34
Silverdale, 74, 79, 84, 95
Simcoe (2), 107, 190, 230
Sinmac, tug, 176
Sioux, tug, 134
Sir Alexander Glen, 50
Sir James Dunn, 17, 26, 63, 209, 223, 228-229
Sir Wilfrid Laurier, icebreaker, 127, 145
Sirius, 177
Skudenes, ferry, 214
Smit-Lloyd 109, tug, 144
Socrates, 125
Solta, 118, 152
Soo Chief, tug, 76

Soo River Belle, pilot boat, 177
Soo River Trader, 5, 25, 30, 32, 49, 56
Soodoc (2), 57, 66, 227
Soren TH, 209
Soren Toubro, 193, 205
South Carolina, tug, 176, 195
South Haven, 127
Southcliffe Hall, 193
Sparrows Point, 5, 77, 112, 127, 167, 236
Spartan (2), 73, 127
Spindletop, 201
Split, 182
Spruceglen, 56, 63, 68, 113
St. Clair (2), 88, 118, 144, 166, 189, 230
St. Lawrence (3), 98-99
St. Lawrence Navigator, 5
St. Marys Cement, barge, 107, 139
Stadacona (2), 72
Stadacona (3), 112, 126, 149, 174, 219, 239
Star I, 235
STC 2004, barge, 168-169
Ste. Marie I, tug, 26
Ste. Marie II, tug, 18, 26
Steelcliffe Hall, 47, 80, 99, 157, 174, 187
Stella Desgagnes, 131-132, 167
Stephen B. Roman, 60, 72-73, 93, 132, 160, 215
Steven H., 179
Steven M. Selvick, tug, 127, 219
Stewart J. Cort, 53, 87, 127, 154, 167, 214, 219, 231
Stolt Castle, 218-219
Stormont, tug, 62, 76, 78, 109, 111, 141-142, 144-145, 156, 181-182, 200, 222, 226-228
Sundew, buoy tender, 237
Superior, tug, 152, 176, 208-209, 234
Susan Hoey, tug, 174, 177, 205
Sylvania, 7, 78

T. R. McLagan, 21, 30, 175, 195, 206
T. W. Robinson, 50, 63, 158, 163, 165
Table Rock, 110
Tadoussac (2), 3, 48, 50, 88, 219
Tarantau, 50, 66
Tegucigalpa, 9
Texaco Brave (2), 46, 145
Texaco Chief (2), 145
Texaco Warrior (2), 83
The International, 196
Thomas De Gauwdief, tug, 170
Thomas F. Cole, 11

Index

Thomas F. Patton, 5, 15
Thomas W. Lamont, 1, 7, 34, 169-170
Thomas Wilson (2), 22, 174-175, 184-185
Thornhill, 17
Thornhill (2), 65
Thorold, 211
Thorold (4), 32, 68, 80, 84, 95, 97, 105
Thunder, tug, 228
Thunder Cape, 113, 119, 151-154, 165, 172, 174, 176, 179-180, 193, 211, 232
Timur Swallow, 96
Tipperary, tug, 51, 89, 97
Tlatoani, 44
Tom M. Girdler, 5, 9, 15
Tove Cob, 220
Trader, 83
Trillium, ferry, 29, 225
Trio Bravo, 20
Trio Trado, 20
Triton, tug, 139
Triumph Sea, tug/supply vessel, 209
Troisdoc (3), 37, 67, 71
Tug Malcolm, tug, 6, 11, 37, 39, 51, 60, 66, 72, 87, 98, 102, 126, 144-145, 215, 223, 231, 234
Tusker, tug, 11, 34-35, 115, 119, 140, 152-153, 155, 158, 163, 165, 169-170, 172, 174, 176, 178, 200, 217

U.S. 265808, 101, 144, 153, 163, 165
U.S. 266029, 101, 144, 154
Ungava Transport, 36, 103
USL 501, barge, 110
USS *Croaker*, 209
USS *Grasp*, 152
USS *Little Rock*, 209
USS *The Sullivans*, 209

V. W. Scully, 160
Vac, tug, 143
Valley Camp, museum ship, 74
Valor, 93
Vandoc (2), 117, 146
Venture, tug, 221
Verendrye, barge, 122
Vermont, tug, 31, 134, 228
Viking (2), 69, 89, 160
Ville-Marie, 51
Vishva Bhakti, 77

W. J. Ivan Purvis tug, 26, 66, 68, 113, 126, 128, 173, 179, 232
W. M. Edington, 84
W. M. Vacy Ash, 167, 217
W. N. Twolan, tug, 173, 181, 192-193, 208
W. R. Woodford, 169
W. W. Holloway, 115-116, 144
Walka Mlodych, 39
Walter A. Sterling, 55, 66, 93, 100-101, 120, 155
Walter R., tug, 161
Weeks 297, barge, 237
Wheat King, 28, 136, 141
Whitefish Bay, 67, 233, 244
Wicklow, tug, 73, 96-97, 114, 218
Wilfred M. Cohen, tug, 7, 49, 56, 60, 62, 67, 164, 203
Wilfred Sykes, 82, 146, 211-212
William A. Irvin, 1, 134, 148, 189
William A. Lydon, tug, 100
William A. McGonagle, 61, 131
William A. Reiss (2), 29, 34
William A. Whitney, tug, 6, 38, 52, 89, 174, 191, 218
William B. Dickson, 183
William C. Selvick, tug, 95
William Clay Ford, 13, 74, 93, 100-101, 103, 144, 154-155, 188
William Clay Ford (2), 101, 105, 109, 164, 188, 200, 215
William G. Mather (2), 84, 133, 183
William H. Warner, 196, 199
William Hoey, tug, 202
William J. De Lancey, 7, 27, 54, 82, 109, 142, 150, 152, 181, 218
William J. Dugan, tug, 231
William K. Field, 2
William McLauchlan, 176
William P. Cowan, 123
William P. Snyder Jr., 41, 62, 136, 165
William R. Roesch, 128
Willis B. Boyer, 41, 62, 136
Willis L. King, 96
Willowglen, 56, 69, 71-72, 74, 102, 163, 176-177
Windoc (2), 187, 232-233
Winnipeg (3), 187, 191
Winter Hill, 117
Wisconsin, tug, 134, 228
Wittransport II, barge, 37, 71, 92, 181
Wolverine (2), 20, 50, 85, 114, 137, 147, 237
Woodland, 135, 174, 183, 199, 205, 208

Index

World Palm, 156
Wyoming, tug, 77, 97, 183

Xenia, 75

Yankcanuck (2), 3, 11, 42, 97, 157, 181
Yasnyy, tug, 141
Yemanja, 50
Yerel, 68

Zapolyarnyy, 171
Zenovia, 113
Ziemia Bialostocka, 70
Ziemia Gnieznienska, 177, 210
Ziemia Krakowska, 218, 234
Ziemia Lubelska, 127
Ziemia Olsztynksa, 113, 155
Ziemia Tarnowska, 200, 204, 235

www.ingramcontent.com/pod-product-compliance
Lightning Source LLC
Chambersburg PA
CBHW081832170426
43199CB00017B/2705